8/93

# DICTIONARY OF AMERICAN CHILDREN'S FICTION, 1985–1989

# DICTIONARY
# OF
# AMERICAN
# CHILDREN'S
# FICTION,
# 1985–1989

## Books of Recognized Merit

ALETHEA K. HELBIG

AND

AGNES REGAN PERKINS

**GREENWOOD PRESS**
Westport, Connecticut • London

**Library of Congress Cataloging-in-Publication Data**

Helbig, Alethea.
    Dictionary of American children's fiction, 1985–1989 : books of
recognized merit / Alethea K. Helbig and Agnes Regan Perkins.
       p.  cm.
    Includes index.
    ISBN 0–313–27719–2 (alk. paper)
    1. Children's stories, American—Dictionaries.  2. American
fiction—20th century—Dictionaries.  3. Bibliography—Best books—
Children's stories.  4. Authors, American—20th century—Biography—
Dictionaries.  I. Perkins, Agnes.  II. Title.
PS374.C454H45   1993
813′.54099282′03—dc20       92–19613

British Library Cataloguing in Publication Data is available.

Library of Congress Catalog Card Number: 92–19613
ISBN: 0–313–27719–2

First published in 1993

Greenwood Press, 88 Post Road West, Westport, CT   06881
An imprint of Greenwood Publishing Group, Inc.

Printed in the United States of America

The paper used in this book complies with the
Permanent Paper Standard issued by the National
Information Standards Organization (Z39.48–1984).

10 9 8 7 6 5 4 3 2 1

# CONTENTS

# PREFACE

As university teachers of literature for children and young adults for twenty-five years and as people trained in the study of literature as literature, we are dedicated to the idea that books for children must be judged by the same criteria as those for adults, keeping in mind, of course, that children are the intended audience. The critical comments found in *Dictionary of American Children's Fiction, 1985–1989: Books of Recognized Merit* judge each book as imaginative literature, not on other values, regardless of the particular emphasis of the award for which it was chosen.

The entries in this *Dictionary* are of several types, chiefly title, author, and character. A book's title entry gives the plot summary and a critical assessment of its literary value. Other entries about a book provide additional information. Taken together, they form a short essay, complete in itself for classroom or library use, or a good starting point for further research.

The *Dictionary of American Children's Fiction, 1985–1989* contains more than 400 entries on such elements as titles, authors, characters, and settings based on 134 books by 93 twentieth-century authors. It is a supplement to our two books of American fiction for children dealing with award-winning books published from 1859 to 1984 and a companion book to *Dictionary of British Children's Fiction* (two volumes) and *Dictionary of Children's Fiction from Australia, Canada, India, New Zealand, and Selected African Countries*. It is the first of a projected series of five-year updates, intended, as are the earlier volumes, for use by anyone who is interested in children's literature: librarians, teachers, literary scholars, researchers in comparative social history, parents, booksellers, publishers, editors, and writers—all those to whom literature for children is of vital interest professionally or personally.

This *Dictionary* brings together in one volume those books that critics have singled out as the best to receive awards or have placed on citation lists during these five years. As with the earlier *Dictionaries*, we have not included translations, books with awards given by strictly regional groups, or those issued by organizations to their members only. We have also excluded books chosen by children, since children as a whole are unsophisticated readers and have limited critical experience.

Because our study is of fiction and not of illustration, we have not included stories in picture book form, since the texts of such books can seldom stand alone and their analysis requires a consideration also of the illustrations. Somewhat arbitrarily, we have set 5,000 words as a minimum; most books must be at least that long to develop a story that can function on its own. Books of more than 5,000 words are included, even if the illustrations are very prominent.

Collections of short stories also require a different sort of analysis and plot summary from novels and are not included, even if technically they are fiction. Retellings from oral tradition appear if the material has been developed like that in novels, as in *The Outlaws of Sherwood*.

In our author entries, we have focused on what in the author's life is most relevant to children's literature and to the particular books in this *Dictionary*. Although several other published sources give biographical information about authors, none considers all the writers whose books are in this study. Having the information in the same volume is not only of convenience for researchers; it is of particular value for those areas where libraries are on limited budgets and do not own the other publications.

In presenting our entries we have tried to follow an arrangement that will be convenient for a variety of users.

A. Title entries. These consist of bibliographical information; the sub-genre to which the work belongs; a plot summary incorporating the plot problem (if any), significant episodes, and the conclusion; a discussion of important themes; a brief literary critical evaluation; a note about sequels, if any; and awards and citations in abbreviated form. A list of the complete names of the awards and citations appears in the front matter. Entries vary in length. The number of words in an entry does not indicate the importance or quality of the book, since plots can be summarized more briefly and critical judgments stated more succinctly for some books than for others.

Most readers will be acquainted with the terms we have used for sub-genres, but a few terms may need some explanation. By realistic fiction, we mean books in which events could have happened some time in the world as we know it, as opposed to an imaginary or fantastic world, and not necessarily that the action is convincing or plausible. Historical fiction includes those books in which actual historical events or figures function in the plot, as in *Streams to the River, River to the Sea* and *Charley Skedaddle*, or in which the specific period is essential to the action and in which the story could not have occurred in any other time, as in *After the Dancing Days* and *In the Year of the Boar and Jackie Robinson*. Books that are merely set in a past time, like *The Whipping Boy*, we have called period fiction. Although all plots are driven by problems, we have used the term "problem novel" in its more recent sense to refer to those stories where social, physical, or psychological concerns dominate, as in *Remembering the Good Times* and *Scorpions*.

B. Author entries. These consist of dates and places of birth and death, when available; education and vocational background; major contribution to children's literature; significant facts of the author's life that might have a bearing on the work; titles that have won awards; frequently titles of other publications, usually with brief information about them; and critical judgments where they can safely be made.

C. Character entries. These include physical and personality traits for important, memorable, or particularly unusual characters who are not covered sufficiently by the plot summary, and focus on such aspects as how they function in the plot, how they relate to the protagonist, and whether the characterization is credible and skillful. Characters are classified by the name by which they are most often referred to or by the name by which the protagonist refers to them, e.g., Old Pepper, Uncle Earl Johnson, Mr. Henry Wheatley. The name is also cross-referenced in the index under the most likely possibilities. If the character's surname does not often appear in the story, it will usually not appear in the index; when it is included, it is usually as a family name: Pratt family, Wallis family, etc. If the plot summary gives all the significant information about characters, as with many protagonists, they are not discussed in separate character entries. All major characters, however, are listed in the index.

D. Miscellaneous entries. These include particularly significant settings and elements that need explanation beyond mention in the title entry.

Every book has title and author entries. Entries are in alphabetical order for convenience. Asterisks indicate that the item has a separate entry elsewhere in the book. A dagger indicates that the book or the author appears in *Dictionary of American Children's Fiction, 1960–1984*. Double daggers are used in the few places where a book or author appears in *Dictionary of American Children's Fiction, 1859–1959*. Entries do not duplicate one another.

A list of awards and their abbreviations appears at the front of the *Dictionary*. A list of books classified by the awards is in the back of the volume. The index includes all the items for which there are entries and such elements as cross-references, major characters for whom there are no separate entries, specific place settings, settings by period, and such matters as themes and subjects, books of first-person narration, unusual narrative structures, significant tone, authors' pseudonyms, illustrators, and genres.

When we compare the books in this five-year period with award winners in our earlier volumes, we find the trends we noted in the late 1970s and early 1980s continue. The majority of the novels are realistic fiction set in the contemporary period. The largest single group consists of stories of family life, some of them light and humorous, like *The Blossoms and the Green Phantom* and *The Agony of Alice*, and others more serious like *Permanent Connections* and *Come a Stranger*. The last three of these happen also to be growing-up stories, which still form a major segment of contemporary realistic fiction. Although some are trivial, others are among the finest books on the list: *Izzy, Willy-Nilly, One-Eyed Cat, Good-bye and Keep Cold, Return to Bitter Creek*, and the emotionally powerful *In Summer Light*.

Sociological and psychological problem stories remain prominent, still dealing with such matters as alcoholism, the death of a friend, and inner-city violence. Some new areas of concern, however, appear among these late 1980s award winners, for example, wife abuse in *Cracker Jackson*, teen suicide in *Remem-*

*bering the Good Times*, child molestation in *Promise Not to Tell*, and the unexplained disappearance of a child in *The Year Without Michael*. Public scrutiny of religious cults and investigations of televangelists are reflected in *A Fine White Dust* and *A Good Courage*. The tendency to exploit the shocking seems less obvious (or perhaps we have become conditioned to it), but it still appears in the extramarital pregnancy of a mother in *The Kindness* and in the intense cruelty of the campers and the callous attitude of the camp directors in *The Goats*. While sociological problems are treated sensitively and often graphically, the underlying causes are seldom examined.

Although we are told by teachers and librarians that they would welcome more historical fiction, this genre is still under-represented. Of historical novels in this volume, a number are from the Civil War period, like *Charley Skedaddle* and *Shades of Gray*, and several are set in the twentieth century, among them *After the Dancing Days*, about the aftermath of World War I, and *The Return*, which concerns the evacuation of Ethiopian Jews to Israel, an occurrence that some might consider too recent to be classified as historical. Interestingly, much of the substantial historical fiction is from the point of view of minority characters, like *Tancy*, about Blacks in the Civil War, *Legend Days*, about Native American Indians, and *So Far from the Bamboo Grove*, set in Korea and Japan at the end of World War II.

Fantasy, long a mainstay in children's literature, is also sparsely represented. Even including some novels that might well be called science fiction, only about twelve percent of the 1985–1989 award books are fantasy. On the whole, these are relatively inconsequential, though some are inventive in concept, like *Heart's Blood*, about an economy based on dragons, and *Through the Hidden Door*, about the discovery of relics of a miniature civilization, and a few stand out, like the grim post-holocaust *Wolf of Shadows*.

While the traditional survival and adventure tale has only a handful of examples, the mystery story is prominent and has become less conventional in characters and plot. Few of the award winners fall into the accepted who-done-it mode, where a murder or a theft drives the story. More substantial and complicated, these novels interweave a mystery with a personal or social problem, for example, *The Other Side of Dark*, in which an assault victim wakes from a coma to deal with a murderer and her own delayed maturation, or *The Sandman's Eyes* and *Following the Mystery Man*, both of which concern the search for an unknown parent.

Although almost all the books are competently written, showing grasp of form and skill with language, many seem underdeveloped or foreshortened, and most would have benefitted from a fuller treatment. Only in a few, like *Sarah Plain and Tall*, does brevity perfectly support the story. Often there is a tendency to exploit eccentric characters or eccentricized events, and the reliance on the topical in language and detail may date these books rapidly.

While most of the writers of these books from 1985–1989 are skillful established authors like Avi, Cynthia Voigt, Walter Dean Myers, and Erik Christian

Haugaard, a number are represented by their first novel for young people, among them Brock Cole, Jenny Davis, Paul Samuel Jacobs, Lyll Becerra de Jenkins, and John Reynolds Gardiner. With the addition of these new voices, American fiction for young people has a promising future.

As with the earlier American books and the companion volumes on British children's fiction and *Dictionary of Children's Fiction from Australia, Canada, India, New Zealand, and Selected African Countries*, we have read every book included in this *Dictionary* and have done all the research and writing in this volume. We have had some valuable assistance from a variety of sources. We wish to express our appreciation to the Eastern Michigan University Library and the Ann Arbor, Michigan, Public Library for the use of their extensive collections. Specifically, we thank the staff of the Ann Arbor Public Library Youth Room, Brian Steimel and Thomas Staicar of the Interlibrary Loan Department of Eastern Michigan University Library for their help in obtaining books not available locally, and Harold Helbig for his careful proofing of the index.

# KEY TO AWARDS AND CITATIONS

| | |
|---|---|
| Addams | Jane Addams Peace Association Children's Book Award |
| ALA | American Library Association Best Books/Notable Books for Children |
| Boston Globe Honor | *Boston Globe-Horn Book* Award Honor Book |
| Boston Globe Winner | *Boston Globe-Horn Book* Award Winner |
| Child Study | Child Study Children's Book Committee at Bank Street College Award |
| Christopher | Christopher Award |
| C.S. King Honor | Coretta Scott King Honorable Mention |
| C.S. King Winner | Coretta Scott King Award Winner |
| Fanfare | *The Horn Book Magazine* Fanfare List |
| IRA | International Reading Association Children's Book Award |
| Jefferson | Jefferson Cup Award for Historical Fiction |
| Newbery Honor | John Newbery Medal Honor Book |
| Newbery Winner | John Newbery Medal Winner |
| O'Dell | Scott O'Dell Award for Historical Fiction |
| Poe Nominee | Nominee for the Edgar Allan Poe Award Best Juvenile Mystery |
| Poe Winner | Winner of the Edgar Allan Poe Award Best Juvenile Mystery |
| SLJ | *School Library Journal* Best Books for Children |
| Spur | Western Writers of America Spur Award |
| Stone | George C. Stone Center for Children's Books Recognition of Merit Award |
| Western Heritage | Western Heritage Award |

# THE DICTIONARY

# A

*THE ACCIDENT* (Strasser*, Todd, Delacorte, 1988), mystery involving a drunk driving accident that kills four teenagers. Matt Thompson, high school senior, has always felt somewhat inferior to his best friend, Bobby Stewart, who is from a wealthy family, good looking, and the best athlete and captain of the school swim team. Even on a visit to the Stewart family ski lodge, Matt is afraid to follow Bobby and their newcomer friend, Jason Ellman, on a daring jump in an off-limits area, and he irrationally blames his girl friend, Karen Shecter, who has warned him that he is not a good enough skier to try it. Although Matt no longer sees much of Chris Walsh, his neighbor in the housing project occupied mostly by fatherless families, as both of theirs are, he attends a drinking party at Chris's home when Mrs. Walsh is out. Because Karen will not come to the party and they have quarrelled, Matt drinks too much and is in the bathroom vomiting when Bobby, Jason, Chris, and two girls pile into Chris's new Blazer and head for the Stewart ski lodge to sit in the hot tub. Matt reacts with shock and disbelief to the news that the Blazer has gone off the mountain road and only Jason is still alive. When questioned by Lee Washington, black police officer whose younger brother, Don, is on the swim team with him, Matt can add very little information except to confirm that they had all been drinking and that Chris was very drunk. Summoned to the Stewart palatial home by Bobby's father, who wants advice on what memorial to erect for his son, Matt suggests a new pool for the school to replace the aging, inadequate "Black Hole" where the team practices. The town naturally blames Chris for the accident, since he has been in trouble before and is suspected of selling drugs in school. The Walshes' windows are shot out at night and trash is dumped on their front lawn, which Matt and his younger brother, Peter, join their mother to clean up before Mrs. Walsh sees it, and they are among the very few at Chris's funeral, a contrast to the big crowd at Bobby's. In the following weeks, a delay in the autopsy report, strange questions from Lee Washington, a record of the alcohol blood levels of all the victims, which appears anonymously in his mail slot, an evasive attitude from Jason, and various other clues make Matt realize that some sort of cover-up is taking place. Although Karen believes he is obsessed by the accident and both the principal and the coach, fearing he will endanger the prospect of the new pool, pressure him to stop, he continues to investigate, finally getting Chris's little sister, Casey, 10, who has a serious speech impediment and seldom talks, to point out the picture of the boy she saw driving the Blazer away that night, confirming that it was Bobby, not Chris, who drove off the mountain road. Mr. Stewart summons him again, explains that he is providing a good special education school for Casey, whose mother knows the truth but is keeping quiet, and is essentially bribing or pressuring all the others who suspect the truth so that it will not affect the political chances of Bobby's uncle, who is running for governor against a corrupt incumbent. Matt refuses Mr. Stewart's implied offer of a bribe but agrees not to say anything. The next summer, however, after Bobby's uncle has been elected, Matt hunts up Lee Washington and learns that the policeman presented the evidence to the district attorney, who said there were no grounds to prosecute. Matt calls an old high school friend who now works on the local paper and prepares to tell the truth at last. The novel is, of course, a strong condemnation of teenage drinking and driving. Since the outcome of Matt's investigation is foreseeable, the ethical question of whether to withhold the truth in a good cause is of stronger interest. Characters are functional, none of them really developed, and the plot seems manufactured to present the questions. Action, however, is fast enough paced to hold the interest. Poe Nominee.

**ADLER, C(AROLE) S(CHWERDTFEGER)** (1932–      ), born in Rockaway Beach, Long Island, N.Y.; educator, prolific writer of novels, mostly for children in the middle grades. She received her B.A. degree, *cum laude*, from Hunter College in 1953 and her M.S. degree from Russell Sage College in 1967. For two years she worked as an advertising assistant in New Jersey and later taught English in the middle schools of Niskayuna, N.Y., for nine years. Since 1977 she has devoted her professional energies to writing, publishing twenty-eight novels from 1979 to 1990, but she has also served as a volunteer working in child abuse prevention and protection programs and as a tutor for foster children. Her first novel, *The Magic of Glits* (Macmillan, 1979), a seaside fantasy, won the Golden Kite Award for Fiction from the Society of Children's Book Writers and several children's choice awards. *The Shell Lady's Daughter* (Coward, 1983) was named to the American Library Association Best Young Adult list, and *With Westie and the Tin Man\** (Macmillan, 1984) won the Child Study Award. Most of her books are about emotional problems, with family relationships as a common subject. Both *The Cat That Was Left Behind* (Clarion, 1981) and *Fly Free* (Coward, 1984) concern foster children. *Kiss the Clown* (Clarion, 1986) is about a dyslexic child, while *Down by the River* (Coward, 1981), one of her books for older young people, is a love story. The death of one of her twin sons in a car accident provided the background for *Ghost Brother* (Clarion, 1990), a sibling-relationship story.

**AFTER THE DANCING DAYS** (Rostkowski\*, Margaret I., Harper, 1986), historical novel of the rejection of crippled and mutilated veterans of World War I, set in Kansas City about 1920. The homecoming of her doctor father, Lawrence Metcalf, from eighteen months in the service is overshadowed for the narrator, Annie, 13, by the sight at the railway station of the blind, legless, and disfigured men he is escorting. She is also aware of a conflict between her beautiful, musical mother, Katherine\*, who wants him to return to practice at County Hospital, and Lawrence, who has decided to treat the war victims at St. John's Catholic Hospital. Annie's maternal Grandfather\* MacLeod, whose son Paul died in France, goes frequently to St. John's to read *Ivanhoe* to Timothy Lewis, a local boy whose eyes were injured. Increasingly curious and annoyed at her Protestant Sunday School teacher's criticism of her father for associating with Catholics, Annie goes with her grandfather one day. While he dozes, she wanders around the lawn and comes upon Andrew\* Clayton, a young man so badly burned by gas that his nose is almost gone, his mouth a lipless slit, and his skin a vivid red, with only his eyes looking normal. Terrified, she runs away. Conscience stricken and resentful of her mother's attitude that everything about the war is best forgotten, she returns another day with her grandfather and talks to Andrew, who has come with Timothy to hear *Ivanhoe*. Their group on the lawn is interrupted by her mother, come to fetch home grandfather, who has not been feeling well. She rudely refuses to be introduced and orders Annie to leave at once. That night grandfather has a heart attack. As soon as he can travel, Katherine takes him, along with her mother, to the Colorado mountains to recuperate, leaving Annie in Kansas City. Although her mother has forbidden her to return to St. John's and she is usually an obedient girl, Annie finds *Ivanhoe* and goes back to the hospital almost every day to read to Timothy and Andrew, with her father's approval. During the next few weeks, her friendship with Andrew deepens, and he begins to socialize more with the other men. She sees his Purple Heart and wonders why her Uncle\* Paul did not receive one. Since the story the family has been told of how he was killed and the date of the telegram announcing his death do not match, she gets Andrew to investigate. He takes her to an officer dying from a shell fragment in his lung who was with Paul when he died, not heroically in battle but of measles. When her mother returns Annie confesses that she has been deliberately disobeying her all summer and lying by not telling about going to St. John's. Her mother is very angry but, when Annie's father strongly defends her, lets her continue her visits. Timothy's eye bandages are removed, his eyes have healed, and he leaves to live with a sister in St. Louis. Andrew starts working in the wards, learning to do dressings. Annie learns with a shock that he is soon going to take a job in a hospital in Topeka and at first can hardly accept the loss. Her mother, to her astonishment, suggests that they invite him to dinner and redeems herself by being a charming hostess. She even agrees to come and play for the men at the hospital the night before Andrew is to leave. When Annie sees him off at the station, he gives her his Purple Heart to keep for him. The novel is both a condemnation of the patriotic citizens who build a war memorial but ignore the men who have returned maimed and ill and the story of a girl's first love. Annie is a proper child whose sense of fairness makes her act more compassionately than the community and who grows up through the experience. Many details give credibility to the period setting, and the characters, even minor figures like the nuns at St. John's, are well drawn. ALA; IRA; Jefferson.

*AFTER THE RAIN* (Mazer*, Norma Fox, Morrow, 1987), realistic novel of a teenage girl's relationship to her grandfather, in a modern American urban setting. Manny and Shirley, the parents of Rachel Cooper, 15, are older than her friends' parents, with two sons twenty years older than Rachel, and her grandfather, Izzy Shapiro, is eighty-three. He has recently seen a doctor for stomach pains, and Rachel goes with her mother when she is summoned to the doctor's office to learn that he has asbestosis, cancer caused by breathing asbestos fibers forty years earlier, a diagnosis the doctor has kept from the old man. A stonemason, Izzy has been strong and seemed invulnerable and is too curt and irascible to encourage sympathy. A few days later when Rachel is home alone a woman named Alice Farnum calls to say that Izzy has fallen in front of her house. Unable to reach her father, Rachel rushes to the address and finds her grandfather sitting in Alice's living room, looking a little gray but enjoying the attention and even flirting a bit with his rescuer. He insists on walking home and tolerates Rachel's company with ill grace. To ease her mother's fears, Rachel starts going to his apartment after school to accompany him on his daily walk. Soon he is tyrannically expecting her, though he converses only in abrupt, usually insulting, phrases. This interferes with her own life, her long-standing friendship with popular Helena Minor and her budding romance with Lewis Olswanger, a skinny, intelligent boy, shy in person but very funny when he assumes zany characters over the phone. Gradually Izzy begins to tell her brief bits about his earlier life and about her grandmother, Eva. Rachel starts to kiss him goodbye when she leaves. One day he takes her on a bus to an old part of town with a creek running through it and examines the bridges where streets cross the creek. On the way home Izzy tells her he built all those bridges, and on one he left his hand print and initials in the cement. As he gets weaker, Rachel feels so obligated that she refuses to go to Helena's birthday party so Helena, her boyfriend, and Lewis bring the party to Izzy's apartment. He is so pleased that he shows off by lifting Helena and almost collapses. The next day he tells Rachel that he saw Eva that night and insists on a long walk, on which he seems to appreciate everything, but he cannot make it back to the apartment. Manny and Shirley come and take him to the hospital. Rachel gets assignments from her teachers and stays out of school to be with him. Finally, as he gets weaker and in more pain, Rachel insists on staying at the hospital through the night and is with him when he dies. Some time later she and Lewis go back to the street with the bridges and examine each one, and at last they find Izzy's hand print and the initials, I.S. Most of the novel is in the present tense, interspersed with entries from Rachel's diary and letters she writes to her brother Jeremy, in which she pours out her frustration with her elderly parents, who depend on her remaining their sweet little girl, and her doubts about her own attractiveness. Dialogue is especially strong, the predictable phrases that make up the parents' conversation, Lewis's flip wise-cracking, Izzy's brusque, dismissive put-downs. Jewish speech patterns add realism without calling attention to themselves. The greatest strength is in characterization, with all the major figures well drawn. Rachel's love for her grand-father grows convincingly, and her loss at his death is moving. ALA; Fanfare; Newbery Honor; SLJ.

**THE AGONY OF ALICE** (Naylor*, Phyllis Reynolds, Atheneum, 1985), realistic novel of an eleven-year-old growing up through the mishaps and triumphs at school and home during her sixth-grade year. Motherless Alice McKinley, new in Silver Spring, Maryland, is not assigned to the class taught by beautiful Miss Cole, whom she has secretly chosen as a role model, nor even to that of Mr. Weber, who takes his group on an overnight camp-out before the term end. Instead, she is in the class of Mrs. Plotkin, a pear-shaped woman with thick legs, to whom at first Alice acts quite rude. This becomes one of the many embarrassments she records on her list titled "Backward," a record of all the humiliating things she has done that make it seem she is reverting to early childhood and that outnumber those on her "Forward" list that show her ma-turing. Mrs. Plotkin wins her over by choosing her for a safety patrol substitute to attend the regular meetings with Miss Cole and by her practice of reading aloud for the last half hour every day. Another recent major embarrassment occurs while her brother Lester, 17, takes her shopping for blue jeans and she opens the wrong dressing-room door and sees a red-haired boy about her age in his blue underpants. To her horror, she later discovers that the boy is Patrick, the regular crossing guard. Her chances of making Miss Cole like her are doomed on Halloween when, as the back end of a horse, she kicks out friskily and connects with the beautiful teacher's arm. Her main problem, she decides, is having no mother to give advice and understanding, though her father, who runs a music store, does his best and her relations with Lester improve when she offers comfort after his girl friend dumps him. To her astonishment, Patrick starts giving her candy bars, turns out to be the sender of an anonymous valentine, and becomes her boy friend. When her father sends her for Easter vacation to her Aunt Alice in Chicago, she learns, with various disasters on the way, to figure out the toilet and the bed in her roomette, to eat in the dining car, and to get off at the right time. She admires her Aunt Alice, whom she scarcely re-members, for her confidence and great organization, although she is exhausted by their thorough tour of museums and appalled at her aunt's choice of a frilly white dress for her. Even more, she enjoys her grown-up cousin Carol, who cuts her hair stylishly, takes her for an easygoing, unplanned afternoon, and buys her some good-looking casual clothes and her first bra. She gives the white dress and shoes to the porter on the return trip. At the end of the year, when they once more turn in their journals, Alice, who has recorded all her intensely embarrassing blunders and paperclipped those pages together so the teacher will not read them, has developed enough self-assurance and trust in Mrs. Plotkin to remove all the paper clips. Alice narrates her "agonies" with excruciating self-consciousness that rings true to a bright girl her age in a voice that remains authentic and remarkably interesting. A reader can share her squirming misery and still laugh at the ways she blows a minor incident out of proportion. Her dry assessment of her father and Lester is amusing. They, her Chicago relatives, and the teachers are well characterized; Patrick and the various sixth-grade girls are types but not overdone. Alice matures through the year convincingly. ALA.

**AKIYAMA NOBUTOMO** (*The Samurai's Tale**), samurai general to whom Takeda Shingen gives the newly captured narrator, a rival samurai's youngest son. Akiyama renames him Taro, and, puzzled at what to do with the four-year-old, says casually that the child "may do to look after his horses," a statement Taro takes as a promise. Akiyama then assigns him to the kitchen for servants and forgets him. Not until some seven years later, when he comes upon the cook, Togan*, just murdered by a ruffian and Taro reminds him of the earlier incident, does he remember the boy and send him to his horse barns. When Taro is almost fourteen, Akiyama chooses him to ride secretly to Toko-ji Temple with the Wakatono, second son of Takeda Shingen, where the Wakatono evidently murders his older half-brother who earlier revolted against their father. Although Taro fantasizes that Akiyama might adopt him, in reality the lord's attitude is ambivalent. He eventually gives Taro a new name, which includes the boy's true family name, obviously trusts him, and seems at times to favor him, but during the siege of Iwamura Castle he assigns Taro to a seemingly doomed position in charge of an expendable group of supply workers. After Akiyama marries the widow of the castle's ruler, he seems to fall deeply in love with her, takes to dressing richly, leads a group of young samurai on hunts and in sports contests, and acts rejuvenated. When the castle falls to his enemy, he is crucified upside down as an added humiliation, and his wife is beheaded. He exemplifies the truly noble among the high-bred samurai.

**ALENA OSTERMANN MALCOLM** (*Edith Herself**), loyal wife to John*, devoted mother to Vernon* and baby Lettie, and overly loving sister of Edith Ostermann. Alena stays with her mother and Edith and her older brothers and sister until their mother dies, probably of tuberculosis, and remains in the house until after the funeral, when her husband insists she come home and care for her own family. Alena's emotions tend to govern her actions. She argues with John about sending Edith to school because she wants to avoid the possibility of Edith having an epileptic seizure there for which the children might tease her. Fortunately for Edith, John prevails, and Edith attends school, where she proves herself quite capable of handling the situation.

**ALEXANDER ARMSWORTH** (*Blossom Culp and the Sleep of Death\**), blond, mop-headed youth of fourteen who accompanies Blossom\* Culp on her adventures in righting wrongs and saving souls. His father is a well-off house builder. Alexander's main interest in this book is in being accepted into the Iota Nu Beta secret fraternity in Bluff City High School. The boys make him do such things to prove his worthiness as smoking a cigar alone at night in Old Man Leverette's privy. To give Alexander such a scare that he will give up all this nonsense about fraternities, Blossom builds a small bonfire near the privy in the middle of the night. The fire gets away and burns up the privy. Thus she is able to blackmail Alexander into helping her with her Egyptian project. When Alexander travels through time with her to the Egypt of fifty years earlier, she points out to him that he also possesses psychic abilities, or the Gift, as she puts it. It is unclear whether or not he has agreed to give Letty\* Shambaugh his fraternity pin, but it is clear from Blossom's narrative that Letty could probably get it from him.

**ALEXANDER†, LLOYD (CHUDLEY)** (1924–     ), born in Philadelphia, Pa.; educated at West Chester State Teachers College, Lafayette College, and the University of Paris (Sorbonne); author, free-lance writer, and translator. He achieved prominence for his novels of fantasy for children, chiefly the five frequently honored Chronicles of Prydain: *The Book of Three†* (Holt, 1964); *The Black Cauldron†* (Holt, 1965); *The Castle of Llyr†* (Holt, 1966); *Taran Wanderer†* (Holt, 1967); and *The High King†* (Holt, 1968), winner of the John Newbery Medal. Based loosely on the legends of the Welsh *Mabinogion* and set in a Wales-like land, they trace the adventures of the youth Taran, a foundling of no known parentage and an assistant pig keeper, and attack questions of identity and self-worth in an atmosphere of heroism and danger. Among his other notable fantasies are *The Cat Who Wished to Be a Man†* (Dutton, 1973), *The First Two Lives of Lukas-Kasha†* (Dutton, 1978), and *The Marvelous Misadventures of Sebastian†* (Dutton, 1970), which received the National Book Award. *Westmark†* (Dutton, 1981), *The Kestrel†* (Dutton, 1982), and the Fanfare book *The Beggar Queen\** (Dutton, 1984) constitute a trilogy that departs from his previous work. They are realistic novels of adventure and conflict set in a fictitious medieval kingdom threatened by democratic revolutionaries. In a more romantic vein is *The Illyrian Adventure\** (Dutton, 1986), one of several suspenseful, fast-moving novels of intrigue featuring high-spirited, resourceful Vesper Holly. It was named a Best Book for Children by the American Library Association. Other books featuring Vesper Holly are *The El Dorado Adventure* (Dutton, 1987), *The Drackenburg Adventure* (Dutton, 1988), and *The Jadera Adventure* (Dutton, 1989). Alexander's style is exuberant, contemporary and slyly witty; his plots are inventive and action filled if superficial, overly intricate, and too patly resolved; his hosts of characters are intriguing if shallow and static; and recurring themes include the triumph of good over evil, treachery foiled, and discovering one's hidden strengths. Before writing for young readers, Alexander wrote for adults, including the novel *And Let the Credit Go* (Crowell, 1955) and translations from the French of Sartre, Eluard, and Vialar. He was nominated for the Laura Ingalls Wilder Award in 1983.

**ALICE SHIPP** (*Come a Stranger**), wife of Tamer* Shipp, a pretty, fluttery, dependent woman, mother of three young children. She leans on her husband, who at first indulges her whims, and is inclined to drink too much. Later, Tamer urges her to take hold of herself and attend to duty. Alice likes to have fun, and in one memorable scene, while at the Smith house, she and Tamer dance in the yard, both having a fine time. She is quite willing to let someone else, like Mina, take care of her children and her house, while she goes out to socialize or watches TV. Tamer urges her to get her high school equivalency diploma, so that she will feel better about herself. After a long period of playing off on that, too, she eventually works at it and is delighted to have secured her diploma before she and Tamer move to the college community where he will serve as chaplain and occasionally teach. She has disliked living in Harlem and looks forward to the change. As Tamer is a foil for quiet, plodding Mr. Smiths, she is a foil for sensible Raymonda Smiths, a loyal and dedicated wife and mother who not only keeps a good house but also works as a nurse and who has mostly become reconciled to her husband's putting his ministerial duties first. Although Alice has many undesirable characteristics, it is hard to dislike her because she projects the charm of the weakling.

**ALISTAIR MACBETH** (*The Moonlight Man**), Canadian Royal Mounted policeman who is young and inexperienced enough to be nervous while questioning Harry Ames about the vandalism of a shed. Harry glibly says he knows nothing about it, a barefaced lie since he himself did it. Later, at Harry's request, Alistair takes Harry, with Catherine along, to local bootleggers for moonshine. When Catherine asks Alistair why he does not arrest them, he says he does, but not on his time off, since they are poor farmers and need the extra money. Harry wants Catherine along because he senses that Alistair is attracted to her, again, as often, using people to advance his drinking purposes. Alistair wants to be known as Macbeth when he is on duty, and as Alistair when they visit the bootleggers. He is an interesting combination of innocence and experience, of idealism and reality.

***ALL ABOUT SAM*** (Lowry*, Lois, ill. Diane deGroat, Houghton, 1988), seventh in a series for middle readers about the Jewish family of Anastasia Krupnik in contemporary Cambridge, Massachusetts, this one featuring her little brother, Sam. The action, seen through the perceptions of Sam, starts with his birth and his egocentric introduction to his family and the world around him. He learns to crawl, to walk, to talk, especially to say, "NO!," and soon progresses to the Terrible Twos, an idea which rather frightens him when his mother mentions it, since he expects the Twos to be lurking under the bed or ready to burst out of the closet at night. The family moves from the apartment to a house, and Sam starts nursery school. Most of the episodes occur when Sam is about three: he goes with his mother to the supermarket, where he slips a package of gum into his pocket and suffers instant remorse; he wants a pet, although his father is allergic to dogs and cats, and finds one for himself, a worm he christens King of Worms; he enters King of Worms in a pet show, only to have him disappear, and he is heartbroken until Anastasia convinces him that his pet has slithered underground back home faster than they can walk, and sure enough, they find him when they dig by the bush in the yard; he takes his father's pipe and lighter to school for Show and Tell, to the consternation of his teacher; he gives himself a punk haircut; he tries to develop muscles; he visits Gertrustein, the old woman next door, and learns to communicate with her in Morse code, using a flashlight. Most of the humor comes from Sam's taking a statement literally when it is meant otherwise, as when he tries to figure out how to pump iron with his mother's steam iron and dress shoe, and when his mother wants him to be trained and he practices being a locomotive. The antics are all those of a normal, lively small boy, not exaggerated but given importance because of the child's point of view. Sam's first day, when he meets his parents and sister, cleverly repeats the exact dialogue from the first book, but as heard by Sam, a device amusing to readers who know *Anastasia Krupnik*. The rest of the earlier chapters, before Sam can talk, are perhaps a bit overcute. Characterization of Anastasia and her parents depends on a familiarity with the other books in the series. SLJ.

**ALMA ALTON** (*Cracker Jackson\**), the young woman who before she married Billy Ray Alton babysat Jackson Hunter and who is beaten by her husband, apparently to vent his frustrations when he meets with some disappointment. Alma is a sweet, warm, naive person, emotional and vulnerable. She likes to address people by affectionate nicknames. She is curiously friendless of people her age and relies on Jackson for support. She had been friends with Billy Ray for several years before they married and had been very much in love with him. She decides to leave him after a bad beating during which he also beats their baby girl, Nicole.

**ALMAZ** (*The Return\**), Desta's* little sister. In the village, she is a pretty, forward, indulged child who craves attention, especially from adults. On the journey, she at first whines, disobeys, and is untrustworthy. Later she becomes intensely sober and puts up with physical suffering and great hardship without a word of complaint. In the refugee camp, she makes friends with a boy her age, Hagos, who has lived all his life there and has become a carrier of gossip and information of all kinds. As a character he demonstrates what life is like for child refugees. Almaz is a round and likeable character, a good foil for Desta.

*AMY'S EYES* (Kennedy*, Richard, ill. Richard Egielski, Harper, 1985), doll fantasy set in the period of sailing vessels, much of it on the high seas. Amy's father, a tailor suffering hard times, leaves his infant daughter along with a nautical doll he has made named the Captain at the gate of St. Anne's Home for Girls. There she is treated well by Mrs. Hill, the High Mistress, finds an enemy in Miss Quince, and a true friend in Miss Eclair. Amy considers the doll her brother, carries him everywhere with her, and reads to him from *Mother Goose*. When she is ten years old, she accidentally jabs a needle sharply into his head. The doll begins to talk, within a few days has become real flesh and blood, and soon starts to grow. Since Mrs. Hill thinks he should be sent to the Boys' Home and Miss Quince wants to shut him in the bread box, the Captain escapes with the help of Miss Eclair, promising to write Amy or return within a month. Miss Quince, however, intercepts his letter, and Amy, thinking him dead, becomes ill and changes into a doll. Mrs. Hill puts her in a shoe box for safe keeping. When the Captain returns, having by bravery and good fortune become master of his own ship, the *Ariel*, he takes her in the shoe box to sea. Before the *Ariel* leaves port, the Captain is approached and threatened by a heavily veiled woman who says she is the bad sister of the deceased previous captain and knows the ship is to seek pirate treasure with a map he gave the Captain. She claims half the loot and insists on traveling with them to make sure she collects. Learning that a woman is to sail on the *Ariel* and hearing rumors that the Captain is talking to a doll, the crew deserts, except the first mate, Mr. Cloud, and one seaman named Skivvy, who was a suit of long underwear to which the Captain read the Bible until he came alive. Unable to sign a crew, the Captain settles for a bag of toy animals. Anchored far out in the bay, he diligently reads *Mother Goose* to the toys and, with the aid of a darning needle poked into their heads, brings them to life. With this odd crew, the *Ariel* sails, pursued by the *Locust*, a ship commanded by Goldnose the pirate. During the voyage the Bad Sister acts as cook and occasionally displays redeeming qualities; the Captain suspects that Mr. Cloud may be her accomplice, although actually the mate is loyal and is seeking a mermaid he once knew; Davy Duck, bent on mutiny, sews a crew of stuffed ducks, reads *Mother Goose* to them, and displays a light at night so the pirate ship can follow; and Skivvy, his brain steeped in the Bible, becomes more and more obsessed. At Vulcan Island, the Captain snips off Amy's eyes, puts them into a bottle which he lets down on a line from the ship's boat, and at last brings her to life with the darning needle so that she can tell him if she sees the pirate gold, which he believes is sunk at that point. As her eyes search, a man wearing gold bracelets and necklaces swims to the boat, saying he was shipwrecked there ten years before and has gradually taken all the treasure to the island. Preoccupied by this Golden Man, who of course turns out to be their father, the tailor, the Captain neglects the bottle with Amy's eyes and it breaks against a rock. The eyes are eaten by a fish. In a complex final scene, Goldnose attacks, Davy Duck, having brought his duck crew to life, attempts mutiny, the Golden Man subverts the ducks to the Captain's side, the combined forces drive the pirates back to the *Locust*, and Skivvy, badly wounded, sets off a powder keg on a raft that destroys the pirates and their ship. Aboard the *Ariel* many are near death, including the Captain. In the meantime, far to the south, Mama Dah-dah, a black islander with unusual powers, has cut open a fish and found the two blue buttons that are Amy's eyes. By looking into them closely, she learns Amy's story and sends her pet albatross to deliver the eyes to the *Ariel*. The Bad Sister, who has protected Amy during the battle, sews them back on, and Amy recognizes her as Miss Eclair. It is explained that after an accident killed Miss Quince, who was pretending to be the previous captain's sister, Miss Eclair took her place to keep an eye on Amy. The Captain dies happy, knowing that Amy has her eyes again, Miss Eclair and Amy go with the Golden Man, who plans to set up a tailor shop, and Mr. Cloud sails off still seeking his mermaid. The plot is full of other misunderstandings, mistaken identities, and impersonations, but action lags during the voyage. There is no explanation of why Miss Eclair does not make herself known earlier. The bizarre way Amy becomes a doll and the use of her eyes, detached from her body, to find the gold are disturbing elements not found in the conventional doll story. Skivvy's tortuous attempt to interpret the Bible with mathematical formulas is a satirical comment on the fanatically religious. ALA.

**ANDREW CLAYTON** (*After the Dancing Days**), young man horribly disfigured by gas in World War I whom Annie Metcalf meets on the hospital grounds. A farm boy who could have been deferred, Andrew enlisted and was in France less than two months. Although his mother visits him when she can, his embittered father will not come into the hospital to see him. Although Annie is still something of a child and Andrew is nine years older, he is so lonely and bored that he appreciates her visits, while she falls deeply in love with him. Through the summer he gradually becomes less withdrawn until, before Timothy Lewis leaves, Andrew acts as manager for the baseball game they hold to celebrate.

**ANDY MEARS** (*Quentin Corn**), three-year-old son of the local constable. Like Emily* Emerson, he is precocious and sees right away that Quentin is a pig, not a runaway boy. Thinking fast, Quentin tells Andy that his identity is a secret, and Andy immediately plays along. Andy is the youngest and only boy in the large, poor Mears family, all of whom are dressed in castoffs or made-over flour sacks. Even on his birthday, Andy is clad in black, his shirt and pants newly fashioned from his father's broken umbrella. Andy grows to have a splendid soprano, which the choirmaster says reminds him of Quentin's. Even those many years later, Andy does not divulge what he knows about Quentin.

**ANDY SCHUYLER** (*A Place To Come Back To**), neighbor friend of both Oliver Shattuck and Charlotte Paige, one of their intimate circle. Andy is determined to run the family farm, the Bullard Farm that has come down through the generations, and enlists the help of his friends in making it go. Thus the young people become very close, and Oliver has used the Bullard Farm as an excuse for staying summers in Concord. In Andy's way he is just as stubborn as Oliver is presented as being (Oliver spends hours and hours alone learning to do ice skating figures), but Andy's emotions are always on the surface whereas Oliver submerges his.

*ANGEL'S MOTHER'S WEDDING* (Delton*, Judy, ill. Margot Apple, Houghton, 1987), amusing realistic contemporary family novel set from May through August in the small Wisconsin town of Elm City, one in a series about the O'Learys. When their friend Edna* informs Angel O'Leary, 10, that weddings mean invitations, cakes, pictures, presents, and the like, Angel and her little brother, Rags*, 5, get worried because so far as they know Mrs. O'Leary has not begun making preparations for her wedding to Rudy* the television clown, which is scheduled for August. When he learns Rudy wants a new car but would settle for a new paint job on his old one, Rags takes the initiative. While Angel is biking with Edna outside of town, when she should be babysitting him, Rags tries to paint Rudy's blue car red. He ends up with red paint all over himself and the garage, and the car turns out striped. Both children feel terribly guilty, each for different reasons, but congenial, accommodating Rudy saves the day. He remarks the car "is probably the most—ah—thoughtful" of any gift he and Mrs. O'Leary will receive, and the whole family bursts out laughing. For weeks thereafter, the wedding receives little attention, since Rudy's station is sponsoring a float for the Memorial Day Parade. The whole family works on getting it ready, enlisting friends to help and be in the show, which consists of a "tin pan" orchestra and trained dog performance. Rain pours down on the big day, and Rags has trouble with the trained dogs, which run away, but everyone has a good time anyway. After school is out, Edna reminds Angel of the wedding, but Angel is almost sure it is off since her mother does not pick up Angel's hint about it. At a spaghetti dinner Rudy cooks for them, however, the children are informed that the wedding will be very small, "important but not showy," so few preparations will be necessary. Some days later, when Mrs. O'Leary tells Angel that Rudy intends to adopt the children and give them his name, Pappadopolis, Angel is not keen on the idea, because she is afraid she will be the laughing stock of the school. Although Mrs. O'Leary's good friend, Alyce, tells her it is all right, Angel is still not sure because Edna roars with laughter, saying the name sounds like a city. Preparations, of the kind Edna means, begin in July with a costume-party shower given by Alyce, where even Rudy shows up dressed as a rabbit. Then Angel learns she is to be junior bridesmaid and Rags the ring bearer, a function he understands as "ring bear." Mrs. O'Leary and Angel drive to the city for new dresses, Mrs. O'Leary finding a becoming teal blue and Angel getting a pretty lavender, both dresses they can also wear later. Other preparations ensue, all low keyed and modest for an at-home wedding attended by close friends and relatives. It turns out beautifully, in spite of several hitches. Since Rudy's suit does not come back from the cleaner's in time, he appears in his clown trousers and short sleeves, and Alyce, the maid of honor, arrives in a dress identical to Mrs. O'Leary's. Even though he now knows what a ring bearer is supposed to do, Rags insists on performing "ring bear" antics through-out the ceremony. When Rudy gives Mrs. O'Leary her ring, he also gives Angel a locket with her new monogram and Rags a small gold watch with his new initials. A surge of love sweeps over Angel for her new father, and she feels proud to be Angel Pappadopolis. Winning characters and Angel's concern that the wedding be done right according to Edna's notions hold this loosely plotted story together. The point of view, which is almost all Angel's (now and then that of Rags), seems typical of imaginative, over-dramatizing children. The gently humorous tone recalls the books about Henry Huggins and the Moffats, although episodes rely less on situation comedy than do the Huggins incidents. There are a similar strong sense of family unity and support, the willing desire to "make do," looking on the bright side, and parental common sense that rescues what might otherwise be thought disasters. Sentence structure and diction are accessible to most readers just beyond primers, but since the book is never babyish or condescending, it can appeal also to middle and later elementary readers. SLJ.

**ANNIE** (*Good-bye and Keep Cold**), best friend of Frances* Combs until it is revealed that she had a brief affair with Ed Combs when Frances was in the hospital. An outsider like Frances, Annie came to the mountains as a Vista worker and lives by preference in a log cabin with outdoor plumbing, a choice that increases the suspicion of her local neighbors. Annie teaches art at the high school and is doing a series of portraits of the mountain people later published in a book. Annie's way of life is much more free than that of Frances, and she apparently considers her extra-marital excursions innocent fun or at least un-important, and tries unsuccessfully to repair her friendship with straight-laced Frances. She is partly the cause of the breakup between Frances and Henry* John, whether unwittingly or purposely is not clear.

**ASHLEY PACKARD** (*Princess Ashley**), influential, affluent fifteen-year-old who heads the pace-setting social set at Crestwood High. Her father's pampered darling, spoiled and manipulative, she dominates her stepmother, whom she openly disparages and tells the girls is not married to her father. On her birthday, she invites her set of aping followers to a "cosmetic consultation" party, after which her father presents his "princess" with a new blue Mustang convertible. She represents over-indulged, callous, immoral contemporary youth.

**AUNT ALICE CUMMINGS** (*Underdog**), Izzy's aunt by marriage. Alice's frosted hair is always perfectly coiffed, and her garments always coordinate with her white and off-white apartment. She and her husband, Izzy's Uncle* Roger, agreed not to have children since both wished to concentrate on their careers. They take Izzy in, however, and are genuinely kind to her, doing the best they can under the circumstances. Aunt Alice is a fine cook and a warm person and pays more attention to Izzy than does Roger. Like Roger, she is a distorted type, the "modern" woman.

**AUNT BEA** (*The Village by the Sea**), Uncle* Crispin's wife and Emma's father's half-sister on his father's side. The house in which she lives was built by her father for her mother and left to Bea in his will. Although the details are not clear, Bea evidently resented her widower father marrying again and often makes snide remarks about Emma's grandmother and a Connecticut estate. She typically puts people down and tries to make them feel guilty or inferior. The brandy bottle deer that Emma finds and puts in the beach village forest symbolizes both Bea's alienation and the alienation she creates for others. If Aunt Bea had been polite and hospitable, Emma would not have sought refuge on the beach and would not have built the village that drives home to Bea her inability to relate. Bea allows Uncle Crispin peace, apparently, only when they are alone. Then she has his undivided attention, and association with others does not remind her of her inadequacies. Bertie and her mother refer to her as "Lady Bonkers," a term that reflects her reputation in the neighborhood.

**AUNT KIBRET** (*The Return**), Desta's* pretty, talkative, loving aunt and foster mother. Kibret has trained Desta for village life and is preparing her for marriage to Dan* when circumstances dictate that Desta leave. Aunt Kibret opposes the children's going to Israel because she is honestly afraid for their safety and also, as Uncle* Tekle, her husband, points out, because she is childless and wants them to look after her (and him) in her old age. Kibret is characteristically indecisive, arguing on both sides of questions so that later she can claim, regardless of the outcome, that she was right. After the children make up their minds to leave for Israel, she takes it in good part and helps them get ready. At the story's end, her fate is unknown.

**AUNT LAURA** (*Borrowed Children**), half-sister of Mandy's mother, some thirteen years younger. Because their emotionally distraught mother rejected her when her older brother died as a result of flu after serving unscathed in World War I, Laura turned to her older sister, who "adopted" her, almost as if she were her own child. The two were inseparable until the older sister fell in love with Jim Perritt and ran off to marry him. Laura, already a self-dramatizing child, felt twice betrayed and has evidently never recovered. She has married a handsome man who does not work, and together they have drunk up and squandered his money. They wear matching raccoon coats but have no furniture in their apartment. In the relationship of Laura and her mother, Mandy sees the parallel to her feeling about little Willie, her newborn brother she has cared for while her mother is bedridden.

**AVI†** (**AVI WORTIS**) (1937–      ), born in New York City and educated at the universities of Wisconsin and Columbia; librarian, storyteller, teacher of children's literature, and author of children's books. Since *Things That Some-*

*times Happen* (Doubleday, 1970), a collection of short stories, Avi's list has grown rapidly into more than twenty books that cover a wide variety of times, places, subjects, and treatments, including mystery-detective novels like *No More Magic†* (Pantheon, 1975) and *Shadrach's Crossing†* (Pantheon, 1983), and the ghost story *Something Upstairs\** (Orchard, 1988), all nominees for the Edgar Allan Poe Award, and adolescent problem novels like *A Place Called Ugly* (Pantheon, 1981), and *Sometimes I Think I Hear My Name* (Pantheon, 1982). More highly regarded are his spirited, adventure-filled parodies on Victorian melodrama, *Emily Upham's Revenge†* (Pantheon, 1978), also a nominee for the Poe Award, and *The True Confessions of Charlotte Doyle* (Pantheon, 1990), a Newbery Honor book, and sensitive, revealing historical novels, like *Encounter at Easton†* (Pantheon, 1980), a Christopher Award book, and *The Fighting Ground\** (Lippincott, 1984), a novel of the American Revolution that was selected by the American Library Association as a Best Book for Children and was honored with the Scott O'Dell Award for Historical Fiction. Avi is ranked as one of the most versatile and inventive of contemporary writers for the young. His best works are marked by fast-moving, imaginative plots, strong characterization, and considerable wit and irony.

# B

**BANKER** (*Good-bye and Keep Cold**), great-uncle, or perhaps great-great-uncle, of Edda Combs's father, she is not quite sure which. Because he and Ed got along well with each other and not well with the rest of the Kentucky mountain family, he has come to live with Ed and Frances*, staying most of the time in his upstairs room, contentedly clipping articles from the several newspapers he takes and carefully filing them in books according to subject. Although he seems removed from the household, his presence provides a stability and a refuge for all the members, and although he seldom gives advice, he is a sympathetic and thoughtful listener. After Ed's death, he suggests that he should be looking for another place, and Frances cries out, "Banker, I need you. Please don't go." He moves with Frances and the children to Lexington, a new home chosen partly so they will not be too far from the mountains where he grew up, but by the end of the book he has died.

**BARNEY PENNIMEN** (*Through the Hidden Door**), eighth grader at Winchester Boy's School who becomes involved with uncovering artifacts of a miniature civilization. Barney's mother is dead and his father is an antique dealer, traveling frequently in Europe and other distant places. He has impressed Barney with the importance of attending the right school, so that he can get into the right prep school, then the right university. When Barney is threatened by Rudy Sader and his gang, his father regrets having stressed this program and tries to get his son to transfer to a second-rate school in Monterey, California, but Barney sticks stubbornly to Winchester, even though he is scared. His father gives him an antique "lady's pistol" to defend himself if necessary.

**BAUER†, MARION DANE** (1938–      ), born in Oglesby, Ill.; teacher, writer of novels for children. She attended La Salle-Peru-Oglesby Junior College and the University of Missouri, and received her B.A. degree from the University of Oklahoma. She has taught high school English in Wisconsin, and creative writing at Hennepin County Technical School in Minnesota and for the University of Minnesota Continuing Education program. Several of her novels have twelve-year-old protagonists, including *Shelter from the Wind* (Seabury, 1976), a story of a girl whose fanatically religious foster father presses his attentions on her, *Rain of Fire†* (Clarion, 1983), about a boy's nearly disastrous efforts to cover up the odd behavior of his brother who has witnessed the horrors of Hiroshima, and *On My Honor** (Clarion, 1986), concerned with a boy's feelings of guilt in the drowning death of his friend. *Shelter from the Wind* was named an honor book for the Golden Kite Award; *Rain of Fire* won the Jane Addams Award; and *On My Honor* was listed as an American Library Association Notable Book, a *School Library Journal* Best Book, and a Newbery Award Honor book. Bauer has also written a novel for young adults, *Tangled Butterfly* (Houghton, 1980), about a disturbed seventeen-year-old girl.

**BEATTY†, PATRICIA (ROBBINS)** (1922–1991), born in Portland, Oregon; educator, librarian, and author best known for her adventurous historical novels for young people. A graduate of Reed College and the University of Washington, she taught high school English and history in Idaho and was a technical and science librarian in Delaware and California. She wrote novels with her husband, John Beatty, a professor of British history, a collaboration that resulted in eleven historical novels for children and young people, many set in the British Isles and including *A Donkey for the King†* (Macmillan, 1966), a story of ancient Palestine. Individually she wrote more than two dozen carefully researched novels of Indians, women's rights, the Old West, pioneer life, and the Civil War. Among these are *Hail Columbia†* (Morrow, 1970), about one woman's campaign to clean up Astoria, Oregon, in the 1890s, and the Civil War novels *Turn Homeward, Hannalee* (Morrow, 1984), about Georgia millworkers shipped North during the war, and *Charley Skedaddle** (Morrow, 1987), about a New York Bowery runaway to the Union forces who deserts and is befriended by a Southern woman, which was honored with the Scott O'Dell Award for Historical Fiction. Other books by Beatty with a Civil War setting are *Eben Tyne, Powdermonkey* (Morrow, 1990) and *Jayhawker* (Morrow, 1991). Although Beatty's characters are often flat and sometimes approach caricature and her plots may be overly complex and contrived, her stories are fast-moving, suspenseful, full of the events and flavor of the times, and highly entertaining. A resident of southern California, she taught classes in writing for children at branches of the University of California.

***THE BEGGAR QUEEN*** (Alexander*, Lloyd, Dutton, 1984), fast-paced, generously cast realistic novel of war, danger, and intrigue, the last of three about the fictitious kingdom of Westmark* and featuring the urchin-queen, Mickle*, and her faithful friend and loyal advisor, Theo*, once a lowly printer's devil. Although Mickle, as Queen Augusta, has been ruling Westmark for about two years with the help of her three consulars, Theo, Justin, and Florian* and the realm has enjoyed peace, some elements are dissatisfied. Justin resents the compromise that produced the consular triumvirate, advocating rule of the people instead, and Cabbarus, the unscrupulous, tyrannical prime minister under Mickle's father, yearns to take over the kingdom from which he has been exiled. With the aid of devious Duke Conrad of the neighboring kingdom of Regia and Ankari mercenaries, he takes the Westmark capital of Marianstat and sets up a directorate. Mickle evades his clutches and takes refuge with Ingo, a pawnbroker, and his friends in The Shambles, an area in Marianstat of cheap wine shops, dicing dens, and flea markets, where she forms a government in exile. Theo has been staying with Keller, a journalist who publishes a small political paper called *El Kasperl*. Thus having escaped the director's dragnet, he joins Mickle, and they persuade Florian to flee to friendly King Constantine of Regia, where the old and ailing rebel can gather forces to restore Westmark to normal. Florian agrees to go to Regia on condition that Theo secure the city for him, that is, incite the people against Cabbarus and prepare them to rebel when Florian attacks. Theo agrees, though very reluctantly, since he knows many lives will of necessity be sacrificed. Count Las* Bombas, a long-time friend of Theo and Mickle, forges false identity cards for the rebels, his dwarf, Musket, gathers information, and numerous other characters assist in a variety of ways. Justin, however, proves difficult, having gathered his own partisans. Theo orders nuisance attacks and thefts of weapons and supplies, which provoke numerous reprisals. Things come to a head when Theo unfortunately catches the attention of Ankari mercenaries, is captured, and taken to Carolia prison. In a humorous passage, Keller tries to get arrested in order to free him but fails, since he is apprehended by friendly constables who refuse to arrest him. Ironically, Theo is released by a prison constable whom once he had helped. As this is going on, street fighting has broken out, the people having turned on Cabbarus for his murderous ways in spite of his superior firepower and trained soldiers, and when Justin arrives with his men later Florian, the city already belongs to the people. Justin is slain in the fighting, and in an attempt to bargain with Mickle, Cabbarus is slain by a supporter he had earlier tried to kill. Las Bombas is put in temporary charge of the government. Mickle and Theo are married, and Mickle relinquishes the throne to Florian, whose ancient line has a legitimate claim. He refuses the crown and sets about preparing elections, and Mickle and Theo join Las Bombas in a tour of the countryside. It is often hard to keep track of characters, since there are so many, some new, some brought over from earlier books. Character development is minimal, and most figures are distinguished by one or two features or by an unusual name, like Weasel, the "water rat" raised by Keller. He sniffs out information, sometimes influences the action, creates the street barricade about which most fighting revolves, and skillfully leads a faction of urchins like himself. The accent is on action, of which the convoluted plot has ample, along with twists, turns, treachery, and surprise to keep the pot boiling. Swift shifts in scene from sector to sector and cliff hangers in abundance tighten the tension as well as give a sense of the commotion in the beleaguered city. Theo's moral problems are awkwardly handled, since they are narrated rather than shown, but the difficulty of making decisions on the personal level when all paths seem wrong comes through clearly, and on the public level the philosophical matter of the sovereignty of the people is supported at every turn. Mickle is properly regal and as astute and gutsy as ever, while Theo seems more acted upon than acting, a follower of conscience and integrity who is content to be second fiddle to the woman he loves. Style is exuberant, witty, sometimes acerbic or satirical, and often calls attention to itself. Fanfare.

**BELLAIRS, JOHN** (1938–1991), born in Marshall, Mich., the small town that provided the locale for his books; college teacher and free-lance writer. After receiving degrees from the University of Notre Dame and the University of Chicago, he was a member of the English faculty at the College of St. Teresa in Minnesota, Shimer College in Illinois, Emmanuel College in Boston, and Merrimack College, North Andover, Mass., before becoming a full-time writer in 1972. He published more than a dozen well-received Gothic novels, mostly for young readers, of which the best known are *The House with a Clock in Its Walls* (Dial, 1973), his first for children, and *The Lamp from the Warlock's Tomb\** (Dial, 1988). One of several starring elderly, birdlike Miss Myra Eells and high-school-aged Anthony Monday, this book was nominated for the Edgar Allan Poe Award. These resourceful amateur sleuths also appear in *The Treasure of Alpheus Winterborn* (Harcourt, 1978) and *The Dark Secret of Weatherend* (Dial, 1984). Bellairs made his home in Haverhill, Mass.

**BENNETT†, JAY** (1912–      ), born in Brooklyn, N.Y.; lecturer, writer of suspense novels for both adults and young people. He attended New York University and has written stage plays and many radio and television scripts. Two of his mysteries for young people, *The Long Black Coat†* (Delacorte, 1973) and *The Dangling Witness†* (Delacorte, 1974), won the Edgar Allan Poe Award for Best Juvenile Mystery, and his novel, *The Skeleton Man\** (Watts, 1986), was a nominee for the award. His adult novel, *Catacombs* (Abelard, 1959), has been translated into eight languages and made into a movie. His books have been commended for being well crafted and having a strong sense of contemporary society. Bennett makes his home in Cherry Hill, New Jersey.

***BEYOND THE CHOCOLATE WAR*** (Cormier\*, Robert, Knopf, 1985), realistic school novel, sequel to *The Chocolate War†*, set some seven or eight months later in the same Vermont town of Monument, in which the corrupt leadership of Brother Leon, now headmaster, and the terrorist rule of Archie Costello at Trinity High are both challenged but endure, promising to become even worse, although Archie is graduating. Love has distracted Obie, Archie's right-hand man in the secret society of the Vigils, his passion for Laurie Gundarson overshadowing the importance of his position and his fear of Archie. As Assigner, Archie devises ingenious tasks for younger boys, usually not physically harmful but psychologically damaging. Like most of the Vigils, Carter, the sports hero president of the club, really hates Archie but fears his cleverness and his ruthlessness. As a final show of power, Archie plans a mass school skipping on the day of the bishop's visit to Trinity, so that Brother Leon will be humiliated as his superior celebrates High Mass in an auditorium empty except for one student, who will be assigned to attend as if everything were ordinary. Chosen for this assignment is Ray Bannister, a new boy whose hobby is magic and who has just built a trick guillotine. Obie, delivering the assignment, is fascinated with the machine and realizes that Archie has always employed sleight of hand to avoid choosing the black ball from the Vigil box, a choice that would mean he had to perform the assignment himself. Annoyed that Obie is slipping from his control, Archie suggests that something be done about "that girl" to his new stooge, Bunting, a sophomore who aspires to be Assigner when Archie graduates. Bunting organizes an attack on Obie and Laurie that stops just short of rape. When Obie learns that Archie was behind the attack, he is consumed with hate, especially after Laurie will have nothing more to do with him. Horrified at the plan for the bishop's visit, Carter sends an anonymous warning to Brother Leon. The visit is called off, but Archie discovers who wrote the letter and warns Carter that he will suffer for it, maybe years later, thus destroying Carter's confidence. Bannister's assignment is changed to being the Fool at Fair Day. With Carter's complicity, Obie substitutes black for white balls, insuring that Archie will have to be the Fool himself. Through intimidation, Archie avoids the usual humiliations of the Fool, but in the culminating skit show, he must place his head on the chopping block of Bannister's guillotine. At the crucial moment, with Carter providing a momentary distraction, Obie reverses the switch that makes the blade harmless, expecting Archie to be decapitated. Bannister, however, has failed to show Obie a safety catch, and Archie escapes injury, now marking Obie for some future retaliation. Meanwhile, David Caroni, a sensitive boy driven by Brother Leon's harassment to the edge of suicide, hears voices directing him to take the butcher knife and attack his tormentor. Before he can really harm the headmaster, he is interrupted, flees, and dives off an overpass bridge to his death. In a minor plot, Jerry Renault, who was badly injured early in the school year when he defied the Vigils, has returned to Monument, still psychologically damaged. His friend, Roland Goubert, known as the Goober, re-establishes contact although he is sick with guilt at having deserted Jerry at the critical moment earlier. Emile Janza, the boy who nearly killed Jerry, starts again to terrorize him and, when Jerry stands up to him, beats him up again. The novel ends with Archie retaining his control after graduation by appointing Bunting the Assigner but insisting that Janza be second in command, since he can feed Bunting ideas through Janza. Under this new arrangement, the Vigils plan to expand into using weapons, collecting protection money, and selling drugs. The unrelenting grimness of *The Chocolate War* continues in this sequel, but without the intensity, since it lacks a sympathetic focus, Obie being less appealing than Jerry was in the earlier book and Bannister, being a secondary character, not much developed. The theme seems to be that corruption will survive and flourish, despite combined efforts to destroy it. Jerry's decision to re-enter Trinity High is brave but foolish, not a gesture of defiance against the system but simply a personal challenge, almost sure to meet further violence. Fanfare.

**BLOSSOM CULP** (*Blossom Culp and the Sleep of Death**), heroine of a series of books set in Bluff City, U.S.A., in which by wit, luck, and courage, she sets things right with the help of her classmate Alexander* Armsworth. A small, dark, frizzy-headed girl of fourteen, who dresses in a motley collection of garments her mother gleans in night foragings about town, Blossom is intelligent, spunky, independent, and endowed with supernatural talents like extrasensory perception and time travel, acquired, she thinks, through her gypsy blood: "It's been given to me by Forces Unknown to unlock the heavy doors of Time and enter history past and future." Blossom and her mother live in a tiny shack by the side of the streetcar line, where Blossom sleeps in a kind of attic whose only access is a narrow ladder. Her mother makes their living by telling fortunes (but Blossom realizes her own psychic talents far surpass her mother's) and mostly by foraging about town and stealing things, like the Egyptian antiquities, which she then sells.

**BLOSSOM CULP AND THE SLEEP OF DEATH** (Peck*, Richard, Delacorte, 1986), lighthearted, humorous fantasy involving extrasensory perception and time travel in the fictitious town of Bluff City, U.S.A., in 1914, one in a series featuring spunky, take-charge, high school freshman Blossom* Culp and her classmate Alexander* Armsworth. Looking back, Blossom tells in loquacious, grandiloquent style how she and Alexander help an Egyptian princess dead more than 3,800 years to regain her mummy and other artifacts stolen from her tomb and assist their history teacher, Miss Fairweather, to keep her job. Blossom's antagonist is wealthy, snooty Letty* Shambaugh, who has set her cap for Alexander. After the students hound their history teacher into quitting, the school board hires no-nonsense Miss Fairweather, who embarks on an Egyptian unit of study. Because Miss Fairweather is tough and no respecter of persons, Letty determines to get rid of her, her ammunition the discovery that Miss Fairweather lost her previous position because she is a suffragette who advocates women's right to vote, a matter Letty and her mother, local president of the Daughters of the American Revolution, consider unwomanly. The plot thickens when Blossom is awakened late one night by an apparition at the foot of her bed, a cobra-crowned young woman who says she is the ka (spirit) of long-dead Egyptian Princess Sat-Hathor and demands that, under pain of a curse, Blossom help her recover her mummy and other precious possessions. Blossom blackmails Alexander into joining her in her school Egyptian project (by threatening to reveal that he has been smoking a cigar in Old Man Leverette's privy). Her project is to search for the Princess's earthly possessions. For her project, Letty organizes the girls in her exclusive club into preparing a float that they will also use for

Homecoming, starring herself as Cleopatra, with asp, and decorating it with some of her mother's Egyptian antiques. Blossom discovers a ruby scarab among her mother's things, and Alexander, undergoing another step in his fraternity initiation in an abandoned circus tent near town, discovers more Egyptian things there, including the Princess's mummy, apparently the place where Blossom's mother found the scarab. Matters rise to a climax when Mrs. Shambaugh leads the school mothers in a march on the principal's office in an effort to oust Miss Fairweather and Blossom reveals that the antiques are stolen. Afraid of being turned in to the police as a receiver of stolen goods, Mrs. Shambaugh, over Letty's vociferous protests, tries to smooth things over by doing an about-face and supporting Miss Fairweather's women's rights efforts. When Miss Fairweather suggests she ship the artifacts off to the Egyptian Museum in Cairo, Mrs. Shambaugh immediately agrees. The Princess, however, is not satisfied, and Blossom, Alex, and the Princess slip back fifty years to just before the tomb is vandalized. Blossom and Alexander frighten off robbers so that the remainder of the Princess's precious entombed possessions are intact, like those in the museum. As the two leave to return to Bluff City, the Princess promises Blossom a gift she will appreciate. It arrives during the Homecoming parade, when "out of an absolutely clear sky a bolt of light sizzled down" and destroys Letty's Cleopatra barge. Characters are distorted to almost tall-tale proportions, and the narrative employs many startling and witty stylistic effects. Action packed, fast paced, and filled with twists and turns for an intricate plot, the story is not only top-notch comic entertainment, it conveys social comment about the behavior and attitudes of high schoolers and their officious and all-knowing parents. Typical of the hilarious scenes is that in which the ninth-grade boys roll runty Collis Ledbetter up in a window blind, from which "like the crack of doom" he falls down right in front of Miss Fairweather on her first day in school. Others in series. ALA.

*THE BLOSSOMS AND THE GREEN PHANTOM* (Byars*, Betsy, ill. Jacqueline Rogers, Delacorte, 1987), lighthearted realistic family novel, third in the series about the close-knit, active Blossoms, set in a rural area with hills, caves, and cliffs somewhere in the United States, possibly South Carolina. Having followed the rodeo circuit until father was killed by a steer four years earlier, the Blossoms are now settled on their farm, although the mother, Vicki, still longs for the old days. Junior, the youngest at about seven, fancies himself an inventor, hopes to become a stunt man, and feels keenly the failure of his two earlier inventions, wings (he launched himself from the barn and broke both legs) and a coyote trap (he caught himself in it). Having secretly fashioned in the barn a flying saucer, or UFO, he calls the Green Phantom, of air mattresses and garbage bags, he is bitterly disappointed because no one has barged in or even asked about his project, all being busy with their own activities. Vicki and Maggie, the eldest at possibly thirteen, spend hours out in back practicing trick riding for a mother-daughter act, and Vern, maybe ten, is intent on developing a friendship with Michael (who has absolutely everything, Vern thinks) from a mile or so down the road. Even Pap (grandfather) and his nondescript, half pointer dog named Mud are busy about their own concerns. When Vicki praises Maggie for her excellent progress, Junior bursts into tears, asserting he is a failure. Prompted by his sorrow, Vicki makes a solemn "Blossom promise" that he will have the "most beautiful, the most wonderful, the most spectacular UFO that the world has ever seen," and orders the other children to help him. Ralphie, who is sweet on Maggie and wants to impress her, steals helium (the last thing Junior needs for launching) from his mother's Balloonerie, and the children haul the contraption to Owl's Cliff. They inflate it and launch it at sundown, as Junior planned. The green raft-like creation floats eerily on the breeze, veers, hits the weathervane on Benson's barn, and collapses on the chicken house roof. Junior, having shinnied up while the others fled, nervously loosens it while Benson sits nearby with his gun in hand, thinking something may be after his chickens. Vicki has missed the launch because she has been waiting by the phone for word about Pap, who has been missing for eight hours. Pap had left in his truck with Mud, as he does early every Monday, to collect cans to redeem for deposit to supplement their meager income. He finally turns up about two o'clock in the morning, having spent most of the day and night trapped in a garbage dumpster, from which he was finally released by police. He had fallen in while trying to rescue a skin-and-bones, brown-and-white puppy, which he names Dump and gives to the children. At the second launching next day, the saucer gets stuck in an oak, but Ralphie and Maggie climb up and, with a cane belonging to Mad Mary, the elderly recluse who lives in a local cave and survives on road-kill animals, pry the contraption loose. It soars upward through the night, Junior's "gift to the world," an achievement of which Vicki assures him his father would have been proud. The situation comedy is less strained than in many books of this genre, and the characters, while of no depth, are carefully and believably individualized, with only mild eccentricities. The pace is lively, sentences and paragraphs are short and uncomplicated, dialogue is abundant and convincing, and tone is affectionate. Although Junior's problems are the story's focus, the narrative also shifts periodically to Pap's dilemma, so the reader is kept apprised of happenings at the dumpster. Maggie and Ralphie's little romance is sweetly and gently handled. Best are the picture of a caring and compatible family, where each member is respected and loved for himself or herself, and the humor that is never demeaning or sensationalized. ALA; SLJ.

*A BLUE-EYED DAISY* (Rylant*, Cynthia, Bradbury, 1985), fourteen realistic episodes about Ellie Farley, 11, and her family and friends, set in a coal-mining region in the West Virginia mountains one year from fall through the following summer probably in the late 1960s or early 1970s. The episodes are connected by the same central characters and rural setting but are otherwise discrete. Of her family of five older sisters, her homemaker mother, and father, Okey, Ellie is closest to Okey, a hard-drinking man, in spite of his occasionally abusive behavior. Okey no longer works since he was hurt in a mining slate-fall, and the family just manages to get by. In various episodes, Okey teaches Ellie to shoot a gun, and when she has become skillful, they go hunting with his beagle, Bullet. Ellie has an easy shot at a doe they flush, but she cannot bring herself to shoot the beautiful creature, and the two both agree the doe's the "*prettiest thing*" they've ever seen. Ellie dreams of a room of her own with roses on the canopy bed and owls on the wallpaper and enjoys supper at which they all happily share scraps with Bullet. She weeps for Uncle Joe, home from the war (probably Vietnam) that a classmate says is stupid and not "real," and bakes cookies for James Meador, the boy whose name she drew in the Church of God Christmas gift exchange. Her Uncle Trapper from Arizona visits with his eccentric wife, Crazy Cecile, and, when the school bus gets mired in the snow on Valentine's Day, the driver takes such tender care of the children that Ellie sees the man she thought cold and unfeeling in a whole new perspective. She also discovers that James Meador saved two of her Christmas cookies all this time. They share them, making Valentine's Day a perfect day for her. She attends the funeral of her classmate Lester Wood, shot accidentally by a brother; gathers pop bottles for spending money with her best friend, Carolyn Oaks, and spends it all on a Saturday in town on delightfully frivolous things; observes a boy having a seizure in school and worries about the possibility of having one herself; attends Carolyn's birthday party where she gets her first kiss during spin the bottle; and prays for her father, injured when his car goes off the mountain road from one glass of whiskey too many. The book concludes with Ellie looking forward to her twelfth birthday on August 26 with some trepidation because Carolyn's party had been so nice. Ellie opts for a quiet evening at home with her family and Carolyn over for pot roast and chocolate cake with white icing. She confides in Bullet's ear that altogether "it has been some kind of year." Characters, except for Okey and Ellie herself, are drawn in minimal strokes, the emphasis being on how little-big, naive-knowledgeable, poor-rich Ellie looks at and reacts to life. Although the book lacks the depth of the Moffat books, which it recalls, is more naturalistic (Ellie has "rotten" teeth which she hides with her hand when she laughs), and is not as overtly humorous, it has a similar warm and affectionate tone, optimistic outlook on life in spite of poverty and setbacks, and accuracy of the child's point of view. The title comes from a song Okey sings, "which made Ellie blush, though she wasn't sure why." ALA.

**BOND†, NANCY (BARBARA)** (1945–      ), born in Bethesda, Md.; librarian and author of fantasy and realistic fiction for children and young people. The daughter of a librarian and an elementary school teacher, she grew up in Concord, Mass., and received her B.A. degree from Mount Holyoke College. She lived for several years in the British Isles, where she attended the College of Librarianship in Aberystwyth, Wales, receiving her diploma in 1972. She was a member of the promotional staff of Oxford University Press in London from 1967 to 1968, then returned to the United States, where she took a position as children's librarian and was for two years director of a library in Massachusetts. In 1979 she became an instructor in children's literature at Simmons College in Boston. Her first book, *A String in the Harp*† (Atheneum, 1976), a fantasy improvising on Welsh folklore, received the International Reading Association Award, among other honors. *The Voyage Begun*† (Atheneum, 1981), also a critically acclaimed fantasy, is set in the future after pollution and energy limitations have resulted in a much reduced standard of living for Americans. *Another Shore* (Macmillan, 1988), set in Nova Scotia, is also a time-travel fantasy. Her realistic novels include *Country of Broken Stone* (Atheneum, 1980), set at an archaeological dig in northern England, and *The Best of Enemies* (Atheneum, 1978) and the Fanfare book *A Place To Come Back To\** (Atheneum, 1984), which together follow the lives of four friends in a small Massachusetts town from pre-adolescence into high school. Although Bond's books are sometimes heavy with detail, they are credible in character and situations, project a keen sense of time and place, and deal especially convincingly with family relationships.

**THE BONE WARS** (Lasky\*, Kathryn, Morrow, 1988), historical novel concerning rivalries of early paleontologists of the American West, set mostly in Montana Territory in the 1870s. Thad (Thaddeus) Longworth, 14, suffers from the memory of the murder of his mother, a prostitute in No Creek, Texas, which he witnessed when he was five, and is glad to get away from the town to join a cattle drive to Colorado with Jim Dundee, a rancher who has sometimes befriended him. By the time they reach Greeley, where Dundee dies of a heart attack, Thad has become a skillful scout and tracker. He hears of a Harvard professor named George Babcock, who is trying to get Buffalo Bill Cody to scout for him in the Black Hills. Thad rides to Ogalla where he comes in on a marital spat between Cody and his wife and gets Cody's recommendation to scout for Babcock. Babcock and his assistants ride west with General George Armstrong Custer's troops from Fort Lincoln, Dakota Territory, included in the expedition because the Indians seem to think there is magic about the Men-Who-Pick-Up-Bones, although the army is really exploring for gold in the hills, which are considered sacred by the Sioux and are deeded to them by treaty. Thad soon learns where to hunt for the best fossils, but he has mixed feelings about the expedition, knowing Custer's real purpose and, having earlier come to know Black Elk, an Indian seer about his age, feeling sympathy for the Indian point of view. When Custer is unable to buy the Black Hills from the Indians, he and his army, having ascertained that there is gold, return to Fort Lincoln, while Babcock's small group go west to the Judith River basin in Montana. There Julian DeMott, 14, from Devonshire, England, is excavating with the expedition of his father, Dr. Algernon DeMott, a cold, arrogant British scholar whose theory of Divine Intelligence attempts to refute ideas of evolution. Also in the Judith River country is a group from Yale, headed by Nathaniel Cunningham. The three paleontological groups have intense rivalry and are not above spying on each other, faking evidence, and distorting the truth to divert the others from a good find or attempting to beat each other in announcing a new discovery. Thad scouts, rides for supplies, and aids in the excavation, in particular devising ways to protect the fragile fossils as they are exposed and to strengthen the larger pieces so that they can be removed whole. On one trip to Fort Benton for supplies, he makes a valuable friend in Rap Stevens, a gambler who owns a number of river boats. Thad and Julian meet by accident, when the British boy has fallen down a deep fissure and Thad saves him. They discover that they have much in common, both being disillusioned by the behavior of their leaders and the narrowness of their visions, jealously guarding their finds and keeping them in private collections. Julian has met Louis Woodfin, a railroad magnate who wants to start the New World Museum to show fossils and reconstructed dinosaurs to the public. Since after a dispute his father has ignored him, Julian is able to devote most of his time to excavating an almost complete skull of a Triceratops he and Thad have discovered, and Thad joins him whenever possible. When it is almost ready to transport, he gets Rap Stevens to supply the riverboat to carry it. In an attempt to kill Thad and claim the huge fossil, Dr. DeMott is killed. After a number of seemingly devastating setbacks, including being diverted to witness the Battle of the Little Bighorn where Custer made his last stand, the boys are able to get their massive fossil to the New World Museum, which will finance their further explorations. The ambitious book contains far too many events and characters, many of the historical ones dragged in unconvincingly for brief or cameo appearances, among them Red Cloud, Crazy Horse, Sitting Bull, Elizabeth Custer, Calamity Jane, General Philip H. Sheridan, Louisa Cody, and Hunkpapa Chief Gall. While the rivalries among the three paleontological groups, based on actual groups with different names, are interesting, some of the other elements are far less believable. Thad learns to ride in one day and becomes an expert scout in a few weeks; he rides great distances in relatively short times; he is implausibly welcomed into the war camps of various tribes at the height of the last of the Indian wars. An author's note at the end explains helpfully which of the prominent figures are fictional, but a map locates the Badlands in the wrong part of Montana. SLJ.

**BORN INTO LIGHT** (Jacobs*, Paul Samuel, Scholastic, 1988), science fiction novel set in a rural area in New England for ten years beginning in 1913. More than seventy years later, Roger Westwood, "aged scientist and dignified winner of prizes," looks back on events that began on a spring morning when he was ten. As if reliving the events, he tells how he awakens to a blaze of light outside his window and then sees a strange form burst from the woods, a wild boy, naked, frightened, and frightening, about whom his sister, Charlotte, 14, throws a blanket. Shortly thereafter, Roger discovers a strangely burned circle on the floor of their woods. Charlotte, their widowed mother, and Dr. Jensen, the local physician, tame the beastlike creature with care and kindness. When Dr. Jensen advises institutionalizing the boy, Mother asserts "he will be one of ours" as long as she can manage to keep him. Ben, as they name him, calms down, adopts civilized behavior, and grows very rapidly, soon eclipsing Roger in build. Intelligent, he acquires a good command of language and does very well in school. Extremely strong, he stands up to bully Jackson Stone, yet seems constitutionally frail. It is discovered that he has healing power in his hands, especially when he employs the strange gray mud from the woods circle. When Dr. Jensen tells Mother about a wild girl named Nell, who has been consigned to an institution, Mother adopts her, too. Nell develops much as Ben did, and after Mother and Dr. Jensen marry and the family move to his house, all are very happy. Tutored by Dr. Jensen, the children progress rapidly, Ben being particularly interested in the stars and Roger in medicine. At boarding school, the boys excel also, and Ben again deals aptly with bullies, though afterward he is physically spent. They make friends with Montrose, a popular boy and fine athlete, who drops dead of exertion after barely defeating Ben in a footrace. Dr. Jensen informs the boys that Montrose was also a feral child. After a period of ill health provoked by the race, Ben recovers, outstrips Roger in his studies, and enters Harvard at an early age. He and Charlotte marry, have a daughter and then twin sons, all extraordinarily quick children. During this time, Dr. Jensen has been collecting information about other feral children, and, as his health declines, Ben becomes convinced that he and they are creatures from space and that by June of 1923 all possible of the second generation ferals must gather at the woods circle for the return to space. Roger and Jackson spend the winter and spring contacting ferals, and eventually more than one hundred families gather. Clustered in the woods circle, the hybrids disappear upwards in a great column of light. Roger theorizes that travelers from earth to a distant star had grown intellectually advanced but physically weak and sent the wild children to mate with humans to restore vigor to their race, and that technological innovations of the twentieth century derive from the ferals. If a little too morally good, Ben holds the center of attention. The other characters revolve about him and lack personality. Predominant are ideas, as in most science fiction, and suspense is high. The reflective "I" mode, known rapid advances in technology, and the factual, journalistic tone also help to make events seem real. SLJ.

**BORROWED CHILDREN** (Lyon*, George Ella; Orchard, 1988), realistic family and girl's growing-up story set in the Depression in the coal country of Goose Rock, Kentucky. Mandy (Amanda) Perritt, 12, loves school and her teacher from Boston, Mr. Aden, but when her new little brother is born and her mother hemorrhages and must stay in bed for weeks, her father takes Mandy out of school to keep house and care for the baby, little Willie. Although, at their father's command, her older brothers, David, 16, and Ben, 14, take over the clothes washing, Mandy must cook, clean, and look after her little sisters, Anna and Helen*, as well as rise in the night to change Willie, take him to her mother for feeding, and then walk the floor as he screams with colic. She works doggedly but her physical and mental exhaustion erupts one night when her mother quietly cautions her not to take more gravy, saving it instead for her brothers. Overcome by the injustice of it all, she hurls the gravy boat at the fireplace, then, as the family pretends nothing has happened, cleans up the mess. A few days later, summoned to the kitchen after her siblings are in bed, she expects punishment but instead is told that since they appreciate all she has done, they are sending her to Memphis for Christmas with her grandmother, Omie. Mandy is ambivalent. She has always longed to go to a big city; she also hates to leave Willie, who now seems like her own baby. Omie and Opie, her step-grandfather, meet her at the station and in the comparative affluence of their home treat her like a little girl, a situation she partly resents and partly enjoys. In Memphis Mandy learns much she has not known about her family, especially about her mother as a joyous girl who loved music and daring card playing, but gave up both when she ran off at seventeen to marry Jim Perritt. She is puzzled to remember that her mother recently ordered a "little emerald" ring, telling Mandy that she needed something pretty, even though times are hard. She also learns about her Uncle William, who died as a result of flu after World War I, and she spends one wonderful and astonishing afternoon with her Aunt* Laura, going to Beale Street and a speak-easy and to Crawfish Alley, where a street musician's trumpet makes her weep with emotion. Her next visit with Aunt Laura, when she is invited to her apartment for lunch, is different. Her aunt is either drunk or hung over; she and Uncle Cress argue. He slaps her, then picks her up and they disappear. Mandy cleans up what looks like weeks of dirty dishes, scrubs the kitchen, and leaves a note. That night Omie apologizes for "using" her, as her mother has used the ring, showing it as collateral to get a loan for her father's timber business, then returning it. Omie admits inviting her to Memphis in hope that being with the daughter of the sister she had loved above everything would work some sort of redemption for Laura. Mandy is shocked that the visit was not a reward by her parents for her hard work but was Omie's idea. Her grandmother is equally shocked when Mandy tells her about her mother's hemorrhage and about staying out of school to care for the family. She would gladly have come to help, she points out, if Mandy's parents had not been too stiff-necked to ask. Mandy returns to Kentucky glad to go back to her loving family but realizing that she has learned to see her mother differently and wondering if any of them really know each other. The novel is slow in starting and loosely structured, but it has the tone of genuine family life, and characterization is strong. Scenes are memorable, especially those of Mandy trying to keep ahead of the housework and baby care and of the lunch at Aunt Laura's home. Most of it is narrated in the present tense by Mandy, though flashbacks to memories are in past tense. The period is well evoked. Mandy's resentment at the preferential treatment her brothers get and of the assumption not only by them but by her parents and the doctor that she, as the oldest girl, should take over the housework, is presented in 1930s terms, an unfair situation she must be resigned to, not as a 1980s feminist rebellion. SLJ

**BORROWED SUMMER** (Doren*, Marion Walker, Harper, 1986), realistic novel for middle-grade readers in which three eleven-year-old girls kidnap two old people from a nursing home and give them new hope and renewed vigor. In an unspecified American small town, Jan Robinson, almost eleven, lives with her parents, the "urchins," David, 6, an Sue-Sue, 2, and Gram, 80, her great-grandmother to whom she is unusually close. When Gram breaks her hip, Jan's life changes. She baby-sits her young siblings and overhears with dread her parents talking about Gram's changed personality and their decision to send the old lady to Dugan's Rest Home, since Mom is pregnant and cannot face caring for an invalid in their inconvenient old home. With her friends, Sylvia Wyndham and Trixie Murphy, Jan volunteers at the nursing home, talking to patients and running errands. There she discovers that Gram acts childish and irritable in response to the condescending staff but summons up her old dignity for Jan and even begins to use her walker, which she refuses to try for the physical therapist. The girls also take an interest in Carl Stringer, an old man recovering from an operation who starts to give up hope and become senile when his son, Leopold, fails to take him home as he has promised. When the girls, exploring on their imaginary horses, find an abandoned house isolated in the woods, Jan gets an idea: the perfect project for their Sunshine Club, dedicated to doing good deeds, will be to clean the place up and somehow get the two old people there to live. Through Sylvia's father, a lawyer, they learn that the little house belongs to a New Yorker who has left it vacant for years. Sylvia's brother, Ronald, and his friend, Frank, with whom he drives the ambulance, learn of the house and want it for a party, but when the girls confide their plan the older boys agree to support it and are extremely helpful. They also enlist the help of Kitty Dugan, daughter of the nursing home owner, and Nona Kincaid, a disaffected nurse's aide. Trixie and Jan forge permission forms to release Gram and Carl for home visits, and Roland and Frank transport them in the ambulance to the little house. Although disoriented at first, Gram and Carl quickly adjust and begin to assert themselves. The girls take turns staying at the little house, letting their parents think they are at pajama parties at each other's homes, and Nona, taking a vacation from the nursing home, stays at night. Roland and Frank bring groceries and carry water from the well. For nearly a week the deception works as the old people regain vigor and interest in life. When Mom calls Dugan's and learns that Gram is supposedly at home with her, the whole scam blows up. Jan returns from her night at the little house to find her parents alarmed and furious. Mr. Dugan appears with Leopold, and after Jan is forced to tell the whole story, they go in three cars to the little house. There they find Gram calmly picking blueberries and Carl fishing with Ronald and Frank. After initial emotional outbursts, Carl calms the group with authority, instructs Leopold to learn who owns the house and buy it, invites Gram to live with him, and hires Nona to look in each day to check on their health and personal needs. While spending winter in the little house does not seem possible, they will at least have a summer of independence, and Jan's parents plan to install a first-floor bathroom so that Gram can move back into their home in the fall. Although the plot is worked out carefully, it greatly oversimplifies the problems of the frail elderly and unnecessarily casts Dugan as a villain. The recovery of the two old people is implausibly rapid, and the cooperation of Nona, Roland, and Frank, all young adults, unlikely. Jan's love and concern for her great-grandmother are the most appealing elements in the story. Her voice, as first-person narrator, is not always convincing. Christopher.

**BOYD, CANDY DAWSON,** educator and writer. Her novel *Circle of Gold\** (Scholastic, 1984), about a poor black girl who enters a newspaper contest to earn money to buy her mother a gold and pearl pin for Mother's Day, was a Coretta Scott King Honor book. The story is based on Boyd's own experiences in entering a Chicago newspaper contest when she was twelve. *Breadsticks and Blessing Places* (Macmillan, 1985) concerns a girl whose best friend dies, and *Charlie Pippin* (Macmillan, 1987) is about a girl's efforts to understand her father, who was traumatized in the Vietnam War. Boyd teaches at St. Mary's College of California at Moraga and lives in San Pablo, Calif.

*THE BOY WHO REVERSED HIMSELF* (Sleator\*, William, Dutton, 1986), fantasy set in an ordinary American town and in other dimensions of space, presumably in the late twentieth century. At her mother's insistence, Laura, the high school-aged narrator, invites Omar, the strange boy who lives with Mr. Campanelli next door, to come over to watch TV or play with her new computer games. He speaks with an accent, has never heard of a Macintosh, and is amazed by the electric can opener and chocolate chip cookies, but he catches on very quickly and is pathetically eager to have a friend. Laura, who is attracting the attention of popular Pete and does not want to be considered weird, shuns Omar at school until strange notes in mirror writing appear in her locker and he retrieves a report from it without using the combination. Studying his face, she realizes that it is reversed: the part in his hair, usually on the right, is now on the left, a missing right tooth now a gap on the left side. She pressures him for explanations and promises, insincerely, to be his friend forever if he tells her his secret. By analogy to the difference between two- and three-dimensional space, he explains that there is a fourth dimension in which he can travel and where, by accident, he reversed himself. Just as anyone from our three-dimensional space could reach from above or below into any spot on a two-dimensional world, he can reach into her locker from 4-space. Using his desire for friendship manipulatively and cynically, Laura persuades him to take her into 4-space several times, although he warns her that it is dangerous and that if they are caught they will have to be killed. Not understanding, she persists and once returns reversed, to find that ordinary food tastes horrible and only ketchup tastes delicious. It also makes her high, so that when Pete, who has been sulking over her interest in Omar, takes her up to the school roof to make love, she goes, against her better judgment. The door swings shut, stranding them on the roof. Laura forces herself into 4-space, gets to the stairway, and opens the door from the inside. Pete pressures her, and although she promised Omar never to tell, she soon explains all about 4-space to Pete. He insists that she take him there. The rope with which they are tethered to her room comes loose, and they are lost in 4-space. Before long they are captured by two beings, whose conversation they can hear as thoughts, but whom they can see only in ever-changing cross-sections. One is kindly Gigigi, who has somehow been made hideous in an accident, and exploitive Ramoom, who puts them in a cage and experiments with them, attempting to make them lead him to 3-space, which he could control with absolute power. Knowing she will probably never get home without his help, Laura nevertheless attempts to mislead him. Pete almost gives the truth away, but Omar intervenes at the critical moment. Laura learns that there are many, perhaps an infinite number of dimensions, with select creatures of each space acting as guardians of the space below it to keep it from being invaded and exploited. Omar is an apprentice guardian of 2-space, training to replace aging Mr. Campanelli. Although she and Pete should be killed to prevent their misuse of their knowledge, Laura convinces a 5-space female that she is reliable and, by feeding Pete numerous plastic packets of the delicious ketchup, makes him think she provided drugs which sent him on a wild psychedelic trip. He drops her cold, but an ending note, telling that all this happened years ago, says that Laura has become a neurosurgeon, aided greatly by her ability to enter 4-space, and is married to Omar, now a full-time guardian. The fascination of the story rests on its ingenious premise of the multiple dimensions and the well-imagined detail of 4-space. Characters are not highly developed but are adequate for their parts. Pace is fast, with an early sense of foreboding and exciting scenes of danger that mask the inconsistencies that appear on closer examination. SLJ.

**BRENNER, BARBARA (JOHNES)** (1925–      ), born in Brooklyn, N.Y.; educator, writer of many books for children, both fiction and nonfiction, most of which have a natural history component. In the 1940s she attended Seton Hall College and took extension courses at Rutgers, The State University; in the early 1950s she studied painting at New York University; and in the early 1960s she attended the New School for Social Research. She has had a varied career, having been a copywriter for an insurance company, a free-lance artists' agent, a writer-consultant for the publications division of the Bank Street College of Education, and an instructor at both the Bank Street College of Education and Parson's School of Design. In 1947 she married Fred Brenner, who has illustrated a number of her books, including *A Bird in the Family* (Scott, 1962), *The Flying Patchwork Quilt* (Scott, 1965), *Summer of the Houseboat* (Knopf, 1968), *If You Were an Ant* (Harper, 1973), *Little One Inch* (Coward, 1977), and *A Dog I Know* (Harper, 1983). Five of her books have won the Outstanding Science Book Award from the National Science Teachers Association and the Children's Book Council: *Baltimore Orioles* (Harper, 1974), *Lizard Tails and Cactus Spines* (Harper, 1975), *On the Frontier with Mr. Audubon* (Coward, 1977), *Beware!*

*These Animals Are Poison* (Coward, 1979), and *Have You Heard of a Kangaroo Bird?: Fascinating Facts about Unusual Birds* (Coward, 1980). Her mystery for older children, *The Falcon Sting** (Bradbury, 1988), about illegal trading in protected species of birds, was a nominee for the Edgar Allan Poe Award.

**BRIDGERS†, SUE ELLEN** (1942–     ), born in Greenville, N.C.; author of several young adult novels set in North Carolina, where she was born and has lived with her husband and three children. She attended East Carolina University in Greenville and received her B.A. degree from Western Carolina University in Cullowhee in 1976. In *Home Before Dark* (Knopf, 1976) a family of migrant workers return to the father's rural home in North Carolina. *All Together Now†* (Knopf, 1979), which won the Christopher Award, tells of the friendship of a twelve-year-old girl and a retarded man and of the lives that their friendship affects. In *Notes for Another Life* (Knopf, 1981) a brother and sister suffer emotional trauma when their father's mental illness uproots their lives and causes them to live with their grandmother. *Permanent Connections** (Harper, 1987) is a story of a spoiled and disaffected boy who is forced to care for his rural uncle injured in an accident and discovers the value and loving support of an extended family. It was named to the American Library Association Young Adult list and to the *School Library Journal* list of Best Books. Bridgers's novels have been commended for their well-rounded adult characters and for their appreciation of the natural beauty of the mountain area. She has also published a novel for adults, *Sara Will* (Harper, 1985).

**BROOKS, BRUCE** (1950–     ), born in Virginia; teacher, novelist for young people. He is a graduate of the University of North Carolina at Chapel Hill and of the University of Iowa Writers' Workshop. Among other jobs he has worked as a newspaper reporter, editor, and movie critic. His first novel, *The Moves Make the Man** (Harper, 1984), a story of a friendship between a young black basketball whiz and a troubled white boy, has been much honored. It won the *Boston Globe-Horn Book* Award, was a Newbery honor book, and was named to the *School Library Journal* Best Books list and to both the American Library Association Young Adult and Notable Books lists. In *Midnight Hour Encores** (Harper, 1986), a highly gifted cellist travels to meet her mother, who gave her up at birth. The novel, which shows understanding and intense love of music in many different forms, was named to the ALA Young Adult, the *School Library Journal* Best Books, and the *Horn Book* Fanfare lists. A later title, *No Kidding* (Harper, 1989), a story set in the near future, has also won critical acclaim. Brooks has made his home in Washington, D.C., and in Silver Spring, Maryland.

**BROTHER DANIEL** (*A Good Courage**), fanatic leader of the Kingdom of Yahweh, a repressive religious sect. Although to the neighboring small town and prospective members of the Kingdom he is a twinkly-eyed bear of a man, sincerely leading a loving flock, in reality he is a tyrant, obsessed by his idea that Satan threatens his people, especially the children, and that only strict rules and harsh punishments can drive out the devil in them. Illness, he thinks, is Yahweh's punishment for sin, and he insists that sick children work in the fields as usual. He has taken the children from public school and built a schoolhouse at the Kingdom to satisfy inspectors, but it has never been used. His son, Benjamin, tells Ty that the Kingdom used to be a place of great joy, but the pleasure in cruelty that Ty has witnessed when Brother Daniel kills his pet rabbit makes the boy doubt this statement.

*BUILDING BLOCKS* (Voigt*, Cynthia, Atheneum, 1984), time-travel fantasy in which a boy is transported back to his father's childhood, where he has experiences that help him alleviate family problems in his own dimension. Brann Connell, 12, of New York State in 1974, hates it when his parents argue and his strong-minded mother browbeats his father. Diane, who works with Legal Aid and wants to become a lawyer, is energetic and ambitious, while Kevin*, a draftsman, is diffident and retiring and, in Brann's eyes, a failure at almost everything. The current dispute revolves around a western Pennsylvania farm that Kevin has inherited from his Uncle Andrew, a place he dearly loved as a child. Diane thinks they should sell it so she can go to law school and thus elevate the family fortunes. Brann retreats from their angry words to his father's basement workroom, where his father's old boyhood building blocks are now stored. To his surprise Brann finds them set up as a kind of fortress, crawls inside, falls asleep, and awakens in the attic bedroom of a ten-and-a-half-year-old boy he learns is his father. The period is the Great Depression just before World War II. Kevin, his hard-driving father, Thomas, a builder, his pregnant, overworked mother, and several younger siblings live with Kevin's aged grandparents in their big old house in Sewickley, Pennsylvania, on the Ohio River near Pittsburgh. Brann keeps his identity secret, pretending he is new in town, and joins the family for a day as Kevin's friend. Breakfast is filled with tension, for Thomas Connell is a stickler for obedience. He is supported in this by his wife, and both demand near-perfection in behavior and great responsibility from Kevin, their eldest. In Kevin's eagerness to please—and to avoid being beaten with a belt by his father—he has become wimpish, fearful but kind, obsequious but solicitous. He yearns for the security and peace of his Uncle Andrew's farm, of which he has a picture on his bedroom wall. His ambition is to become an artist, but his mother discourages this vocation as impractical. The climax of the story comes through Brann's taking advantage of Kevin's lack of assertiveness. Although Kevin tells Brann the children have been strictly forbidden to investigate the river caves, Brann has found Kevin easily bullied and pressures him to go. In an exciting but not wholly credible episode, they get lost in a cave, but Kevin's artist's sense of space and proportion save them. When they arrive home tired and dirty, snippy and willful Suzanne, about eight, gets them to go swimming in the pool of a vacant mansion nearby. The caretaker catches them, and Thomas whips them, even Brann, and Brann harder than the others

because he will not scream or beg and refuses to lower his pants. That evening
Kevin experiences a terrible blow. Thomas and Uncle Andrew inform him that
it has been decided that he will not go to the farm that summer, since his mother
needs him in the house and his father needs him at work. Kevin takes the blow
philosophically. He tells Brann his father's hardness is born of fear of failure
not of meanness. He rationalizes his disappointment by saying he is needed,
speaking with a quiet courage that Brann respects. That night Brann falls asleep
among the blocks again and awakens in his own dimension, only a few hours
in real time having elapsed. Brann has learned something about why his father
gives in so easily and encourages him to assert himself. Together the two persuade
Diane that they should sell their house and move to the farm, which Kevin will
work and where he will produce drawings for sale, and that she should enroll
in law school in Pittsburgh. This story of compassion and fortitude in two
dysfunctional families has strong and aptly foiled characterizations, real-sounding
dialogue, a gripping problem, clearly delineated family relationships, and a
motif—the building blocks—that works well on two levels of meaning. SLJ.

BUNTING, (ANNE) EVE(LYN BOLTON) (1928–      ), born in Maghera,
Northern Ireland; highly prolific writer of fiction for children and young people,
much of it with an Irish background. She is a graduate of Methodist College
and attended Queen's University, both in Belfast. With her husband she emigrated to the United States, became a citizen in 1967, and has made her home
in Pasadena, California. A class at Pasadena City College started her on her
writing career, and since 1969 she has been a free-lance writer and has also
taught writing at the University of California, Los Angeles. In her first fifteen
years as a professional writer she published more than one hundred books, most
of them fiction, some under the name Evelyn Bolton and a few as A. E. Bunting.
Her work has won many awards. *One More Flight* (Warne, 1976) won the
Golden Kite Award from the Society of Children's Book Writers, was named
an Outstanding Science Trade Book for Children by the National Science Teacher's Association and the Children's Book Council, a Notable Book by the National Council for Social Studies and the Children's Book Council, and a Child
Study Association Book of the Year. *If I Asked You, Would You Stay?* (Lippincott, 1984), was named to the Young Adult list of the American Library Association. *Is Anybody There?** (Lippincott, 1988) was a nominee for the Edgar
Allan Poe Award. Among her books set in Ireland are *Ghosts of Summer* (Warne,
1977) and *The Haunting of Kildoran Abbey* (Warne, 1978). Many of her novels
deal with contemporary issues. She has been both praised as a highly competent
writer and criticized for the shallowness of treatment in many of her books.

*THE BURNING QUESTIONS OF BINGO BROWN* (Byars*, Betsy, Viking,
1988), humorous realistic novel set for several weeks in the late 1980s mostly
in a public school in the town of Marshfield somewhere in the eastern United
States. Although he is shy and often assailed by self-doubt, Bingo (Harrison)

Brown, 12, finds life satisfying in most respects if frequently perplexing. He enjoys his classmates in Roosevelt Middle School, where most of the action takes place, appreciates his earnest, young teacher, Mr. Mark (John Markham), and gets along well most of the time with his parents. When Mr. Mark passes out notebooks for the class to write in every day, Bingo decides that his will be a book of questions, burning questions, the first one being, "Has there ever been a successful writer named Bingo"? While some of the ensuing questions are incidental reactions to specific events or people or just convey his feelings, most revolve around three matters that unify this loosely knit story: the three girls he falls instantly and madly in love with in a single hour; his archenemy Billy Wentworth; and Mr. Mark's unfortunate love life. Bingo's three romances, never openly declared, gradually fade to one, Melissa, a bright, perceptive, and highly assertive girl whose ambition to become both a scientist and a rock star intrigues him. Billy, a new boy who sits in front of Bingo, persists in belittling him with such put-downs as "Worm Brain" and complicates his life by moving in next door. The two boys establish an uneasy and gradually improving friendship after Bingo spends a weekend at Billy's house and suggests that Billy lead a rebellion against the principal's interdict against T-shirts with words on them. His relationship with both Melissa and Billy solidifies over Mr. Mark's unfortunate romance with a girl named Dawn. The class becomes aware of her existence when he asks them, as an assignment, to write letters to her extolling his virtues. When Mr. Mark becomes more and more moody and abstracted, Melissa, who knows Dawn, informs the students that Dawn has persistently refused Mr. Mark's advances. The class becomes very concerned about their lovelorn young teacher when he makes an assignment to write a letter to a friend trying to talk the friend out of suicide. Their concern about his well-being and also about the moral issues involved reaches its peak when Mr. Mark is critically injured when his motorcycle leaves the road and he is not wearing his helmet. Billy and Bingo investigate the scene and conclude that it was no accident. When, however, Mr. Mark writes the class from the hospital that he feels lucky to be alive, the troubled students relax. Bingo's various experiences at working out vexing interpersonal relationships and being chosen, along with Melissa, to represent the class on a visit to the hospital, leave Bingo with a "VIP feeling" and more confidence in his ability to deal with life's issues. A fast pace, contemporary tone, and mostly hyperbolic humor combine for consistently entertaining reading about a boy who discovers that it is all right to be a follower and that adults also have problems they cannot handle. Although Mr. Mark's infatuation seems strained, since according to Melissa, Dawn has never encouraged him, he is likeable because he is a patient, understanding, and skilled teacher, and the students' concern for him seems well motivated. The school scenes, though blown out of proportion, carry the ring of truth, and the possible suicide attempt is handled without sentimentality and didacticism. Others in series. SLJ.

**BYARS†, BETSY (CROMER)** (1928–      ), born in Charlotte, N.C.; for more than twenty years a popular writer of realistic novels of contemporary family life for early adolescents, ideas for which come from her personal experiences at home and with her family. She grew up in Charlotte and was graduated from Queens College, where she met her future husband, later a professor of engineering at West Virginia University. Among her many critically cited books are *The Summer of the Swans†* (Viking, 1970), which won the John Newbery Award, *The Midnight Fox†* (Viking, 1968), *The House of Wings†* (Viking, 1972), *The Pinballs†* (Harper, 1977), *The Cartoonist†* (Viking, 1978), and *The Night Swimmers†* (Delacorte, 1980). *Cracker Jackson\** (Viking, 1985), in which a boy tries to help an abused wife, was a best book of both the American Library Association and the *School Library Journal* and was named to the Fanfare list. Also included on the ALA and SLJ Best Book list is *The Blossoms and the Green Phantom\** (Delacorte, 1987), one of a series of lighthearted realistic novels about an unusual family. *The Burning Questions of Bingo Brown\** (Viking, 1980), also an SLJ book, deals humorously with the serious problem of a teacher's attempted suicide. Byars's style is lively and contemporary and her plots usually fast, but her characterization is shallow and often distorted for effect, her plots unfocused and occasionally thin, contrived, and improbably concluded, and her attempts at humor are sometimes heavy-handed. A dynamic and amusing speaker, she has made many personal appearances at professional conferences.

# C

CAMERON, ANN (1943–      ), born in Rice Lake, Wisc., daughter of a lawyer and a teacher; writer mainly of books for early readers. She received her B.A. with honors from Radcliffe College and her M.F.A. from the University of Iowa. She has held a variety of positions, as a teacher of creative writing at Queens College in New York and an educational consultant, among others. Her first book for children, *The Seed* (Pantheon, 1975), presents the growth process from the standpoint of a seed sprouting from the ground. The first of her several easy-reading books about black Julian and his family and friends, *The Stories Julian Tells* (Pantheon, 1981), arose from stories told her by a friend about his own childhood. *More Stories Julian Tells*\* (Knopf, 1986) was named a Best Book by both the American Library Association and the *School Library Journal*. Further adventures of the earnest, irrepressible Julian appear in *Julian's Glorious Summer* (Random, 1987), *Julian, Secret Agent* (Random, 1988), and *Julian, Dream Doctor* (Random, 1990). Cameron divides her time between New York City and Guatemala. The latter is the setting of *The Most Beautiful Place in the World*\* (Knopf, 1988), the story of a few years in the life of a poor family in a Guatemalan mountain village. It received the Child Study Award. Her stories are sharply focused on the child's viewpoint and are told with warmth and affection in easy but never condescending language. Cameron has also contributed stories to *Iowa Review* and *Northwest Review*.

CAMPBELL BITTNER (*Return to Bitter Creek*\*), mother of Lacey. Originally called Ann, she switched to her middle name after she fled the mountain community when her illegitimate daughter was two years old to keep her mother from getting the legal custody she sought. In the ten years since then, she has lived with and lost various men, but she has taken good care of Lacey and has settled with David\* Habib in what they both consider a permanent relationship. A skilled leather worker and a competent blacksmith, she is capable of supporting herself and her daughter, but without David's emotional support she is at first unable to think ahead. Her feelings about returning to Bitter Creek are mixed.

Although she loves the North Carolina country and retains some affection for her brother and father, she is deeply afraid of falling again under her mother's control, and she still resents the narrow-minded morality of the local people.

**CARRICK, CAROL (HATFIELD)** (1935–      ), born in Queens, New York; artist and writer for children. She received her B.A. degree from Hofstra University and was staff artist for *Coronet* magazine and for an advertising agency in New York. From 1961 to 1965 she was a free-lance artist, and since 1965 she has been primarily a writer. She married Donald Carrick, an illustrator and a landscape and portrait painter, who died in 1989. Thirty-seven of Carrick's books were illustrated by her husband, many of them receiving critical honors. The first was *The Old Barn* (Bobbs, 1966), based on a farm where they were living in Vermont. She has written books of nonfiction, among them *The Blue Lobster: A Life Cycle* (Dial, 1975), which was named an Outstanding Science Trade Book by the National Science Teacher's Association and the Children's Book Council and one of the Best Children's Books of the Season by the *Saturday Review*. Many of her other books, both fiction and nonfiction, have a nature subject. She has also written books with a historical period setting, including *Stay Away from Simon!*\* (Clarion, 1985), which was named to the *School Library Journal* list of Best Books and to the Child Study Association of America list of Children's Books of the Year, as were several of her other books. She has made her home in Edgartown, Mass.

**CASSEDY, SYLVIA** (1930–1989), born in Brooklyn, New York; teacher and writer for children and young people of fiction and poetry. After graduating from Brooklyn College, she studied creative writing at Johns Hopkins University, and throughout the 1970s and early 1980s, she taught creative writing to children and trained teachers to teach creative writing to children in the New York area. Her first publications were stories for picture books, among them *Little Chameleon* (World, 1966) and *Marzipan Day on Budget Lane* (Doubleday, 1967). Her three novels are notable for how sensitively they depict the innermost thoughts and feelings of early adolescents, especially of those on the fringes socially. The first, *Behind the Attic Wall* (Crowell, 1983), about a neglected orphan who hears ghostly voices, was acclaimed by the American Library Association and *School Library Journal*. *M. E. and Morton*\* (Crowell, 1987), also an ALA and SLJ best book, is about a socially maladjusted girl and her relations with her retarded older brother and with a new girl in the neighborhood. Her last novel, *Lucie Babbidge's House* (Crowell, 1989), a fantasy about an orphan girl who creates an existence for dolls she discovers, came out posthumously. She translated and edited *Birds, Frogs, and Moonlight* (Doubleday, 1967) and *Red Dragonfly on My Shoulder* (HarperCollins, 1992), both haiku anthologies, and *Moon-Uncle, Moon-Uncle: Rhymes from India* (Doubleday, 1973). She also published *Roomrimes* (Crowell, 1987) and *Zoomrimes* (Crowell, 1993), books of her own verse, and *In Your Own Words: A Beginner's Guide to Writing* (Doubleday, 1979).

**CELIA PACKARD** (*Princess Ashley\**), Ashley Packard's stepmother, whom Ashley despises and dominates. When Chelsea Olinger's mother, the school counselor, quits her job, Chelsea asks Celia to try to persuade her mother not to quit because Mrs. Olinger has been working hard and is in line for a promotion. Celia tries, half-heartedly because she is weak and has not exerted herself to keep Ashley in line. She admits that she has been trying too hard not to be a "wicked stepmother." She is a pathetic figure, a foil for Mrs. Olinger.

*CHARLEY SKEDADDLE* (Beatty*, Patricia, Morrow, 1987), historical novel of a boy's involvement in the American Civil War that begins in the New York City Bowery early in 1864 and then shifts to the region of the Wilderness battlefield in Virginia. Disgusted because his older sister, with whom he lives, is marrying a man who will not tolerate his street fighting, filled with gallant spirit to avenge the death of his brother at Gettysburg, lured by the honeyed words of his brother's friend, newly enlisted Con* Sullivan, feisty, red-haired, orphaned, Irish Bowery boy Charley (Charles Stephen) Quinn, 12, runs away with Con to join the New York Volunteers against the Rebels. Smuggled aboard a crowded troop ship, Charley arrives in Alexandria, Virginia, with mixed feelings about his situation, having learned from observation and another soldier, Jem* Miller, that Con is a disagreeable troublemaker not to be trusted. At Culpeper camp, uncertain about what to do with Charley since he is too young to be a soldier, an officer orders sixteen-year-old drummer boy Silas* Gorman to teach Charley drumming. The boy's spirits rise again as Silas shows him about the camp and he catches glimpses of General Meade and General Grant, whose presence means a major engagement of some sort is not far off. Charley finds discipline stern (no more Bowery boy behavior, he is told). For two months Silas drills him in the Virginia countryside, amidst sobering remains of past battles, but when in May the troops are ordered out, Charley's enthusiasm can hardly be contained. The march is hard going, a night slog across the Rapidan River and down the Orange Turnpike. When the conflict comes, in the tangle of vines, bushes, and scrubby trees called the Wilderness, and the Union forces are lured into a trap, Charley gives in to his terror. Union soldiers are slaughtered, including Jem, who goes down before Charley's eyes. In fear, anger, and revulsion, Charley grabs Jem's gun and shoots the nearest Rebel, then horrified that he has actually killed a man, flees headlong. Taken prisoner by a Rebel soldier who asks his name, in his shame he responds, "Charley Skedaddle." A Rebel ex-schoolteacher officer, not wanting to send the boy to Andersonville, tells him to head west for the mountains. Charley gradually makes his way to the highlands, through the tangled woods, sometimes by road. Scrounging food and water from slain soldiers, he is given a ride on the wagon of an ancient black man, and stays a night in an abandoned cabin, hiding from Rebel conscriptors. In the Blue Ridge Mountains, he comes upon a little cluster of buildings, where he is caught in the act of stealing eggs by the owner, tall, spunky Granny* Jerusha Bent, in whose rude hut he lives for about a year. A widow, a "wise woman" who doctors the mountain people with her "yarbs" (herbs), she keeps Charley for his labor, locking him in the henhouse whenever she leaves, setting her watch-goose, Malindy, to guard him, and instructing him to pretend to be mute so people will not know that he is a Yankee. She is a kind woman, and gradually Charley warms to her, enjoys the beauty of the area, and acquires the new and better sense of self-worth that comes from work well done and practical skills learned. The only time he fights, with young Cois MacRae (the MacRaes and the Bents are long-time feuders), he gets trounced. Later he beats up Cois for insulting pretty Sarie Giffen, for the first time feeling good because he has actually used his fists to help someone and not just for the pleasure of fighting. When a black man, a Yankee soldier on leave, visits, Charley learns to his amazement that for fifteen years the Bent farm had been a station on the Underground Railroad. Winter brings a "painter" (panther), and, when Granny leaves to help deliver a baby, the "painter" eats most of the hens one night and then attacks Charley, who kills it with Granny's old gun. Uneasy when she does not return, he searches and finds that on the way home she and Canaan the mule fell from a ridge and she suffered a hurt leg. Now accepted as a man by Granny, his self-respect enhanced by his redeeming acts, Charley even makes peace with Cois. April of 1865 brings news that General Lee is on the run and may carry the war to the mountains. Granny says that it is too dangerous for Charley to stay and that Sarie Giffen (on whom Charley is now sweet) will live with her in his stead. He heads west, hoping to come back after the war. Since Granny seems not hurt badly enough to have lain in a ravine for two days and nights, Charley's redeeming acts seem overly fortuitous. Charley matures convincingly. His ambivalent feelings about himself, people, and the war are natural for a boy his age, particularly one so concerned about pride and appearance and so prone to visions of grandeur. Settings are skillfully contrasted: the hubbub of the New York streets, the seaminess aboard the troop ship with the brutish behavior of the drunken, loutish, gambling soldiers, the rigors of training and the griminess of the camp, where the soldiers are under guard lest they desert, the confusion and horror of battle, the peaceful and healing mountains with the emphasis on neighborliness and cooperation. Best is the picture of the war from the standpoint of a naive youth who thinks he is worldly. The reader learns about the progress of the war as Charley does, from conversation, reports, and limited participation. General Lee appears once, in a memorable scene in which on horseback he valiantly struggles to lead a charge but is sensibly restrained by his men. Some mountain dialect reinforces the setting. O'Dell.

**CIRCLE OF GOLD** (Boyd*, Candy Dawson, Scholastic, 1984), realistic novel of family and school life set in the early 1980s on Chicago's black South Side. Life has grown difficult for Mattie* Mae Benson, 11, during the six months since her father was killed, his car struck by a drunk driver. Her ordinarily sweet mother now works two jobs, in a factory, often overtime, and as superintendent of their apartment house, and is short-tempered, snappy, and worried from trying to make ends meet. Mattie, who was close to her father, is sure that her mother loves her twin, Matt*, more. She feels left out and unappreciated, in spite of doing her best at cooking, cleaning, and baby-sitting after school. Mattie has problems at school, too, where bullying Angel Higgley and Angel's cowed shadow, Charlene, threaten with a "skull and crossbones" note to get even when Mattie refuses to let Angel copy her math test. Mattie is sure things will be better at home if she can give her mother for Mother's Day the beautiful round gold filigree and pearl pin she saw while shopping at Stern's department store with her best friend, Toni* Douglas. Mattie puts twenty dollars down on the fifty-five dollar pin, the balance to be paid in a month. Since she has just lost her baby-sitting job, she worries about the money, but Toni and Toni's friend, old Mrs. Stamps, encourage her to enter the Mother's Day essay contest run for the *South Side Daily*, with a fifty dollar first prize. No good at writing, although she struggles hard, Mattie persuades Toni to write one for her. Problems accelerate when Angel accuses Mattie of stealing her expensive new pearl and gold bracelet. Suspicious that Angel may be lying, Toni pretends to be Angel's friend to learn the truth. After the parents have a meeting in the principal's office about the missing bracelet, Toni discovers that Charlene took it in retaliation for Angel's being mean to her in spite of her constant loyalty. One problem resolved, another looms larger. Just before Mother's Day, Mattie goes to Stern's to ask for an extension of time and discovers the pin has been purchased. Fortunately, a letter from the paper informs her she has won third prize in the contest. At the newspaper office with her mother, Matt, and Toni, she reads her essay aloud, and thus the reader learns that Mattie did not mail Toni's essay but a simple, heartfelt one of her own composition, saying, among other things, that, although tempted, she cannot cheat. Her prize is the pin for her mother, which she had also mentioned in her essay. Mrs. Benson has begun seeing a therapist, Matt having urged her to seek counseling at Mrs. Stamps's suggestion. With the therapist's help, Mrs. Benson has grown confident enough to ask for a two-year superintendent's contract, and the future looks brighter for the Bensons. Characters are well-known types and events proceed as anticipated. Extensive, convincing dialogue keeps the story moving, and complications build judiciously. Best is the sense of a close, loving family who have encountered tough times but struggle together with the help of friends and some luck toward a better life. C.S. King Honor.

**CLASS CLOWN** (Hurwitz*, Johanna, ill. Sheila Hamanaka, Morrow, 1987), brief novel of elementary school life set in an unidentified American town in the contemporary period. Third grader Lucas Cott is very bright but bored and restless in school. Although he likes his teacher, Mrs. Hockaday, he always seems to be in trouble for calling out without raising his hand, marking on his desk, and generally acting up. His nemesis is Cricket Kaufman, the smartest girl in the class, who always has the answers and keeps a sharp eye on Lucas to report his wrongdoing. At home his parents are too busy with his two-year-old twin brothers, Marcus and Marius, to be overly concerned about Lucas. Still, when Mrs. Hockaday gives Lucas a note to take home, saying he is obstreperous (which Cricket interprets to mean a doctor for ladies), both parents have a talk with him, and he promises to try harder to behave. His first efforts go astray. Thinking that Arthur Lewis's new glasses make him look serious, Lucas fakes eye trouble, only to give himself away in the nurse's office. Determined to outdo all the others in their homework assignment to bring a leaf to class, he brings a big garbage bag of leaves in his wagon and accidentally rips the bag, scattering leaves over the whole classroom. When Cricket bets him a dollar that he cannot stay quiet a whole school day, he fakes a cough to keep from responding to Mrs. Hockaday's questions and writes the answers on the blackboard. Cricket tricks him into gloating before they are out of of the classroom and refuses to pay up; since the bell has already rung, Lucas says he has won and their bet ends in a draw. When a mime comes to entertain the school, Lucas keeps quiet as directed but sticks his head through the cut-out section in a heavy plastic folding chair, gets stuck, and interrupts the program. To his surprise, Cricket comes to his defense after he has been extricated and talks Mrs. Hockaday out of the extra homework she is assigning him as punishment. In the class play, a mini-circus, Lucas is told to be a clown, and although the circus was his idea, he is unhappy, since he is unable to be funny on demand. Fortunately, the ringmaster gets tonsilitis, and Lucas takes his part with great success. At the end of the term, Mrs. Hockaday sends another note home, saying that Lucas is no longer rambunctious. Reading this one for himself, Lucas decides she means he is no longer like a male sheep, and since he has just had a haircut, he thinks she is stating the obvious. School scenes are interspersed with a few of home and family life, notably at the barber shop where Lucas, who has practiced wrestling holds on the twins to their great delight, clasps first Marcus then Marius in headlocks so the barber can trim their hair without their usual wriggling and fighting. Although not written in primer language, the book is designed to be read by children Lucas's age or a little older. The humor is mild, but not overly slapstick, the best of it coming from Lucas's genuine efforts to improve and his misunderstanding of why he gets into trouble. SLJ.

**CLEARY†, BEVERLY (BUNN)**, (1916–      ), born in McMinnville, Oreg.; librarian, prolific author best known for her amusing, episodic books for eight- to ten-year-olds. She received her B.A. degree from the University of California, Berkeley, and her degree in librarianship from the University of Washington, Seattle. She served as children's librarian in Yakima, Washington, and during World War II, in an army hospital in Oakland, California. Of her many books, the most popular have been in three series: *Henry Huggins‡* (Morrow, 1950) and its sequels, including *Henry and Ribsy‡* (Morrow, 1954) and *Ribsy†* (Morrow, 1964); the fantasies about Ralph the mouse, including *The Mouse and the Motorcycle†* (Morrow, 1965) and *Runaway Ralph†* (Morrow, 1970); and, best-loved of all, the Ramona series, about the sisters who first appear as friends of Henry Huggins. The earliest of these, *Beezus and Ramona‡* (Morrow, 1955), was followed by *Ramona the Pest†* (Morrow, 1968), *Ramona and Her Father†* (Morrow, 1977), *Ramona Quimby, Age 8†* (Morrow, 1981), *Ramona Forever\** (Morrow, 1984), and several others, all starring the spunky little girl who is so often a trial to her older sister. A somewhat more serious but still amusing tone dominates *Dear Mr. Henshaw†* (Morrow, 1983), an epistolary novel of a boy's difficult adjustment to his parents' divorce, which won the Newbery Medal. It has been followed by a sequel, *Strider* (Morrow, 1991), in which Leigh Botts acquires a dog and grows up to new responsibilities. Cleary has also written novels for teenagers and an autobiography, *A Girl from Yamhill: A Memoir* (Morrow, 1988). She has been the recipient of many honors, the most prestigious being the 1975 Laura Ingalls Wilder Award from the American Library Association for total contribution to children's literature and the 1983 George G. Stone Recognition of Merit Award for her body of work.

**COLE, BROCK** (1938–     ), author and illustrator of picture books and novels. Before turning to full-length fiction, Cole gained attention for several picture books he both wrote and illustrated in pen and ink and watercolors, among them *The King at the Door* (Doubleday, 1979) and *The Giant's Toe* (Farrar, 1986). His first novel, *The Goats\** (Farrar, 1987), the tense story of an unpopular boy and girl who are stripped of their clothes by their summer campmates and marooned on an island in a lake, was selected for Fanfare by the editors of *The Horn Book Magazine* and recognized as a Best Book by the American Library Association and by *School Library Journal*. He has also published *Celine* (Farrar, 1989), about a precocious, artistic, sixteen-year-old girl forced to spend the summer with her stepmother, and has illustrated novels for other writers, including *Gaffer Samson's Luck* (Farrar, 1984) by Jill Paton Walsh and *The Indian in the Cupboard* (Doubleday, 1980) by Lynne Reid Banks.

**COME A STRANGER** (Voigt\*, Cynthia, Atheneum, 1986), realistic novel, a companion to *Dicey's Song†*, also set in Crisfield, Maryland, about 1980. It tells of several years in a young girl's life in which she is in conflict with self and society. Life-loving, assertive, outgoing, Mina (Wilhelmina) Smiths, 10, second youngest in the large family of a minister, leaves in high elation for summer ballet camp on scholarship, confident of her ability and dreaming of becoming a ballerina. She enjoys herself thoroughly in the exercises and with a close group of girls her age, so busy and excited she never really notices that she is the only black. The following summer, she is dismissed as lacking ability, the teacher saying puberty has made her too awkward to continue, but Mina soon understands that she has been rejected as much for her color as for the clumsiness of her body. At home she experiences instances of discrimination, too: white employers exploit her when she baby-sits; white girls also out for tennis refuse to play with her; teacher Mr. Bryce resents her asking questions and providing information about black contributions to the development of the United States. She comes to see what her mother, a nurse, means when she says that history continues to influence the lives of blacks and that being female contributes an additional hurdle. Over the next several years, Mina learns that color and sex, while barriers, need not prevent happiness and that life can be satisfying if she uses her talents and reaches out to others. Though the girls cut her, for example, she is a natural athlete and soon is invited to join the junior varsity tennis team, and she maintains an "A" average in her classes. Coincidentally, the summer she must leave camp, her father's interim minister is Tamer* Shipp, a young preacher from Harlem who arrives with his pretty, dependent, "butterfly" wife, Alice*, and three small children. Mina soon loves people-oriented, active, philosophical Tamer with a deep and abiding but never revealed affection. While she spends much time ruminating on her own situation and feelings, she also does a good deal to help others. She helps her family take care of Miz Hunter, the old ex-schoolteacher who lives next door, and continues to feel great joy singing in the choir. She encourages Alice Shipp to get her high school equivalency diploma, an achievement of which Alice informs Mina with pride at the very end. Her ultimate act of reaching out involves Tamer himself and a white classmate, aloof, independent, surly Dicey* Tillerman, a new girl in town. Tamer confides in Mina his crisis in faith, due in great part to the untimely death in Vietnam of a much respected fellow track runner, Bullet Tillerman. Attracted by the name Tillerman as well as by Dicey's academic ability and aloneness, Mina cultivates Dicey's friendship and learns that Bullet was Dicey's uncle. Her friendship with the Tillermans helps the family through the difficult period of their mother's death and her introducing them to Tamer (she invites them all to come to church to hear him) helps him to come to grips with his lingering grief over Bullet. Through the Tillermans she comes to know Jeff Greene (of *A Solitary Blue†*), whose high school graduation she attends with Dicey and whose friend, Dexter Halloway, a black youth, she gets to know and thinks of as a possible romantic interest. The book ends with Mina, having just said goodnight to Dexter after the graduation, "leaping down off her porch into the dark yard," where she "danced around in circles." She feels that "sometimes there was nothing but dancing to really say what you felt. Even if someone had told you years ago that you couldn't dance, and you'd been silly enough to believe them, even if they were right." Characters in the very large cast are created with clarity, even very minor ones, like Miz Hunter who warns Mina that maybe her closest friend Kat would not be entirely without jealousy about Mina's good fortune in winning the scholarship; Kat, pretty enough to be a model; Louis, Mina's little brother, who wants Maybeth Tillerman at his birthday party but whose mother thinks Maybeth will feel out of place among all blacks; pugnacious little Sammy Tillerman, whom Mina coaches at tennis; Rachelle, who gets pregnant and about whom Mina wonders what will happen since her family has dumped her out; Mina's practical, hardworking mother, Raymonda; Miss LaVelle, Mina's ballet instructor who never achieved her ambition of becoming a ballerina because she is black and blacks do not become ballerinas. Scenes are richly drawn, at the Smiths house, the Tillerman place, the Shipp home, school, church—a fine panorama of family and community life. The themes of family love and friendly affection, finding happiness in caring for others, confidence in one's self and the essential goodness of life, and of keeping faith in spite of injustice and hard knocks appear naturally and without specific statement. If the ending is too pat it is still an acceptable, pleasing, and hopeful one for Mina. Although Tamer's crisis in faith is inadequately delineated, it is still satisfactory if allowances are made for Mina's point of view. Even though Mina's mischievous nature (Mina's "T-rou-ble") is more described than shown, she is a winning protagonist, whose outward behavior and inner doubts, hopes, joys, yearnings, and ambitions exemplify these blacks, who are consistently depicted not as ethnic oddities but as real people. This richly crafted book is a worthy companion to those several in what has come to be known as the Tillerman series. SLJ.

**COME SING, JIMMY JO** (Paterson*, Katherine, Dutton, 1985), novel of family life in a group of country singers from Blue County, West Virginia, in the 1980s. Although his mother, Olive*, his father, Jerry* Lee, his grandfather, and his Uncle* Earl are all regular performers at fairs and tent meetings, James Johnson, 11, never sings for anyone but Grandma, who has raised him and who was once lead singer in the group but retired and returned to the hardscrabble mountain farm when her voice began to crack. She has also taught him to play his guitar, Chester. Together they keep the marginal place going and await the return of the Johnson Family between engagements. As they sit on the porch one evening, Jerry Lee starts playing his banjo to drown out the usual quarrel between Olive, Earl and Grandpa, and James, to help him out, sings in harmony to his father's gentle baritone. They are overheard by the agent Olive has been trying to foist on the group, and he insists that James join the others. Soon they have a regular contract for Countrytime TV in Tidewater, Virginia. Olive changes her name to Keri Sue and his to Jimmy Jo, claims that he is just ten years old, and will not let him wear his glasses on the stage. James misses Grandma deeply and senses that Olive and Earl resent him. At school, he tries to be invisible but makes two friends, Will Short, the smartest boy in the class, who volunteers to tutor him during recess so Will can escape the playground where he is hassled, and Eleazer Jones, an older black boy, undisputed king of the classroom, who becomes his protector. Although James comes to love performing, he is uncomfortable with Olive and worried by the way she and Earl want to become a duo and drop the country style for a brassier Nashville sound. He is also disturbed by a tall, skinny stranger who hangs around the schoolyard trying to talk to him and eventually claiming that he is James's real father. Olive, Earl, and Grandpa take a Sunday job singing at a club, but Grandpa is soon fired and replaced by a man playing an electric bass. When Olive and Earl go to Nashville to make a demonstration tape with their new, brassy sound, Jerry Lee puts up the money, and while they are playing at the club, he takes James home to Grandma for Christmas. Their holiday is spoiled when they get Nashville on the new radio and hear "Broken Bird," the song Jerry Lee wrote for James, sung with electric backup and introduced as written and sung by the new brother-sister team, Keri Sue and Earl Johnson. James is furious and feels betrayed that Jerry Lee does not upbraid the others when they arrive. Back in Tidewater, James brings the situation to a head by choosing "Broken Bird" when they offer to let him sing whatever he likes. When Jerry Lee will not back him against Olive and Earl, he throws the name and telephone number the stranger gave him at his mother and sees that she recognizes it. Then he locks himself in his room. Since his identity as Jimmy Jo has been discovered at school, he cannot stand the attention and spends the day with Eleazer in a boat on the river. At home he stays locked in his room, refusing to go to rehearsal or even to the regular Countrytime program despite Earl's threats, Olive's pleading, and Jerry Lee's reasoning. After the others have left, the stranger calls, saying he is coming over to get acquainted. At first James panics, locking all the doors and hiding behind the sofa. Then, realizing that he must face the truth, he sits on the front porch, meets the man, tells him that although he may be his father, Jerry Lee is his real daddy, a man who would not run out on his pregnant girl friend. A short time later, Grandma and Grandpa arrive, having been summoned from Blue County by Jerry Lee. They take James to the studio where he joins the program already in progress and sings, "Let the Circle Be Unbroken," realizing at last how Jerry Lee has been trying to keep them together and how he belongs to the Johnson Family, no matter who his biological father is. The novel is made moving by good characterization of all the major figures and by strong evocation of both the fear and the joy James gets from playing in public. The sleazy promoters, the avid fans, and the rivalry and jealousy of performers, even those who love each other, are strong and convincing elements. Country dialect is used effectively. ALA; SLJ.

**CONRAD, PAM** (1947–      ), born in New York City; poet and writer of fiction for children and young people. After graduating from the High School of Performing Arts, she attended Hofstra University and received her B.A. degree from the New School for Social Research. She has written stories for picture books, like *The Tub People* (Harper, 1988), and books for those children who are just reading, like *Seven Silly Circles* (Harper, 1987). Her most acclaimed novel is for early adolescents and young adults, *Prairie Songs** (Harper, 1985), which concerns a family of pioneers and their neighbors in Nebraska at the turn of the twentieth century. It was a *Boston Globe-Horn Book* Honor Book and won the International Reading Association, Spur, and Western Heritage awards. Her other novels for young people include *Taking the Ferry Home* (Harper, 1988), *My Daniel* (Harper, 1989), which is also set on the prairie, and a time-travel fantasy, *Stonewords* (Harper, 1990). Although from the New York City area, she has also lived in Colorado and Texas, where she developed a keen interest in the pioneer period. She teaches creative writing at Queens College.

**CON SULLIVAN** (*Charley Skedaddle\**), aptly named deceitful Union soldier who persuades Bowery boy Charley Quinn to run off to the Civil War. Charley encounters this friend of his dead brother, Johnny, killed at Gettysburg, as Con is marching, half-drunk (Charley thinks gallantly), on parade along Broadway with other enlisted men en route to his ship. On board the steamer, Charley learns that Con, who had brought the news of Johnny's death to the Quinns along with Johnny's silver watch, had kept Johnny's prized knife because, Con says, he won it fairly in gambling. Charley also learns Con joined up for bounty and not out of conviction. At Culpeper camp, Con gets into trouble and is punished by having to stand tiptoe on the rim of an open, vertical barrel. As Charley runs from the battle at the Wilderness, Con yells in derision, "Charley, skedaddle! Go on. Run away. Run, ye coward Bowery bummer!," words that ring in Charley's ears. In self-punishment, Charley calls himself Charley Skedaddle.

**CONTRARY THE DOG** (*The Secret Life of Dilly McBean\**), Dilly's hound-type dog, bought at the local pet shop. Dilly names him Contrary because the dog always does the opposite of what he is told. He appears in numerous scenes, providing companionship for Dilly and giving Dilly someone to talk to and share his thoughts with. Dilly believes that he knows what Con is thinking.

**CORALEE DICKSON** (*Permanent Connections\**), aunt of Rob who has always stayed home at the Appalachian farm, helping to care for her brothers and sisters, her mother in her long illness, and now her aging father. In the past Coralee was devoted to her garden, both vegetables and flowers, but suddenly she became terrified of something she seemed to see in the wind and has been unable to leave the house for three years, even to step onto the porch. With the encouragement of Ginny\* Collier, who patiently helps her make the first venture out the kitchen door and then comes by every day to lead her a little further and a little longer, she is at last able to walk into the yard. When her father is hurt, she makes an immense effort, runs to the truck, and cradles the old man in her arms as Rob drives to the hospital. A little simple, Coralee likes shiny doo-dads, rings and necklaces, from the dime store, but she is aware of how her life has been deprived and admits that she longs for a time when she does not have to serve the menfolk.

**CORMIER†, ROBERT (EDMUND)** (1925–      ), born in Leominster, Mass.; author of popular and highly controversial novels for young adults. He attended Fitchburg State College and became a scriptwriter for radio, then a newspaper reporter and columnist and later an associate editor of the Fitchburg *Sentinel and Enterprise*. *The Chocolate War†* (Pantheon, 1974), a story of corruption and violence in a Catholic boys' school, is one of the best-known and most discussed books for young people in the second half of the twentieth century. Its ending on a tone of helplessness and defeat is shared by some of his other novels, including *I Am the Cheese†* (Pantheon, 1977), in which a family is given a new identity to escape the revenge of organized crime, and *After the First Death* (Pantheon, 1979), about a school bus highjacked by terrorists. *Beyond the Chocolate War\** (Knopf, 1985) carries on the story of Trinity High and its vicious student organization, the Vigils. He has also written novels for adults and a book of short stories for young people, *Eight Plus One* (Pantheon, 1980). Among his other novels for young people are *The Bumblebee Flies Anyway* (Pantheon, 1983), which explores medical ethics in an experimental facility, and *Fade* (Delacorte, 1988), a gripping fantasy.


**THE CORPORAL** (*The Fighting Ground\**), American soldier who comes to Jonathan's area looking for men to fight against the British near Trenton, New Jersey, during the American Revolution. Impatient, knowledgeable, determined, he is a capable leader in battle but one not completely trusted by the men. Jonathan thinks he sees him through the fog near the deserted cabin and later learns that he was one of those responsible for killing the little boy's parents, an act Jonathan finds repulsive but which the Corporal justifies as necessary for eliminating the enemy within. The Frenchman tells Jonathan that the Corporal is a good man to have on your side in a war because he is a good fighter, but "when the fighting stops . . . you hope that he . . . is not there." The Corporal is an ambivalent figure about whom Jonathan and the reader have mixed emotions.


**CORPORAL MATSUMURA** (*So Far from the Bamboo Grove\**), wounded soldier whom Yoko Kawashima visits in the military hospital and who, having become a family friend, is instrumental in getting them aboard a hospital train out of Nanam. After the mother has died and the girls are living above a warehouse in Kyoto, he sees Yoko's name in the newspaper as having won an essay contest, and he writes from the hotel where he is staying to ask if it could be the same Yoko he knew in Korea. Because it is unthinkable for girls to visit a man in a hotel, especially without a chaperone, they cannot rush to see him, but Yoko writes a postcard, and he comes to her school to find her, then goes to their home to see Ko\* and eat with them. He has survived the wreck of the ship bringing him from Korea, having clung to a log for four days. When he arrived home, he took over his family silk thread and textile business, his marriage was arranged, and they are expecting a baby. He has saved the piece of calligraphy saying, "Good Luck in War," which Toko gave him as they parted in Nanam and has it framed in his office. When the girls refuse his monetary help, he gives them his watch, saying they must keep it to give their brother when he arrives.

**CRACKER JACKSON** (Byars*, Betsy, Viking, 1985), contemporary realistic sociological problem novel set in an unspecified United States town. When earnest schoolboy Jackson Hunter, 11, receives an anonymous note saying, "Keep away, Cracker, or he'll hurt you," he immediately knows who sent it. Only sweet, loving Alma* Alton, who had been his favorite baby-sitter, ever calls him Cracker, a special name she gave him when he was younger because she thought him sweet like Cracker Jack. His fear is immediately aroused, not for himself so much as for her because he knows the "he" of the note refers to her husband, Billy Ray, a garageman. Jackson suspects Billy Ray is abusing her, the evidence being a black eye Alma said she got from walking into a door. Although he is terrified that Billy Ray will spot his Day-Glo bike in the gathering dusk, Jackson rides across town to her house. Alma denies being assaulted and makes Jackson promise not to tell his mother about the bruises. Jackson communicates his concern, however, to Mr.* Hunter (divorced from Mrs.* Hunter) in his father's weekly phone call. His father insists that he inform his mother, who tells Jackson about a safe house in Avondale, a neighboring town. When Jackson's mother, an airline stewardess, is in Chicago, Alma phones Jackson that Billy Ray has hit her baby, Nicole, and Jackson and his "best, most loyal friend," Goat, decide to transport her to the safe house in the Hunter car, a hilarious and often precarious ride with the boys driving. Half-way there, Alma becomes nostalgic over her once happy relationship with Billy Ray and asks to go home. Since Jackson's concerns continue, Mrs. Hunter decides to talk to Alma, but when Alma does not appear at the Hunter house as agreed, Mrs. Hunter races over to Alma's, and, when Jackson arrives later, on his bike, he finds the place a shambles and learns from a neighbor that Alma and the baby have been rushed to the hospital. Having herself suffered several broken bones and her baby a concussion, Alma agrees to go to the safe house, and the Hunters, including Mr. Hunter, take her there. Two weeks later, Jackson receives a letter from Alma that indicates that she is rebuilding her life and has taken a job in a day nursery. Since later pre-teens form the intended audience, incidents are not developed as they might be for an older audience, background information is sketchy, and the conclusion is anticipatory and foreshortened. The result seems a "classic" case of helping an abused wife. While the plot exploits the emotional force of a hitherto largely ignored social problem, some aspects seem strained and unconvincing, for example, Jackson's strong attachment to Alma, who has not baby-sat him for years, has never been a friend of the Hunter family, and lives some distance away. Conversely she seems extraordinarily dependent on him for emotional support. Her quick reversal in attitude toward Billy Ray and her placement in a local, apparently known safe house, also are not convincing and seem to contradict accepted facts about wife abuse. That Alma can take a job in a nursery so soon, in spite of her extensive injuries, and that the two boys can manage the car, even in traffic, also strain credulity. Characters are flat and minimally developed for the plot, and extensive dialogue keeps the pace up. Flashbacks and interludes of life with Goat and his family provide relief, humor, and texture. ALA; Fanfare; SLJ.

**CRAIG KETTERING** (*Princess Ashley**), high school youth Chelsea Olinger's age, boy friend of Ashley* Packard. Chelsea first meets him when he comes with his father to look at Chelsea's father's hunting dogs. She is struck by his good looks: "He blew me away," she says. A sophomore, he sets about becoming leader of the "in-group" of boys, the C-Stars. Mrs. Olinger finds him with drugs when he is sent to her for in-school suspension. After he is arrested for selling liquor to minors, Mr. Kettering asks Mrs. Olinger to alter the school records so that the possibilities of Craig's getting into a good college will not be jeopardized. Mrs. Olinger tries to get Mr. Kettering to see that Craig's drinking is out of hand but fails. Craig is a foil for Pod* Johnson.

# D

**DAD MCALLISTER** (*December Stillness**), once a hippie, who changed after law school, according to his wife, Mom* McAllister. Kelly, his daughter, who is always at odds with him, thinks of him as the stereotypical corporation lawyer. He resents what he thinks is Vietnam veteran "freeloading." Late in the book, Kelly and the reader learn that he never really got over the war and is even upset by the death of an animal. At the end, it is learned that he feels guilty for surviving when close buddies died. He is a type figure who suits the plot.

**DAN** (*The Return**), sober, pious, proper son of a village *kess* (priest) to whom Desta* is betrothed. Dan takes his position as priest's son very seriously and on the journey is attentive to everyone's needs, proving himself a worthy leader. Where once she thought Dan domineering and patronizing, Desta gradually comes to see him as capable, reliable, and caring. At the border into the Sudan, he draws the guards' attention to himself with a loud shout so the others can make it to freedom. He is captured and detained for some time. Later in Jerusalem, when Desta* says she does not want to marry him at that time, he seems relieved. He is ready, he says, to do his duty by her, but he really wants to study (as does she) and to prepare himself for the future in this new land. He is a round character, gradually revealed.

**DANNY BECK** (*The Keeper**), junior-high school friend of Nick Karpinski, a good-natured boy from an untroubled family that contrasts sharply with Nick's. Danny is given to harebrained schemes, as when he suggests that he call Lois Mueller, pretending he is Nick and asking for a date, and then that Nick call Karen Zimmerman pretending to be him. Though both girls realize that the boys are pretending, the scheme works. Later, Danny, who has a date with Karen to the school dance, asks another girl as "insurance," not wanting to lose a ten dollar investment in the ticket if Karen should decide not to go, and ends up with two dates and two girls annoyed with him.

**DAVID HABIB** (*Return to Bitter Creek**), Iranian-born blacksmith with whom Campbell* and Lacey Bittner live. A tactful, friendly, loving man, he gradually gets most of the Bittner family and the mountain community to accept him and his relationship with Campbell, but he is firm with Grandmom* when she tries to dominate Lacey. His background is somewhat mysterious. Lacey knows that his parents were tortured and killed in one of the Middle Eastern conflicts and that he came to the United States when he was about twelve, her present age in the story, but he speaks English with no accent and always replies, "Colorado" when asked where he is from. Lacey loves him deeply and considers him her true father.

**DAVIS DICKSON** (*Permanent Connections**), father of Rob, a management consultant in New Jersey. Youngest of the southern Appalachian family, he always wanted to get away from the marginal farm, has dropped the family middle name of Lee, and has returned for brief visits only three times during his son's seventeen years. Prompted by the realization that he has been no closer to his city-bred son than his cantankerous father was to him, he admits that he always longed for a more polished family and has done little to mend relationships.

**DAVIS, JENNY (SCHNEIDER)** (1953–        ), born in Louisville, Ky.; educator, novelist for young adults. Davis received her Associate degree from Allegheny Community College and from 1973 to 1975 worked as a child advocate for Appalachian Region Hospitals in Hazard, Ky. She then returned to school and earned her B.A. and M.A. degrees from the University of Kentucky. Her experience as a sex educator for Fayette County Health Department in Lexington from 1983 to 1985 served as background for her second novel, *Sex Education** (Orchard, 1988), a sensitive story of young love and tragedy, both the indirect result of an innovative high school class. Since 1985 she has taught at The Lexington School, in Lexington. Her first novel, *Good-bye and Keep Cold** (Orchard, 1987), a family story set in eastern Kentucky, was named to both the American Library Association Young Adult and the *School Library Journal* Best Book lists.

*DECEMBER STILLNESS* (Hahn*, Mary Downing, Houghton, 1988), realistic sociological problem novel with girl's growing-up story aspects set just before and after Thanksgiving in the 1980s in Adelphia, an affluent suburb of Washington, D.C., and told by underachieving, rebellious, only child Kelly McAllister, 14. Slovenly in appearance and studies, to her friends a "goof off" and exhibitionist, Kelly lives with her corporate lawyer father, Greg (Dad*), and commercial artist mother, Martha (Mom*). In spite of her father's prodding, which she increasingly resents, and her mother's encouragement, she does poorly at school, seeing no relationship between academic pursuits and art, where she excels, though she enjoys Mr. Hardy's literature class with its discussion of the

*Iliad* and other war poems. Nearly failing in global perspectives, where she cannot think of a topic for her term paper, she goes to the library with her best friend, Julie* Sinclair (now into boys and clothes) and old buddy Kevin* Myers (Julie's sweetheart), where she spots the local bagman, Mr.* Bob Weems, gets the idea of writing about the homeless, and, for kicks and sensationalism, decides to interview him, which she does to the accompaniment of her own and her friends' giggles. That night, lying in bed, she has an awakening of conscience. The next day, from an old friend, Mrs. Hunter, children's librarian, she learns that Mr. Weems is a vagrant Vietnam veteran. Although her father insists that Weems is using the war as an excuse for not working and cites himself as an example of what Vietnam vets can accomplish, Kelly decides to try to help the man, fearing that, as winter deepens, he will be cold and hungry. She tries persistently to talk to him, takes him food, which he dumps, and gives him her father's mittens, cap, and scarf, which he wears. The two talk a little while feeding ducks at the lake, but mostly he avoids her, insisting he does not need friends. On Thanksgiving, since her parents refuse to let her invite him to dinner, she and Great-Aunt Eliza take him leftovers. In the library she offers to share an article on post-traumatic stress disorder with him, but he flares up, yells, and throws the magazine at her. This behavior, interpreted as dangerous (plus his body odor), provokes complaints from patrons and leads eventually to his being told he can no longer come to the library with his bags, and hence effectively ousts him. Kelly takes very seriously what has happened to him, blaming herself, and her social consciousness thus having been raised, she joins for the first time in the literature class discussions about war and also ponders her father's and mother's relationship, having learned that her father was once a hippie. One day she and Dad, driving home from the library, observe that Mr. Weems has been hit and killed by a car, a death that upsets her father because it brings back Vietnam memories. Then Mr. Hardy tells the class how people bring mementoes to the Vietnam War memorial in Washington, and Kelly decides to take a picture she sketched of Mr. Weems and a portion of Siegfried Sassoon's poem ''December Stillness'' to the memorial in his honor, deeming him just as much a casualty of the war as those actually slain there. At Mom's suggestion, she asks Dad to drive her to the memorial. Both are deeply moved by the experience, and Dad compliments her on what she did for Mr. Weems. The visit is cathartic for him, and for the first time since Kelly was a little girl she feels close to her father again. Although Kelly's about-face may seem sudden and predictable, it is not inappropriate for her stage in life, and, as she grows more concerned about Mr. Weems, she becomes more likeable to the reader and the story exerts a greater hold on the reader's attention and emotions. Characters are carefully foiled types, the various teenagers and adults respectively with one another, and are superficially or expectedly developed. Dialogue often sounds contrived to present prevailing views. Scenes at home, with the teens in school corridors, classrooms, library, and shopping mall focus on generational discords, clothes, makeup, and similar teen items, the details carrying conviction. The sympathetic presentation of Great-Aunt Eliza, the eighty-year-old soup kitchen volunteer who encourages Kelly in her unconventional ideas, and Mr. Hardy, the literature teacher who develops a unit on war, makes the author's sentiments transparent. Mr. Weems, although he says very little, is focal in the novel, a clichéd figure if not sentimentalized. He appears as an ordinary guy, not very bright, sent to a conflict he never understood and cannot forget. Child Study.

**DEEP WIZARDRY** (Duane*, Diane, Delacorte, 1985), fantasy in which two young American children, both wizards, help the whales and other creatures of the deep defeat an evil that threatens the ocean and all communities along the shore, sequel to *So You Want To Be a Wizard*. Summoned by dolphins, Nita (Juanita) Callahan, 13, and her friend, Kit Rodriguez, 12, who are vacationing with Nita's family at Southampton, New York, come to the rescue of the whale-wizard, S'reee, and heal her of the wound made by an explosive harpoon, which killed her senior whale-wizard. They learn that S'reee must summon the participants to the TwelveSong, a ritual to break the evil, known as the Lone Power, again rising from the deep. Because she cannot carry a tune, Nita volunteers to take the part of the Silent One, learning only after the others are assembled and it is too late to back out that this part requires a willing sacrifice of self to the teeth of the Master Shark, the Pale One, named Ed'Rashtekaresket, the only fish and non-wizard who is one of the twelve. With Nita in the form of a humpback whale and Kit, who is not part of the TwelveSong but goes along as backup in the shape of a huge sperm whale, they travel down the Hudson Canyon, an undersea cleft greater than the Grand Canyon through ridges to the great deep around Caryn Peak, a phenomenon that rises more than eight thousand feet under water, at the base of which the ritual is performed. Although terrified, Nita converses with the shark, whom she calls Ed, about his role in the sea. It is to cure distress, he says, since he dispatches any frightened, hurt, or ill creature expeditiously. She tries to persuade him that he misses the greatest thing in life, which is love, since sharks do not form lasting pairs when they mate, but he coldly says that he has no use for that sort of thing. At the crucial moment, when the evil rises from the sea floor in the form of a huge serpent, Ed knocks her out of the way and continues her part of the song, then dives willingly to his death as he attacks the fiery snake. All this takes several nights and their participation is complicated by the worry of Nita's parents, who do not know what is going on and at first suspect that the two young people are getting sexually involved. Finally, it becomes necessary to tell them and, since of course they doubt the story, to convince them of their wizardly powers by taking them for a quick trip to the moon. Nita and Kit's realization at the end that they will be called back for other confrontations with great powers and their discovery that Nita's younger sister, Dairine, is also a wizard, leave an opening for further sequels. The plot and cast of characters are extremely complex and references to people and events in the previous book create complications for a reader unfamiliar with it, but the sense of being a whale and traveling through the deep ocean, evoked with strong sensory detail, is very compelling. Theme and action are primary; characterization is less important. The seriousness of the central theme, which of course parallels the idea of salvation by willing sacrifice in the Christian story and other mythologies, is lightened by some humor, as in the conversations with the Callahan's feckless dog, Ponch, and some of the actions of Hotshot, the dolphin. SLJ.

**DELTON, JUDY** (1931–      ), born in St. Paul, Minn.; elementary school teacher, prolific and versatile writer of mostly lighthearted novels of family life and fantasy for later elementary and junior high readers, and teacher of creative writing in various Minnesota colleges and schools. Since the publication of her first novel, *Two Good Friends* (Crown, 1974), a Junior Literary Guild Selection and an American Library Association Best Book, she has published about sixty books and more than two hundred essays, articles, and short stories. She has written several books in series, among them the autobiographical Kitty books about her own experiences growing up Catholic in the forties, including *Kitty in the Middle* (Houghton, 1979), *Kitty Goes to High School* (Houghton, 1985), and *Kitty from the Start* (Houghton, 1987), and the humorous books about Brimhall the bear, among them *Brimhall Comes to Stay* (Lothrop, 1978) and *Christmas Gift for Brimhall* (Houghton, 1986). Very well liked have been the family stories about Angel O'Leary, her mother, and younger brother, including *Backyard Angel* (Houghton, 1983), *Angel's Mother's Boyfriend* (Houghton, 1986), and *Angel's Mother's Wedding\** (Houghton, 1987), a *School Library Journal* Best Book. The Angel books are amusing, lively looks at contemporary, unconventional family life. Delton attended the School of Associated Arts and the College of St. Catherine and married Jeff Delton, a psychologist.

**DESTA** (*The Return\**), Ethiopian Falasha girl who escapes to freedom. Desta matures considerably during her flight. In the village she is dutiful, modest, and obedient, but also chattery and mostly concerned with appearances and her own feelings. The responsibilities of insuring the survival of her sister, Almaz\*, and herself, and later of other relatives on the long journey change her. She becomes less egocentric and also acts in ways she never would have at home. For example, she assumes authority over elders and even lies, out of necessity, though not without some shame. In the village she has mixed emotions about marrying Dan\* because he is so serious. Later, she sees him as steady and sturdy and admires his courage. In Jerusalem, she seizes the chance for an education previously denied her because she is Falasha.

**DICEY TILLERMAN** (*Come a Stranger\*, Sons From Afar\**), new girl in town who becomes a close friend of expansive, practical, outspoken Mina Smiths. Dicey is aloof and sullen at first, with such things on her mind as lack of money and the illness and subsequent death of her mentally ill mother. She and Mina become lab partners in science, and thus Mina has the opportunity to cultivate her. Mina is curious about what relationship Dicey might have to the Bullet (Samuel) Tillerman whom Tamer* Shipp so admired when they both ran track in high school, and learns that Bullet was Dicey's uncle. In a memorable scene, which repeats that in the earlier *Dicey's Song†*, Dicey is accused by her English teacher of plagiarizing a paper, and Mina, who recognizes Dicey's ability, stands up for her. Through Dicey, Mina meets Jeff Greene, an older boy and another loner, who has become very fond of Dicey, and then Dexter Halloway, who the reader feels sure will become Mina's romantic interest and eventual sweetheart. In *Songs From Afar*, Dicey is at college.

*DOGSONG* (Paulsen*, Gary, Bradbury, 1985), realistic boy's growing-up novel that begins in a contemporary Eskimo village. When he sees that his son dislikes the changes modern technology has brought to their village and that the boy is at the stage in life where he is unhappy with himself, the father of Russel Susskit, 14, suggests he visit Oogruk*, the almost blind old man of the village, because, he says, Oogruk knows the old songs and songs are true. Russel does so, cooking for Oogruk, admiring his traditionally made, museum-quality weapons and skin garments, feeding his dogs, and listening to his stories about the way it once was in the Arctic. After one particularly heavy meal, Russel falls into a kind of trance (from which comes the title of the novel's first section, "The Trance"), where the old man speaks but also seems to transfer thoughts. Russel learns to handle Oogruk's five now seldom-used but tundra-wise dogs, traditional sled, and the old weapons, getting a caribou in his first real hunt. When lost on the ice in a storm, he survives because of the dogs' judgment, becoming during the critical time one with the dogs, as Oogruk says it should be. Russel moves in with Oogruk, abandoning regular school for the old man's instruction. On another hunt, for seal, the old man asks to go along, and, at a certain place near the sea, he tells Russel to go on without him on what will be Russel's "long journey" to become a man. Doubling back later, Russel finds Oogruk dead in the snow and leaves him there as he wished. The last half of the book, entitled "The Dreaming," concerns Russel's solitary run with the dogs steadily northward toward the mountains and the sea, a journey of many miles and many days through the Arctic winter, in which he and the dogs survive hunger, forty-below temperatures, storms, ice, and snow. They grow ever closer to one another, and Russel gradually adds to an obviously symbolic song that forms in his head. Interspersed among the camps, hunts, and runs are dreams in which Russel sees himself as a man, an Eskimo hunter, who kills a great mammoth and returns home to find his wife and two children dead of starvation, their bodies devoured by foxes, dreams that instruct, encourage, and warn the boy. Finding snowmobile tracks, he follows them, comes upon a pregnant girl-woman lying in the snow, half-frozen, and revives her. He and Nancy* go on together for ten days, and when they run out of food, he hunts, like the dream hunter, killing a bear with the help of his dogs and returning after four days to find Nancy near death. He revives her, but the baby comes early and dies. When Nancy is still sick after five days, Russel begins a race to the coast for a doctor. The narrative ends with them drawing near a coastal village. Russel and the dogs together have proved themselves. In a kind of coda entitled ''Dogsong,'' Russel sings a song to honor them and himself and celebrate his coming of age. Though there are exciting moments, plot and characters are stock. The book's power comes from its clear, detailed descriptions of traditional ways of surviving in the tundra; the affectionate descriptions of the terrain, the dogs, and even the elements, which though seemingly hostile are hospitable to those who make the effort to know them; and of the traditional beliefs about closeness to nature, respect for the elements and animals, and the symbiosis of all things. The style is a major element. Verbal pictures sometimes seem not quite in focus, producing a surrealistic fuzziness that emphasizes the mystical aspects of the indigenous coming-of-age practices. Sentences sometimes flow, other times seem restricted, and fragments are sometimes strung together in a cumulative, repetitive progression, all to heighten a particular effect. Some parts of the plot seem improbable, even given Russel's determination and allowing for possible thought transference, and presume more ability than he would be expected to acquire in so short a time. The conclusion is open and ambiguous. It is unclear if or how this experience might change Russel's life, since there is no indication that he has thought ahead, and, although Russell abhors snowmobiles and other such technology from the outside world, he heads ironically for a modern doctor to save Nancy. ALA; Newbery Honor; SLJ.

**DOREN, MARION WALKER,** (1928–      ), born in Glen Ridge, N.J.; elementary school teacher, writer. She received her B.A. degree from Connecticut College for Women and has also studied at Central Connecticut State College, Southern Connecticut State College, Framingham State College in Massachusetts, and the College of Charleston. From 1949 to 1950 she taught elementary school in Connecticut, and, after a twelve year hiatus during the early years of her marriage, again taught from 1962 to 1981 in Massachusetts. Since that time she has devoted her professional energies to writing, winning both the *Post and Courier* Prize and the Fiction Award from the South Carolina Arts Commission for short stories. Her first novel, *Borrowed Summer** (Harper, 1986), a story for middle-grade readers about children who abduct two old people from a nursing home and prove that they can live independently, won the Christopher Award and the Juvenile Fiction Contest Award from the National League of American Penwomen and was named to the Mark Twain Award list. Her stories and articles have appeared in a number of periodicals. She has made her home in Mount Pleasant, S.C.

**DUANE, DIANE (ELIZABETH)** (1952–      ), born in New York, N.Y.; nurse, novelist, and television writer, known mostly for science fiction and fantasy for young adults. She has worked as a registered and psychiatric nurse, as a staff writer for Filmation Studios, and has managed a graphics company.

Her early novel, *The Door into Fire* (Dell, 1979) and its sequel, *The Door into Shadow* (Bluejay Books, 1984), which follow the adventures of a young sorcerer in a world where bisexuality is the norm, has been praised for expanding "the limits of the sword and sorcery genre." Two other novels, *So You Want To Be a Wizard* (Delacorte, 1983) and *Deep Wizardry\** (Delacorte, 1985), feature the young wizards Nita and Kit. *Deep Wizardry*, in which they are transformed into whales and avert a world catastrophe, was named to the *School Library Journal* Best Books of the Year list and to the list of best science fiction and fantasy for young adults by *Voice of Youth Advocate*. She has also written two novels based on the *Star Tick* television series, *The Wounded Sky* (Pocket/Timescape, 1983) and *My Enemy, My Ally* (Pocket, 1984). She has made her home in Bala Cynwyd, Pa.

**DUNCAN†, LOIS (LOIS STEINMETZ ARQUETTE)** (1934–        ), born in Philadelphia, Pa.; writer best known for her novels for teenagers. She sold her first story to *Calling All Girls* when she was thirteen, and she was three times winner in contests for *Seventeen* magazine. Since 1960, she has written some two dozen books as Lois Duncan and as Lois Kerry. Versatile as well as prolific, she has written for slicks and also for such national popular magazines as *McCall's*, *Reader's Digest*, and *American Girl*. Two of her mystery-suspense novels, *Ransom†* (Doubleday, 1966) and *They Never Came Home†* (Doubleday, 1969), were nominated for the Edgar Allan Poe Award. Though unsubtle, these are well-plotted, suspenseful, and consistently entertaining. She has written love stories like *Debutante Hill* (Dodd, 1958), about romance between teens from different social backgrounds, *Major Andre, Brave Enemy* (Putnam, 1969), a biography, and *Chapters: My Growth as a Writer* (Little, 1982), a book of personal experience. Also nominated for the Poe Award are *The Third Eye\** (Little, 1984), about a young girl who is called upon by police to use her psychic powers in a kidnapping case, *Locked in a Time\** (Little, 1985), a fantasy about a family that never ages, and *The Twisted Window\** (Delacorte, 1987), a psycho-thriller of a mistaken kidnapping.

***THE DUPLICATE*** (Sleator\*, William, Dutton, 1988), fantasy set in a seaside American town in the late twentieth century of a boy who finds a way to make a clone of himself and of the troubles that ensue. The narrator, David, 16, is upset that on the very Sunday when fascinating Angela has asked him to help her with math problems and has suggested that they will have fun afterward, he must go to his grandmother's house with his parents. Walking on the beach and worrying about how to keep both commitments, he comes on a strange box labeled Spee-Dee-Dupe, and he sees a seagull, hopping on top of it, suddenly become two gulls. He takes the box home and soon discovers that it will not duplicate inanimate objects but makes his single tropical fish instantly into two. Spurred by his need to be in two places at once, he duplicates himself. The duplicate, however, is not as tractable as he might wish, insisting on flipping a coin to see who goes to Angela's house, and winning. This is just the first of a series of difficulties they encounter: only one can be at each meal; one must stay unseen while the other is in school; clean clothes are used up twice as fast as usual. Stratagems for getting in and out of the house without David's parents seeing both get more and more complex. Most disconcerting is that the duplicate, endowed with all David's memories, thinks that he is the original and that David is the clone. Also, neither entirely trusts the other, and each is jealous of the other's time with Angela. Part of their problem seems to be solved when the duplicate finds a hide-out in the old World War II lookout tower, avoided by local young people because it was the scene of a brutal murder. Two events cause David's worries to mount: one of his fish develops black marks on its back and fin, and the other dies, its flesh having been ripped to pieces. Persuaded by the duplicate to skip school while he attends, David narrowly misses being brained by a concrete block balanced on a door in the lookout tower. He discovers that the duplicate has used the machine to clone himself, producing Duplicate B, and that the two of them are conspiring to kill him. David notices black marks appearing on one hand and the back of the neck of both duplicates. He paints similar but larger marks on his own hand and neck and tries to convince Duplicate B, who is far more aggressive and heartless than the first clone, that the marks are signs of advancing illness and that since his are largest, it must mean that he is near death. The only chance for Duplicate B to survive, he says, is to kill Duplicate A. Extremely distrustful, Duplicate B rigs a trap to kill Duplicate A, and then, seeing Angela approaching, knocks David out, gags and ties him, and goes to meet her. Duplicate A arrives, evades the trap, and eventually, after hearing Duplicate B in the next room trying to rape Angela, releases David. By this time, however, Duplicate A is so weak and disoriented from the advancing disease and David is so numb from being bound that they cannot overcome Duplicate B. In the culminating scene on the roof of the tower, Duplicate B pushes Duplicate A off, tries to do the same to David, and, when tripped by Angela, falls over the edge himself. Together David and Angela bury the two bodies. Characterization is not strong and does not engage a reader's emotions. Only David is a developed character; Angela is a functional figure, adequate for her part. Subtle differences in appearance make it possible for the three boys to be distinguished from each other, and the strong difference in the personalities of the two duplicates motivates the main tension of the novel. The ingenious plot dominates. Setting, beyond being an Atlantic seacoast area, is not exploited. SLJ.

# E

EDITH HERSELF (Howard*, Ellen, ill. Ronald Himler, Atheneum, 1987), realistic period novel of family life set on a well-run, prosperous farm in Illinois in the 1890s. Two problems unify the loosely plotted story: the protagonist's epilepsy and her need to adjust to a new home. After her widowed mother dies, orphaned Edith Ostermann, about six, goes to stay with her eldest sister, Alena* Malcolm, and Alena's husband, John*, who live with his parents, Grandma* and Grandpa* Malcolm, in their strict, rigidly Christian household. Although Edith knows Alena loves her dearly, she sorely misses her other older sister, Faithie, and her five older brothers. Nothing belongs to her in this house, she feels, and she finds the Malcolms harsh and forbidding, is much afraid of John, a schoolmaster and operator of his parents' farm, is repelled by misanthropic Grandma, who she thinks smelly, and is intimidated by Vernon*, her nephew her age, hostile lest she replace him in his mother's affections. Lonely and afraid, she retreats to the barn, where she finds a nest of tiny mice. When she proudly shows them to John, he dashes them viciously out of her hands and stamps them to death on the ground. His action brings on the first of several seizures she suffers during the book, what the others call ''fits'' and are considered mysterious and demeaning. A partial breakthrough in her relationship with the Malcolms comes when, isolated in her room for not eating, Grandpa Malcolm, then Alena, and finally Vernon smuggle her food. The pressure becomes too much again when Faithie comes to help Alena with the threshing dinner and brings Edith some of her dead mother's things as keepsakes. ''The beauty and pain of it clutched in Edith's chest,'' and she suffers another seizure. Grandma Malcolm disapproves of her, says she is just trying to get out of work, and, using Biblical language, cautions her against laying up treasures on earth. Because she associates the fits with these possessions, Edith puts away her mother's things and the rag doll the missionary ladies give her that she calls Pansy Violet Rosebud, her first doll ever. When school starts, she becomes aware of tension between Alena and John over enrolling her, Alena fearing she will have a spell in school and be laughed at. John reminds Alena that the Bible admonishes wives to be subservient and wins out. He also argues that no child of his will go uneducated. Edith is intelligent, and she must not be coddled because of her disability. School appeals to Edith very much, and she progresses rapidly, but her worst fears occur on Thursday of the first week. The children do laugh and taunt her afterward about the seizure, but Vernon, her seatmate, Rosa, and, unexpectedly, a big boy stand up for her, and she herself ignores the taunts. Later she is pleased when she overhears John telling Alena that she has proved herself worthy. The book ends with her snuggling up against Grandpa Malcolm on the way back from the church service at which baby Lettie is baptized and helping Vernon set the table. She has come to enjoy school and to feel at home in the Malcolm house and no longer craves living with Faithie and her brothers. Characterization and setting are the book's strengths. The figures are sharply drawn, revealed through Edith's eyes (though the story is in third person), and develop as they change in Edith's thinking, except for Vernon, who is shown as becoming her friend. The sense of the times, especially attitudes about Edith's malady, is clear. The book is more a series of vignettes or snapshots of a few months in Edith's life than a plotted novel, though whether or not the seizures will continue provides some suspense. There is humor—Vernon diving through the window at her suggestion lest he be found in her room and later crying in the school outhouse because he has wet himself; poignancy—Edith hiding under the porch singing to herself, "I come to the garden alone . . . ," when her mother dies; horror—the killing of the mice, and snide, pitying Mrs. Runyon, the head of the church ladies' missionary society, intent on doing her duty to an orphan but showing little sympathy for the fearful child; warmth—the understanding doctor who examines her, looking after her doll first in order to calm her; nostalgia—she and Rosa having a tea party with their dolls; but the author carefully avoids sentimentality. Edith's little-girl reactions to people and situations add charm and authenticity; for example, when John calls Grandpa Malcolm father, she thinks it strange for a grown-up person to have a father, but then it occurs to her that Alena is grown up and had the very same mother as she herself. The book offers a good look at farm life in an extended, very religious family, at a time when epilepsy was a feared disease. SLJ.

**EDNA** (*Angel's Mother's Wedding\**), Angel O'Leary's talkative, know-it-all friend. Angel often feels inferior to Edna because Edna seems to know so much more about the world than she does. Edna tells Angel about weddings and showers, and, whenever she discusses the wedding with Angel, worries. When Edna laughs about Angel's new name, Angel knows she will also be teased at school, even though it is a good Greek name and she likes Rudy\* very much. Edna is horse crazy and pretends her bike is a riding horse. She is a common kind of middle elementary-aged girl, a contrast to the less self-assured Angel.

**ELSIE POTTER** (*Sirens and Spies\**), small, deft teenager, whose intense desire for order has made her rebel against her disorganized family and wall herself off in her own immaculate room, which she allows neither her sister Mary\* nor their two younger siblings to enter. Her relationship to Miss Fitch, her violin teacher, has gone beyond even the usual pride in a promising student to a special closeness of understanding until, through the window one evening, she sees Miss Fitch passionately embracing a man. Elsie refuses to continue lessons, sells her violin, and buys an elaborate desk set and notebook, where she keeps a record of the visits of an assortment of men to Miss Fitch's house. To her family and the outside world, Elsie seems hard and uncompromising. Although the reader is never told directly, it is apparent that she is hurt and feels betrayed. In Miss Fitch's story of her youth, Elsie recognizes her own qualities and realizes that she might have acted as the French girl did.

**EMILY EMERSON** (*Quentin Corn\**), daughter of the local rector who befriends Quentin Corn, the pig who masquerades as a runaway boy. Bright, nosy, opinionated, grandiloquent, Emily is a source of town gossip for Quentin and shares it generously with him. She is the first to tell him that she knows he is a pig, but since she is a social misfit herself, she never tells anyone else about him. She comes down with a mysterious ailment after the horse breaks into the parlor, and when she recovers from the delirium that accompanies the malady, Quentin has left town. She ends up believing Quentin was just a figment of her illness, for the reader an emotionally unsatisfying conclusion to their relationship.

# F

***THE FACTS AND FICTIONS OF MINNA PRATT*** (MacLachlan\*, Patricia, Harper, 1988), realistic, humorous girl's growing-up novel set in an unnamed contemporary American city. Imaginative, romantic Minna (Melinda) Booth Pratt, 11, who is "waiting to be a woman," enjoys her offbeat family: McGrew\*, 10, who hums what he wants to say and is a failure at baseball; her abstracted psychologist father, Mr.\* Pratt; and her juvenile novelist mother, Mrs.\* Pratt, an indifferent housekeeper always at her typewriter. Minna takes the bus regularly and happily to her cello lessons with Mr. Porch\* at the conservatory, though she seldom practices until after Lucas\* Ellerby, violist with a marvelous vibrato, swells their chamber group to four, and Minna falls in love. She has several problems: getting her mother to discuss love and other important things, figuring out the meaning of the mysterious quotation her mother has taped above her typewriter: "Fact and fiction are different truths," and, mainly, acquiring a vibrato, for which she practices diligently and has when she plays on her knee, the dining room table, and the nightstand but which eludes her on the cello. She is invited to dinner at Lucas's house, a beautifully organized and appointed place with a young maid, Twig\*, and conversation that seems to Minna civilized and genteel compared to that at home. His room, on the third floor, is filled with tanks and aquariums of frogs. Minna's problem with vibrato becomes more urgent when Porch announces that the group, which also includes Imelda\* and Orson\* on violins, will perform in a competition at concert hall in two months. Before the big occasion arrives, Minna writes a fan letter pseudonymously to her mother, complaining that her mother does not talk to her; suggests her father teach McGrew to catch; discovers that McGrew has been making up "facts" for his science report on beavers; helps Lucas dispose in various ponds of his large collection of frogs, suddenly discovered by his horrified mother ("alien creatures"); and observes the progress of the romance between Twig and Willie\*, a musician who picks up extra money playing violin on the street corner. The big night arrives, the four play their Mozart beautifully, even though the lights go out, and Minna and Lucas give their $200 winnings to Willie and Twig. That night, at 12:30, Minna awakens, feels compelled to pick up her cello, and discovers she now has a vibrato. She immediately phones Lucas, who answers on the first ring with "Congratulations." Minna has learned that things come in their own time. Events are so closely seen from Minna's vantage and the narrative is so made up of her thoughts, observations, and reactions, that it almost seems she is speaking. Present tense intermingles with past, giving the story immediacy and vigor. Humor comes from revelation of and interplay between characters, which are richly drawn, eccentric but distorted kindly, and behave as one might expect of intelligent people almost totally engrossed in what they most like to do. The style is distinctive and witty, often alliterative and appealing to the intellect: "the dog collapsed in a fury of friendship against them" and wagged his tail "a little on the slow side, like a stubborn metronome." Humor also comes from the child's inexperienced yet logical way of considering things; for example, Emily Parmalee, McGrew's baseball-loving chum, who favors bright pink, feathered earrings, ponders kissing: "Do they breathe through their noses, or do they leave a bit of free space at the edges of their mouths . . . ," after observing Minna's parents in a long, passionate clinch. Minna's casual parents are deftly contrasted with Lucas's formal ones, her positive feelings about his family contrasted with his positive ones toward hers, and, while the conclusion seems rushed and it is not clear that Minna grasps how much she has grown, these problems are of no great moment and do not keep this from being a very funny and very insightful book that improves with repeated readings. ALA; Fanfare.

**FAIRLEE DICKSON** (*Permanent Connections**), uncle of Rob who falls through a rotting hayloft floor and breaks his hip. Having worked most of his life handling road-building machinery, he is retired and supports his father and sister, doing a little farming on their marginal land. A cheerful, tolerant man, he puts up with the family eccentricities, makes friends with Ginny* Collier and her daughter, Ellery, outsiders from Charlotte who build a house on the mountain above the farm, and welcomes Rob to help out while he is recovering, understanding the boy's frustration and overlooking his surliness. When Rob comes home drunk, he assures the boy that it is not the first time that has happened in the family, and when Rob is arrested, he arranges for a lawyer.

*THE FALCON STING* (Brenner*, Barbara, Bradbury, 1988), novel of mystery and suspense set in the Arizona desert concerning the illegal collection and smuggling of rare hawk eggs and chicks. Bored with the little town of Serenity, Marina Cassidy, probably sixteen or seventeen, has entered a summer ACE — Accelerated College Experience—program in creative writing offered at the local high school. Her real interest, however, is in bird watching in the desert near the isolated home built by her now dead artist father, where she lives with her mother, Isobel, a half-Mexican potter who supports them by running a catering service. Helping her mother serve a party for a wealthy client, she meets his son, Nick Menaker, a handsome blond biker whom she has noticed in the ACE class, and she overhears conversation between guests that indicates that he has been in trouble with the law. Learning that she is interested in desert birds, Nick invites her to go with him when he flies his prairie falcon, Roxanne. Although she is fascinated, Marina dislikes the killing for sport, and their parting is less than friendly. Nevertheless, she gives him a copy of her story about discovering a nesting pair of rare peregrine falcons with four eggs. When she hesitates to take him to see them, despite his eagerness, he introduces her to Cheryl Harper at the raptor rehabilitation center where he sometimes works, thereby proving that he is not one of the smugglers known to be taking eggs and eyasses from nests in the area. Cheryl is tense and evidently angry with Nick for some unexplained "stunt" he has pulled. She tells them that federal authorities trying to catch the smugglers are setting up a sting, hoping to pull in low- and middle-level operators who will eventually lead them to the ringleaders, and she knows she and especially Nick are under suspicion. Although wary of infiltrators, she welcomes Marina's offer of aid at the center, where she meets Sam Spenser, who introduces himself as an old friend of Cheryl, but whom Marina recognizes as the man she saw near Montenegro, a steep rock outcrop where she sighted the falcons, and her suspicions are rekindled about Cheryl and Nick. Nevertheless, she takes Nick, as she has promised, to Montenegro, and, when she inquires about his limp, he tells her his story. After his mother ran off with a young man, he was upset and wild and did a lot of hunting for the sake of killing, even taking eggs from falcon nests and selling them. Having been sighted shooting an eagle, he was injured in trying to escape on his motorcycle. As a result he lost a foot, paid a stiff fine, and was sentenced to community service at the raptor rehabilitation center. Cheryl has changed his attitude, taught him falconry, and helped him train Roxanne; her recent anger is because he broke probation, which forbids him from flying a falcon until fall, to show off to Marina. Now with understanding and trust and on Nick's part great difficulty, they climb the rock formation and see the nest with just one chick, white like his extremely rare albino mother. When they descend, they discover and report the body of a young man who is identified as Jimmy Toddy, an Indian game warden. The next day they are summoned to the raptor center, where Detective Murdoch, Sam Spenser, and two men from the U.S. Fish and Wildlife Service are planning strategy. They admit that they have used Marina's information about the white peregrine falcon as bait, spreading the word where smugglers might hear it and waiting for them to make a move, as those did who took the three falcon chicks and presumably murdered Toddy. Now they recruit reluctant Nick and Marina into their sting, getting the boy to place ads cleverly worded to imply that he will buy illegal eggs, the story being that he has reverted to his old ways and wants a falcon for his new girl friend. Eventually he gets a call to meet in the elaborate Alhambra Hotel, but the smugglers fail to show up, evidently alerted by the police van in the parking lot. Foreseeing the next move, Marina calls Murdock, and they race to the airport, where the detective meets them and apprehends an Arab couple about to fly off with the three chicks. The couple, however, seem to have nothing to do with Toddy's murder. Returning to Montenegro alone, Marina discovers in a pack rat's nest an identification tag that leads the police to a long-time criminal who was cactus rustling when Toddy was staking out the falcon egg thieves. This last set of coincidences is unlikely, but the story as a whole is well knit, using Marina's vacillation between trust and suspicion to good advantage, as well as Nick's personality changes from surly to charming to vulnerable and the clumsiness of the police and federal agent operations. A good deal of information about saving endangered hawks and injured birds is included unobtrusively, and the harsh beauty of the desert, seen through Marina's eyes, is evoked well. The girl's relationship to her mother, warm and appreciative despite teenage irritations, is a good element. Poe Nominee.

*FALLEN ANGELS* (Myers*, Walter Dean, Scholastic, 1988), historical fiction of the Vietnam War, exemplified in the tour of duty of one black seventeen-year-old from Harlem. Richard Perry, the narrator, has enlisted, not from any thought-out conviction but because, although his grades are good enough for City College, he has no money for clothes, and no other options offer themselves. On the trip to Vietnam, Richie meets a white nurse, Judy Duncan, and a fellow enlistee, Peewee Gates, a joking fellow with brown skin and reddish hair from Chicago. Both of them, and almost everyone else he meets, think they will probably see no action since the war is almost over. Richie also knows that he should have a medical profile because of a knee hurt in basketball at training camp and that this should exempt him from fighting. In the next months he and Peewee see some of the worst action of the war in the Tet offensive, along with others on their squad: notably Monaco, a little Italian who acts as point man; young Jenkins, son of a colonel, who is visibly terrified; Jewish Lobel, a movie buff, son of a director, who thinks of the whole war as a scenario in which he chooses various roles; Brewster, a religious boy hoping to enter a seminary; Jamal, a medic, probably gay; Johnson, a huge black soldier; Sergeant Simpson, who is counting the days until his tour of duty is up; and Lieutenant Carroll, the decent, concerned platoon leader from Kansas. Returning from their first patrol, Jenkins steps on a mine and is killed. In the next months they see all kinds of action, including a "pacification mission," which involves going into a village to give food and candy to the natives, and later, after the Viet Cong have infiltrated the same village, going in, burning the huts, and shooting anything that moves. On one mission Lt. Carroll is killed. Richie writes a letter to his wife. He is replaced by inept Lieutenant Gearhart, whose blunders almost cause disaster for the squad. When Richie is wounded, not seriously, he meets Judy again at the medical facility. Returning to his company he finds that Sgt. Simpson has gone back to the World, as they call anywhere outside Vietnam, and has been replaced by a racist, so obvious that both blond Lobel and little, dark Monaco say they will stand with the blacks if it comes to a showdown. In their last action, Richie and Peewee go off to check a ridge, get separated from the rest of the squad, see a huge contingent of Viet Cong passing through the area, and spend the night in a "spider hole" dug under an embankment, killing the Cong soldier who comes to hide out there. Peewee is wounded, but in the morning they make their way back to the pickup zone and see Monaco sitting against a tree, set there as bait by the Cong who hope to shoot down the rescue helicopter. As it comes in, Richie and Peewee open fire on the bushes, alerting the chopper, which clears out the Cong and picks up all three of them, Richie's leg being seriously wounded as he boards. After surgery, he and Peewee are sent home together. Just before they leave, Richie's medical profile from Fort Devens finally arrives. A personnel sergeant who looks up friends for ten dollars reports that Judy Duncan was killed in a hit on a field hospital. They also learn that Captain Stewart, who continually volunteered the company for dangerous assignments in order to get credited with a high enemy body count, has been promoted to major. Throughout the experience, Richie wishes he had a girl to write him and to go home to, and he worries about his young brother, Kenny, and about his own uncertain relationship with his mother, who drinks too much. The prevailing tone of the novel is ironic. It is impossible to know who is the enemy or why, and some of the greatest damage is done by blundering attacks on their own side. The horrors of combat are described graphically, as are the mud, bugs, discomfort, and sheer boredom that oppresses them between actions. All this is leavened by the genuine affection of the men in the squad and their humor, in the tradition of battlefield stories. Dialogue is sharp, clever, and convincing, probably the best feature of the novel. C. S. King Winner; SLJ.

**FELICE SMITH** (*Fran Ellen's House**), Fran Ellen Smith's younger sister, seven years old. At the beginning of the book, Fran Ellen thinks Felice is fat, mean, and whiny and resents the attention Felice gets from little Flora, their younger sister who used to choose Fran Ellen over the others. Later, Fran Ellen and Felice become close, especially after Fran Ellen takes Felice shopping for a jacket and Felice is caught swiping a little golden-haired doll that looks like the missing Goldilocks of the Bears' House. Fran Ellen immediately comes to Felice's defense and tries to take the blame upon herself. By this time also, Felice has been fixing up the Bears' House on her own by placing found objects inside. The two sisters then form a solid friendship through the Bears' House.

**FERNANDO** (*The Honorable Prison**), handsome young teacher of whom Marta Maldonado becomes infatuated and to whose sexual advances she almost succumbs. Polished, poised for the most part, he became responsible for his mother and sisters at an early age, a situation he resents, and he yearns to leave the mountain village. He urges Marta to join him in teaching at the school his mother runs because, being genuinely lonely, he wants her company. His uncle, the mayor, refuses to allow it, however, and when Fernando continues the friendship, the mayor has the young man beaten publicly. Marta observes the incident and feels shaken by the implications for the safety of her family. Fernando leaves the village soon after. The romance between the two young people seems believable, since they are the only ones of their age in the village, but the extent to which the relationship progresses does not fit Marta's character as presented. Fernando is not particularly likeable because by the time he is introduced the reader's sympathies lie firmly with Marta.

**FERRIS, JEAN** (1939–      ), born in Fort Leavenworth, Kansas; author of novels for teenagers on sociological and psychological subjects. After receiving her B.A. in 1961 and her M.A. in 1962 from Stanford University, she worked as an audiologist until 1976, when she began writing full time. Her first novel, *Amen, Moses Gardenia* (Farrar, 1983), concerns teenage depression and suicide, and her second, *The Stainless Steel Rule* (Farrar, 1986), is about the demands of friendship. Her most honored book is *Invincible Summer** (Farrar, 1987), a moving story about teenagers with leukemia, which is a *School Library Journal* Best Book. Her other novels include *Looking for Home* (Farrar, 1988) and *Across the Grain* (Farrar, 1989).

**THE FIGHTING GROUND** (Avi*, Lippincott, 1984), historical novel of the American Revolution set from April 3–4, 1778, about twenty miles from Trenton, New Jersey. Moved by patriotic fervor, farm boy Jonathan, 13, runs off at 9:58 in the morning to fight the British, deceiving his mother and disobeying his war-wounded father whom he regards as cowardly and who has refused him permission to go. The next twenty-four hours see a radical change in Jonathan's attitude toward war and his father. At the local tavern he joins a motley dozen men who have responded to the bell summoning them to report, is loaned a gun by the tavernkeeper so large that he can barely manage it, and marches down the road led by the mounted, commanding Corporal*. At the crest of a hill the Corporal orders them to form two lines, the shortest men, including Jonathan, in front, the rest behind, to await the enemy troops, who turn out to be the much dreaded, mercenary Hessians. Under fire, a friend of his father dying beside him, another friend, the Frenchman, wounded, Jonathan breaks and runs, soon to be captured by three Hessians. They tether him on a rope and take him with them, the time now toward evening and the weather foggy. When they hear a cow mooing, they follow the sound until they come upon a deserted cabin. While searching for a milk pail, Jonathan discovers a small boy huddled alone in a shed and soon after the boy's parents lying dead, shot, in the woods. Fearful, angry, desperate, Jonathan tries to bury the bodies, then enlists help from the Hessians to complete the job. That night, they settle to sleep, Jonathan tethered to the ankle of the eldest Hessian. Guilt stricken, Jonathan thinks he should try to kill them, but he finds that he does not have the stomach for it and decides to escape. He unties the rope, grabs the sleeping boy, and makes an arduous way to the road, comes upon the American remnants of the battle, and tells the Corporal about the Hessians. At dawn they sneak up to the cabin, and Jonathan is sent to reconnoiter. Horrified that the Hessians may be killed without a chance, he awakens them. They grab him for a shield, but he breaks away and trips the eldest by the still attached ankle rope, and they are slain. The other Americans leave, as does Jonathan, who rejects the Corporal's company and goes home by himself. He finds his father at work in the field, sees relief and gratitude on the man's face, and realizes that the fear he had earlier seen in his father's eyes was not cowardice but true apprehension for his son. Jonathan is very happy to be home and deeply grateful to be alive, having learned that war is a cruel, hard business that poses severe dilemmas even for common soldiers. This essentially single incident story is told in spare and unadorned language. The pace is rapid, although for Jonathan events come to seem endless, and the frequent chapter headings in hours and minutes enhance the sense of the rapid passage of time and point up how dramatically Jonathan changes in his perceptions about war and his father. Finding the child and the burial are poignant scenes. In the latter Jonathan sees that even the Hessians have feelings when the younger one murmurs what appears to be a prayer. Jonathan also learns that for some soldiers like the Corporal the political issues are so important that they lead to such atrocities as the slaying of the child's parents simply because they were British-sympathizing Tories. Some ironically humorous scenes ensue: Jonathan can barely manage the gun, which takes him a full five minutes to load, and when he is captured the reader learns that the Hessians, whose language Jonathan cannot understand, are just as scared and lost as he is. Jonathan's emotions cover a broad spectrum and are completely credible as presented. ALA; O'Dell.

*A FINE WHITE DUST* (Rylant*, Cynthia, Bradbury, 1986), realistic contemporary boy's growing-up novel set in a small North Carolina town. A year later, Pete Cassidy, 14, looks back on his fateful eighth-grade summer, when he discovers what is really important to him in life. Although his parents attend church only occasionally, Pete says he started "loving church" at a very early age, fascinated by Jesus and "afraid of Hell just because of Him." He takes very personally the preaching he hears about heaven and being judged. The first time he sees him, the Preacher Man is hitchhiking on the 19–21 bypass. The young man's light blue eyes so impress Pete at that time that, when he sees him later in the drugstore, he thinks maybe he's a "lunatic who hitched into town to murder people with a pickax." That night, at the revival meeting, Pete is astonished to find the hitchhiker is the current revival preacher and is so moved by his words and demeanor that he loses his heart to this new Preacher Man, who blesses him and tells him that he is born again. After this, all Pete thinks about is the Preacher Man, whose real name, he learns, is James W. Carson. Pete even turns away from his best friend, Rufus*, with whom he has chummed since he was a little boy and who regards the Preacher Man with intense skepticism. When the Preacher Man, who is obviously lonely and who says he sometimes feels like Jesus Christ but lacks disciples, invites Pete to join him when he moves on, Pete eagerly accepts. He secretly packs his bag and leaves a note for his parents, certain that joining the Preacher Man is God's will. Rufus remonstrates angrily with him, but Pete goes to the designated meeting place at 10:00 at night anyway. He waits and waits, until 2:00 A.M., when he gives up and starts home. Rufus appears, having observed from hiding in the bushes, and tenderly walks Pete home. The next morning, Rufus's news that the Preacher Man left last night with Darlene Cook, the drugstore girl, adds to Pete's pain to such an extent that he rages at Rufus and kicks him out. Pete describes the next weeks with characteristic understatement: "I never knew life could be so hard." Three weeks later, Darlene returns, but she never says a word about the Preacher Man, and rumors about the minister explode through the little community. Pete becomes so abstracted his parents worry about him, but he gradually comes out of his anger and hurt. He even feels compassion for the Preacher Man in his loneliness and accepts what happened philosophically. Perhaps God's purpose in all this was to help him realize the riches in his life: his parents, who have stood by him, and Rufus, with whom his friendship is restored by summer's end. Although Pete considers throwing away the dusty pieces of his little broken ceramic cross, fished from the duffel bag he packed, he realizes that they are part of a whole he can never lose or do without, his belief in God. Pete tells the story of his infatuation with such honesty, compassion, and self-control that the Preacher Man never assumes the proportions of a villain and emerges as a lonely, haunted young man. Since Pete does not indulge in self-pity, the reader sympathizes more deeply with him and accepts him as impressionable, naive, and overly earnest. Economy of words, understatement, and skillful use of irony make this reminiscence emphatic and enhance the few developed scenes, such as that when Rufus accompanies Pete home, when Pete's mother tries to comfort him, and when the Preacher Man tells the story of the older man who helped him grow up, a conversation that serves both as character revelation and foreshadowing. The theme that love, faith in the basic goodness of life, and forgiveness transcend even the worst of situations comes through strongly. ALA; Fanfare; Newbery Honor; SLJ.

**FLEISCHMAN, PAUL** (1952–      ), born in Monterey, Calif.; poet, author of picture books, short stories, and novels for young people. He attended the University of California at Berkeley and received his B.A. degree from the University of New Mexico at Albuquerque. He is the son of Sid Fleischman†*, the well-known author for children. In 1989 his *Joyful Noise: Poems for Two Voices* (Harper, 1988) won the Newbery Medal. His two books of short stories, *Graven Images: Three Stories* (Harper, 1982) and *Coming-and-Going Men: Four Tales of Itinerants* (Harper, 1985) are both set in New England in earlier times and full of haunting irony. *Rear-View Mirrors** (Harper, 1986) is a young adult novel of a girl, newly graduated from high school, who spends the summer with the eccentric father she has never known and learns much about herself in the process. His writing has been commended for its musical quality and sensual use of language.

**FLEISCHMAN†, SID (ALBERT SIDNEY)** (1920–     ), born in Brooklyn, N.Y.; reporter, writer of screenplays; for more than twenty-five years noted in children's literature for his tall-tale, fast-action novels for elementary-age children. After service in the Navy in World War II, he was graduated from San Diego State College with a B.A. degree and wrote for the San Diego *Daily Journal* until 1950, when he became a full-time writer. A number of his novels have won awards or citations, among them his first book, *Mr. Mysterious and Co.†* (Little, 1962), and several others with an American historical background: *By the Great Horn Spoon!†* (Little, 1963), which established his reputation as the master of the comic novel and was made into the movie *Bullwhip Griffin; Chancy and the Grand Rascal†* (Little, 1966); *Humbug Mountain†* (Little, 1978); and several short, outrageous fantasies about Josh McBroom, including *McBroom Tells the Truth†* (Norton, 1966); and a pirate novel, *The Ghost in the Noonday Sun†* (Little, 1965). Among his many awards are the John Newbery Medal for *The Whipping Boy** (Greenwillow, 1986), a facetious, rollicking farce revolving around the mistaken identities of an English prince and his whipping boy look-alike that recalls Mark Twain's‡ *The Prince and the Pauper‡* (Osgood, 1881). *The Whipping Boy* was also a Best Book of both the American Library Association and *School Library Journal*. Fleischman has also written a series of mysteries featuring the Bloodhound Gang (Greenwillow, 1991) and a dozen other robustly amusing stories of action, suspense, and villainy. His son, Paul Fleischman*, also an author for children, received the Newbery Award for his book of poems, *Joyful Noise* (Harper, 1988).

**FLOATING ILLUSIONS** (Yarbro*, Chelsea Quinn, Harper, 1986), mystery of suspense and detection, set in the first-class section of the *Duchess of Malfi*, a luxury liner traveling from the United States to Genoa about 1911. Millicent Cathcart, 14, is returning to school in Switzerland after visiting her wealthy father, accompanied by her father's sister, Mehitabel Reyns. Although ostensibly chaperoned by the widowed Mrs. Reyns, Millicent is not only a much more seasoned traveler, but also far more intelligent and sensible than her aunt. Among the widely varied first-class passengers, some stand out: General Cuernos, an autocratic Spanish officer; Geoffrey Wingham, a handsome smooth talker, who seems to be playing up to Aunt Mehitabel; Auralia Dovecote, an affected woman who neglects her invalid husband and holds seances in Aunt Mehitabel's cabin; Cloris Gordon, a young woman assertively interested in education and political rights for women; Milton Homes, a meek middle-aged man who joins in the seances; and most prominent, the Incredible Anton, a stage magician who agrees to provide some entertainment during the voyage. Millicent, who is frequently censured by Aunt Mehitabel for her conduct and for even knowing such things as that her mother lives with her lover in Europe and her father keeps a mistress in New York, tries to exert some independence from her silly aunt while still maintaining good manners and proper decorum. She strikes up a friendship with Anton by guessing how he does some of his stage tricks. She learns, by something she overhears his assistant, Sabina, say, that he is actually an archduke in Bohemia, but that he abdicated when he was a boy and has no interest in reclaiming the title. Early in the voyage, an understeward disappears and is assumed to have been washed overboard in a storm. Then other people are found dead—another understeward, General Cuernos, and Wingham—each in some circumstance that seems to point to wizardry and each with a spangle from Sabina's costume found near the corpse. Suspicion falls upon Anton, and he is shunned by most of the other passengers. Millicent, determined to defend him by discovering the true murderer, interviews all the passengers. Captain Symington institutes patrols, directed by the chief steward. Millicent learns from Jibben, Anton's gypsy servant, that attempts have been made upon the magician's life before, evidently by a Bohemian group that fears he has political ambitions. When Miss Gordon, who has severely criticized the growing clamor to blame Anton, confesses to her that she has seen a shadowy figure in her room, despite the locked door, Millicent points out that it may have been an illusion, and she goes to the room in the hold where Anton's equipment is stored to ask Jibben whether any of it is missing. She overhears a conversation between Sabina, who has a Cockney accent, and her newest lover, clearly showing that he has been using her and now is threatening her life if she does not continue to help him. Before she can identify him, Millicent is seized from behind and forced into the Iron Maiden, the prop for a trick in which steel spikes are driven through the holes, and evidently through the body of the woman inside. Using her head, Millicent discovers that the five essential spikes can be unscrewed from within, so she is not skewered as her attacker has assumed. Rescued, Millicent is taken to the captain, who is at first skeptical but agrees to talk to Anton and turns Millicent over to the chief steward, who attempts to drug her. Anton agrees to put on one last performance, at which, having created the illusion that Sabina, who has been missing and is assumed murdered, has come back from the dead and is floating over the stage. Anton is able to uncover the murderer, who turns out to be Milton Homes, an international criminal, in league with the chief steward, both trying to discredit Anton so that he will be unable to return to his dukedom, as they suppose he plans to do. The shipboard scene and the period setting provide an interesting background for the complicated plot. Characters are more fully developed than in many mystery books for young people, and the pace is well handled to keep suspense high. Poe Nominee.

**FLORIAN** (*The Beggar Queen**), bold, idealistic, hard-nosed leader of the revolutionaries in a trilogy of novels set in the fictitious kingdom of Westmark* by Lloyd Alexander*. In *Westmark†*, Florian has gathered around him a small corps of insurgents who become known as "Florian's children." They wish to bring about democratic reforms in the government. Born a noble, Florian is the son of the Count of Montmollin, but he was moved by conscience and ideals to champion the peasants. In *The Kestrel†*, he takes his followers into battle on the side of the monarchy in return for a constitution guaranteeing equal rights for all and becomes one of the three consulars who advise Queen Augusta (Mickle*). He is old and ailing in *The Beggar Queen*, and when the kingdom is invaded, he flees to Regia to seek help from its friendly king. Once the usurper has been deposed, he prepares to hold general elections.

**FLOSS BREWER** (*In Summer Light**), mother of Kate, who gave up her own painting career when she married Marcus* Brewer. Although she defers to him completely and runs their home and family to suit his needs, she sees that her daughter has genuine artistic talent, which she lacked, and should not give up painting. At the end of the summer, Kate realizes that it was her mother, not her father as she had thought, who brought her good paints when she was a child and arranged that he take her to museums and let her paint in his studio.

*FOLLOWING THE MYSTERY MAN* (Hahn*, Mary Downing, Clarion, 1988), realistic mystery novel with girl's growing-up story aspects set in the small town of Hilltop, Maryland, in the 1980s. Madigan Mahoney, 12, learns that people can be betrayed by their emotions and good intentions. Half-orphaned, living with her grandmother, Mrs. Porter, Madigan tells how, one hot August afternoon, she and her best friend, Angie Wilkins, are at Sweeney's Drugstore sipping Cherry Cokes, when a handsome, bearded, young stranger comes in, consults the community bulletin board, and asks if Mrs. Porter's room is still for rent. Her romantic instincts aroused, Madigan quickly takes Clint James, Angie accompanying them, home. When Clint quotes from Wordsworth, says he is in electronics, just wants "to get away from it all," and offers $100 a week, Grandmother* rents the room to him for an unspecified length of time, over the vociferous objections of Miss Lucas, fifth grade teacher and long-time boarder. Madigan jumps to the conclusion that this mysterious man is her father, who abandoned her and her deceased mother when Madigan was a baby and has come incognito to claim her. Although Angie is highly skeptical and Clint does not respond properly when Madigan poses test questions, she becomes obsessed with the notion. Disturbing events occur, which alert the reader but do not influence Madigan. She and Angie, who plan to become detectives, inspect his room looking for evidence that he is her father and find a pistol hidden in one of his cowboy boots and a picture of him holding a baby. Reports of burglaries in neighboring towns appear in the newspaper, and the girls see Clint in lively conversation with Alice Wilkins, Angie's sister of nineteen, estranged from her family because she ran off and returned unmarried with little Chad six months earlier. Then burglaries occur in Hilltop, curiously on wealthy Locust Hill, where Madigan pointed out leading citizens' homes to Clint. Lonely one day, Madigan goes to her mother's grave in Ivy Hill Cemetery, falls asleep, is awakened by voices, observes Clint put an expensive necklace around Alice's neck and the two kiss, and overhears Alice call Clint Chad's daddy. Madigan blurts out that Clint is her father, not Chad's. Clint kindly but firmly says she is wrong, and she runs home weeping and feeling stupid. That evening she goes back to Ivy

Hill, her tomcat Holmes trailing her, to see if the burglary loot is there because she is now convinced that Clint is the thief and finds it in garbage bags in a secluded mausoleum. Clint and Alice return, find her (given away by Holmes), take the loot, put it and her in Clint's van with Chad, and speed off, heading west. Many hours later, when they stop so she and Alice can use the "ladies' room" in a woods, she reminds Alice that kidnapping is a federal offense, and Alice stalls while she runs away. Tired, hungry, bedraggled, she comes upon a little town north of Columbus, Ohio, where authorities contact Grandmother, who brings her back to Maryland. After a fast start, the predictable events move rapidly with ironic humor and more human interest, deeper characterizations, especially of the principals, and less sensationalism than typical for this genre. Clint, who is revealed as a dangerous escaped convict, also has admirable features. Ironically, it turns out that he came to Hilltop because he loves Alice and wants to be with her and his son. He shows a warmth, tenderness, and consideration for Madigan that arouse mixed feelings toward him. Grandmother is memorable, and the boarders are individualized: disapproving Miss Lucas, who has a man friend on the sly, and easygoing Mr. Schumann, who delights in teasing Miss Lucas because she irritates so easily. Pretty, blond, flirtatious Angie is remarkably well behaved, considering her miserable home life, and even none-too-bright, weak Alice, whose parents refuse to forgive her, evokes sympathy. The reader suspects long before Madigan that she is thinking wishfully, but Madigan is completely convincing as presented. Poe Nominee.

**FOX†, PAULA** (1923–      ), born in New York City; author best known for her contemporary realistic problem novels for later elementary readers and early adolescents. After studying at Columbia University, she held various positions as a reporter, a machinist, editor, reader for a film company, and teacher of emotionally disturbed children and English to Spanish-speaking children. In 1974 she won the Newbery Medal for *The Slave Dancer†* (Bradbury, 1973), a historical novel that departs from the bulk of her work by being set against the slave trade just before the American Civil War. Other novels singled out for critical attention have been *Maurice's Room†* (Macmillan, 1966), *How Many Miles to Babylon?†* (White, 1967), *The Stone-Faced Boy†* (Bradbury, 1968), *Portrait of Ivan†* (Bradbury, 1969), *The King's Falcon†* (Bradbury, 1969), and *Blowfish Live in the Sea†* (Bradbury, 1970). *One-Eyed Cat\** (Bradbury, 1984), about a boy taking responsibility for an animal he thinks he has maimed, won the Child Study Award and was accorded Newbery Honor and Fanfare status, as well as being named a Best Book by the American Library Association. In two books girls must cope with alcoholic relatives, *The Moonlight Man\** (Bradbury, 1986) and *The Village by the Sea\** (Orchard, 1988). Both are ALA and SLJ best books, and the latter was also a *Boston Globe-Horn Book* Winner and selected for Fanfare. Fox's books deal sensitively with emotional situations children might face and often revolve around lack of communication and understanding, but her plots sometimes employ extraneous surrealistic details and unconvincingly distorted characters and may be disturbingly inconclusive. In 1978 she received the Hans Christian Andersen Medal for her collected work for young readers.

**FRANCES COMBS** (*Good-bye and Keep Cold*\*), young woman who, at twenty-eight, becomes a widow with two children and an old man to look after in a Kentucky mountain community. An orphan, she was raised by restrictive grandparents, from whom she fled at fifteen, and her husband, children, and great-uncle-in-law are the center of her existence. Although she is attracted to Henry\* John Fitzpatrick, who courts her after her husband's death, she rejects him, saying that she is still married to Ed. Later she bitterly regrets it when she learns of her husband's infidelity. An emotional woman, she cries easily and tells exaggerated stories to make the children laugh. She has a rigid moral sense that makes her "divorce" her dead husband and cut off her former best friend, leaving her with no confidants except Edda, who is burdened with the knowledge of her mother's hurts and desires. When Henry John brings her his baby, she is delighted, not hesitating for a minute to take in the handicapped child to raise as her own.

**FRAN ELLEN'S HOUSE** (Sachs\*, Marilyn, Dutton, 1987), short, realistic novel of family life set from August to January in the late 1960s in New York City, sequel to *The Bears' House†*. Two years after the events in the previous book, Fran Ellen Smith, 12, describes the problems that confront her in her two houses—her real one and the house in which the three bears live that was given to her by her former teacher, Miss Thompson. Now that Mama has been released from the mental institution, she and the children, who have been living in foster homes for two years, are together again: Fletcher, 15, Florence, 14, Felice\*, 7, little Flora, 3, as well as Fran Ellen. Their apartment is cramped, dingy, almost unfurnished, and cockroach infested. Fran Ellen feels Florence, now interested in makeup, clothes, and boys, picks on her and avoids responsibility. She also worries about Flora, always her favorite. Flora has grown close to her foster family and pleads to go back to them, avoids Fran Ellen's overtures, and switches her affections to Felice, who is chubby, like Flora's foster sister. Even Fletcher can be a problem because, fearing Mama may have a relapse, he pushes the girls to do more about the place. At school, Fran Ellen runs into trouble, too, especially with an obnoxious showoff named Joey Rupp. After their caseworker convinces the family that Flora would be better off with her foster parents, Fran Ellen gradually warms to Felice, while her school science project on cockroaches not only gains her an A, which elevates her self-esteem, but also wins her needed positive attention from the students, who make her pair of cockroaches class mascots they call Romeo and Juliet. Fran Ellen's second house, the Bears' House, was damaged while she was away and needs considerable repair and even the bears must be cleaned and fixed up. Moreover, Fran Ellen, who has all along imagined the life of the bears inside, feels that they blame her for their problems and thus will not speak to her. Felice and then gradually the whole family begin to take an interest in sprucing up the Bears' House. This activity brings them all closer together and relieves the bickering. Christmas finds them happily exchanging small but carefully selected gifts. Mama is proud of Fletcher's achievement in school and looks forward to college for him and taking a job outside the home herself. At the end, Fran Ellen has begun to make friends at school and lose interest in the bears. Felice takes her place with the Bears' House, imagining the bears' doings and conversations. The italicized, imagined story about the bears parallels and supports whatever problem Fran Ellen is having in the real world. It is easy to identify with Fran Ellen, who is less naive than in the first book but still open and honest. Except for her, the characters are drawn with broad strokes: chubby, impetuous Felice; patient, enduring Mama; hardworking, worrying Fletcher; snippy, appearance-conscious Florence, just as Fran Ellen, very concerned about herself and narrow sighted, might indeed see them. Buildup is lacking, there is no proper climax, and for the most part scenes are underdeveloped. The effect is of a series of isolated events, the chapter headings by months being the only clue to the time sequence. The conclusion with Felice assuming Fran Ellen's role with respect to the bears seems completely appropriate to Fran Ellen's stage in life. Vocabulary is easy, sentence structure uncomplicated, and the pace fastmoving. ALA; Stone.

**FRANK BROUGHTON** (*Park's Quest**), uncle of Park and stepfather of Thanh*, the Vietnamese child whose birth or impending birth was the reason Park's parents were divorced. There is no explanation in the novel of how Frank found Thanh and her mother and brought them to this country, but the housekeeper says that people of the area were shocked and that his father, the Colonel, had a second stroke at the time. A quiet, patient man, Frank has firmly controlled the wild little girl, insisting that she milk cows, work in the garden, and behave herself, but he has not quelled her spirit. Park's mother, Randy, says that Frank has spent his life "cleaning up other people's messes," referring to her husband, father of both Park and Thanh, and also perhaps to his father, the Colonel. Frank lives in a little house, not the decaying mansion, and does all the work on the farm.

*THE FRIENDSHIP* (Taylor*, Mildred D., ill. Max Ginsburg, Dial, 1987), short realistic account of racial tension set in Mississippi during the Great Depression, told by black Cassie Logan, 9, who with her family appeared in the Newbery Award winner *Roll of Thunder, Hear My Cry†*. While Cassie and her brothers, Stacey, 12, Christopher-John, 7, and Little Man, 6, are at the store of white John Wallace fetching headache medicine for an old neighbor lady, Mr. Tom Bee, a black man so old he "had seen the slavery days," stops in from fishing to get sardines. Refused by John's sons because he owes money, he demands to see their father, referring to the elder Wallace by his first name without the prefix of Mister as the blacks are supposed to do. The sons angrily and spitefully respond that his behavior is inappropriate for a "nigger." When John arrives,

Mr. Tom Bee repeats his request, addressing the elder Wallace as "John." John sternly reminds the old man that using the Christian name of a white "ain't seemly" for a black person, to which Mr. Tom Bee replies: "An' I done tole you, it ain't seemly t' me to be callin' no white man mister when I done saved his sorry hide when he wasn't hardly no older'n them younguns standin' out yonder!" After John gives Mr. Tom Bee what he asks for, Tom leaves and explains to the Logans that he had saved John's life when John was a boy and reared him, and that John had promised him that Tom need never call him Mister, since he had been like a "daddy" to the boy. Remembering he has forgotten to get "tobaccie," Mr. Tom Bee re-enters the store and again addresses the store-keeper as John, without prefix. Intimidated by the presence of other white men and wishing to save face, John pulls out his shotgun and shoots Mr. Tom Bee in the right leg. The book ends with the children watching Mr. Tom Bee dragging himself down the road, in a loud and penetrating tone repeating the white man's promise of friendship and defiantly shouting his name, John! John!, over and over again. The story's title aptly foreshadows the ironic and tragic nature of this single incident narrative, which is made more powerful because it is seen through the eyes of the nervous and only partially informed children and is understated and very economical of words. Based upon an actual incident told to the author by her father, it carries the conviction of lived racial discrimination and tension. The story can stand by itself as dramatic evidence of the period and is not dependent for understanding upon the other books about the Logan family. ALA; Boston Globe Winner; C. S. King Winner.

# G

---

**GARDINER, JOHN REYNOLDS** (1944–      ), born in Los Angeles, Calif.; aerospace engineer, novelist for children. He received his B.A. and M.A. degrees from the University of California at Los Angeles and since 1968 has worked as a thermal analyst for aerospace engineering firms in Los Angeles. He is also an inventer for Num Num Novelty Company. His first novel, *Stone Fox*\* (Crowell, 1980), won the George C. Stone Center Children's Book Recognition of Merit Award, as well as several more localized honors. It is a story based on a Rocky Mountain legend of a dog sled race, in which a young boy with an aging dog wins through the help of an enigmatic Indian. It has been adapted with an audiocassette by Listening Library. His second book, *Top Secret* (Little, 1984), is about a nine-year-old boy who chooses to do a science project on human photosynthesis, despite opposition from his parents and teacher. Another Gardiner title is *General Butterfingers* (Houghton, 1986). He has three daughters and has made his home in the Los Angeles area.

*THE GHOSTS OF NOW* (Nixon\*, Joan Lowery, Delacorte, 1984), realistic mystery-detective novel set in a West Texas oil town at the time of publication. Angie Dupree, 17, tells how she and her family, her oil man father rising rapidly on the corporate ladder, her socialite mother inclined to drink too much, and her brother, Jeremy, 15, newly arrived from Los Angeles, find the people of Fairlie hostile and unfriendly because of the Duprees' association with oil. Only handsome "kicker" (farmer) Del Scully, also a senior, goes out of his way to be welcoming to Angie. He shows her about town in his pick-up, including the old Andrews place, overgrown with trees and bushes, secluded and said to be haunted. The terror starts for Angie at 10:45 one Friday night, when, alone in the house, she lifts the ringing phone and hears a whispering voice telling her her brother is dead. Afraid and horrified, she locates Jeremy in the hospital in intensive care, where he lies in a coma severely injured by a hit-and-run-driver. After this swift and dramatic beginning, the novel traces Angie's persistent efforts to learn the identity of the driver so he or she can be brought to justice. All she has to go on at first is a sliver of blue paint she finds under one of Jeremy's fingernails. With Del's help, she learns a matching blue car belonging to Debbie Hughes, her contemporary and the daughter of Grandy Hughes, respected local banker, has been repaired at a body shop. She also discovers that Mr. Hughes reported to the police that the car was stolen and found wrecked. Boyd Thacker, 16, another local youth of good family who was Jeremy's school tennis partner, informs her that Jeremy had been at a party with him, drank too much, and ran into the street intent on suicide, a story she also takes, like that of the stolen car, as a lie. In spite of threatening phone calls, police harassment, and Del's warning that she is pushing things too hard, Angie continues to try to learn the truth. She investigates the old mansion, because the accident took place near there, because Jeremy had sharply told her to stay away from it, because she finds a poem he wrote about "Ghosts of Now," which she associates with the place, and because she finds a stolen watch in his desk. She discovers a room upstairs filled with such property as television sets and cameras, obviously stolen. She returns later to the place to see who might come for the goods and finds Boyd there. He tells her that the stuff was taken by town youth to relieve their boredom. He said Jeremy refused to prove himself in the accepted way by robbing his own house and ran away. Boyd admits that he drove the car that struck Jeremy—Debbie's car—having gone after Jeremy to keep Jeremy from going to the police. Although Del arrives just in time to help Angie, Boyd gets away. When Angie tells her parents the story, she insists that the implicated families be informed so that they will know what their children have been up to but realizes that the police will do nothing lest the "old guard" Fairlie families be upset. She also persuades her parents that the Duprees need help in learning how to be a family, since this might not have happened to Jeremy if the family members had known each other better. The story ends with Angie talking to Jeremy as he lies unconscious in his hospital bed, as she has done so often during the novel, hoping that her words will somehow be the therapy he needs to come back to them. This time she is rewarded with a long, gentle sigh and pressure on her hand. Events are overforeshadowed with Boyd cast as the "charming villain" from the outset and Del as the "good guy," in spite of a few hints otherwise that serve to build suspense and throw the reader off. Other characters are equally conventional. The book is a fast-paced thriller, with stock tight spots, obstacles, and red herrings, and well-depicted Gothic scenery set against a clearly drawn small-town atmosphere. Fairlie is shown as close-knit to the point of being claustrophobic, a place where longstanding local loyalties transcend the law and even common morality. Poe Nominee.

**GINNY COLLIER** (*Permanent Connections*\*), new neighbor of the Dickson family, having come from Charlotte with her daughter and built a simple, rustic house on the mountain above the Dickson farm. After about twenty years of marriage, she has broken free of her husband, whom she describes as ponderous, and of the social expectations that his business required of her. Realizing that she went from home to college to marriage without striking out for herself because she was always afraid, she understands Coralee* Dickson, who is too terrified to leave the house, and she patiently helps the older woman take first steps toward recovery. In her relationship with her daughter, Ellery, she suffers from the girl's rejection of her love and interest, but she is determined not to let it spoil her new life. She signs Rob's bond when he is arrested and is supportive to him, even though she fears his influence on Ellery.

**THE GOATS** (Cole*, Brock, Farrar, 1987), contemporary realistic sociological problem novel set in a wooded region somewhere in the United States. The gripping opening scene occurs at dusk on an island (later identified as Goat Island) on a lake at a summer camp for privileged young people. Two campers, Laura* Golden, 13, daughter of a divorced career woman, and Howie* Mitchell, about her age, son of archaeologists on a dig in Turkey, are selected as "goats" by campmates, stripped naked, and marooned on the island. She whimpers in fear and humiliation; he pulls himself together and persuades her that they can paddle to shore using a log he has found. There he breaks into a cottage, where they find some food and makeshift garments and spend the night. Ironically, they leave the island just as a counselor, Margo Cutter, and her helper come to rescue them. This pattern of near misses with authorities and rescuers continues throughout the novel, as do the thefts and break-ins, all of which they scrupulously keep track in order to make good later. At the beach, Laura, now composed, steals money from a truck and calls home, but Maddy, her mother, misinterprets the request for help as just another example of Laura's inability to socialize and says she will come to camp two days hence, on Saturday, for Parents' Day. This avenue of rescue closed, they steal some bathers' clothes and, when they put them on, ironically feel an incredible sense of joy, freedom, and control. They decide simply to disappear, and between this point and midday Saturday they have a variety of sometimes frightening and also exciting adventures that give them a new sense of independence and capability and bring them close, so they feel sincere concern and responsibility for each other and affection like brother and sister. Among other experiences, they fall in with inner-city campers, whose buses have stopped at a gas station, and are taken to their camp. Teenagers Calvin and Tiwanda, both black, and Lydia, take a special interest in them, ironically referring to them as Bonnie and Clyde, particularly after they stand up to a bully named Pardoe, share their beds with them, and give them clothes and advice. The next night, Thursday, Laura cleverly manages to get them a motel room, but the next day, the cleaning woman, who suspects that they are misbehaving sexually, reports them, and while they are manipulating a meal at the restaurant, Laura is caught. Howie escapes, and by setting off car alarms, enables her to get away, too. They spend the next night in a car they find unlocked, their difficulties compounded by the onset of her period and a cold Howie has caught. Saturday morning, while walking along the road in the direction of the camp to connect with Maddy for Parents' Day, they are apprehended by a disagreeable, "goat smelling" man, who says he is a deputy, has a badge, and knows that they are the runaways now the object of a massive search. While he reports by phone, leaving the key in the ignition, they steal his truck and get some distance down the road, where an old man who sells honey befriends them. Laura contacts her mother by phone, but the boy insists that he will not give up, certain that the law will make him go back to the camp. He wants to live with Laura in the woods, free and independent as they have been these last few days. They come to blows over this idea, but finally he gives in to her insistence that things will work out and somehow they will be able to stay together. The narrative switches from the children to the adults, so that the reader is kept aware of Maddy's frustrating attempts to find Laura and also get information about what precipitated the flight from the camp administrators. They evade and dissemble, and Maddy and the children are made to seem in the wrong. The several near contacts contribute to the tension and the simple horror of the story. The callousness of most of the adults, particularly the camp director, and the brutality of the campers, who continue what has evidently been a traditional hazing, contrasts starkly with the warm acceptance of the inner-city youngsters. The open conclusion leaves the reader to wonder how things will work out, especially for Howie. Laura's mother has a new confidence in Laura's judgment, as does Laura herself, but Howie's parents are older and often away from home, creating special problems for him. Although the children's relationship is chaste, sexual innuendo appears throughout. ALA; Fanfare; SLJ.

*THE GOLD CADILLAC* (Taylor*, Mildred D., ill. Michael Hays, Dial, 1987), realistic story of barely 5,000 words that starts and ends in a busy residential neighborhood in Toledo, Ohio. 'lois, perhaps ten, tells how she and her older sister, Wilma, learn about prejudice against blacks because of their father's spanking new car. One Saturday father surprises the family by proudly coming home with a beautiful brand-new Coupe deVille Cadillac, painted shining gold outside and upholstered in rich gold cloth inside. The girls race through the house to tell their mother and inform the aunts and uncles who have emigrated from Mississippi and are living upstairs until they have their own homes. The aunts and uncles and neighbors admire the car, and everyone is very impressed, except mother, who adamantly refuses to have anything to do with it. She insists that their money was to go for a bigger house, not a fancy car. She even walks the girls to church the next day, right past the car, leaving 'lois feeling let down because she had hoped to show off. Then father decides to drive to Mississippi to visit grandfather on his farm even though the uncles, aunts, and neighbors try to talk him out of it as being too dangerous for a black. "It's like putting a loaded gun to your head," says one uncle. But father stubbornly sticks to his plan, asserting that, since he's worked for it, he ought to be able to do what he wants with his car. Mother then shocks everyone by announcing that she and the girls will go along. Then the uncles say they will, too, and picnic baskets filled with food, the Cadillac, a Ford, a Buick, and a Chevrolet head south in caravan. In Kentucky, father sternly tells the girls that whenever whites are around, they are not to say a word. Soon they see signs prohibiting blacks from using water fountains, entering restaurants, staying at motels, and the like, and 'lois feels as though she is in a foreign land. In Memphis heavy traffic separates them from the others, and, alone, just over the Mississippi state line, they are stopped by police, who search father, insist he has stolen the car, and take him to the police station. After three hours in the station, father returns, having paid a fine for speeding, and they continue, the police following them for some miles. That night father pulls off the road among some trees to sleep, and in the morning he decides to return to Memphis to borrow a cousin's Chevy. At grandfather's farm, father explains to the girls about conditions for blacks in the South and the meaning of the signs they saw, holding out the hope that some day things will change for the better. Back in Toledo, the Cadillac sits in the garage until one Saturday father takes it downtown and sells it, saying it had pulled the family apart and they can use the money for a new house. Although at first 'lois feels embarrassed riding around in an old 1930s Model A Ford, she thinks his decision was for the best. She also knows she will always remember the gold Cadillac that took them on a revealing ride south. The joy of the beginning of the book sets into relief the subdued tone at the end of the story, and it strains credulity and logic that the girls should not be aware of conditions for blacks in the South, if only from hints in overheard conversations. Though events along the way sober them, the happenings are related too factually for much emotional impact, and what should be the tensest scene of all, the search and seizure, lacks drama. The scenes of extended family fellowship and togetherness at the beginning stand out vividly as not only a way of life for emigrating, upwardly mobile blacks of the period but also for their symbolic value of greater freedom and opportunity. They carry the clarity and impact of the author's own experience. The numerous, brown-toned, full- and two-page spread pictures depict events and family scenes in bold composition—like posters—point up the Cadillac's symbolic value, and emphasize the social didacticism. Christopher.

**GOOD-BYE AND KEEP COLD** (Davis*, Jenny, Orchard, 1987), realistic novel of family life in eastern Kentucky from the death of the father, Ed Combs, in a strip-mining accident to the time of the writing, about fourteen years later. The narrator, Edda Combs, is eight when her mother, Frances*, rushes off to the hospital, leaving her and her two-year-old brother, Jimmy, with Banker*, her father's great-uncle, who lives with them. Before the funeral, Edda meets Henry* John Fitzpatrick out in the dusk behind the house playing with Jimmy, while neighbors crowd the living room and kitchen in the traditional country visit to the home of the bereaved. She thinks that he has the saddest eyes she has ever seen in a human and only later learns that he is responsible for her father's death, having set off a dynamite charge too soon. More frightening than the loss of her father is her mother's emotional withdrawal, the feeling that she is no longer really with the family. For several days she takes to her bed, being finally roused by Annie*, her best friend who came to Appalachia with her husband as a Vista worker and stayed to teach art in the high school when he took off with another woman. Henry John starts coming by, first to bring some of Ed's belongings, later to do small handyman jobs and to tell Frances of a job opening for a secretary at the mining company, and finally, over the next couple of years, to court her. When he asks her to marry him and she says she cannot, that she is still married to Ed, they have a loud, emotional fight and he moves to Lexington. For some time, the Combs family stays in Cauley Creek, although they are always treated like outsiders, since Frances is from Pittsburgh. When she is eleven, Edda makes her first real friend in Charlie Henson, a mathematical whiz whose family has recently come to town. The next year in the school yard Otis Spicer taunts Edda, saying that her father had V.D. and got it from that "hippie art teacher." Edda, who has no idea what V.D. is but knows that this is an insult to her father's memory, attacks and thoroughly beats up Otis and is suspended from school. Although it turns out that it is Otis's father who got herpes from Annie, the incident leads to the revelation that Edda's father did have an affair with Annie when Frances was pregnant with Jimmy and was in the hospital with a broken leg. Furious, Frances cuts off her friendship with Annie and is physically sick for some days. Then she insists that she is going to divorce Ed, and, though Edda is afraid for her sanity, goes through some sort of formality in the cemetery and thereafter considers herself not widowed but divorced. That summer she moves the family to Lexington, where she works part time and takes nurses' training. After about a year, Banker, walking to the store for his newspapers, runs into Henry John, who has long since married. He drops by occasionally until he asks Frances to make love, and, refusing to be any man's mistress, she angrily sends him away. Two years later, he shows up with a baby only a couple of weeks old, his daughter Alexandra, he says, rejected by her mother because of a deformed foot. With amazing simplicity, he gives the baby to Frances, and she accepts with delight. Only Edda, who has taken over handling the family finances and other practical matters, thinks to ask if this is legal. Soon he has divorced his wife and, by giving money for Ali, as they call the baby, helped out the family, and he begins courting Frances again. After being propositioned out of wedlock, she is leery, but by the time Edda finishes high school, they have decided to marry. Edda is telling the story when she is twenty-two, has graduated from college, and is living with Charlie Henson, who looked her up again after finishing at MIT. She says she is "resting from her childhood." The title is from a poem by Robert Frost, spoken by a farmer who, having done all he can for his young orchard, leaves it for the winter, as Edda now feels she must leave her family to cope without her. As protagonist and narrator, a child burdened with responsibilities beyond her years in caring for her little brother and worrying about her mother, Edda is thoroughly convincing and likeable. The Appalachian community is shown through her eyes to be both bigoted and beautiful. The main character, however, is Frances, a complex woman whose strong moral principles nearly destroy her already damaged life. The novel is compelling, with a ring of authenticity. SLJ.

*A GOOD COURAGE* (Tolan*, Stephanie S., Morrow, 1988), realistic novel of a youth caught in a repressive religious sect and his struggles to escape, set somewhere in the United States in the late twentieth century. Ty (Tie-Dye) Rainey, 14, was born in a hippie commune and has lived in one anti-establishment group after another as his mother's mood dictates, so he has hope of adjusting to the rural Kingdom of Yahweh, which at least seems to have plenty of kids and good food. He endures his renaming to Tobias (Tie-Dye is a devil name, Brother* Daniel, leader of the Kingdom, says) and watches his mother, formerly Jasmine, become Jordana* and a True Servant. As a child-servant, Ty must live in a closely guarded dormitory with the other boys between five, when they leave their mothers, and sixteen, when they Pledge and become full adults. With the others, he works all day in the fields, seven days a week, and does after-dinner chores of dishwashing, all on very skimpy rations, the good food which he saw earlier being reserved for guests and True Servants. At first he believes, as he was told when he and his mother were guests, that the children are out of school for spring Busy Time, but he learns with a shock that this is a story concocted for the outside world and that the children no longer go to school at all. Although it is a tenet of the Kingdom that no child shall be struck, there are other more devastating punishments. When he gets out of bed to comfort little Noah, 5, who is having a nightmare, Abner, the adult in charge of the dormitory, chains him to a tree on a hill, where he spends the night shaking with cold and terror. Fast days are common for minor offenses. Illness is considered a punishment from Yahweh, and sick children are kept working as usual. Conversation as they work and in the dormitory is forbidden, but Ty gradually learns something of the other youngsters: Ezekiel, who is a Chosen, having been born in the Kingdom; Caleb, who is often punished for singing or dancing but seems to use music to endure; Gideon, at fifteen almost ready to Pledge and already bullying the others; and notably, Samarah, whom he privately calls Sam*, a girl whose parents defected, leaving her at the Kingdom, and who is now considered a devil-child and avoided by the others. Brother Daniel's son, Benjamin, a top leader newly returned to the Kingdom, is especially to be feared, he learns. When he tries to tell his mother about the life of the child-servants, she turns a deaf ear, praising Brother Daniel and emoting about the joy she now feels in the true faith. There are a few bright spots: Jeremiah, one of the leaders, seems to like him; he is assigned to care for the animals before going to the field each day and likes the rabbits, becoming especially attached to one doe he calls Ophelia; and Sam shows him a cave that she has found and kept secret. When little Noah begs Ty to teach him to read, they risk sneaking out at night to the never-used schoolhouse but are caught. Ty is condemned to spend a fast-week in the Cage, a windowless shed exposed to the blazing sun, so small he cannot stretch out, with only a small door through which someone slides a bottle of water each day and lets him hand out his waste can. Only once he is allowed out, when Brother Daniel escorts him to the barn and kills Ophelia in front of him. At night Sam sneaks out of the girls' dormitory and whispers to him through the shed door. Ty concocts a plan and writes a letter, with paper and pen he stole earlier, to Polaris*, a man from an earlier commune who is the closest Ty has ever had to a father, and gets Sam to give it to Jeremiah to mail. Sam saws the padlock off the door, but just as Ty gets out Jeremiah intercepts them. Sam attacks and bites him, and Ty runs away, gets to the neighboring town, alerts the police, and returns to the Kingdom with them. There, to his dismay, Brother Daniel talks them into believing Ty is a misguided adolescent making up stories. Benjamin shuts Ty into an office with a phone, briefly tells him that he can use it and escape that night, that his own interest is in saving his father from extreme action that will endanger the Kingdom, and that he has already let Sam escape and wants them both out for good. Ty calls Polaris, lets himself out a window, and finds Sam in the cave, ready to leave with him. The book involves a reader completely in Ty's growing horror and anger at the Kingdom, with strong use of sensory detail and enough parallels to known abusive sects to be believable. The contagious fear among the children is chilling. Jeremiah's duplicity is predictable, but Benjamin's aid at the end is not convincing, and the question of what will happen to Caleb and Noah and the other children keeps the denouement from being satisfying. SLJ.

**GORDON, SHEILA** (1927–      ), born in Johannesburg, South Africa; writer for both adults and older children of fiction and nonfiction often revolving around racial issues. She received her B.A. from the University of the Witwatersrand, married a physician, and has three children. Her first novel, *Unfinished Business* (Crown, 1975), for adults, concerns a South African doctor exiled to England for helping an ill black soldier. Her most celebrated novel, *Waiting for the Rain*\* (Orchard, 1987), received the Jane Addams Award and was an American Library Association Best Book. Set in contemporary South Africa, it contrasts ten years in the lives of two boys who are friends, one white and the nephew of a prosperous farmer, the other black and the son of the farmer's foreman. Gordon has made her home in New York City and has lived in the British Isles. *A Modest Harmony* (Seaview, 1982) is the account of her summer vacations in rural Scotland. Gordon has won praise for her ability to evoke the moment and for her fairness toward the cultures of which she writes. She has published *World Problems* (Batsford, 1971) and *3rd September 1939* (Dryad, 1988), both nonfiction, and *A Monster in the Mailbox* (Dutton, 1978), a novel for children about a boy who buys a mail-order monster, and has contributed to various periodicals.

**GRANDFATHER MACLEOD** (*After the Dancing Days*\*), stubborn father of Annie Metcalf's mother. He, his wife, and his youngest son live across the street from the Metcalfs, where he keeps chickens. He shocks Annie by scolding her mother for her rudeness to the injured soldiers, although Annie has also resented her mother's attitude. He has stoically accepted the death of his most promising son, Paul, and with equal courage learns that Paul did not die a hero's death but succumbed to measles, but he keeps this information from his wife, who dwells constantly on Paul's memory. After Timothy Lewis regains his sight, Grandfather finds another blind soldier and starts reading *Ivanhoe* to him because, he says, there is nothing like Sir Walter Scott to stir up the blood.

**GRANDMA MALCOLM** (*Edith Herself*\*), wife of Grandpa\* Malcolm, mother of John\*, and mother-in-law of Alena\* Ostermann Malcolm, Edith Ostermann's sister. Edith sees her as "tiny, with wrinkled hands and small narrow feet [that] did not seem to belong to the rest of her, which was huge and shapeless inside her dark heavy dress. Edith had to be careful not to knock over Grandma Malcolm's canes. . . . '' She is disapproving of the child and tends to dominate the house. She is very religious and speaks in Biblical language. When Edith is more sure of herself in the Malcolm house, she feels sorry for Grandma Malcolm because she is "old and ill and smelly" and sees her for what she is, an aged, unpleasant, unhappy woman.

**GRANDMOM BITTNER** (*Return to Bitter Creek*\*), Eva, domineering mother of Campbell\* and grandmother of Lacey. Determined to have her own way, she evidently drove her daughter into the arms of Wally Palmer, then made her life miserable when she had Wally's illegitimate child. Two years later, her efforts to get custody of Lacey forced Campbell to flee to Colorado, where she has lived a hand-to-mouth existence but raised Lacey well. Their return to Bitter Creek seems to Grandmom an opportunity to control again, but Campbell's determination to be independent, Lacey's wariness, and the gentle, good-natured persistence and tact of David\* Habib finally win out. Although they are at odds most of the time, it is clear that Grandmom and Campbell share the same uncompromising spirit.

**GRANDMOTHER PORTER** (*Following the Mystery Man*\*), Madigan Mahoney's mother's mother, who teaches high school English and rents a room to mysterious Clint James because she needs the money to repair the house and generously does not want to raise the rent on her long-term boarders. Events show her that she should have told Madigan more about Madigan's father. She held out because she thought Madigan's mother's fatal cancer was induced by shock and anxiety after he abandoned her and Madigan. After the kidnapping, Grandmother tells Madigan that Madigan's father contacted her after Meg's death but that she refused to let him see his daughter. Unforgiving like Alice Wilkins's parents, she says her biggest mistake "was thinking I could be everything to you.''

**GRANDPA MALCOLM** (*Edith Herself*\*), father of John\* and father-in-law of Alena\* Ostermann Malcolm. When she first meets him, Edith is reminded of St. Nicholas because he has a "halo of gray hair" and a "full gray beard.'' She wonders if he is jolly but is frightened by his loud voice. He proves to be gentle, however, genuinely liking the motherless child. Edith later feels closer to him than any of the adults except her sister, Alena. He is practical about his religion. When John decides to hire a man to help with the harvest, Grandpa thinks it extravagant and says that they can handle things by working all weekend. John protests on the grounds of the sanctity of Sunday. Grandpa argues that since God lets things grow on Sunday, he would surely understand the need to work on Sunday. John's will prevails, however, because John is supported by Grandma* Malcolm, whom Grandpa fears to cross. When Edith is isolated in her room because she refuses to eat the meal that nauseates her, Grandpa slips in with a slice of ham, still warm, for her. He is one of the most attractive figures in the novel.

**GRANNY BO** (*Night Cry**), really named Alma Goff, old woman in her eighties who lives alone in an isolated cabin, having outlived three husbands and raised five children. Full of superstitions, she is locally suspected of being a witch, and when, on rare occasions, she rides her mule into town and hands pennies to little boys, people fear that she is putting a spell on them. As her nearest neighbor, Ellen Stump feels obligated to visit her a couple of times a week to see that she is all right, but the girl is a little afraid of her, especially when she learns that Granny predicted the death of her mother five years previously from spinal meningitis. Because people have seen her hand something to little Jason Cory at the auditorium dedication, she becomes a prime suspect in his kidnapping and is almost the target of a vigilante raid. Granny tells Ellen that her youngest son is dead, and when the man claiming to be Gerald Hawkes turns out to be Sam Goff, the old woman still says that Sam is dead, having convinced herself of this after he got into trouble and left the area.

**GRANNY JERUSHA BENT** (*Charley Skedaddle**), the old "wise woman" of the Blue Ridge Mountains who takes in Charley Quinn and for whom he works for about a year. At first she calls him Boy, but after he kills the "painter" (panther) and rescues her from her fall in the mountains, she addresses him as Charley, an action that makes him feel redeemed and accepted. She lifts much of his burden of guilt when she tells him that since his bullet lodged in the Rebel soldier's shoulder, he probably did not kill the man. Granny is chiefly responsible for Charley's maturing. She is a foil to Noreen, Charley's matronly sister.

# H

**HAAS, DOROTHY F(RANCES)**, born in Racine, Wis.; longtime editor and author of books mainly for primary-grade children. After receiving her B.S. degree from Marquette University, Milwaukee, in 1955, she was an editor for Whitman Publishing Co. until 1968, for Worldbook Childcraft until 1970, and for Rand McNally and Co. until 1983. Her writing career has spanned thirty years, beginning with such picture books for young readers as *Little Joe's Puppy* (Whitman, 1957) and *Mimi, the Merry-Go-Round Cat* (Whitman, 1958) and moving through somewhat more complex plots like *Tink in a Tangle* (Whitman, 1984) to full-length fantasies like *The Bears Upstairs* (Greenwillow, 1978) and *The Secret Life of Dilly McBean*\* (Bradbury, 1986), which was a nominee for the Edgar Allan Poe Award. A sprightly story full of action and human interest, *The Secret Life of Dilly McBean* concerns a boy whose gift of magnetism in his fingers motivates villains to attempt to kidnap him in order to exploit his talent. Under her own name or as Dee Francis, Haas also wrote original stories based on television programs and movies and edited several series of fiction for preteens and picture books for younger children. She received the Children's Reading Round Table Award in 1979 for "distinguished and continuing service" to children through books. She has made her home in Chicago.

**HAHN, MARY DOWNING** (1937–     ), born in Washington, D.C.; teacher, artist, librarian, and writer best known for contemporary problem and mystery novels for later elementary and adolescent readers. She received her B.A. and M.A. degrees in English and art from the University of Maryland at College Park, has been an art teacher in junior high school, was a free-lance artist for Washington, D.C., television, taught English at the University of Maryland, and since 1975 has been a children's librarian in Laurel, Md. Her own experiences provide the ideas for her novels, the most acclaimed of which have been *Daphne's Book* (Clarion, 1983), a *School Library Journal* Best Book and a Library of Congress Children's Book; *Following the Mystery Man*\* (Clarion, 1988), about a girl who becomes involved with a stranger she is sure is her father, which was nominated for the Edgar Allan Poe Award; and *December Stillness*\* (Houghton, 1988), which relates a girl's efforts to help a homeless Vietnam veteran and received the Child Study Award. Hahn's books have been praised for their contemporary tone and speech and their well-paced plots. Her other titles include *Tallahassee Higgins* (Clarion, 1987), about the adjustment problems the daughter of a single mother faces when she goes to live with her aunt and uncle, and *Stepping on the Cracks* (Clarion, 1991), which tells of a girl in World War II who becomes involved with an army deserter.

**HAMILTON†, VIRGINIA (ESTHER)** (1936–      ), born in Yellow Springs, Ohio; writer whose novels of black life in New York and the Midwest have won many honors. She attended Antioch College, Ohio State University, and the New School for Social Research in New York. Among her many novels, *Zeely†* (Macmillan, 1967), *The House of Dies Drear†* (Macmillan, 1968), and *M. C. Higgins, the Great†* (Macmillan, 1974) are set in southern Ohio, where she has returned to live on the family farm with her husband, writer-anthologist Arnold Adoff. *The Planet of Junior Brown†* (Macmillan, 1971), which was an honor book for the Newbery Medal, and *Sweet Whispers, Brother Rush†* (Philomel, 1982), also a Newbery honor book and winner of the *Boston Globe-Horn Book* Award and the Coretta Scott King Award, are both set in New York City, while *Junius Over Far*\* (Harper, 1985), honor book for the Coretta Scott King Award, is set on a Caribbean island. Another honor book for the Coretta Scott King Award, *A Little Love*\* (Philomel, 1984), is a romance in which the overweight protagonist, with the help of her boy friend, seeks her father who departed many years before. *Arilla Sun Down†* (Greenwillow, 1976) explores the problems of a family of a black mother and an American Indian father. Although much admired and containing memorable scenes, her novels have been criticized for having prominent bizarre elements difficult to accept as realistic yet intrusive as symbols.

**HANNIBAL TATE** (*Rear-View Mirrors*\*), father of Olivia, who after sixteen years of neglect summons her abruptly to come to New Hampshire and "try out" as his heir. Besides gardening, collecting butterflies, and playing classical music, Hannibal is a baseball fanatic, so hooked on the game that out of season, when he cannot listen to his beloved Red Sox on the radio, he has invented a French league, including the Bordeaux Bombers, the Toulouse Guillotines, the Avignon Popes, and his favorites, the Arles Impressionists, with such star players as Vincent Van Gogh, the scrappy leadoff man, Renoir, a good long-ball hitter, and Monet, in center field where he can study the grass. He sets up a schedule and flips a ten-franc coin to decide who wins each day's games. Hannibal is a hypochondriac, assuming that because he has heart palpitations he is near death, although this does not deter him from his annual seventy-mile bike trip to Lake Kissadee and back. He dies accidentally, being struck by lightning while repairing his roof.

**HANSEN, JOYCE** (1942–     ), born in New York City; English teacher and novelist for children and young people about the black experience in New York City and during the American Civil War and Reconstruction periods. She received her B.A. degree from Pace University in 1972 and her M.A. from New York University in 1978. Her contemporary novels draw upon her own experiences while growing up in the Bronx and her observations of West Indian immigrants in New York. *The Gift Giver* (Houghton, 1980) and its sequel, *Yellowbird and Me* (Houghton, 1986), see inner-city life from the perspective of a ten-year-old girl, while *Home Boy* (Houghton, 1982) alternates between the Caribbean and New York City. More highly acclaimed have been her two historical novels for young adults, *Which Way Freedom?** (Walker, 1986), a Coretta Scott King Honor Book and a Best Book of the American Library Association, and its sequel, *Out from This Place** (Walker, 1988), also an ALA Best Book. These novels follow two young slaves, a man and a woman, through the Civil War and into the initial rebuilding after hostilities cease. Hansen has won special praise for her characterization and for her ability to show clearly the problems of black life while at the same time maintaining a spirit of optimism. She has made her home in the Bronx.

*HATCHET* (Paulsen*, Gary, Bradbury, 1987), realistic survival novel set in the late 1980s in the Canadian wilds. His parents having recently divorced, Brian Robeson, 13, leaves Hampton, New York, in a Cessna 406 bushplane to spend the summer with his father, a mechanical engineer, on the treeline in the Canadian oilfields. In a memorable, naturalistic scene, the plot suffers a fatal heart attack. Frightened but not panicked, Brian tries unsuccessfully to radio for help. When the plane runs out of gas, it crashes into a small lake in a vast forest. After scrambling to the surface, Brian manages to get his battered body to shore where he spends a painful night. His first full day is miserable, with aches and pains from the crash, swarms of biting mosquitoes, and sunburn. His survival instinct is strong, however, and although he hopes for a speedy rescue, he realizes that the possibility is dim because the plane veered off course. He thinks positively, as a teacher had always recommended, and sets about providing for such basic needs as shelter and food. He finds an overhang on a rocky ledge overlooking the lake for living quarters, drinks lake water, exists on chokecherries and raspberries for a while, and manages with much effort and trial and error to produce a fire using a special kind of rock in his overhang and the hatchet his mother had given him as a going-away present. His lowest point comes five days after the crash, when he fails to attract the attention of a passing plane. He is so dispirited that he tries to take his life, but the next morning awakens with the "tough hope" that he can survive. The next forty-nine days of his marooning are filled with activities, as he survives through luck, pluck, observation, logic, and knowledge gained from school and, surprisingly, television. He discovers the lake teems with fish and the area with a species of ground bird he calls "foolbirds" because they seem so stupid. He collects turtle eggs, which he greatly enjoys, and fashions a spear and a bow and arrow. He has some ticklish times with animals, encountering bears, a timber wolf, a porcupine, whose painful quills he endures, and a skunk, which invades his shelter to get his turtle eggs and sprays him liberally. He learns from his mistakes and even comes to appreciate the natural beauty of his environment and the richness of its resources and to trust himself and his instincts. His story rises to a climax with the attack of a she-moose, for some reason gone wild with fury, and a raging tornado that wrecks his shelter. Luckily when the tornado strikes the lake, it raises the plane's tail. With tremendous physical and emotional effort, because he remembers the plane contains the body of the pilot and because the moose has severely injured his ribs and chest, Brian constructs a kind of raft, chops open the tail of the plane with his hatchet, and salvages the survival kit. In another vivid naturalistic scene, he notices that the fish have devoured the dead pilot's head. The kit contains, among other "treasures," a transmitter, which he attempts to activate and then sets aside while he enjoys the food. Within a few hours a trader who deals with the Cree by floatplane puts down on Brian's lake, having picked up the signal from the transmitter, which Brian accidentally left on, and the boy's ordeal is over. Brian despairs but briefly, matures as expected, recovers from his hurts quickly, and never seems to yearn for human companionship or so-cialization of any sort, as might be expected of a city boy. Coincidence and luck play an expected, big role. The depiction of nature as both benign and beautiful and as worthy antagonist is one of the book's strong features. The details by which Brian survives, the way he learns from nature, for example, and fashions his tools, give the story its greatest force and contribute a more intellectual tone to the book than in most survival stories where the accent is on adventure. The book also has growing-up story aspects. Occasionally Brian flashes back to, among others, events involving his mother and another man that lead up to the divorce, what Brian calls the Secret. Although at the beginning he looks forward to divulging the Secret to his father, at the end he is tougher emotionally as well as physically, has more self-control, and is less dependent. He decides to keep what he knows to himself since there is no useful purpose in sharing it. The sequel is *The River*. ALA; Newbery Honor.

**HAUGAARD†, ERIK CHRISTIAN** (1923–      ), born in Copenhagen, Den-mark; historical novelist who has lived most of his life in the United States, writes in English, and publishes his novels in this country. He emigrated to the United States, after his parents moved here, and attended Black Mountain Col-lege, N.C. During World War II he served in the Royal Canadian Air Force, and later studied at the New School for Social Research in New York. After the death of his first wife in 1981, he married a Japanese woman and has lived in Japan, the setting for *The Samurai's Tale*\* (Houghton, 1984), a psychological novel of sixteenth-century warlords, which was named to the American Library Association Notable Books list. Many of his earlier novels have been honored. *The Rider and His Horse†* (Houghton, 1968) won the Phoenix Award of The

Children's Literature Association, given for the novel published twenty years previously that has stood the test of time. *The Little Fishes*† (Houghton, 1967), a story of World War II Italy, won both the Jane Addams Award and the *Boston Globe-Horn Book* Award. Settings in time and place are diverse. *Hakon of Rogen's Saga*† (Houghton, 1963) and *A Slave's Tale*† (Houghton, 1965) are both about the last part of the Viking period; *Orphans of the Wind*† (Houghton, 1966) concerns the American Civil War; *A Messenger for Parliament* (Houghton, 1976) and *Cromwell's Boy* (Houghton, 1978) are both about the English Civil War of the seventeenth century; *Chase Me, Catch Nobody!*† (Houghton, 1980) is set in Germany just before World War II. Though very different in period, place, and even style, all his novels concern a child without the ordinary protection of a family who is thrown somehow on the mercy of strangers. He has also written picture books and translated the fairy tales of Hans Christian Andersen.

**HEART'S BLOOD** (Yolen*, Jane, Delacorte, 1984), futuristic fantasy novel of intrigue, second in the Pit Dragons series and sequel to *Dragon's Blood*, set on Austar IV, the fourth planet in the Erato Galaxy. Austar is a semi-arid, metal-poor world with two moons that was once a penal colony and is now an independent Protectorate of the intergalactic Federation. Dragon fights held in arenas called Pits are central to Austarian economy. Young Jakkin Stewart, once a bondman, is now a trainer at the dragon nursery owned by Sarkkhan and master of his own dragon, a powerful, smart, beautiful red called Heart's Blood, with whom he has extraordinary powers of communication by mental telepathy. Proud that Heart's Blood has birthed a large clutch of eggs, Jakkin is very content with his life as it is and resists when Darrah Golden, an off-worlder who speaks in flute-like tones, is a Senator on Austar, and has been introduced to him by Sarkkhan, suggests that he infiltrate the rebels who are increasing in number and threatening the government. Jakkin consents only when Golden asks him to help locate Akki, Sarkkhan's daughter and Jakkin's sweetheart with whom he has quarreled. Akki, a physician's assistant in the capital city of The Rokk, has disappeared while on assignment for Golden, who Jakkin learns is a double agent. He distrusts Golden and is warned away from the man by Dr. Henkky, the woman for whom Akki had worked, but after Heart's Blood's eggs hatch, Jakkin goes with Sarkkhan to the capital, where he gets his orders from Golden. He is eventually contacted by a courier, finds the cell of which Akki is a member, and together they are given the task of delivering a small case that looks like an athletic equipment bag and contains explosives to the fighting pit area, where it will be picked up the next day. After Heart's Blood wins her match, although she sustains a wound Akki tends, they leave for home, having planted the case and leaving Sarkkhan to watch to see who picks it up. Not far out, they hear a tremendous explosion and observe the pit area of the city go up in smoke. Golden awaits them at Sarkkhan's, and when the Federation forces arrive to arrest them, they flee on foot over the desert for the distant mountains, all the way just ahead of their pursuers. Golden dies of injuries sustained in a fall, and Heart's Blood saves them on several occasions, finally, in the showdown fight, sustaining a fatal wound. Things so fall out that Jakkin and Akki take shelter inside the dragon's body to avoid the terrible planetary cold that follows night called Dark After. In the morning they emerge from her body, reborn as it were and able to see Austar as dragons do, in myriads of colors. Heart's Blood's five dragonlings wing over the desert to join them, and all complete the journey to the mountains and safety. Tension starts early and persists, and memorable moments with the dragons abound—the birthing of the eggs, the hatching, the fights, the rebirth. Although most characters are conventional faceless functionaries, Jakkin's bond to his dragon and his conscientiousness distinguish him. The details about the training of and life with the dragons and the history, government, and ways of the Austarians are carefully and ingeniously worked out, convincingly thorough, and fascinating, clearly the best part of the book. ALA.

**HELEN PERRITT** (*Borrowed Children\**), Mandy's sensitive little sister. A preschooler, Helen takes literally everything she hears. When her father whips her brothers with his belt, as he has threatened, "so they will never sit down again," she weeps because she thinks they will not be able to go to church or ride in the wagon if they must always stand. Because she worries that Mandy will not come back from Memphis, Mandy tells her that she has a round-trip ticket, and has difficulty making her understand that she will go and come back on the same track, not in a circular pattern. Helen considers Mandy the authority on all subjects and always asks, "Is that true, Mandy?" when their brothers tease her or when she does not understand something.

**HENRY** (*Tancy\**), ex-slave brother of Mary, Jemmy's mother. Henry's master was a lawyer who trained Henry as his clerk and paid him a salary. A slender, stern, bespectacled young man, he has thrown his considerable energies and all his savings into the development of Shantytown. Through Henry, Tancy finds her mother, Sin*. Although Henry tries to persuade her to take the teaching position at the school he has started in Shantytown, Tancy remains adamant in refusing the offer because she feels that it is important for her to run her own life. She does, however, realize that she is becoming fond of him, and the reader expects that some day they will marry. Henry represents the idealistic, strong-minded freedman devoted to the betterment of his people and is the foil of conscientious, uneducated ex-slave Stud and of spoiled white Billy Gaither.

**HENRY JOHN FITZPATRICK** (*Good-bye and Keep Cold\**), the man who accidentally causes the death of Ed Combs and later courts and finally marries his widow. A quiet, soft-spoken man with sad eyes, he is genuinely grief-stricken at what he has done and tries to make it up to the family by repairing broken pipes and leaky roofs and anything else that goes wrong in their house. An outsider like Frances* Combs, he discovers that they grew up not far apart in

Pittsburgh, both orphans. He plays the guitar very well, writes songs, and is a skilled craftsman. He is scornful of the jerry-building prevalent in the Kentucky mountains. Although Edda Combs thinks that she should hate him, she cannot help liking him and can see that he and her mother are in love.

**THE HERO AND THE CROWN** (McKinley*, Robin, Greenwillow, 1984), sword and sorcery fantasy of the kingdom of Damar, a companion novel to *The Blue Sword* (Greenwillow, 1982), but set many years earlier, telling the events that led to the legend of Aerin Firehair and the blue sword. Although daughter of King Arlbeth, Aerin has always been excluded from court circles because her mother was his second wife, and, rumor has it, a witchwoman who enspelled the king, then died at the birth of a daughter rather than a son as she hoped. Moreover, although she has her mother's flame-colored hair, she seems to have none of her magic or the *kelar*, the second sight that most members of the royal family possess. When she is fifteen and her jealous cousin Galanna taunts her, Aerin deliberately stuffs into her mouth some leaves of surka, the plant that poisons all but those with the royal gift, and she becomes very ill. During her long convalescence she reads deeply in the royal library and discovers an old recipe for ointment that is proof against dragon fire. She also goes to the paddock of her father's old war stallion, Talat, wounded long ago in a battle, and gradually gains his confidence until she is able to ride him. Over the years she has been a favorite of her cousin Tor, who is now first sola, in line to be king at her father's death, and he has taught her sword play. Now, although Aerin at almost nineteen does not realize it, he is deeply in love with her, having escaped the matrimonial traps Galanna has set for him. When a small dragon is reported harrying a village, Aerin slips out ahead of the group sent by the king and with both herself and Talat smeared with the ointment, dispatches the dragon and its mate. Returning with the heads, she is given a sword and spears by the king and soon becomes the official dragon slayer. Damar is threatened at this time by trouble in the north, thought to be caused by demons from across the border that have subverted some of the outlying nobles. Arlbeth and Tor lead a large army to quell the rebellion, but Aerin is refused permission to accompany them. Just as they set off, a report comes that Marl, the huge Black Dragon thought to be dead for generations, has arisen. In a tremendous duel, she kills him, being badly wounded herself, and at the banquet in her honor Maur's skull, hung in the great hall, seems to mock and taunt her. In her subsequent illness she dreams of a blond man who can heal her, and she sets off secretly, leaving a note for Tor. After a long, dream-like journey on Talat, she comes to the house of Luthe, the blond wizard who loved her mother and who cures her, partly with the waters of a wide silver lake, which make her no longer completely mortal. He teaches her lore of the mage and, after some seasons, sends her off toward the north to engage Agsded, the master mage who is creating trouble for Damar, a wizard who was her mother's brother. As she travels on Talat, bearing Gonturan, the blue sword, she is joined by huge hunting cats and dogs. In a black tower where she climbs stairs for what seems an eternity, she encounters Agsded and finds him wearing the Hero's Crown of Damar, which was lost generations earlier and is badly needed to protect the kingdom. She defeats him with a red dragon stone, a wreath of surka, and the blue sword. The tower crumbles and the forest turns into a wide plain. From the rubble, the queen of the wild dogs brings her the dragon stone and the Hero's Crown. Luthe, having come to meet her, makes love to her, but they realize that their time is far in the future. Aerin takes the Hero's Crown back to the city, where she finds a fierce battle raging. With its help, Tor is able to defeat the horde of northerners, although Arlbeth is killed in the fighting. Aerin marries Tor, loving him with her mortal part and Luthe in a different way. The first half of the book, until the trip to Luthe, is compelling, with well-developed characters and enough realistic details to make the fantasy believable. The dragon fights, especially, are well drawn and exciting. The second half, while highly imaginative, is less convincing. Luthe's background and position in the total story of Damar seems to be held for a future book. Fanfare; Newbery Winner; SLJ.

**HIDEYO KAWASHIMA** (*So Far from the Bamboo Grove**), 18, brother of Yoko* and Ko*. He tries to join the Japanese Student Army, against his mother's wishes, but fails the written examination, evidently having changed his mind and put down wrong answers on purpose. When the ammunition factory to which he is assigned is invaded by Korean Communist soldiers, he hides in a box and escapes with two friends. Together they walk, wearing Korean clothes, to Wonsan, where they part, with Hideyo going on toward Seoul, as his mother has instructed him in a note she left for him. Only because he is able to speak Japanese and Korean equally well is he able to escape challenges from soldiers on both sides, but he is almost crushed by a train in a tunnel and almost frozen before he stumbles into a peasant's cottage, where he is taken in and treated as one of the family. When spring comes, he swims the Imjon River, shot at by Korean soldiers, and gets south of the thirty-eighth parallel, safe from the Communists. Eventually he gets to the Japanese port of Maizuru and sees the poster of his name pasted up by Yoko, giving the girls' address.

**HIGHWATER, JAMAKE** (1942–      ), born in Glacier County, Mont.; Native American (Blackfeet) activist, lecturer, and writer of fiction and nonfiction for teenagers and adults. He received his B.A. and M.A. degrees from the University of California-Berkeley and his Ph.D. from the University of Chicago. He has been with the San Francisco Contemporary Theatre, served as editor for Fodor Travel Guides, and held teaching positions with New York University, Columbia University School of the Arts and Graduate School of Architecture, and the University of Texas Health Science Center. He has contributed widely to periodicals and founded, wrote, and narrated the Public Broadcasting Service Network series "Songs of the Thunderbird." Among his many other accomplishments are a novel for adults, *Journey to the Sky* (Crowell, 1978), and several works of nonfiction for adults, including *The Primal Mind: Vision and Reality in Indian America* (Harper, 1981). His best-known writings for children are his Newbery Honor book *Anapao: An American Indian Odyssey* (Lippincott, 1977), his Jane Addams Award-winning *Many Smokes, Many Moons: A Chronology of American Indian History through Art* (Lippincott, 1978), and his Ghost Horse Cycle of novels that trace the life of a Blackfeet woman, *Legend Days*\* (Harper, 1984), a *School Library Journal* Best Book, *The Ceremony of Innocence* (Harper, 1985), and *I Wear the Morning Star* (Harper, 1986). Highwater has also written under the name J. Marks.

**THE HONORABLE PRISON** (Jenkins\*, Lyll Becerra de, Dutton, 1988), historical novel set for some months in an unnamed South American country in 1955 involving political repression of speech and movement. A popular journalist and champion of peasants' rights, Miguel\* Maldonado is arrested by soldiers of the dictator known as the General, ironically on the very night he had planned to flee with his family to Costa Rica. He, his wife, Margarita\*, and their two children, eighteen-year-old schoolgirl Marta, who tells the story in present tense as if it were happening, and Ricardo, 13, are taken by car during the night to an isolated military post above a pueblo (village) in the Andean highlands. There they are confined in a small white-washed house, servants' quarters of an old hacienda, on a hill above the base, Miguel's "honorable prison," as the arresting officer puts it. Inconveniences are many: boxes for furniture, a hole in the ground for a toilet, the cold weather, and later the penetrating rains, for example. The family strives to remain cheerful. They write compositions, Miguel of a political nature on his Remington, and Miguel even conducts English lessons. Ricardo acquires a chicken, Perico, for a pet, and they try to celebrate Marta's eighteenth birthday. Since they refuse out of principle to eat at the army mess, Marta and Ricardo, accompanied by Polo\* Beltrán, a campesino (peasant) soldier, go to market every Saturday, outings they look forward to. Problems accumulate, however. For Marta the loneliness and monotony become oppressive, and she longs for a friend, especially to discuss her growing attraction to Fernando\*, the handsome twenty-five-year-old local school teacher and nephew of the mayor whom she meets on market days. Their relationship culminates with a sexual encounter in the mud behind the church that is interrupted before consummation by a passing peasant. The isolation brings Marta closer to her parents, particularly her mother, whom she comes to see as a woman. Fear is a constant companion for the family, for themselves and for those who associate with them. Honorio, an elderly peasant, grateful for the help Miguel had once given him, comes from the hills to bring a bouquet of herbs for medicine and is summarily shot. As their money runs low, Margarita hoards food, but their diet becomes so meager that they grow gaunt and thin, and Ricardo suffers boils caused by malnutrition. Their worst problem revolves around Miguel's health; his tuberculosis worsens because of the damp climate and lack of proper food to the extent that eventually he can only lie in bed, so weak he can hardly cough. They try unsuccessfully to get word to Miguel's friends in the city for money and medicines, and Margarita even humbles herself to beg the commandant for help. Unknown to them, however, the political climate has begun to change, and one day a Doctor Martinez arrives to examine Miguel and gives them medicine and vitamins. He has been dispatched by the base commandant, who fears reprisal under the new regime if it seems he has not cared properly for his prisoner. Pedro*, another campesino soldier, Honorio's godson, brings a food basket, and Marta accidentally kills Perico with a bar during an argument with Ricardo. This food, as it turns out, tides them over. One day they hear shouts and church bells and notice the base is deserted. A political turncoat now on the revolutionary side, the mayor comes and orders an ambulance for Miguel. The attending doctor, a family friend, calls the spirit of celebration that pervades the city nonsense, cynically wondering how long freedom will last anyway. Although Marta and Ricardo know that Miguel will probably not survive, they agree with their father's philosophy that lives given for human rights are not given in vain. The novel shows political tyranny in terms of its effect on an upper-class family, but ironically the plot lacks tension, since the reader is never made to feel that anything really terrible will happen to them, except Miguel's death from neglect. The central irony is that Miguel's idealism causes the imprisonment of his family, and the conclusion suggests that their struggles are probably in vain. Ironically the understated style and first person mode work against creating the fear that would give the story strength. Characterization is good, even of minor figures like Pedro, who helps them out of reverence for Miguel and his godfather; Fernando's haughty invalid mother; Polo, whose sympathies for them deepen as their conditions worsen; and Don Nicanor, the compassionate storekeeper who provides aspirin and soup bones out of genuine goodness. The bleak mountains, the birds of prey, the village seen as through a mirror contribute to the sense of oppression and hopelessness. Marta's mixed feelings of bitterness, resentment, admiration, and pride for her father are made understandable. Miguel, idealistic, stubbornly tenacious of his beliefs, stands at the center of the novel, a symbol of loyalty and devotion to cause to the very end, never bitter and never complaining, always optimistic. As he speaks with the children about past events and shares his hopes and his writings with them, the reader becomes acquainted with the political realities. O'Dell.

**HORACE MORRIS** (*Unclaimed Treasures**), boy about Willa's age who lives next door and becomes a good friend of the Pinkerton family, whom by the end of the story Willa accepts as her true love, and whom eventually she marries. Horace is calm and steady and likes to eat apples, his most distinguishing feature throughout the story. Willa gradually comes to see that he is perceptive and decisive. When, for example, Nicholas shows Matthew the picture he has drawn of Willa kissing the bedpost, Horace saves the day for Willa by diverting attention to the chicken potpie Willa's mother is serving, and he alone realizes that Willa engineered the reconciliation between his father and mother. He is a consistently interesting figure, slightly comic as are they all.

**HOWARD, ELLEN** (1943–      ), born in New Bern, N.C.; author mostly of problem novels for children and young adults. After holding positions as an office and library worker, she received her B.A. with honors from Portland State University in Oregon in 1979 and became a secretary for the Collins Foundation in Portland and a volunteer worker for various social causes. Her novels include *Circle of Giving* (Atheneum, 1984), about a girl's friendship with a cerebral palsy victim, which was nominated for the Golden Kite Award; *Gillyflower* (Atheneum, 1986), about sexual abuse; and *When Daylight Comes* (Atheneum, 1985), a historical fiction set during an eighteenth-century slave uprising in the Virgin Islands. All three were named Notable Trade Books in the Field of Social Sciences. *Edith Herself\** (Atheneum, 1987), the poignant and occasionally humorous story of a little girl's adjustment to a new home after her mother dies that is outstanding for its characterization, is a *School Library Journal* Best Book. Another novel, *Her Own Song* (Atheneum, 1988), concerning an adopted girl's search for her identity, was a Junior Literary Guild Selection. *Sister* (Atheneum, 1990) and *The Chickenhouse House* (Atheneum, 1991) are companion novels to *Edith Herself*, revolving around Edith's elder sister, Alena. Howard currently lives in Kalamazoo, Mich.

**HOWIE MITCHELL** (*The Goats\**), shy youth of about thirteen, who wears glasses and is regarded as a wimp by the other campers. He is by nature watchful and hesitant, the child of older parents who, he thinks, never seem to know what to do with him. He is the leader at first as he and Laura\* Golden run away from camp because he is determined not to go back to face the sadistic campers and also because he subconsciously needs to prove himself. Later Laura becomes an equal partner in their enterprise, and when he suffers from a cold, she assumes responsibility for them both.

**HURMENCE, BELINDA** (1921–      ), author most acclaimed for her historical novels for junior and high school readers about the black experience before and just after the American Civil War, which have been praised for their strong sense of the times. *A Girl Called Boy* (Clarion, 1982), a time-slip fantasy in which a pampered modern black girl is projected back to 1853 where she gains new insights into her slave heritage, received the Parents' Choice Award. *Tancy\** (Clarion, 1984) follows the experiences of a sixteen-year-old ex-slave girl as she searches for her mother at the end of the Civil War. It was a *School Library Journal* Best Book for Children. She has also written novels with modern settings like *Tough Tiffany* (Doubleday, 1980), a girl's growing-up story set in a poor rural area of North Carolina, and *The Nightwalker* (Clarion, 1988), a mystery in which a girl thinks fires on the North Carolina coast may have been set by her sleepwalking brother.

**HURWITZ, JOHANNA (FRANK)** (1937–      ), born in New York City; librarian, author of more than twenty books for early elementary and middle-grade children. She received her B.A. degree from Queens College, Flushing, N.Y., and her library degree from Columbia University. She has worked both in public libraries and as a school librarian in New York, and has taught children's literature at Queens College and the writing of books for children at Hofstra University. Some of her books are for early readers, one step beyond picture books in difficulty, among them *Busybody Nora* (Morrow, 1976), *Superduper Teddy* (Morrow, 1980), and *Rip-Roaring Russell* (Morrow, 1983). Some are for later elementary children, like *Baseball Fever* (Morrow, 1981) and *Teacher's Pet* (Morrow, 1988). *Class Clown** (Morrow, 1987), about a third grade boy, labeled by his teacher as "rambunctious," whose sincere efforts to improve only get him into further trouble, was named to the *School Library Journal* list of best books of the year. In most of her books, Hurwitz treats ordinary situations with humor, not delving into deeper meanings but not ridiculing her young characters.

*I'LL MEET YOU AT THE CUCUMBERS* (Moore\*, Lilian, ill. Sharon Wood-ing, Atheneum, 1988), brief poetic novel of a country mouse who visits the city, probably New York, since there are bridges, a subway, and museums with dinosaur skeletons. Adam Mouse likes to sit and think, eventually reciting his thoughts for his friend, Junius, a more adventurous mouse who rides to the city each week in the farmer's truck. Although Junius tries to entice Adam to ac-company him by describing the sounds and smells of the Farmer's Market, Adam declines. He does agree to become a pen friend to Amanda Mouse, who lives near the market, responding to her lively notes by "thinking aloud" on paper to describe life in the country. When Junius brings a note with a special request that Adam visit the city for Amanda's birthday, he agrees with some trepidation to go and meet her at the cucumbers. Adam is especially worried because Junius is considering moving to the city permanently. Amanda is just as charming as her letters. While Junius runs off on his own, she shows Adam the sights. He gives her the birthday present he has brought, a large, fat sunflower seed, which she insists on sharing with him. As she escorts him to her home, he is startled by the noise of the subway, delighted with the beauty of traffic lights, and uncomfortable in the passageways for pipes under the street. At Amanda's home, which is next door to a small boy's room, they take rides in the boy's Silver Racer toy automobile. Impressed by the "thoughts" that Adam has written her, Amanda takes him to the library, where he reads from a poetry anthology and discovers that his thoughts are poems and that he is a poet. Back at Amanda's house, they find that Junius has been rounding up friends for a surprise birthday party, with food, good company, and a recital of poems by Adam. Junius decides to return to the farm, and Amanda, though terrified of open spaces, agrees to visit sometime in the country. Although not written in primer vocabulary, the story has short sentences and a simple style. Some of the poems Adam recites are by Valerie Worth, Judith Thurman, Carl Sandburg, and Langston Hughes. The others, presumably, are written by Moore. Inevitably, the book invites comparison to Randall Jarrell's *The Bat Poet* (Macmillan, 1964), to which it is a distant second, being less inventive, deriving incidents from a number of books about mice, and having less interesting poems. It is, however, a pleasant and sensitive story for younger children. SLJ.

*THE ILLYRIAN ADVENTURE* (Alexander*, Lloyd, Dutton, 1986), rousing, lighthearted realistic adventure novel set in 1872 in the fictitious kingdom of Illyria on the eastern seacoast of the Adriatic Sea. Beautiful, clever, headstrong Vesper Holly, 16, is determined to verify the theory of her late scholar father that the treasure and the magical army mentioned in the twelfth-century epic, the *Illyriad*, really existed. The *Illyriad* tells of the conflict between the native Illyrians, led by Vartan, and their Turkish conquerors, the Zentans, under King Ahmad. After studying the language, she and her reluctant, stodgy guardian, her father's close friend and colleague, Prof. Brinton Garrett, called Brinnie, sail to Illyria. The two soon become embroiled in two modern conflicts: first, an Illyrian rebellion against the oppressive Zentans and, later, a scheme to overthrow the current Zentan king, proud, idealistic, young Osman. Events are numerous and start fast. Shortly after Vesper and Brinnie arrive they visit Old Town, the Illyrian section of the capital of Zenta, where they encounter rioting and Vesper is inexplicably stabbed in the arm. They engage Nilo, a young Illyrian as their *dragoman* or handyman, to help them with equipment and guide them to the area of the legends. With the encouragement of King Osman, they set out, but Nilo, though willing, proves frustratingly inept and is only one of several enigmatic figures they encounter before they arrive at their destination. Others include Ergon Pasha, the prime minister, army Captain Zalik, both antagonistic to their venture, and Dr. Helvitius, a loquacious, evasive scholar, all three of whom turn out to be traitors to Osman; Milan, a bearded blacksmith, who turns out to be a rebel leader; and a seer called Matrona Mira, also involved with the rebels. They attend an annual Illyrian village folk festival, are captured by rebels, and are set upon by Zentan forces, among other excitements and dubious doings that keep the pot boiling. When they finally arrive at Vartan's stronghold in the Petrosias Mountains, they discover that Nilo is the current "Vartan," or rebel leader, and that his fecklessness is merely an act to throw off the Zentans. Investigating an ancient temple called Vartan's Castle, they discover a set of foot-high chessmen in the form of Zentan and Illyrian soldiers, and Vesper is sure that they have found the magical army of ancient lore. Dr. Helvitius unexpectedly turns up, trusting Brinnie unsuspectingly tells him about the soldier-chessmen, and Brinnie, Vesper, and Vartan (Nilo) are taken prisoner. Helvitius wants the chess piece representing ancient King Ahmad and dynamites the room, thinking thus to dispose of his prisoners. With luck they survive, discover the piece, escape, and make their way to Zenta with the help of rebels disguised as gypsies. Since Helvitius has dropped the information that he, the prime minister, and Zalik are plotting to assassinate the king, Vesper is determined to save Osman's life and bring him and Vartan (Nilo) together. She discovers an inscription on the King Ahmad chessman that indicates that Ahmad had sent a gift to Vartan, after Vartan had saved his life, as indicated in the *Illyriad*. The gift was a parchment secreted in the chessman's arm and contained a message from Ahmad to Vartan offering peace and indicating that henceforth the only conflict between them is to be on the chessboard. Vesper has proved her father's theories about the *Illyriad* are true. Since, as did his ancient ancestor, Vartan (Nilo) has helped to save the life of Osman, a descendant of Ahmad, Osman extends friendship to Vartan, the two are reconciled, and Vartan becomes Osman's adviser in the effort to improve the quality of life for everyone in the country. The traitors flee, and Vesper and Brinnie return to Philadelphia. Although it is easy to see that Nilo will turn out to be Vartan, coincidences, twists, close encounters, and cliffhangers abound, insuring that there is never a dull moment in this action-packed romantic adventure. Characters are flat and conventional but interesting and appropriately melodramatic, especially Vesper, whose lively mind comes up with answers to almost every problem, with the diffident Brinnie her foil. Style is spirited, distinctive in its diction, and deliberately sensationalistic. Others in series. ALA.

**IMELDA** (*The Facts and Fictions of Minna Pratt\**), Minna Pratt's co-musician in the chamber group. She has "black braids slick as snakes," perfect pitch, and "pronounced varied facts even when not asked," most of them of curiosity value but of little practical moment. Her tendency to dominate and organize comes in handy when, as first violin and hence their leader, she keeps the group going during the competition at concert hall when the lights go out.

*INCIDENT AT LORING GROVES* (Levitin\*, Sonia, Dial, 1988), contemporary realistic mystery novel with problem story aspects set for a couple of weeks in the affluent small town of Loring Groves, California, in the late 1980s. Two high school juniors conclude that morality takes precedence over loyalty to peers and even family. Cassidy Keaton and Ken Farquar are big people in Loring Groves High. Quick and intelligent, she writes a popular column called "Street Seen" for the school paper and is a member of the flag squad. Sensitive and artistic, Ken has been elected to the exclusive boys' service set called Hawks and nominated for the Young Humanitarian Award. When on Monday classmate Mary Lou Davenport disappears, foul play is feared since the mutilated bodies of three girls were found recently in the hills, believed to have been slain by a serial killer. The next Saturday, Ken and Cassidy date for the school dance, after which Cassidy is to stay the night with her best friend, Patty\* Osborne. Although he is not keen about the idea, Ken persuades Cassidy to go after the dance with him, Ross Schultz and Patty, Ross's date, and several other fellows and their dates, to a summer house on Canyon Cove belonging to the Park Service. The idea is Wayne\* Wagger's, who supplies Ken and Ross Schultz with marijuana in return for their doing his English compositions. Although Ken and Cassidy mostly opt out, some youths drink and drug, and there is joking, dancing, and some making out. Down by the lake, Wayne and his girl stumble upon Mary Lou's partially decomposed body. Although they all get panicky, Ross stays cool and suggests that they keep mum, lest the murder be deemed a group effort and they all get into deep trouble. Later in the basement rumpus room at Patty's house, Patty smokes a joint and soon gets so sick from strain, drugs, liquor, and diet pills that she must be taken by ambulance to the hospital. Cassidy's mother holds Cassidy partly to blame for Patty's illness, since she did nothing to stop Patty from drinking and using drugs, and grounds her. Mr. Farquar organizes a horseback search for Mary Lou, which he insists Ken join. Ken suggests the summer house area, thinking this a solution to the youths' dilemma, but the searchers find nothing, to the amazement of Ken and Ross. Cassidy is questioned by Police Detective McAllister, as is Ken. From him, they learn that Reggie Taylor, a black football player Mary Lou often watched at practice, is a prime suspect, and that Mary Lou's body was found at an old quarry. They are present when McAllister examines her school locker, where he hunts particularly for a hoop earring to match the single one found on her body, and tells them that the murder appears to be a "copycat killing," that is, Mary Lou's murderer tried to make his crime match the serial ones. Various strands now come together for Cassidy and Ken independently to identify the killer. In particular, Ken remembers that Wayne missed track practice Monday afternoon, while Cassidy, having accepted a ride from Wayne, feels frightened by his attitude, particularly after she finds a hoop earring in the seat, but she manages to get away from him and into a shopping mall. Ken confides his suspicions about Wayne to Ross, who rationalizes matters, and both get high. Ken later goes to Wayne's house, where he gets Wayne to admit to the crime, apparently committed partly out of egomania and partly because he thought Mary Lou led him on and then backed out. At first, Ken cannot bring himself to confide in his father, who is riding high on political ambitions, and Cassidy cannot tell her mother either. When Ken does tell him, Mr. Farquar says he will throw Ken out if he goes to the police. Caught in still another moral dilemma, both youths independently come to the conclusion that they must go to the police, both arriving at the station on the same morning, Cassidy a little ahead of Ken. Ironically, later Mr. Farquar makes political hay with the media by praising Ken publicly and asserting that he himself has always stood by the truth. The story is set up in chapters that alternate between Cassidy and Ken, describing in third person their thoughts and things that happen to them alone and together. Since so many characters are introduced at the beginning in school scenes, it is hard to keep them straight for a while. Eventually they sort out as easily recognizable types, as are the parents. For example, Cassidy's people are the community auto dealer who advertises on TV as Smilin' Jack Keaton and her mother is a successful realtor, while Ken's father is the conventional joiner, the pillar of the community who always manages to get along through contacts and loyalties he has built up over the years and who expects his sons to play the same game of not rocking the boat. The story starts slowly as the author establishes the school and community setting, then picks up and moves very fast as the two "good kids" sort out their situation and finally declare on the side of morality rather than expediency. Cassidy and Patty are foils, as are Ken and Ross Schultz, who is the kind that smooths things over like Mr. Farquar. The book exposes not only the selfishness and superficiality of contemporary teens but also their elders' lack of integrity, false values, poor parenting, and materialism. Tension and mystery relieve the didacticism. The narrative consists almost entirely of dialogue. Poe Winner.

*IN SUMMER LIGHT* (Oneal*, Zibby, Viking Kestrel, 1985), psychological novel of the talented daughter of an artist who struggles for self-identity in a family dominated by her egotistical father. Because she is suffering from mononucleosis and cannot get a summer job in New York as she planned, Kate Brewer, 17, is spending the vacation from boarding school on the New England island where her family has its home and her father his studio. Her enforced idleness makes her notice more than ever how home life revolves around her father, Marcus* Brewer, who is generally considered to be a genius. When a red-haired California graduate student, Ian Jackson, comes to catalog Marcus's paintings for an exhibit, Kate finds someone she can talk to and their friendship gradually deepens, although their trips to the beach or into town usually include her little sister, Amanda, 7, and often Frances Hilmer, the ten-year-old daughter of the cleaning woman. Kate struggles to write a make-up paper on *The Tempest*, finding her anger at Prospero blocking her way. When her roommate, Leah, comes for a weekend, her father is charming. Kate, under Leah's questioning, finally admits that she stopped painting when she won first prize at the school exhibit for an oil of the meadow on the island. Expecting her father to be delighted, she was crushed when he dismissed it as "a nice little picture." Kate's mother, Floss*, worries a bit that Ian at twenty-four or -five is too old to be a romantic interest for Kate, but he encourages her to return to art, suggesting, when she mentions that she used to paint the big beach rocks on the other side of the island with red clay, that they spend an afternoon painting rocks. The experience is exhilarating and makes her root out a child's box of watercolors from the attic and experiment with them. Ian insists that she buy good paints, and after he sees the painting of the meadow, kept wrapped in her closet, and is genuinely impressed, she starts trying in earnest. When he must spend a week in Boston looking up Brewer drawings in the museum, Kate asks him to take her. He refuses, explaining that it would not be fair to her father, and she is humiliated. Once again it seems that the world runs for the convenience of Marcus Brewer. Ian, however, brings her a museum card of a painting she once told him was her favorite and holds her gently, so she knows he thinks of her and returns her love. All summer Mrs. Hilmer has been harping on a preposterous proposal that Marcus Brewer paint a picture of Frances, although he does not do portraits and certainly would not choose that subject if he did. After Ian returns to California, Kate makes a painting of Frances, partly to quell Mrs.

Hilmer's resentment and partly to be different from her father, who is interested in color and light and not in people. She also finishes her paper, castigating Prospero for his treatment of other people but in the end forgiving him, since she sees that he, like her father, is an old man, with his magic powers almost gone. Restraint is one of the fine and telling characteristics of this subtle novel. The parallel between the island in *The Tempest* and the Brewers' island is obvious, but it is never pressed. Kate's romance is touching, but there is neither a seduction nor a pledge of undying love. There is no confrontation scene in which Kate blows up at her father. The relationships, however, are intense and are handled tactfully and convincingly. The style is skillful, dwelling frequently on the color and shape of things as Kate, a naturally gifted artist, sees them. ALA; Boston Globe Winner; Fanfare; SLJ.

*INTERSTELLAR PIG* (Sleator*, William, Dutton, 1984), science fiction novel of a conflict between weird characters from various distant stars and an American boy, carried out as a game in which all the losers and their home planets will be wiped out. The action occurs in a resort area on the Atlantic seaboard, presumably in the 1980s. The narrator, Barney, 16, is bored at the old vacation house his parents have rented, isolated by a marsh from everything but an ugly cinder-block cottage built not ten yards away. His interest is caught when the landlord tells him of a nineteenth-century sea captain who owned the house. The story goes that the captain's vessel picked up a shipwrecked sailor, who that night was strangled by the captain's brother. The murderer raved about the victim's being the devil and after being keelhauled was locked for the rest of his life in the room that is now Barney's. Throughout his ordeal, he clung to a "trinket," which he had evidently taken from the dead man. Barney also becomes fascinated by the three people who move in next door, a woman named Zena and two men, Manny and Joe. Strangely, the three seem middle-aged to Barney's parents and to Barney only a little older than he is. They clearly are curious about the captain's house and take the first opportunity, when Barney's parents are gone, to search it thoroughly, even going through drawers and cupboards. Zena introduces Barney to a board game, a sort of space fantasy with dream-like but detailed planets, called Interstellar Pig. The object is to hold the character card of the Piggy at the end of the game. He deduces that the three are after the trinket of the long-dead seaman and realizes that the scratch marks around the window of his room converge on a rocky point on an island nearby, where the captain must have hidden it. When the three neighbors go there via sailboards, Barney wheedles his way as a passenger with Joe, although he has acquired a painful sunburn. There he finds a small box containing a pink disk with the identical single eye and idiotic smile of the Piggy card of the game. Slowly, Barney realizes that the board game is just a simulation of the real game, in which Zena is Zulma, a spider lady from Vavoosh, Manny is Moyna, an octopus-like gas bag from Flaeioub, and Joe is Jrib, a water-breathing gill man from Thrilb. The three have joined forces to regain the Piggy, each hoping to trick or force the other two to give it up before the end of the game. Each tries to bribe Barney to give him the Piggy, one with an elixir of youth, another with super-intelligence, the third with the power of space travel. Barney finds that when he plays the board game with them again, he is a new character, Homo Sapiens, and that the game is real and will end with the destruction of all the planets except the one that holds the Piggy. As the horrifying game progresses, he finds that he can mentally communicate with the Piggy, and he begins to think that they may all have it wrong and that the one who holds the Piggy at the end is destined for destruction. Disguised as a sapient carnivorous lichen from Mbridlengile, he fights off the other three and listens to the Piggy, which he has hidden inside an old high school yearbook. In the end he realizes that the Piggy is not capable of destroying any of the planets, but is essentially a recording device that tricks the other characters into thinking that it has cosmic power. Barney allows the real lichen to find the Piggy, and all the non-earth characters depart for their own planets. The strength of the novel lies in its vivid depiction of the contest, starting as a complex but harmless board game and progressing to a fearful battle of creatures with highly varied attributes, all single-mindedly set on one goal at whatever cost to others. Characterization is minimal, and the seacoast setting is not developed beyond bare essentials. The plot, imaginative but extreme, is made acceptable by control of the mood, with strong tension, foreboding, and terror. ALA; Fanfare; SLJ.

*IN THE YEAR OF THE BOAR AND JACKIE ROBINSON* (Lord*, Bette Bao, ill. Marc Simont, Harper, 1984), realistic novel set in New York City during the Chinese Year of the Boar, the American 1947, in which each of the twelve chapters relates the experiences of an immigrant Chinese girl for a particular month. When her engineer father, who has emigrated to the United States from China against the wishes of his large, traditional Wong family, sends for them, Sixth Cousin, also known as Bandit, and her mother leave for America. Before they depart, Bandit is allowed to choose another name, a real one. She selects Shirley Temple because she thinks that it is properly American. Her father's apartment is small but adequate, though Mother deplores having to cook and not having servants. Shirley is soon enrolled in fifth grade, having, in the Chinese way, told her teacher that she is ten, although by American reckoning she is really nine, and she takes seriously Mother's admonition to remember that she is "China's little ambassador." Since she is the only Chinese in her grade at P.S.8, her classmates regard her as a curiosity and seem friendly, but after the novelty wears off, the students exclude her because they think she is the teacher's pet (she is very deferential in the Chinese way, and the teacher gives her extra help to catch up), they think her ways funny, and she cannot play their games. To ease her loneliness, Father gets her roller skates, with which she has trouble, and Mother enrolls her for piano lessons with Mrs. Rodriguez, their eccentric landlady, who lives downstairs. These efforts to ease her loneliness do not help much. The turning point comes in May, when she is given two black eyes by the "tallest and the strongest and the scariest" girl in the class, Mabel, who is black, because Shirley blunders into a baseball game and disrupts the action. When she does not tattle, Mabel accepts her, teaches her to play baseball and roller skate, and becomes her first American friend. For her ability at the game, the class sings a Jackie Robinson playground chant-rhyme to her, and after she finds out who Robinson is, she becomes his avid fan. Following the Dodgers avidly on the radio eases the loneliness of the summer months, and in the fall she makes another friend, Emily Levy, at whose house she visits and of whom Mother approves because Emily is studious and reads a lot. With the baseball lovers in her class Shirley suffers through the Dodger loss to the Yankees in the World Series. In December Shirley campaigns to elect Emily as class representative for the Christmas assembly. When they learn that Jackie Robinson is coming as a special guest, Emily gives up the post so that Shirley can present the school key to her baseball hero. The book's strongest points are Shirley's naive, uninformed reactions to American customs and the warm, sensitive way the author captures her feelings. Although she wishes to be accepted, Shirley is a strong figure and remains true to herself, a combination of fears and courage, timidity and boldness, never despairing and never whining. The other children and the adults are drawn in broad terms as foils for Shirley or to serve the plot, but Shirley herself seems real and genuine. The abundant humor forestalls sentimentality and didacticism. Language is uncomplicated, and the style is fast moving. Some scenes stand out: Emily getting Shirley to swear an oath in blood not to tell they have looked in Dr. Levy's anatomy book; Shirley reciting, "I pledge a lesson to the frog of the United States of America, . . . " and Shirley getting lost on an errand to buy "Rukee Sikes" for her father. ALA; Jefferson; SLJ.

*INVINCIBLE SUMMER* (Ferris*, Jean, Farrar, 1987), realistic physical problem novel set in a farming area near Bennett, Iowa, for one year in the late 1980s, in which a girl comes to terms with her own leukemia and with the death of her boy friend from the same illness. Robin Gregory, seventeen and a high school junior, lives on a small but prosperous farm with her widower father, Will*, and her mother's mother, Libby* Clayton. She enjoys school and has been dating but looks forward to a more exciting life away from Bennett. In late spring, she experiences fatigue and loss of appetite that become chronic, and she notices alarming black and blue bruises on her body. Ordered into the hospital in Jefferson for tests, which eventually diagnose leukemia, she meets tall, blonde, Rick* Winn, 19, son of a wealthy farmer near Moreland, who is in for therapy for the same disease. Rick is comfortable, amusing, gentle, encouraging, optimistic, and intelligent. He tells her that he comes once a month for "beetle squeezings," as he calls his chemotherapy. They form a friendship that develops into romance. He phones her in the hospital and at home and visits her at home both before and after she has the treatments that make her summer an agony. They have some good times together. In one amusing episode, on a date in

Bennett, they pretend he is a foreign relative who cannot speak or understand English. Unlike Rick, Robin has strong family support, her father gradually coming to terms with the situation, although the threat to her life hits him hard, especially since his wife died in an auto accident not long before. Libby not only ministers to Robin's physical needs but shares events from her life with the girl, and the two grow very close. Robin and Rick have long discussions about how they feel about their disease, talking about their fear and anger, and he prepares her for such aspects of the therapy as the vomiting and loss of hair. He tells her about his strong interest in organic farming and tries to persuade Will to adopt these new procedures. In the fall, while she still recovers from her course of treatment, he enrolls at agricultural college, faithfully calling her to ease her through the dreaded effects of the chemotherapy. He visits at Christmas, and they exchange gifts and make plans to be in the hospital together for tests at the end of January. In spite of difficult weather, Robin makes it, and they spend much of a night together in his hospital bed, their first lovemaking, and the next night in a motel as planned. He shares one of his frequent "quotes of the week," this time one from Camus about "in the depths of winter, I finally learned that within me lay an invincible summer." Then he gives her the terrible news that he has relapsed, the cancer having spread dangerously, and must start chemotherapy again. Robin's return home is filled with a sense of impending loss, and some days of bad weather keep her close to Libby. After the weather breaks she visits Rick in the hospital, sitting by his bed holding his hand when he rambles from the treatment, making up as best she can for the physical and psychological comfort that he fails to get from his distraught parents. After he returns home and she learns that the cancer is terminal, they have some idyllic love trysts in what is now their favorite motel, and then he goes down hill rapidly. By summer she has come to see that his death must be accepted and confronts the possibility that her own may not be far away. She comforts herself with her dead mother's words, that whatever happens, there is really nothing to worry about; one must take life, and death, when and as they come. Holes appear in the plot, for example, after being so extremely fatigued at home that she can barely finish finals, Robin is remarkably alert and vigorous in the hospital when she meets Rick, and in the days before his terrible announcement, Rick seems also quite normal. The relatives are obvious foils and shallow, except for Libby, who has dimension and personality. The book's strength lies in its nonclinical look at the disease, its stress on the victim's need for love and support, and the sweet, unsensational romance. SLJ.

***IS ANYBODY THERE?*** (Bunting*, Eve, Lippincott, 1988), mystery for middle readers, set in southern California in the contemporary period. The narrator, Marcus Mullen, 13, lives with his mother, Caroline, who, since the death of his father, has worked in a department store, which is especially busy during the Christmas season. Two elderly neighbor sisters, Miss Sarah and Miss Coriander Clark, keep an intent eye on the goings and comings at the Mullen house, noting the activities of Marcus and his friends and also of Nick Milardovich, the high school coach and physical education teacher who rents an upstairs apartment, accessible by its own outside stairway. Marcus does not mind the surveillance of the two ladies, as long as he does not have to stay at their house while his mother is gone, but he resents Nick's presence and his growing friendliness with Caroline. Every morning Marcus locks up the house and hides his key on a nub of the live oak tree in the yard. When he finds it is missing, he at first suspects that Nick borrowed it but learns that his mother has given Nick an extra key and later finds his own key hung on the tree, but in a different place. In the next few days minor things begin to disappear, part of a meat loaf, a clock, a flashlight, a sleeping bag, bread, and peanut butter. Marcus discusses his suspicions with his best friend, Robbie Roberts, and finally tells his mother, who confronts Nick. He denies taking things from their house, and even sleeps on their sofa as protection until they can have the locks changed. For Christmas Marcus has been secretly building his mother a bicycle from parts, all done except for the Campagnolo pedals, on order but not yet arrived. Nick, who knows about the bike, gets a set of the special pedals from a different store. Marcus partly resents the interference and partly appreciates it, since he can finish the gift. A series of strange noises and other happenings reawakens Marcus's suspicions about Nick, including coming upon him in the garage hiding something behind his back, and with Robbie distracting the Clark sisters, he sneaks up to Nick's apartment to hunt for clues. Although he does not find the clock or other missing items, he sees a number of photographs, including a lovely, pensive shot of his mother, but mostly of a boy with Nick's blond, curly hair, all carefully dated and labeled "Blake, age—," so that Marcus knows that the boy is about as old as he is. He also finds a closet full of wrapped Christmas gifts, all for Blake, some with paper faded as if from age. He learns from his mother that after Nick's divorce, his ex-wife disappeared, taking their son with her and that Nick has been hunting for them for seven years. On Christmas Eve, Marcus goes to the attic for the tree decorations and is troubled by an unusual smell. His gift from Nick, a photograph of the bike, carefully labeled, matted, and framed, explains the incident in the garage and makes Marcus feel guilty. That night Marcus hears a noise in the laundry room and discovers a boy he recognizes as Blake. They get in the car to talk, and Marcus learns that Blake has discovered that his real name is not Miller, as his mother has said, but Milardovich, and having seen his father with a winning team on television, has set off to find him while his mother is in Mexico with a friend. He has gained entrance to the house with the key Marcus hid in the tree and has hidden in the attic but, having heard from his mother that his father is a terrible man, has not dared to make himself known and has subsisted on what he can swipe from the kitchen. To his own surprise, Marcus tells Blake what a great guy his father is, and with Caroline's help they effect a happy reunion. The story is predictable, without much genuine suspense, but characterization of Nick, who is remarkably patient and understanding with Marcus, wins the reader and makes the ending satisfying. A subplot about

Anjelica Trotter, an assertive classmate of Marcus, who spikes her hair and wears red-and-green lipstick when she goes to school but is much more ordinary, and much nicer, when they meet her with her parents, and her clumsy pursuit of Marcus, is amusing but not essential to the story. The narrative voice of Marcus is uneven, sometimes too literary for his age. Poe Nominee.

*IZZY, WILLY-NILLY* (Voigt*, Cynthia, Atheneum, 1986), contemporary physical and psychological problem novel set in an unidentified American city during the late fall and early winter months. Pretty, popular, slightly above-average student Izzy (Isobel) Lingard, 15, tells of her puzzlement, hurt, and shock when she wakes up one Monday in a hospital room and learns that her right leg has been amputated after being crushed in a car accident. She thinks back to the events that led up to the Saturday night crash, how proud she was to be invited to the post-game party by senior football star Marco Griggers, how, though he has been drinking and drugging, he sets out to drive her home to keep her curfew, and how he loses control and the car swerves into an elm tree. Contrary to the reader's expectations, the sociological and legal ramifications of Marco's behavior are not explored. The writer concentrates on the moral aspects as revealed by the difficulties Izzy faces in rebuilding her life and describes how she becomes a more mature, less self-centered young woman. A number of people affect her, among them such medical personnel as Mrs. Helen Hughes-Pincke, the pregnant psychiatric nurse, and Izzy's husky, black physical therapist, Mrs. Adelia Jones, who is aloof and harsh but also capable and caring and who suggests that Izzy wear pants; and her parents, beautiful, homemaker mother and handsome tax expert father, who are ready to help her in any way possible. To her surprise, her best friends from school are slow to make contact. She discovers later that they consider her a threat to their accustomed way of life, especially beautiful Lauren, who does not want anything less than perfect around her, and Suzy*, who accepts Marco's letter sweater. Ironically, the person who helps her the most is gauche, plain, practical Rosamunde* Webber, who visits her several times while she is in the hospital, bringing interesting gifts, helping her keep up on news, and, in particular, forcing her to face her disability squarely. After Izzy comes home, where her mother has redone the parents' first floor bedroom for her, Rosamunde continues the association, helping her with school assignments at home, pushing her into returning to school after the cast on her left leg comes off and she has graduated from walker and wheelchair onto crutches, and then keeping an eye on her at school. The second person outside the family who significantly affects her is handsome, big-man-on-campus Tony* Marcel, the senior who is editor of the school paper. He invites her to join the staff, an activity that eases the pain of losing her cheerleading post, introduces her to potential new friends, and makes no physical demands on her. Several incidents are especially important in showing the degree of maturity Izzy achieves. She helps Rosamunde become more socially adept, and she helps Tony accept the fact that his girl will soon be out of his life, most likely forever, because she has received a scholarship to Stanford. Izzy wants her name to be Isobel Lingard on the list of staff writers, since she feels she is a different person and now is no longer comfortable with the "little girl" nickname. She grows to see how shallow her "best friends" really are, and she herself was, and admits that even "nice" girls like herself can be unlucky. Even her grades improve, so that she makes the honor roll for the first time. Most significant is her confrontation with Marco, who never contacts her after the accident even to ask how she is. When at school she sees him flirting with pretty freshman Georgie Lowe, the girl who has replaced Izzy on the cheerleading squad, she jokingly remarks to Georgie, in Marco's presence, that Georgie must "look out for Marco": "I only went out with him once, but it was quite an experience." He angrily calls her a "bitch," and she takes the name-calling as a sign that he regards her as a person to be reckoned with and not just a cripple. Izzy has accepted her disability and is going beyond it to make a good, more worthwhile life for herself. Although plot is intentionally subordinated to character and dialogue and the Lingards indicate that they will not sue, it is curious that there is no mention that the police or insurance company are preparing a case against Marco. The story's emphasis remains entirely on Izzy, so that her feelings and psychological maturation provide the book's core. She experiences loneliness, homesickness, denial, self-pity, sorrow, anger, revulsion at her maiming, fear of what people will think, worry about whether boys will be interested in her, depression, tears, gloom, and also happiness and fulfillment at being able to help others in spite of and because of her disability. Family scenes, especially those with her jealous, spoiled younger sister, Francie, and rambunctious college-aged twin brothers, Joel and Jack, are convincing. The overall tone is upbeat and positive. Fanfare.

# J

**JACOBS, PAUL SAMUEL,** journalist for the *Los Angeles Times* and novelist for children. His *Born into Light\** (Scholastic, 1988), named a Best Book by *School Library Journal*, began as a story for his three children. An inventive and thought-provoking novel of science fiction, it hypothesizes that the remarkable technological advances of the late twentieth century derive from a group of feral children in New England in the early twentieth century who are really extraterrestrials. *Sleepers, Wake* (Scholastic, 1991) is about a space voyage. He has lived in Sacramento, Calif.

**JAMES TILLERMAN** (*Sons From Afar\**), a skinny, dark boy of fifteen, elder brother of Sammy\*, sibling of Dicey\* and Maybeth. A fine student, intellectually gifted, curious, philosophical, he is ambitious to become a lawyer and make "gobs of money," something the Tillermans are always short of. He is proud of his academic achievement but in the story learns that doing the right thing is more important than grades. He also begins to think that helping people might bring him more personal satisfaction and considers becoming a doctor. One of the book's most amusing scenes is that in which in class James reveals to the French teacher that Andy Walker did not do the work for a paper he turned in. James trips Andy up by asking him astute questions. Although he is not good at sports and hates baseball, he goes out for it anyway, all spring suffering through practices and games, because he thinks having a sport on his record would be additional ammunition for getting a scholarship to a good college. At the end he decides that life is too short to not do what you really want to and makes up his mind to go out for chorus in the fall. James is a well-drawn figure, a foil for his father, Sammy, and Andy Walker.

**JASON** (*Out From This Place\**), child of eight when the story begins. When Easter finds him on the Phillips plantation, he has become the special favorite of Mistress Phillips, a spoiled whiner who thinks that he is far more important than he is. She has dressed him in a ruffled shirt, buckled shoes, and velvet breeches. At first he whimpers for "Missy Phillips," shirks his work, and is a general annoyance, but later he does his share more willingly. Among the book's most notable scenes are those in which he attracts attention by his dancing and singing, for example, for Union soldiers and for Dr. Taylor's traveling medicine show. On both occasions Easter hauls him away as fast as she can.

**JEFF CLINTON** (*The Other Side of Dark**), handsome new boy in school, in reality a narcotics officer of twenty-three assigned to help crack the Stacy McAdams case. Jeff looks younger than his age and hence has been assigned to the local high school because police feel sure drugs were involved in Stacy's mother's murder and Stacy's own injury. Jeff has let it be known that he is from Michigan and is uninterested in girls because he has a sweetheart back there, until Stacy arrives. Stacy's friend, Jan, arranges for Jeff to meet Stacy, and thereafter he is a "johnny-on-the-spot," turning up whenever she needs help. Associating with Jeff helps Stacy to sort out her values. It also advances the plot and provides a little romance. Like the other characters, Jeff is conventional for the genre.

**JEM MILLER** (*Charley Skedaddle**), sensible, reliable, kind Union soldier whom Charley Quinn meets on the steamer after Con* Sullivan lures the boy into running away to the Civil War. Jem befriends Charley with food, his jacket, and advice. He helps Charley see Con's deceit and keeps his spirits up. At the camp, Jem advises Charley to write to his sister, having much the same stabilizing, maturing effect on Charley as does Granny* Jerusha Bent later. Jem rises to corporal and is killed at the Wilderness. His death stimulates Charley to what he feels is murder—to shoot a Rebel soldier—and cowardice—to flee from the field. It also stimulates, and prefigures, Charley's redeeming acts of killing the "painter" (panther) and rescuing Granny.

**JENKINS, LYLL BECERRA DE,** raised in Colombia, South America; writer. She received the Scott O'Dell Award for Historical Fiction for *The Honorable Prison** (Dutton, 1988), a "fusion of personal experience and invention." The book is a graphic and gripping story of a family imprisoned for the political beliefs of their father, an outspoken newspaper editor who has persisted in attacking the dictator of their unidentified Latin American country. Her short stories have been published in the *New York Times* and the *Boston Globe*, among others, and the story upon which the novel was based first appeared in the *New Yorker*. The book has been translated into Spanish. A resident of the United States for more than twenty years, she lives in Connecticut and teaches writing at Fairfield University.

**JERRY LEE JOHNSON** (*Come Sing, Jimmy Jo**), husband of Olive* and real leader of the Johnson Family singing group, although Grandpa still plays the standing bass fiddle and sings. A scrawny little man, Jerry Lee married Olive when she was seven months pregnant and has been a devoted father to another man's child. When it is apparent to him that Olive and Earl are thinking of going off together and changing to an electronic sound, he generously gives them money and does not challenge their theft of his song, hoping to keep the family together. He not only writes the best songs for the group, plays a hot banjo, and sings a sweet baritone, he also provides much needed stability.

**JIMMY-CLYDE** (*Night Cry\**), retarded boy of fourteen with a mental age of about eight who delivers groceries on his bicycle to the remote Stump farm, carefully unloading his bag and naming each item as he sets it on the table. He is fond of Ellen because she once stuck up for him when he was being taunted by kids in town, and he is immensely proud of being hired to care for Sleet, the horse Ellen fears. When the television people are trying to interview Ellen after she rescues the kidnapped child, she insists that Jimmy-Clyde share the spotlight with her because he did just as she told him to do. He found Dr. George, even though it was his day off, and "banged his door" until the doctor came and could get the message to send an ambulance to help Granny\* Bo, who supposedly had broken her hip, the story Ellen dreamed up hoping to alert someone that she was in trouble on the farm. Jimmy-Clyde is a well-drawn and sympathetic retarded character.

**JOAS** (*The Return\**), older brother of Desta\* and Almaz\*. He leads them on their flight to freedom to the Sudan. A bright, articulate youth, he attended school until it was closed to Falashas and is very proud of knowing some Hebrew. While looking for food on the journey, he is shot and killed by bandits. Desta and Almaz laboriously bury him in the hard and stony ground, Desta wrapping him in the new holiday *shamma* (shawl) that her Aunt\* Kibret had proudly made for her. Desta had loved Joas greatly, and not until Dan\* talks about his own deep love and great respect for Joas can Desta release her grief in tears.

**JOE STUMP** (*Night Cry\**), father of Ellen, a man of unquenchable and impractical enthusiasms. His latest idea is that he will make good money selling calendars to businesses for promotional gifts, and he leaves his thirteen-year-old daughter alone on their isolated farm while he travels the area trying to make sales. When he first sees Gerald, he thinks that the man looks familiar and asks him whether he might be related to the Hawkeses who live near the Tennessee line, giving the stranger a lead to say that his name is Gerald Hawkes, although actually he is Sam Goff, whose older brother Joe knew. Joe thinks any man who sticks to his work as Gerald does around the farm must be a good fellow and does not hesitate to go off again while the man is around. When Ellen is to receive a reward for rescuing Jason Cory, Joe admits that he might not be cut out for the calendar business and that he should stay closer to home.

**JOHN MALCOLM** (*Edith Herself\**), husband of Alena\* Ostermann Malcolm and brother by marriage of orphaned Edith Ostermann, who is about the same age as his and Alena's son, Vernon\*. Edith thinks him overpowering and frightening at first, but time shows him as not wanting Alena to coddle Edith and Edith to fall into self-pity. A good farmer, he kills the mice she wants as pets, in Biblical language referring to them as vermin: "We cannot suffer vermin to live." Edith thinks that he begrudges her presence on the place. She likes it that he insists that she go to school, however, and that he makes no issue of her epilepsy. He is a strict Christian and the stern schoolmaster of the local country school, where he is a staunch disciplinarian and extremely capable. At the end, Edith no longer thinks of him as forbidding and cold, and neither does the reader, but as a man of principle and responsibility. He is the most interesting figure in the novel, next to Edith, the protagonist.

**JORDANA** (*A Good Courage\**), formerly Jasmine, and before that Faith, Eowin, Sunshadow, Jane, Lucy, and originally Martha Lynn, mother of Tie-Dye Rainey. A dissatisfied woman, she has moved from one communal living group to another since before Ty was born, always starting with great enthusiasm and becoming dissaffected, her one constant being her strong love for her son until they join the Kingdom of Yahweh. The fanatic religious passion of the community so grips her that she does not listen to his complaints about the overwork, lack of food, and harsh punishments of the children, and only dwells on the "joy" she experiences in the services. When Ty brings the police, she is present but just weeps and says, "Brother\* Daniel's right, Tobias," and tells him that if he cares about their life together, he will accept Yahweh and his rules. Polaris\*, who has known her as Sunshadow, tells Ty that she will tire of the Kingdom and come to find him, but the boy feels betrayed and abandoned and realistically doubts that he will ever live with her again.

**JOSEPH** (*Waiting for the Rain\**), Tengo's older cousin, from the township near Johannesburg. He first informs Tengo about police searches and the need for passbooks. When Tengo arrives in Johannesburg, Joseph is engaged in some secret activity the nature of which he refuses to divulge to Tengo lest Tengo become the object of police interest. At that point, Tengo does not care much about what Joseph is doing, since he is single-minded about getting an education and is only dimly aware of revolutionary activity. Later Joseph informs Tengo that he is an activist with and recruiter for the African National Congress. He is an obvious foil for Tengo and a means by which the writer can convey black aspirations and frustrations.

**JOSH CLANCY** (*Sweet Creek Holler\**), with his mother the owner of the coal mines in the area of Sweet Creek Holler. A caring and understanding man, he finds the house in the Holler to which the Shortts move after Jed Shortt, an employee of his, is shot to death. Josh is liked and respected in the area, although set aside socially because of his wealth and position and because the Clancys are regarded as "strange." When Ginny stops at his house on her rounds, selling punches on her punchboard to make a little Christmas money, he buys all the punches that are left, then accidentally backs his truck over her dog, Buddy. In spite of his profuse apologies and many kindnesses thereafter, she holds a grudge until he sensibly convinces her it is time to forgive and forget. Although only sixteen when his father committed suicide, Josh gradually assumed responsibility for the family business, giving up thoughts of further education. When the Clancys return to Pennsylvania, he intends to pursue an engineering degree. A rounded figure, he is the opposite of the typical greedy, grasping, hardhearted mine boss.

*THE JOSIE GAMBIT* (Shura\*, Mary Frances, Dodd, 1986), realistic novel of family and neighborhood life, centering on junior high youngsters who play chess, set in the 1980s. The narrator, fatherless Greg Farrell, 12, is spending six months in Pineville, Ill., with his grandmother, since his mother must travel in Europe for her job. He stops in to see the Nolan family, friends from earlier trips to Pineville, although Grandpa Nolan, who taught him to play chess, has died since his last visit. He finds Josie, 12, whom he remembers as a stocky little girl, slimmed down and quite attractive. She is baby-sitting for her younger sister, Lollie, and introduces him to her best friend, beautiful, blond Tory Mitchell, who is deliberately rude, speaking scornfully of his chess ability and calling him a freak, "a mile high with beaver teeth." Then she walks out. Because Tory is supposed to be staying at the Nolans while her mother is away, Josie is worried, but neither she nor Greg connects Tory with the police cars and commotion at the end of the block until they hear, the next day, that she was the victim of a kidnapping attempt by her paternal grandparents, who want custody after a bitter divorce. She and her mother move to another part of town, but she continues to attend the same junior high, traveling to and from in a taxi. Josie, snubbed and insulted by Tory, is hurt and dejected. Her mother tries to be understanding, saying that Tory is going through a difficult time, but her brother Jason, 16, is furious, and he uses Greg as a sounding board to let off steam. He also decides that Greg's height makes him a natural for basketball and that he will teach him the skill. At school, Greg, always shy, is shepherded around by Josie and joins the chess club, becoming the sixth member. Since the other junior high has challenged them to a match, with the top three in each club playing, their sponsor organizes a play-off to determine their team's players. In the first round, Greg wins but Josie is defeated by Tory who uses psychological tricks to throw her off. That evening, while Greg and Jason are at a fast food stand, they learn that the tree house built by Grandpa Nolan is afire and their home damaged. Greg invites the Nolans to stay at his grandmother's. The next day he learns that Tory was briefly reported missing, but turned up later, and that Jason has been accused of setting the fire by smoking "one substance or another" in the tree house. In the chess play-off, Greg and Tory tie and play again for first place. Greg, partly to avenge Josie's defeat, plays fast and talks glibly, both very uncharacteristic, to throw Tory off. To his astonishment, she tries the Queen's Gambit, a high-risk series of moves, and when she is called on a rule violation she flips the board over and stalks out. Because her mother must be out of town for a week, Tory is to stay at the Nolan house, but when dropped off in the morning she is rude to Mrs. Nolan, refuses to unpack, and sits on her suitcase by the front door. About noon her father comes with a lawyer and a court order removing Tory from the Nolan home because of their consistent record of child neglect, of allowing their teen-age daughter to entertain a male friend without a chaperone, of their son's smoking of illegal substances and starting a fire, and so on. Greg finally puts it all together and sees that Tory is sacrificing her friendship with Josie and the reputation of the Nolan family to get her way, just as she was willing to sacrifice her queen in the risky chess gambit. He boldly speaks up, accusing her of calling her grandparents to come and get her on the first night, of starting the fire, and of slandering Jason, all so she could live with her father. In the end she loses, since she is placed with the grandparents she dislikes. Josie is chosen to be coach of the chess team, and Greg looks forward to a happy time in Pineville. An explanation of chess, the man and the moves, is given at the end. The story roughly follows the patterns of a chess game, but the parallel is strained and the plot predictable. The strongest elements are the good, joking relationship between Greg, his mother, and his grandmother, and the way his thoughts convincingly dwell on food, of which he never seems to get enough. The Nolan dog, Miss Pod, a spoiled and vicious Lhaso Apso, is a nice change from the usual devoted pet. ALA.

**JULIA** (*Tancy**), imperious doctor-cook at the Gaithers' plantation. She mothers Tancy and tries to help her remember her place as a slave. From Julia Tancy learns that Miss* Puddin Gaither's blurted statement about Tancy and Billy Gaither's being siblings is literally true. Julia, however, reminds Tancy that, while the two share blood, under the slave system they cannot be considered brother and sister. Julia informs Tancy that her mother, Lulu or Lucy, was sold off the plantation to keep Miss Puddin from finding out about her relationship with Mas Gaither. At the end of the war, Julia leaves without a farewell, and Tancy assumes some of her responsibilities.

**JULIE SINCLAIR** (*December Stillness**), Kelly McAllister's best friend, an attractive, popular, red-gold blonde who, at book's beginning, chides her for not being more serious, but, who, after Kelly becomes interested in Mr.* Weems's plight, chides her for being too serious. After Mr. Weems is killed, Julie extends sympathy to Kelly and wants to resume the friendship that had lapsed while Kelly was intent on Mr. Weems. At that point, Kelly realizes that they have grown so far apart that they have little to talk about. Julie's main interests are boys, especially Kevin* Myers, with whom she makes out as often as possible, and clothes, although she also wants to do well in school. She is a foil for Kelly as well as for their mutual friend, Courtney, an overachiever, who seems bent on compromising personal achievement for popularity with boys.

**JUNIE SHORTT** (*Sweet Creek Holler**), June Marie, older sister of Ginny. Her outspokenness occasionally causes trouble or embarrassment for her family. For example, on the bus home from a revival, she challenges the town gossip, spiteful Mrs.* Moore, saying she hates people who go to church and then spread lies. Mrs. Moore says she will make the Shortts pay for that remark and does by causing trouble for Mama* Shortt. Junie also speaks up to Poppy* Shortt about going back on his promises. At first, Junie and Ginny are very close, but later, though still affectionate, they develop independent lives.

*JUNIUS OVER FAR* (Hamilton*, Virginia, Harper, 1985), realistic novel set mostly on Snake Island, once called Island of Passage, in the Caribbean, presumably in the 1980s, involving the relationship of a father, son, and grandson with each other and with their island heritage. In a town in the northeastern United States, Junius Rawlings, 14, misses his grandfather, Jackabo, who has returned to the home of his youth on Snake Island. Junius, who was cared for from infancy by Jackabo while his parents worked, has identified with the old man and copied his island accent, although his father, Damius, has tried to disassociate himself from his Caribbean past. Until bright Junius starts tutoring and falls in love with pretty Sarrietta Dobbs and her mother treats him as an inferior, he does not realize that American blacks look down on those from the islands. Jackabo has gone back to the dilapidated Rawlings estate, now owned by his distant cousin, Burtie Rawlings, a white man he grew up with and calls his "old enemy." The two elderly men bicker and insult each other, but they have worked out a system of living together and depending on each other, though Jackabo is often confused, particularly after drinking Burtie's planter's punch. When Burtie disappears, Jackabo at first cannot remember what he thought was a dream of Burtie being carried off by pirates. When he does recall the incident and decides it was real, his letter seems so disoriented that Damius flies to the Caribbean, taking Junius with him. They discover the old man unwashed and half-starved, but delighted that they have come, as he was sure they would. They find that not only Burtie, but his gun, his binoculars, and much of his furniture are gone, although Jackabo is sure that they were there after Burtie left. Damius and Junius take Burtie's story to Lawrence, the only town on Snake Island, and report the story to Chief of Police Downing, an impressive, bemedaled black man. He tells them that Burtie is not lost or stolen, that he has bought a house in Lawrence, having come into an inheritance at his wife's death, and has said that Jackabo's son would come for him. When an officer brings Burtie in, he shouts racial insults and insists that the "American Negroes" get off his land. Downing points out that Burtie has Jackabo's Social Security check, that his wife is still living in Florida, and that he must have bought the house with other money. Burtie is held in jail and, at Downing's request, Damius and Junius return to stay at the Rawlings estate until further notice. It develops that they have wandered into a major arrest of arms and munitions smugglers, centered in a house on the hill beyond the estate. Watching through his binoculars, Burtie evidently got valuable knowledge and traded his silence for cash. Before they leave, taking Jackabo with them, they spend a couple of idyllic days snorkling and picnicking, and Damius promises his father that they will return, with Junius's mother, for a long time the next summer. The experience has made Damius ashamed of his rejection of his island past and has confirmed the desire Junius has to be a real island man himself. The story is told in chapters alternating between the point of view of Junius and, usually, that of his grandfather, both of them talking and thinking in Caribbean dialect. The place is slow, despite the sensational disclosure at the end, with long descriptions usually made palatable by being seen through the eyes of the excited boy but sometimes sinking into the tone of a travelogue. Jackabo, the most interesting character, seems older than his age of seventy-six. C. S. King Honor; Fanfare.


*JUSTIN AND THE BEST BISCUITS IN THE WORLD* (Walter*, Mildred Pitts, ill. Catherine Stock, Lothrop, 1986), realistic contemporary novel of domestic life from the boy's point of view. Justin, 10, whose passion is one-on-one basketball, chafes at being required to do what he calls women's work, like picking up his room, making his bed, washing dishes, and helping with cooking. So when his Grandpa Ward, a widower, arrives and invites him for a visit to his ranch in the Missouri hills, Justin eagerly accepts. Grandpa's Q-T spread was established back in the late 1800s by Justin's Great-Great-Grandfather Wiley Ward and his family, "exodusters," black emigrants from Tennessee fifteen years after the Civil War. Justin helps Grandpa feed and water the animals and rides fence with him. He soon sees that Grandpa does "women's work" matter-of-factly and well. Grandpa shows Justin how to make his bed and cooks for them. In conversations with Grandpa, Justin also learns about famous black cowboys and about his family's perilous trip west in 1879 from an old book of memoirs. They attend the annual cowboy festival in town, where Justin thrills to various events like the big parade, Grandpa takes first prize for the best biscuits, and Justin gains, among others, a blue ribbon in the bean bag toss and a cowboy hat for plucking a red ribbon from the tail of a baby Brahman bull. Just before they leave to take Justin home, he asks Grandpa to show him how to make biscuits. At home the next day, Justin surprises everyone by diligently cleaning his room and making a tasty supper, like Grandpa's, of pork, raisins, and the best biscuits in the world. The simple and straightforward story is aimed at those just beyond primers. Print is large and sentence structure uncomplicated. Its intent to raise self-esteem is obvious. As through contact with Grandpa, the only man in his life, Justin begins to feel better about himself, his attitude toward his mother and sisters improve, and he is surprised to find that he is even happy to be home again. The story also seeks to acquaint readers about little-known aspects of black history. The tone is warm and the pace fast. The typical characters serve to advance the plot. Best are the convincing picture of the tensions of home life and the snatches of black history. C. S. King Winner.

# K

**KATHERINE METCALF** (*After the Dancing Days**), pianist, mother of Annie. She has been extremely hurt by the death of her favorite brother, Paul, who was also musical, and by the breakup of the group of young men from the music school who used to congregate at her house. Her reaction is to close her eyes to the aftermath of the war and pretend that it is all over, even though her husband is treating the badly injured veterans. When Annie says that she was wrong to forbid her to go to St. John's, she is too furious to talk about it, but bows angrily to her husband's opinion that she must let Annie face the truth, even if she herself cannot. Eventually, she forces herself to accept the idea and even goes to play for the men when Andrew* Clayton invites her.

**KAY CHAPMAN** (*The Year Without Michael**), seventh-grade sister of Jody and Michael. Very bright and slightly spoiled, Kay is often at odds with her siblings and rightly sees that her mother does not like her as well as the other children. She reacts to the great strain put on the family by Michael's disappearance with anger, resenting the preoccupation of her parents and the curiosity of her friends, and frankly saying what none of the others will say, that she hopes they find out that he is dead so their tension will be relieved. The fact that no one comes to her birthday party is not entirely convincing in the story, but it probably happens because she has become so touchy and disagreeable. On Christmas, when their mother insists that they get presents for Michael, she puts a beautifully wrapped gift under the tree. Jody, peeking at it before she stores it away, finds that it is a rock. Her genuine effort to help, by putting the advertisement in the paper, is misunderstood by her parents and precipitates a furious rejection from her mother. In the end, she has returned from Florida to try to make a new start with the rest of the family.

**THE KEEPER** (Naylor*, Phyllis Reynolds, Atheneum, 1986), realistic problem novel of a family attempting to cope with the father's mental illness. At thirteen, Nick Karpinski has moved many times when his father changed jobs, but after two years he is settling into his Chicago neighborhood and making friends in his junior high school. His mother, Wanda, who gives piano lessons in their apartment, is a warm, outgoing person, but his father, Jacob, is reserved, not close even to his brother, Thaddeus. Nick's first intimation of his father's illness comes when Jacob appears at home in the middle of the day, saying that he no longer works for the insurance company. He gives no explanation, and Nick and his mother assume that he has been fired until a friend brings things cleared from his desk and tells Nick that no one at the firm knows why he suddenly walked out. Jacob confides in Nick that the Communists are after him and are sending subtle warnings that the only way he will leave Chicago is in a box. He becomes more and more suspicious, sure that the apartment is bugged and that the building superintendent and the neighbors are paid to spy on him. For a while he works at the post office sorting mail, but he soon leaves the job and spends both days and nights pacing the apartment and peering out the window. Because of embarrassment and fear of humiliating her husband and also in an effort to deny his illness to herself, Wanda does not tell anyone of his bizarre behavior and cautions Nick not to say anything. One evening Nick discovers Jacob lying behind the car with the motor running, breathing the exhaust. This suicide attempt prompts Nick to consult the school nurse, Miss Etting, pretending to be concerned about the father of a friend. When she urges him to have his friend get some help, Nick calls Uncle Thad. In his brother's presence, however, Jacob acts nearly normal, and Nick's uncle says that Wanda can cope best with him. Over the next few months, Nick suffers from his father's wild swings of mood, anger and defiance alternating with panic and childish fear. At the same time the boy's social life is developing as he has longed, with his friend Danny* Beck, Lois Mueller, a girl he has admired, and Karen Zimmerman, a girl who lives in Nick's apartment building, whom Danny wants to date, starting to be a regular foursome at school. Nick does not confide in any of his friends and makes excuses to keep them from visiting his apartment. Wanda rents a room in a church to give her music lessons, and Nick gets a part-time job at a deli to help with expenses. Eventually Wanda consults a priest, who visits and invites them to a retreat. He points out what Wanda has already learned in her anonymous calls to local social services, that unless Jacob will admit himself to a hospital, there is nothing that they can do unless the police believe that he is a clear danger to himself or to others. Finally one night, Jacob, in terror, agrees to go to a hospital, but instead he drives Nick and Wanda around, changing from fear to suspicion and anger. Seeing a patrol car, Nick presses the horn until the police come to investigate. Nick says what they have been trying to hide for so long, that his father is mentally ill and that they are trying to get him to a hospital before he hurts someone. With the help of the police, they take Jacob to a veteran's hospital, where the examining doctor explains again that without some evidence of a long-term condition, he cannot admit Jacob. Nick calls Miss Etting, who comes in the middle of the night to the hospital and talks to the doctors, convincing them that for months Nick has known and tried to get help for his father. With Jacob in the hospital, Nick and Wanda pick up their lives, feeling sadness and some guilt, but also relief. After Nick tells his friends, Lois breaks her date for a dance with him, but Karen, who has been two-timed by Danny, is understanding and is destined to become Nick's girl friend. The book's greatest strength is in its nightmarish tone, and in Nick's emotions, running from exasperation and concern at his father's paranoia to horror when his father buys a rifle and nearly shoots Karen. Inevitably, the ending is simplified, since there is no guarantee that Jacob will continue to be hospitalized. The dilemma of mental illness for the family, however, the difficulty of getting help, and the fact that there is no certainty of a cure are all faced squarely and movingly. ALA.

**KENNEDY, (JEROME) RICHARD** (1932–     ), born in Jefferson City, Mo.; author of experimental and complicated fantasies. He received his B.S. degree from Portland State University, Oregon, and studied further at Oregon State University in Corvallis. From 1951 to 1954 he served in the U.S. Air Force. He has worked in a number of different fields, including teaching elementary school, and since 1974 he has been custodian of the Oregon State University Marine Science Center in Newport. His more than fifteen novels vary in style and sub-genre. *The Blue Stone* (Holiday, 1976) is a literary fairy tale full of complicated transformations. *Amy's Eyes\** (Harper, 1985) also contains transformation, mainly from doll to human and the reverse. It was named to the American Library Association Notable Book list. Other titles by Kennedy include *The Leprechaun's Story* (Dutton, 1979), *The Mouse God* (Little, 1979), *Song of the Horse* (Dutton, 1981), and *The Boxcar at the Center of the Universe* (Harper, 1982). He has also published a book of verse and *Collected Stories* (Harper, 1987).

**KEVIN CONNELL** (*Building Blocks\**), Brann Connell's father in the 1974 dimension and his playmate for a day in the 1930s time period. Kevin almost always gives in to his more confident and articulate wife, who ironically is the counterpart of his mother. A family story, which ironically his wife enjoys telling, recounts the only time Kevin prevailed in an important argument with her. The dispute involved naming Brann, when Kevin so strongly insisted upon that name that he won out. Ordinarily, Kevin dismisses setbacks of all sorts as due to "fate," meaning that something is bound to happen a certain way and cannot be changed regardless of anything he might do. After his experience with Kevin in the 1930s dimension, Brann understands that this attitude is a defense mechanism.

**KEVIN MYERS** (*December Stillness\**), Kelly McAllister's best buddy since she bit his leg in kindergarten. From this incident he has a pet name for her, Mad Dog. Although Kelly says that she is not romantically attracted to him, she is not comfortable with the blossoming romance between him and her best friend,

Julie* Sinclair, especially since they are openly very affectionate. When he sees how serious she is about helping Mr.* Weems, Kevin compliments her on her dedication and supports her efforts, not always in front of the other teens, however. He also tells her mother how "cool" she was in defending her views about war in literature class. A tall, thin gangly boy, he loves basketball and is a foil for the "heroics of war" faction in school.

**KIDD, RONALD** (1948–      ), born in St. Louis, Mo.; writer and producer of educational and entertaining films, filmstrips, and recordings for radio, television, and screen; author of light fiction for children and young people. He graduated from the University of California at Los Angeles with a B.A. degree in 1971 and received his secondary teaching certificate from California State University in 1972. He was affiliated with several film companies before founding RK Associates in Altadena, Calif., in 1979. In 1975 he was nominated for a Grammy Award from the National Academy of Recording Arts and Sciences for "Mr. Popper's Penguins," and in 1982 he received the Golden Eagle Certificate from the Council on International Nontheatrical Events (CINE) for "Winnie-the-Pooh Discovers the Seasons," a Walt Disney production. He has written stories for picture books and books for middle-grade readers, including *The Glitch* (Lodestar, 1985), a fantasy about a computer kingdom, and several young adult novels, among them *Second Fiddle** (Lodestar, 1988), which was nominated for the Edgar Allan Poe Award and is the sequel to *Sizzle & Splat* (Lodestar, 1985). Lively and amusing, these books are based on Kidd's experiences as a member of a youth orchestra when he was in high school.

**THE KID IN THE RED JACKET** (Park*, Barbara, Knopf, 1987), realistic novel for middle-grade readers of a boy's adjustment to a new home and school set mainly in Rosemont, Massachusetts, in the 1980s. The narrator, Howard Jeeter, 10, is determined not to like anything about the trip or the town to which the father's job has dragged them across the country from Arizona, away from his friends and his soccer team. Having observed new kids in his old school, he knows how long it takes even to be called by name, not just "the kid in the green shirt." His younger brother, Gaylord, is still a baby, unable to talk or be a companion, and his parents, though they try to be helpful, are hopelessly out of touch with fifth grade mores. They have just arrived when a little red-haired girl appears and introduces herself as Molly Vera Thompson, a first grader whose parents are "divorced from her" so she lives with her grandmother across the street. In the next couple of weeks Howard suffers the agonies of starting in a new classroom, eating by himself in the cafeteria, and hanging around alone on the playground. Most of all, he fears that he will become known as a weirdo because Molly insists on being with him and treating him as her best friend. She attaches herself firmly to Howard and does not seem to understand his efforts to discourage her. His first breakthrough with his classmates occurs when two boys, Pete and Ollie, suggest that he join the Saturday football game. They stop by for him and are inspecting his room when Molly shows up with her dilapidated doll, Madeline. Ollie gets hold of Madeline, tosses her to Howard, and they play keep-away until Molly starts to cry. Pete calls them both jerks and walks out. Feeling terrible, Howard goes out of his way with some success to impress Pete, who reminds him of his best friend in Arizona. For three days Molly stays away. When she returns, Howard tries to explain to her that they cannot be best friends because they like different things. Molly points out that they both like to color and suggests that, if Howard will not be divorced from her, she will use the crayons he wants her to use. Stung by compassion, Howard promises not to get divorced from her. The book's strength is its tone, conveyed in a wise-guy voice that is in convincing fifth grade vocabulary and is intended to be amusing while conveying home truths about understanding, tolerance, and the need to see beyond one's own egocentric concerns. Characters are well drawn, especially Howard and his parents. SLJ.

*A KINDNESS* (Rylant*, Cynthia, Orchard, 1988), realistic novel set for one year in Seattle, Washington, in the 1980s, in which a singleton son learns to accept his mother's illegitimate pregnancy and new daughter. Bright, practical Chip Becker, 15, has lived all his life alone with his painter mother, Anne, whose ex-hippie husband ran out on them to Australia when Chip was a baby. Since imaginative Anne tends to be impractical, Chip has grown protective and possessive of her, assuming most of the responsibility about their place and feeling secure in this insulated environment. One day in October his tidy, safe world crashes. Anne informs him that she is pregnant and will not even name the father. He feels threatened, angry, and afraid and immediately assumes she will have an abortion. Yet, fearing that she might have the baby, he discusses the matter with his steady, Jeannie Perlman. Jeannie is sympathetic to him but reiterates Anne's own contention: it is Anne's life and not really Chip's business. Chip realizes that he is worried about what people will think and does not want his life to change. He wants to continue to have Anne to himself and pleasant, intimate meals like the Friday night one at which their friend Randy, owner of an antiquarian bookshop, makes linguine for them and Jeannie. When Anne tells him that she intends to have the baby, he is furious and asserts that he does not want to have to take care of a baby, too. For the first time Anne realizes that somehow their positions have become reversed. She tells him gently that she does not expect him to. She will manage, she says, and they come to an uneasy truce. By March, Chip has accepted the situation and even hopes that the baby will be a girl, but in a pretend computer letter to the unknown father, he pours out his anger and reviles the man. At the same time, his relations with Jeannie deteriorate. Since he has become possessive of her and much concerned with sex, she asks for some time out from their relationship. Anne gives Chip the privilege of naming the baby, who turns out to be a dark-haired girl. He calls her Dusky Anne, after his mother and a now-extinct sparrow that being nature lovers they both had admired. He soon loses his heart to little Dusky, marveling at the tremendous miracle that has entered their lives. Fear then sets in—fear of losing her to the unknown father. By this time, the readers know that the father is Anne's New York agent, a happily married man whom she has loved for years, though she sees him only on her annual business trip to New York. A family problem had propelled him into her arms for one night's solace. Anne's reaction when Ben George, the agent, phones on a business matter tips Chip off. He discusses his knowledge with Randy, who tells him to stop being possessive. Ben, up to this point ignorant of the baby, learns about Dusky from mutual friends. A proud, responsible man, he is determined to do his duty and phones, getting not Anne but Chip. Frightened, angry, Chip tells him to stay out of their lives, maintaining that if Ben comes to Seattle, as he wishes, it will be out of selfish motives of respectability and responsibility and not out of concern for their well-being. Ben thinks things over and when he next calls Anne asks her if she wants him to come and gratefully receives the response that she does not. This emotionally powerful but never sensationalized story has italicized passages for Anne's story and regular print for Anne, Chip, and Dusky's section. The author often sketches in scenes with pithy general comments about characters or actions that are then demonstrated in the scenes to come. Sometimes the lead-in is in second person, the author addressing readers directly and asking them to imagine themselves in, for example, Chip's place, a technique that emphasizes Chip's dilemma. Chip changes believably as he learns to give up trying to control his environment, while Anne learns to take more control. Ben, who barely appears but has a major role in events, learns that the "manly" thing is not necessarily morally correct. The elemental emotions of love, anger, and fear hold sway in this exploration of how one seemingly small event can have tremendous repercussions, in this case on an unconventional family. Tension increases steadily as the story scrutinizes the meaning of responsibility, caring, and acceptance. SLJ.

**KO KAWASHIMA** (*So Far from the Bamboo Grove\**), elder sister of Yoko\* whose cleverness and stamina are the main reasons the girls and their mother survive their terrible journey through Korea to Kyoto, Japan. A strong, sturdy girl, she passes easily for a soldier with her head shaved and learns quickly to lie and scrounge for food. Because she is bossy, Yoko at one point says she hates her, but the same day Ko rescues her little sister by carrying her on her back across a railway bridge on which Yoko is stuck, paralyzed by fear. Often impatient with Yoko, Ko once says it would be better if her little sister had been killed, then is overcome by remorse. She smuggles her mother's little sword, a family treasure, aboard the refugee ship by binding it to her leg and pretending she wears a cast. In Kyoto she is accepted by the university in a home economics program and does very well designing and sewing beautiful garments, although she wears the ragged remains of a Korean soldier's uniform. To earn a bit of money for food, she shines shoes after school and so is not at the station when her mother dies. After they find the money in their mother's wrapping cloth,

Ko insists that they continue to sell the little garments and toys that she makes of scrap fabric from school, scrounge for cans and bottles, shine shoes, and salvage garbage so that they can save the money for a real emergency.

**KONIGSBURG†, E(LAINE) L(OBL)** (1930–      ), born in New York City; popular author noted for her lively and humorous novels about contemporary life in family or neighborhood situations like *Up from Jericho Tel** (Atheneum, 1986), a fantasy of two children who become acquainted with an aging actress who sounds and behaves like Tallulah Bankhead and who engages them in a mysterious quest. It was named a Best Book of the American Library Association. She graduated from Carnegie Institute in Pittsburgh with a B.S. degree in 1952, studied chemistry further at the University of Pittsburgh, married David Konigsburg, a psychologist, and made her home in Jacksonville, Fla., where she taught in a private girls' school. She began writing when her children were in school and uses her own family experiences as a basis for her books. Highly acclaimed, she received the Newbery Award for *From the Mixed-up Files of Mrs. Basil E. Frankweiler†* (Atheneum, 1967), which was also a Lewis Carroll Shelf selection, *Jennifer, Hecate, Macbeth, William McKinley, and Me, Elizabeth** (Atheneum, 1967), *About the B'Nai Bagels†* (Atheneum, 1979), all realistic novels, and the biographical novels *A Proud Taste for Scarlet and Miniver†* (Atheneum, 1973), an engaging book about Eleanor of Aquitaine, which was a finalist for the National Book Award and a Phoenix Award Honor Book, and *The Second Mrs. Giaconda†* (Atheneum, 1975). Konigsburg's style is lively, amusing, and contemporary, and her plots move along well, but her characters are occasionally shallow, and her attempts at cleverness sometimes fall short. She has almost always illustrated her own books.

# L

**THE LAMP FROM THE WARLOCK'S TOMB** (Bellairs*, John, Dial, 1988), mystery novel with detective story aspects, involving magic of the occult set in Wisconsin near the Mississippi River in the 1950s. A high school youth and his elderly lady friend obviate satanic powers. Miss Myra Eells, an "old, birdlike little woman" of almost seventy, the head librarian of the Hoosac Public Library, buys a small, white china oil lamp with Dutch scenes painted in blue on its base at Mrs. Grimshaw's antique shop and sets in motion disturbing events that take place over half a year's time. As Miss Eells and Anthony Monday are driving home that night, they almost hit an old man with a long, tattered black overcoat and cobwebby face. For days afterward Anthony feels tense and Miss Eells is snappish. Anthony borrows the lamp for a science project, and the night he works late at the high school setting up the display, he sees the old man again, then finds the nightwatchman dead, concludes the old man is a ghoul who killed the watchman, and is certain that the lamp is somehow connected with the murder. Tension builds when he and Miss Eells see Mrs. Grimshaw lurking about the cemetery the day of the funeral and feel strange sensations in the library. Miss Eells contacts her brother, Emerson, a wealthy, peremptory, rabbity Minnesota lawyer who knows much about the occult. He informs them that the lamp had been stolen thirty years earlier from the trash of a wealthy eccentric lawyer named Willis Nightwood of Stillwater, Wisconsin, north of Hoosac. After Mrs. Grimshaw mysteriously disappears and the lamp is stolen from a locked oak cabinet at the high school, Miss Eells decides to drive to Stillwater to investigate. At the former Nightwood residence, she and Anthony run onto strange ritualistic objects, are almost the victims of magical illusion, and return gratefully to Hoosac. At the end of February, Emerson shows up and, for various reasons, says he is certain someone is trying to become the ancient moon goddess, Ashteroth, an exceedingly evil spirit, and will probably conduct the incarnation rites at full moon on March 10 in Stillwater at the Nightwood house. The roaring climax occurs just after midnight on March 10, with Emerson and Miss Eells helicoptering (Anthony stowed away in the cargo hold) to Stillwater and being captured by Mrs. Grimshaw (who has been behind all the skullduggery, her disappearance a hoax). As she is about to assume the evilness of Ashteroth and annihilate them with her magic, Anthony fortuitously saves them by breaking the lamp with steel balls and a catapult. Mrs. Grimshaw, an unhappy misanthrope who sought to elevate herself by acquiring satanic powers through occult information contained in the base of the lamp, dies, wrapped in flames as the ghoul appears, and the three friends escape just before the house collapses in fire. Numerous, skillfully integrated, conventional Gothic elements keep the pace moving and the thriller atmosphere high. Though shallowly drawn and eccentricized, the outgoing, somewhat flighty old woman and the introverted, quiet teenager make an unusual and likeable pair of protagonists. Others in series. Poe Nominee.

**LAS BOMBAS, COUNT** (*The Beggar Queen**), mountebank of many names and disguises who figures prominently in the Westmark* trilogy of novels by Lloyd Alexander*. In *Westmark*, he gives refuge to Theo* when he is fleeing for his life from the king's men, and in *The Kestrel*, he accompanies and advises Mickle* (Queen Augusta) as she leads her army against the rebels. In *The Beggar Queen*, he helps in various ways to overthrow the murderous Cabbarus, who has usurped the government and deposed Mickle. After the rebel army is defeated, Las Bombas is put in temporary charge of the government.

**LASKY, KATHRYN** (1944–      ), born in Indianapolis, Ind.; writer of both novels and nonfiction for young people. She received her B.A. degree from the University of Michigan, has done graduate study at Wheelock College in Boston, and has made her home in East Boston. Many of her books are illustrated by her husband, photographer and filmmaker Christopher Knight, including *The Weaver's Gift* (Warne, 1980), which won the *Boston Globe-Horn Book* Award for Nonfiction and *Sugaring Time* (Macmillan, 1983), which was named a Newbery Award Honor Book. Other works of nonfiction they have produced jointly include *Tugboats Never Sleep* (Little, 1977), *Tall Ships* (Scribner, 1978), and *A Baby for Max* (Scribner, 1984), told from the point of view of a five-year-old and based on the reactions of Lasky's son to her second pregnancy. Her first novel, *The Night Journey* (Warne, 1981), a story of a family's escape from czarist Russia, won the National Jewish Book Award for Children. *The Bone Wars** (Morrow, 1988), a historical novel about nineteenth-century paleontology expeditions in Montana, was named a *School Library Journal* Best Book.

**LAURA GOLDEN** (*The Goats**), plain girl of thirteen, who wears glasses and is regarded as a "real dog" by the campers at her and Howie* Mitchell's exclusive camp. The child of ex-hippies, reared by her divorced mother, Maddy, she had been christened Shadow, a name she reverts to as their adventures progress. The IOU she leaves for the old man who loans her sixty cents to call Maddy is signed with that name. Laura grows in self-confidence and self-respect, as does Howie. Although at first he is the one who shows initiative, at the end Laura is more realistic and pragmatic than he and takes charge.

*LEGEND DAYS* (Highwater*, Jamake, Harper, 1984), realistic period novel of a Blackfeet Blood girl growing up on the Northern American Plains in the late 1800s during the hard times of the white encroachment. Disasters strike after a huge white owl, accompanied by a violent crash of thunder, bursts into the tepee of Amana's family and scatters their fire, igniting the tent and burning it to the ground. Then a smallpox epidemic sweeps the tribe, leaving the camp empty and desolate. Their parents dead, Amana's older sister, SoodaWa, drives the younger girl out into the night, hoping to save her life. Amana, 11, escapes threatening owls with the help of a she-fox, who leads her to a cave, where a grandfather fox blesses her and presents her with a trove of magical objects. This mystical experience gives her strength and resolve: "Amana changed into a man." Back at the camp, she discovers two survivors, old women, Crow Woman and blind Weasel, who recognize a new, great power in her and inform her that her sister, extremely ill, and her sister's much older husband, Far Away Son, have left on horseback, hoping to find a place beyond the epidemic. Dressed in the regalia given her by the foxes, their sacred songs strengthening her, Amana hunts for the women and herself, and thus they manage until winter approaches. They load their travois with preserved food, break camp, and follow the Old North Trail along the Backbone of the World until they encounter a Gros Ventre encampment. To Amana's delight, SoodaWa and Far Away Son are there, but SoodaWa's beauty is gone, since she was horribly disfigured by the disease. They continue to live with the Gros Ventres for some seasons. At twelve, Amana becomes the "little-child" wife of Far Away Son, although with mixed emotions because the marriage seems to go counter to her fox-vision of becoming someone special and doing man things. Far Away Son is kind and patient, and she comes to feel a filial love for him. She longs to hunt, however, and have heroic adventures, and helps reluctantly about the tepee. Events include a visit to a white trading post, where Amana marvels at certain wonders but dislikes the smell and behavior of the whites and where Far Away Son points out the whites' hypocrisy. Her best friend, Yellow Bird Woman, also married to an older man, is scarred facially by the men of the tribe when she and her lover are caught eloping at the annual Sun Dance. Yellow Bird Woman comes to live in Amana's tepee, since no one else will have her, and soon she becomes half-mad, degenerating into a whimpering, whining, fearful imitation of her former beautiful and confident self. During a very hard winter, SoodaWa dies, and half the tribe with her, but Amana is so successful at hunting that the men are in awe of her. She makes a solo trip to a trading post where the trader tries to cheat her. On the way home, she avoids being raped by a white man by pressing handfuls of sand into her groin. She continues to hunt with Far Away Son and the men of the tribe and joins a horse raiding party, dressed in her fox regalia. She and Far Away Son move to Canada where they have learned that there has been a treaty between the Blackfeet and the English. Life is difficult there, too; game is very scarce, and when the railroad is finished, still more whites come. One day buffalo are sighted, and the hunters, including Amana, ride forth excitedly, although some still feel that a woman may spoil the luck. Amana is successful as usual, but Far Away Son is thrown and trampled to death. Amana weeps hard for him, and for herself, since she realizes she now has no family at all and is alone in the world. She begs the sky for a sign that she will survive, hears the song of her vision again, opens her arms to the sky, sees a fox, and runs into the dark night. The plot moves unevenly, being an amalgam of incidents that show life among prairie Indians, and characters lack dimension, even Amana who is the stereotypical girl who resists the accustomed sex role. The novel's beginning is puzzling. Amana's mystical experience with the owls and foxes is later referred to as a vision, but she returns from the foxes with tangible objects. Best are the descriptions of traditional customs and of the deterioration of life due to white inroads. The title comes from a speech of Nez Perce Chief Joseph's widow, in which she refers to the "old days" of the Indians as "legend days," but this book certainly does not depict those times. Sequels continue Amana's story through the third generation. SLJ.

**LETTY SHAMBAUGH** (*Blossom Culp and the Sleep of Death**), bratty high school girl, a social snob who is determined to get Alexander* Armsworth's fraternity pin. At the end of the novel, the pin lies on the floor of the Princess's tomb, having fallen from Alexander's clothes. Letty dominates the small girls' club she heads, the S. T. & B. F. S. (Sunny Thoughts and Busy Fingers Sisterhood), from which she excludes Blossom* Culp as unworthy, being quite literally from the wrong side of the tracks, streetcar, that is. When Letty complains that their house will be bare if her mother sends the stolen antiques Mrs. Shambaugh has purchased from Blossom's mother to the Egyptian Museum in Cairo, Mrs. Shambaugh hits her over the head with her reticule, effectively silencing her. Mrs. Shambaugh does not want to be arrested for receiving stolen goods. Blossom is happy no one brings up the matter of who Mrs. Shambaugh's source is, since the thief is Blossom's mother, who earns their living by snitching and scrounging.

**LEVITIN†, SONIA (WOLFF)** (1934–      ), born in Berlin, Germany; teacher and author of books for children and young people that range widely in subject and approach. After emigrating to the United States with her family when she was four—her experiences under the Nazi regime are re-created in her first novel, *Journey to America†* (Atheneum, 1970)—she grew up in Los Angeles, attended the University of California at Berkeley, received her B.S. degree from the University of Pennsylvania, and studied further at San Francisco State College. She has taught in elementary and junior high schools and at adult education centers. Among her some twenty books are picture books for the very young, fantasies for later elementary readers, and novels for teenagers, like *The Year* *of Sweet Senior Insanity* (Atheneum, 1982), and an Edgar Allan Poe Winner, *Incident at Loring Groves\** (Dial, 1988), a murder mystery. She excels at fictionalizing real-life events for older readers, like the 1841 Bidwell-Bartleson expedition to the Far West in *The No-Return Trail†* (Harcourt, 1978) and the evacuation of the black Jews known as Falasha from Ethiopia to Israel in *The Return\** (Atheneum, 1987), which was named to both the American Library Association and *School Library Journal* lists of Best Books. She received the Jewish Council of America Award for *Journey to America* and has written for magazines and newspapers.

**LIBBY CLAYTON** (*Invincible Summer\**), Robin Gregory's grandmother, who has lived with Robin and her father, Will\*, since her daughter, Julie, was killed in an auto accident. Libby is a sensible, practical, warm woman, typical in her worries, loving nature, and domestic skills. She shares with Robin her experiences with her three husbands, particularly with the second who beat her and her third, who dropped dead at her feet of a heart attack. Her support, and that of Rick\* Winn, keep Robin afloat. Libby is the foil of Mrs. Winn.

**LISLE, JANET TAYLOR** (1947–      ), born in Englewood, N.J.; journalist, novelist. She received her B.A. degree from Smith College in 1969 and has also attended Georgia State University. Besides working for VISTA in Atlanta, Ga., and as a reporter for the *Atlanta Journal*, she has written for *North County News* in Westchester, N.J. Her *Sirens and Spies\** (Bradbury, 1985), a novel of misunderstandings caused by wrong assumptions, was named to a number of critical lists: the American Library Association Young Adult and Notable lists, the *School Library Journal* Best Books list, the Junior Literary Guild, and *Booklist's* Children's Editor's Choice list. It also won the Parents' Choice Award for Children's Literature. *The Great Dimpole Oak* (Orchard, 1987) was also a *Booklist* Editor's Choice and was an honor book for the Golden Kite Award for Fiction. *Afternoon of the Elves* (Orchard, 1989), is a story of the friendship of a girl from a conventional family with a disadvantaged but highly imaginative neighbor.

*A LITTLE LOVE* (Hamilton\*, Virginia, Philomel, 1984), romantic girl's growing-up novel set in a large Ohio town in the early 1980s. Black Sheema Hadley, 17, very overweight and not retarded but mentally slow, attends the food service unit of a vocational high school and lives with her grandparents, her mother having died and her father departed. Although she used to sneak out at night and walk the street, to be picked up by whoever was cruising, she stopped these promiscuous ways when Forrest Jones, a fellow food service trainee, chided her and took over as her sole boy friend. Forrest is tall, slim, good looking, protective, and understanding when Sheema has sudden panic attacks or bursts into tears. At cooking she is competent, and she does most of the housework at home, where Grandmom Jackson is increasingly forgetful and arthritic and Grandpop spends most of his time at the Senior Center or out, Sheema fears, with other women. Despite their love, Sheema feels a hole in her life not for her dead mother but for Cruzey Hadley, the father she has never known. She persuades Forrest, who has an old Dodge, to take her to look for him. When she hints that she has this in mind, Grandmom, who believes she can sometimes read minds, gives her an album her father once sent, a record of the signs he has painted in his itinerant career, from huge banners and sides of buildings to fine lettering on doors or shop windows. She also tells Sheema that he left because her mother died in childbirth and he could not bear to stay where she had been. Nevertheless, he has always sent money for Sheema's expenses, and the morning they start, Grandmom gives Sheema a hundred dollars saved from these payments and the last address she has for him, in Jellico, Tennessee. With considerable misgiving, Forrest heads south. In the dark out of Knoxville, which is hosting a World's Fair, one of his tires blows out, and he has no spare. At the house of a white family they ask to call a wrecker and are scared off when the woman seems to be alerting someone else, they fear a Klan member, but they are picked up by the black garage owner she has summoned who also rents them a room. He overcharges them but turns out to have known Sheema's father and tells them he has left for Dalton, Georgia. In Dalton they find a neat building with a sign saying Cruze Signs Pro-art and advertising all kinds of signs and studio classes, one of which is in session. The man who limps to answer the door Sheema recognizes from pictures, and she begins to sob. He takes them into a small lounge, gets rid of his class, and tells them about his life, two marriages since he left their town, the present one with two children. He says he always meant to get in touch and is not proud of himself. He recognizes her rage and assures her that he will keep sending money so she can continue her education. He suggests that they stay, but Sheema says they are leaving. On the way home, for the first time that she can remember, Sheema cannot eat. Forrest tries to comfort her, then asks her to marry him, not right away but some time in the future. At home, Grandmom is delighted to hear that Cruzey is doing well, and Grandpop goes with Forrest to try to make peace with his father, who does not like Sheema and is furious that they went off together. The story is slow and predictable. The first half shows Sheema as an insecure girl, worried about her own weight, her slowness at reading, her grandparents' aging, the nuclear bomb, and a variety of other concerns but comforting herself by eating, all elements that are established in the first few pages and so seem repetitious. The psychology of her resilience after meeting and leaving her father is questionable; she seems not crushed by the collapse of her dreams of a loving father but ready to take charge of her life and even to resist excessive food. Forrest is altogether too forbearing to be plausible, and his attraction to her is never convincingly explained, although he does enjoy sex with her and thinks that with his brains and her cooking ability they will make a good team. The best characters are the old grandparents, afraid of senility and clinging together for comfort. Point of view is usually Sheema's, but sometimes it shifts jarringly and occasionally is the author's voice intruding. C. S. King Honor; Fanfare.

*LOCKED IN TIME* (Duncan*, Lois, Little, 1985), fantasy novel with mystery aspects set in the 1980s. Nore Robbins, 17, tells how, bitter and angry that her very successful novelist father should marry so soon after her mother's death, she flies from Boston to Baton Rouge to spend the summer with her father, his new wife, Creole Lisette Berge, and her two children, handsome Gabe, 17, and rebellious Josie, 13, on Lisette's antebellum plantation, Shadow Grove. Strange things occur immediately. Among others, Lisette's glances at Nore seem sinister, the three Berges appear to carry on secret conversations with their eyes, and the house, remote and phoneless, seems suspended in time amidst the lush and jungly grounds. Josie, rambling on about the many places they have lived in, mentions being in Hartford, Connecticut, during the Ringling Brothers circus fire, fully forty years earlier. One evening, Gabe and Josie drug the parents' bedtime anisette, sneak out, and with Nore along, drive to town to take in a disco. Nore makes friends there with Dave Parlange, son of Lisette's roofer and a Harvard freshman, who has also noticed that the family seems strange. Then Gabe, who had at first attracted Nore, tries to drown her, toppling her from his boat and leaving her in the water, although he knows she cannot swim. Her father refuses to listen to her fears about the Berges, deeming them the result of jealousy and resentment. She contacts Dave, who arranges a meeting with an old resident of the area. He gives her some information about the family that confirms her suspicions, and then alone she investigates an old slave cabin filled with family records and diaries. She discovers to her amazement that Lisette's family is indeed suspended in time. Lisette, now more than one hundred years old, had through voodoo magic stopped her aging at thirty-five, her children at their respective ages also, and thenceforth married a succession of wealthy men whom she killed for their money, returning with each new marriage to Shadow Grove and giving the neighbors to believe that she is the daughter of the previous generation. After other mysterious and tension-filled happenings, the book reaches its climax when Nore and Dave are locked in the cabin and it is set afire. Gabe and Lisette leave for town, ostensibly to summon the fire department. Before leaving, Gabe slips Josie the key to the cabin, and she releases Nore and Dave in the nick of time. On the way to town, Lisette and Gabe are killed when the fast-moving car veers out of control and hits a tree. The story abounds in skillfully executed Gothic elements, and, since the reader like Nore early realizes that the Berges are much older than they look, two main questions hold the attention: how can it be that the family never ages and when and how will they attempt to kill the Robbinses. The concept driving the fantasy—age suspension—raises important social and ethical issues that derive from the interruption of the natural order. The Berges are more interesting than the Robbinses, who serve merely to introduce the other family. Poe Nominee.

**LORD, BETTE BAO** (1938–      ), born in Shanghai, China; naturalized as a United States citizen in 1964; public servant and writer for adults and children. She received her B.A. from Tufts University in 1959 and her M.A. from Fletcher

School of Law and Diplomacy in 1960. In 1963 she married diplomat Winston Lord, who later became U.S. ambassador to the People's Republic of China in Beijing. She has held many public service positions, among them assistant director of the East-West Cultural Center at the University of Hawaii, program officer of the Fulbright Exchange Program in Washington, member of the selection committee for White House Fellows, and member of the National Committee on United States-China Relations. She received the National Graphic Arts Prize in 1974 for her photographic essay on China. Her first book, *Eighth Moon: The True Story of a Young Girl's Life in Communist China* (Harper, 1964), concerns her own sister. Her first novel, *Spring Moon: A Novel of China* (Harper, 1981), also for adults, was nominated for the American Book Award and appeared on the *New York Times* bestseller list for thirty-one weeks. Her own experiences in immigrating to Brooklyn, New York, with her father are fictionalized in the amusing and sometimes poignant *In the Year of the Boar and Jackie Robinson*\* (Harper, 1984), which was a Best Book of the American Library Association and *School Library Journal* and received the Jefferson Cup Award. She has also written for adults *Legacies: A Chinese Mosaic* (Knopf, 1990), a book of social life and customs. She was given an honorary LL.D. by Tufts University in 1982 and has made her home in New York City.

**LORD ZAKOJI** (*The Samurai's Tale*\*), a wealthy retainer of Akiyama\*, and father of Aki-hime. Because he can no longer hear well, he holds himself aloof from other men and is thought to be proud. Having been brought up in the palace in Kyoto, where his father served the emperor, he is extremely formal and a lover of beautiful things, drinking his tea from exquisite cups even on journeys and wearing tortoise-shell combs, their tops framed in silver. Since he has no son and his older daughters have married well, becoming part of their husbands' families, he suggests that he may let Aki-hime marry a poorer man, whom he will adopt as his heir. Although he makes no promise, he clearly has Taro in mind, but after the death of Takeda Shingen, when the situation for Akiyama's followers appears to be hopeless, he shaves his head and takes up the ways of a Buddhist monk. This does not save him from a humiliating death, being crucified upside-down and naked by the enemy. He is a foil for Akiyama, equally noble but less brave and realistic.

**LOU JEAN PURVIS** (*Sweet Creek Holler*\*), best friend of Ginny Shortt. A pretty, outgoing child, she loves to play make-believe and have and go to parties. She sings in a sweet, clear soprano, and tends to be emotional. After attending a revival when she is about twelve, she becomes religious and fears the fires of hell. After she becomes pregnant by Will Jenkins, who then leaves for the army, she loses her zest for life, feeling very strongly the shame that she has brought upon her already looked-down-upon family, and even becomes masochistic, especially after her sullen, angry, guilt-ridden mother tries to sell her, to punish her and get rid of her, to an old encyclopedia salesman. Lou Jean develops a fascination for fire, sets some, and finally burns herself to death. The contrast between the ebulliently happy child at the beginning of the story and the dejected, self-reproachful, ostracized teenager at the end is marked and pathetic.

**LOWRY†, LOIS (HAMMERSBERG)** (1937–     ), born in Honolulu, Hawaii; novelist whose many books vary in tone and setting, but all have questions of family relationships at their core. She attended Brown University and received her B.A. degree from the University of Southern Maine. Her sensitive first novel, *A Summer to Die†* (Houghton, 1977), which concerns the leukemia and death of the protagonist's sister, was inspired by the death of Lowry's own sister. It won the International Reading Association Award. Better known are the books in her Anastasia series, starting with *Anastasia Krupnik* (Houghton, 1979), lighter, humorous novels dealing with ordinary concerns of early adolescents. *All About Sam\** (Houghton, 1988) switches the focus to Anastasia's little brother. *Rabble Starkey\** (Houghton, 1987), about a single-parent family, won both the Child Study and the *Boston Globe-Horn Book* Awards. Departing from her usual American setting, *Number the Stars* (Houghton, 1989) is about a Danish family who shelter a Jewish friend during the Nazi occupation of Denmark during World War II. Lowry has also written several textbooks. She has two daughters and two sons.

**LUCAS ELLERBY** (*The Facts and Fictions of Minna Pratt\**), violist in Minna Pratt's chamber group with whom she falls in love and whose vibrato she envies. A kind and helpful boy, he encourages her and tells her to call him when she gets one. She does, in the middle of the night, a call he takes in the right spirit. Tall, homely, slim, with one "wandering" blue eye, he wants to be a naturalist or biologist when he grows up. When Minna first meets him, he has a frog in his pocket that he has rescued from a biology laboratory and that they release in the park pond together. Minna discovers that he has many tanks and aquariums of frogs in his room. When his parents discover them and argue so civilly about them, Minna thinks that it is the worst argument she has ever heard, no angry words, no raised voices, no tears. Willie\* and Twig\* help him get the tanks out.

**LUCY FOREVER & MISS ROSETREE, SHRINKS** (Shreve\*, Susan, Holt, 1987), detective novel set recently in Charlottesville, Virginia, near the campus of the University of Virginia. Lucy Childs and Rosie Treeman, both eleven, have been best friends since nursery school. Lucy is the only child of Dr. Anthony Childs, an eminent child psychiatrist formerly on the university faculty and now in private practice in an office over the family garage, and Mrs. Childs, an accomplished painter and sculptor. Rosie is one of the ten children of a construction worker. The two girls have carried out many "projects" together and now are deeply involved in an imaginative game called Shrinks, Incorporated. Their "business" operates everyday after school in the basement of the Childs house and has the two pretending to be the world-famous psychiatrists, Dr. Lucy Forever and Miss Rosetree. One day while the girls are engaging in their make-believe practice, complete with grown-up costumes and perplexing, imaginary cases, a tiny, mute, terror-stricken girl with a jagged red scar at the base of her throat appears at their door. It is Cinder, fresh from a session with Lucy's father and obviously very frightened. She is soon claimed by her nurse, a cold woman named Miss Brill. The girls' curiosities and sympathies are aroused, and though Lucy has been specifically instructed never to enter her father's office, she does so to look for Cinder's address. She finds it, bikes there—846 Cedar Tree Lane out past the university and beyond the limits of Charlottesville—and discovers that the place is the Albemarle County Home for Children. She finds the little girl tied to a tree and clutching tightly the doll the two girls had given her. Astonishingly, Lucy's piano teacher, Mr. Van Dyke, turns up, takes Cinder into the house, and bundles Lucy and her bicycle into his car and takes them home. He tells Lucy that Cinder has a great talent and unless she leaves Cinder alone he will tell her father what she has done. Since Rosie has also spotted Cinder in the back of Mr. Van Dyke's car, looking very scared, the girls are convinced skullduggery is afoot at the home. They ponder the problem, in between school, various responsibilities, and "sessions" at Shrinks, Incorporated. Lucy reads on child abuse in one of her father's books and cancels her piano lessons with Mr. Van Dyke so she can be in her "office" when Cinder arrives. They forge a note to Miss Brill from Lucy's father changing the length of Cinder's session so that they will have a longer time to work with her. When Cinder appears, Rosie hypnotizes her in an effort to get information. When Cinder comes one day with more scratches and then is missing when Miss Brill arrives to pick her up, Lucy knows that the gig is up and runs away. She encounters Cinder, who has also run away, and soon both girls are found by Miss Brill, who takes Cinder with her and warns Lucy to stay away from Cinder. Undaunted, Lucy again bikes to the home, where she sees Miss Brill strike a little boy and where she is soon captured by Miss Brill and locked up. With Rosie's help, Lucy's parents and the police are able to trace Lucy. Miss Brill, who, it has been discovered, forged her resume to conceal a history of child abuse, has fled but is soon apprehended by police, and Cinder is found wandering in the road. Mr. and Mrs. Childs take her home, and to Lucy's delight, since she has longed for a sibling, decide to adopt her. When last seen, Cinder is happily playing the shrink game with Lucy. Characters are drawn in the broadest outlines, the plot depends heavily on coincidence, and Mr. Van Dyke is an obvious red herring. The style sometimes jars ("Staring in the window was a tiny girl the color of pears with long, silky black hair and eyes shiny as polished silver—full of terror."), the humor is overly broad, incidents are melodramatic, the outcome is overfore-shadowed, and the convention that children are brighter than adults drives the story. Counterbalancing these aspects is the clever invention of the business, which seems totally in character, and the carefully calculated suspense that builds and holds to the very last page and provides just plain good entertainment for middle-grade readers. Poe Winner.

**LYON, GEORGE ELLA** (1949–      ), born in Harlan, Ky.; college teacher, poet, playwright, and novelist. She received her B.A. degree from Centre College of Kentucky, her M.A. from the University of Arkansas, and her Ph.D. from Indiana University. At the University of Lexington she has been an instructor of English and creative writing and has been a lecturer at Transylvania University in Lexington. In addition she has taught at Centre College and at Radford University and in 1985 was Writer in Residence at Centre College. In 1983 her poetry chapbook, *Mountain* (Andrew Mountain, 1983), won the Lamont Hall Award. Other books of poems include *Growing Light* (Mill Springs, 1987). Her two-act play, *Braids*, was first produced at Transylvania University in 1985. Her novel, *Borrowed Children*\* (Orchard, 1988), a story of family relationships in eastern Kentucky, was named to the *School Library Journal* Best Book list. Among her other writings are a young adult novel, *A Throne in Goose Rock* (Orchard, 1987), two picture books, *Father Time and the Day Boxes* (Bradbury, 1985) and *A Regular Rolling Noah* (Bradbury, 1986), and many scholarly articles.

# M

**MACLACHLAN†, PATRICIA** (1938–     ), born in Cheyenne, Wyo.; teacher of English and creative writing and highly regarded author of picture book stories and novels for middle elementary and early adolescent readers. She was graduated with a B.A. from the University of Connecticut. Her books deal humorously with the serious matter of interpersonal relationships within family situations and are related with engaging wit and verve. She received the Newbery Award for *Sarah Plain and Tall\** (Harper, 1985), a warmly ironic story about how eagerly two motherless children on the plains in the early part of this century await the arrival of a potential stepmother. Her most honored book, this amusing and poignant story also won the Scott O'Dell and Jefferson Cup awards for historical fiction, received the Christopher Award, and was selected for the Fanfare, American Library Association, and *School Library Journal* lists. Well received have been *Unclaimed Treasures\** (Harper, 1984), featuring a girl intent on finding her "true love," and *The Facts and Fictions of Minna Pratt\** (Harper, 1988), about a budding girl cellist who yearns for a vibrato, both of which were selected for the Fanfare list and were American Library Association Best Books. Her home is in western Massachusetts.

**MAGGIE** (*Sarah, Plain and Tall\**), young woman who was a newspaper advertisement bride and came west to the prairie from Tennessee to marry Anna and Caleb's neighbor. Maggie visits Sarah, bringing gifts, important signs of welcome, but she also gives Sarah practical advice. When Sarah says that she misses her brother and the sea, Maggie sensibly and reassuringly replies, "There are always things to miss. . . . No matter where you are," and urges Sarah to plant a garden and drive over to her house to visit, for she is often lonely. Her invitation gives Sarah the idea of learning to drive the horses and wagon.

**MAMA SHORTT** (*Sweet Creek Holler\**), Olivia Shortt, widow of Jed Shortt, who was shot to death, and pretty, shy mother of Ginny and Junie\* Shortt. She struggles to raise her girls on a meager Social Security check, which is only seldom supplemented by help from Poppy* Shortt, her late husband's father. She has some self-taught learning but only an eighth grade education, has therefore no opportunity for a job except domestic work, and eagerly applies for the vacant position of postmistress, sure she will rank highest on the exam. Because Ginny in anger drops this information to spiteful Mrs.* Moore, Mrs. Moore applies, too, and even though Mama scores higher, gets the post through political patronage. Then Mrs. Moore meanly offers to hire Mama to care for her house and children. Strapped for money, Mama accepts. Mama often reads to the girls, thus helping them become superior students, insists on obedience, propriety, and responsibility, and encourages them to have friends, but she herself socializes little. She does, however, dress up and go around the neighborhood with the newspaper clipping about the conviction of her husband's murderer to allay rumors that Jed was shot while stealing. Mama is often the target of gossip because she is attractive and the other women, who tend to be dowdy, are jealous. Mama is a round and dynamic character, a fine foil to both Mrs. Moore and Mrs. Clancy.

**MARCUS BREWER** (*In Summer Light**), egocentric artist, elderly father of Kate. Generally considered a genius, he is interested in color and light, so that his one picture of a human figure, Kate at ten, he titles ''The Studio: Morning,'' and explains that the figure does not matter; it is just a color occupying space. He loves being lionized, likes to hear himself talk, and accepts the family deference to his whims as his due. When Kate was a little child, he let her paint in his studio and liked to explain the technical problems to her, but when she starts being a really skillful painter he dismisses her work, clearly not wanting to share the spotlight. Through the summer on the island, part of the strain has been caused by his inability to finish a canvas. He finally admits to Kate that he is out of ideas, and she sees that he is getting old, a revelation that helps her forgive him.

**MARGARITA MALDONADO** (*The Honorable Prison**), Marta's pretty, dark-haired mother, loving wife of Miguel*, imprisoned with him and their children because of his outspoken political beliefs. Most of the time Margarita loyally supports her husband and always in his presence, but when away from him she sometimes appears to be sullen and unhappy, especially because his health is deteriorating rapidly. At first she adopts the role of hostess, Marta notes, but later, when the money runs low, she becomes more of a dietician. When she becomes aware of Marta's attraction to Fernando, she asks her daughter to consider carefully whether under normal circumstances Marta would feel this way about this young man, a tactful way of indicating her displeasure about the relationship. Margarita holds the family together during the months in the mountains.

**MARIS** (*The Year Without Michael\**), flighty friend of Jody Chapman, whose hectic family life has always been in sharp contrast to Jody's. Her divorced mother drinks heavily and picks up men, spending more money on wild clothes than on her daughter's needs. Maris is present on the evening when Michael is first missing, and she sticks by Jody throughout the year, during her moods and spells of depression and anger. As the year progresses, however, Maris becomes more unrestrained and starts going out with older boys, choosing motorcycle types or men in their late twenties with sports cars. When Jody decides to go to New York to hunt for her brother, Maris agrees to pretend that she and Jody are staying with her aunt because, as she says, she loves a conspiracy.

**MARY POTTER** (*Sirens and Spies\**), older and softer sister of Elsie\*. Mary has inherited her mother's build and her wide, flat hands, which prevent them both from being good violinists, and she has the same sympathy for any hurt being that makes her mother invite derelicts to a meal and heap them with unwanted favors. Mary knows that Miss Fitch merely tolerates her as a violin pupil because Elsie is so promising. She cannot help resenting the special attention her sister gets, as well as the way Elsie considers it her due and scorns Mary's clumsy and soft-hearted attempts to win the teacher's favor. When they decide to confront Miss Fitch with the evidence of her past, Mary's strong sense of fairness contrasts with Elsie's arrogant condemnation, and she is horrified at the blunt way Elsie produces the picture and demands an explanation. In the end Mary realizes that the dramatic teacher often puts on an act and wonders how much of her story is true.

**MATT BENSON** (*Circle of Gold\**), Mattie\* Benson's twin, a good student and talented artist. He has a paper route to help with household expenses. When Mrs. Stamps tells Mattie that her mother needs counseling and Mattie mentions it to Matt, Matt suggests it. At first Mrs. Benson becomes furious with the children for discussing family problems outside the home, but later she takes the advice. Matt tries to be the man of the family although he is only eleven.

**MATTIE MAE BENSON** (*Circle of Gold\**), good student, talented singer in school and church, conscientious daughter. She baby-sits to help pay for household expenses and resists using any of her money for clothes until her mother insists. Because her mother often snaps at her, as she is overworked and worried about money, Mattie thinks that her mother favors Matt\*, her twin, and is sure that if she gives her mother the beautiful pin she sees at Stern's for Mother's Day everything will be fine between them. The reader gets the idea that Mattie triumphs in the newspaper contest because she remains virtuous and does not cheat. To this extent at least, the book is didactic. Mattie is described as being thin with coppery-colored skin and large dark eyes. She and Toni\* Douglas are foils for saucy, lazy, hateful Angel Higgley.

**MAZER†, NORMA FOX** (1931–      ), born in New York City; writer noted for realistic novels for adolescents. She was educated at Antioch College, Yellow Springs, Ohio, and Syracuse University in New York. Her first novel was published in 1971. *A Figure of Speech†* (Delacorte, 1973), about the close relationship of a girl and her grandfather who must enter a nursing home, was a finalist for the National Book Award. Intergenerational closeness is again explored in *After the Rain\** (Morrow, 1987), which was a Newbery Honor book and was named to the *School Library Journal* Best Books list, the *Horn Book* Fanfare list, and both the American Library Association Notable Books and Young Adult lists. *Saturday, the Twelfth of October†* (Delacorte, 1975), which was chosen for the Lewis Carroll Shelf, is a time-slip fantasy. *Taking Terri Mueller†* (Avon, 1981), about a girl whose father has kidnapped her from his divorced wife, won the Edgar Allan Poe Award. On both *The Solid Gold Kid* (Delacorte, 1977) and *Heartbeat* (Bantam, 1989) she collaborated with her novelist husband, Harry Mazer. Her book of short stories, *Dear Bill, Remember Me?* (Delacorte, 1976), received the Christopher Award. The Mazers have three daughters and one son.

**MCGREW PRATT** (*The Facts and Fictions of Minna Pratt\**), Minna Pratt's small, squat younger brother, who with his best friend, Emily Parmalee, often accompanies her on the bus to her cello lesson at concert hall. He hums his words, loves headlines, which he also hums, sings subtitles in movies, and is a failure at baseball. He helps Minna understand the meaning of her mother's quotation about facts and fictions being true. When he makes up material for his science report on beavers and she insists made-up facts cannot be true, he replies that their mother, Mrs.\* Pratt, produces made-up facts all the time. Minna sees that since they are about people and feelings her mother's fictions are indeed true in their way.

**MCKINLEY†, (JENNIFER CAROLYN) ROBIN** (1952–      ), born in Warren, Ohio; editor, novelist, best known for heroic fantasy and fictionalized retellings of stories from the oral tradition. She attended Dickinson College, Carlisle, Pa., and received her B.A. degree from Bowdoin College in Brunswick, Me. Most of her professional career aside from writing has been in editing, although she has also worked in book stores, on a horse farm, and as a teacher and counselor in a private secondary school in Massachusetts. Her first book of original fantasy, *The Blue Sword†* (Greenwillow, 1982), is set in the imaginary country of Damar, which resembles colonial India. *The Hero and the Crown\** (Greenwillow, 1985) is a companion novel, telling of the origin of the legendary sword. It was awarded the Newbery Medal, as well as being listed on the American Library Association Young Adult and the *School Library Journal* Best Books lists. Among her retellings of stories from the oral tradition are *Beauty†* (Harper, 1978), based on the folk tale, "Beauty and the Beast," and *The Outlaws of Sherwood\** (Greenwillow, 1988), a romantic version of the tales of Robin

Hood. These books, all of which were named to the *Horn Book* Fanfare List, feature protagonists who are shy, bumbling, and diffident, but emerge through trying circumstances to be intelligent and courageous heroes. McKinley has also written *A Door in the Hedge* (Greenwillow, 1981), a collection of four stories, some of them borrowed from Grimm, and other retellings: *Tales from the Jungle Book* (Random, 1985), *Black Beauty* (Random, 1986), and *The Light Princess* (Harcourt, 1988).

*M. E. AND MORTON* (Cassedy*, Sylvia, Crowell, 1987), realistic contemporary novel of friendship, growing up, and family problems set from June to September mostly in or near an apartment house called Jefferson Arms in a large American city. Imaginative, sensitive Mary Ella Briggs, 11, who tells the story and wants to be called M. E., yearns for a best friend. She knows that the neighborhood children think that she is bossy and snooty (she likes to remind everyone that she goes to a private school for academically advanced youth). She is ashamed of her older brother, shy, pleasant Morton*, 14, and avoids him because he is a slow learner, has been held back in school, and the other kids tease him and take advantage of him. A new girl, Polly*, who has come to live with her grandmother, wears long skirts and outsized shirts, and does her hair in frizzy loops, visits M. E.'s apartment. At first M. E. is delighted, then let down, because Polly has really come to play with Morton and his train, and M. E. tries unsuccessfully to dominate the activity. Polly, however, is independent, and she and Morton do as they please. They take one car up to the roof to play, over M. E.'s protests that they are not allowed up there. The car falls over the wall onto the roof two stories down, where it stays in spite of their efforts to recover it. The girls visit back and forth as the summer wears on, and M. E. grows happier and less prissy, although in her efforts to soften the blow to her parents, particularly Mrs.* Briggs, about Morton's being held back still another time, she adopts some of his behavior. She emulates his walk, for example, so well that people think that they are twins. The story peaks when the parents decide that it would be better for both children if Morton were sent to a special school on a farm. Since Mrs. Briggs will not let him take his several collections along, Morton decides to take his train. In the effort to retrieve the car, at Polly's suggestion, he falls. While he lies unconscious in the hospital for many days, M. E. and her mother come to a better understanding, and M. E. realizes how nice Morton is. Polly climbs down a ladder attached to the wall, one the children had not noticed before, and gets the car. When she puts it in Morton's hand, he awakes, like a "miracle," thinks M. E., and steadily improves, even returning to school three weeks into September. After her school starts, M. E. answers the girls' questions about Morton, even explaining that he is in seventh grade like her because he is a slow learner, the first time that she has openly acknowledged his disability and indeed that he is her brother, and is pleased when one of the girls asks her to join her club. M. E. attributes to Polly a "magic" that "can make things wonderful. . . . She made Morton wonderful. Maybe she made me wonderful, too.'' The book seems disjointed because most of it consists of M. E.'s reflections on life and flashbacks to earlier events, but, although the story is overextended, everything fits together with jigsaw puzzle precision. Characterizations are deep, and humor relieves the seriousness and poignancy of a family attempting to cope with two dissimilar children, one of them with obvious adjustment problems. Such scenes as Polly introducing M. E. to bug races in her dingy apartment and M. E. spilling her milk to draw attention away from Morton's similar mishaps are bittersweet in their humor, and the roof scenes foreshadow the climax and contribute suspense. Left unresolved are some moral problems, in particular, Polly's blatant disobedience. Mrs. Briggs's dilemma over her children is all too realistic. ALA; SLJ.

*MEGAN'S ISLAND* (Roberts*, Willo Davis, Macmillan, 1988), mystery set mostly on a lake in northern Minnesota in the 1980s, in which the family pattern of sudden moves with no forwarding address is finally explained. When their mother, Karen Collier, drops and shatters her prized crystal bowl, red-haired Megan, 11, and Sandy, 10, realize that she is frightened but only later remember that she was looking at the television at the time. That evening they pack up and drive all night to the lake where their Grandpa Davis is spending the summer, without waiting for the last two weeks of school or taking Megan's friend, Annie VanDow, as promised. Grandpa, who has broken his foot and rented a lakeside cottage with no phone while it heals, is surprised but welcomes them. Megan overhears Grandpa advise his daughter to tell the children, and Karen, or Caro, as he calls her, ask how she can do this when she has lied to them for so long. Then she departs as suddenly as they arrived, leaving the children with their grandfather. Megan and, to a lesser extent, Sandy are very disturbed by this inexplicable behavior. They nevertheless appreciate Grandpa's relaxed attitude, letting them explore the area on their own, asking only that they wear life jackets when they go out in the rowboat or canoe. On the nearest of the small islands that dot the lake they find an overhang to which they build a makeshift front wall of branches to simulate a cave, where they store food and old sleeping bags. Their hide-out is discovered by the only other youngster on the lake, Ben Jamison, 12, who immediately takes over, makes plans to ferry scrap lumber and tools over in their rowboat and build a tree house. Megan resents Ben's bossiness and cannot quite believe his stories of being expelled from three schools, treated as a nuisance by his mother and stepfather, and ignored by his writer father, who is staying at a lakeside cabin to finish a book. Although she knows that Grandpa might not approve, Megan writes to Annie, apologizing for leaving without saying goodbye or explaining why she cannot visit at Grandpa's as planned. A few days later Ben reports that a man has been asking in the nearby town for a red-haired brother and sister, saying that he is their uncle. A letter from Annie says that there have been inquiries by strangers about them at their old home. While Megan hides in the woods nearby, a man with an Illinois license plate and later two other men snoop around the cottage. Among some papers her mother left, Megan finds a birth certificate bearing the name Margaret Ann Kauffman but showing her date of birth. The truth, they finally learn, is that their father, a spoiled rich boy, did not die eight years before but only recently in prison, where he had been serving a term for embezzlement and bank robbery. Their paternal grandfather, millionaire Daniel Kauffman of Chicago, tried to get legal custody of the children, declaring Karen, actually Caroline, unfit. Afraid of his high-powered lawyers, she has been running ever since. Their recent flight was triggered by a "Have You Seen These Children?" television spot, featuring their picture, at four and three but still recognizable. The children hide out on the island while Grandpa talks to the detective from Illinois and is assured that Daniel Kauffman now simply wants to know the children, not to get custody. Their mother, having returned, cautiously calls and talks with her ex-father-in-law. In an exciting finale, the two other men, minor thugs from their old home trying to kidnap the children, return and beat up Grandpa. Ben runs their car into a tree while Megan and Sandy help Grandpa to the rowboat. In a wild chase, a dog Sandy has adopted upsets the canoe of the thugs, and Ben's father, having finished his book and begun to notice his son, calls the police. Though predictable, the plot is far more logical and plausible than many mysteries for middle readers, and Megan's confusion and dismay at the truth are convincing. The natural appeal of a hide-out on an island is exploited reasonably. The question of the ethics of lying in a serious situation like this is raised but not resolved nor really explored. Poe Winner.

*ME, MOP, AND THE MOONDANCE KID* (Myers*, Walter Dean, ill. Rodney Pate, Delacorte, 1988), sports novel for middle-grade readers set in Chicago in the 1980s, involving a Little League team made up partly of orphans and newly adopted youngsters. Before they were adopted, the narrator, T.J. (Tommy Jackson), 11, and his younger brother, The Moondance Kid (Billy), lived at the Dominican Academy run by Sister Marianne, and they keep up their ties mainly through Mop (Olivia Parrish), who is T.J.'s age and best friend, and whose greatest desire, like that of the other orphans at the academy, is to be adopted. She persuades T.J. to get her a place on the Elks, the Little League team coached by Jim Kennedy and his wife, Marla, because she knows that the Kennedys have been to the academy looking for a child and she wants to be in a position to impress them. Unfortunately, she becomes tongue-tied and clumsy every time she is around Marla. Since the academy is to be closed soon and the remaining children sent to another institution, the need to get Mop adopted is critical. At first the Elks are a terrible team, and even though T.J. refers to himself as the star, it is apparent that he is one of the worst members. His pressure to succeed is increased by his adoptive father, who once played on a major league team. Surprisingly, Moondance shows real promise as a pitcher; at least he throws hard, but often wide of the plate. When Jim Kennedy must go on a business trip and Marla takes over the coaching, the team begins to win, although they are taunted and derided by Mr. Treaster, the coach of their archrivals, the Eagles. They are helped by two unlikely coaches, Sister Carmelita, who was once Titi, star neighborhood pitcher, and Peaches, a wino who happens by their practice field. As the season progresses, Mop has a new worry. What will happen to Taffy, the llama owned by the academy? Peaches helps out in several ways. When Sister Carmelita, who is accident prone, is bilked out of her money for needy families by Buster Greene, he borrows a fierce cat named Four Times Seven, releases it in Buster's living quarters, and with friends braced against the door and T.J. and Moondance holding the window shut, demands the money. Buster slides it under the door and emerges at a run, his face badly scratched. Before the animal protection people come for Taffy, Peaches, who now does odd jobs for the academy, takes the llama to an empty store where he sometimes sleeps. He also gets Sister Carmelita to bring Moondance, T.J., and Mop, and, having diagnosed Moondance's pitching problem as the fear of hitting someone, teaches him to pitch with a store dummy in the batter's position and Mop catching. In the final game, a play-off between the Elks and the Eagles, with Moondance pitching and Mop catching, the score is tied. In the final inning, the Elks have the bases loaded and T.J. is up. The first two pitches are strikes because T.J., who is really afraid of the ball, moves back. On the third pitch, determined not to flinch, he closes his eyes and lets it hit him, thereby winning the game. Mop discovers that Marla has been as afraid of making a bad impression on her as she was afraid of Marla, and she is happily adopted. The academy is turned into a day-care center, and Taffy is returned to be a pet for the children. As in many baseball stories, games are described in detail. The conventional and somewhat implausible plot is strengthened by the narrator's voice, streetwise but young and worried below the surface, and Mop's character, tough, smart-alecky, yet touchingly vulnerable. Illustrations and some dialogue clues indicate that T.J., Moondance, and Peaches are black, while Mop and the Kennedys are white, and Sister Carmelita is probably Hispanic, but this interracial mix is never mentioned in the story. ALA.

**MICKLE** (*The Beggar Queen**), heroine of a trilogy of novels by Lloyd Alexander* set in the fictitious kingdom of Westmark*. In *Westmark*, she first appears as a pitiful waif, "drab as a street sparrow" with "a beaky nose in a narrow face," whose unusual talent for throwing her voice Count Las* Bombas employs in a spiritualist act. She is eventually revealed as the lost princess of Westmark, whom the unscrupulous prime minister had attempted to assassinate. In *The Kestrel*, she is the sturdy, resilient Queen Augusta, field general of the army, and bride-to-be of Theo*, former printer's devil now known as Captain Kestrel. In *The Beggar Queen*, she, Theo, and their supporters defeat Cabbarus, who has usurped the throne.

***MIDNIGHT HOUR ENCORES*** (Brooks*, Bruce, Harper, 1986), novel of a virtuoso cello artist and her father, publisher of a liberal ecological newsletter in Washington, D.C., and her discovery of the depth of their relationship. When the narrator, Sibilance T. Spooner, 16, was less than two days old, her mother, Connie, deeply involved in the more superficial aspects of hippie culture, decided that caring for a baby would limit her self-realization, and told her husband, Taxi (Cabot), to take the infant, whom she named Esalon Starness Blue, and go east. Now, sixteen years later, Taxi takes the girl, who has renamed herself, to see her mother in San Francisco, as he once promised to do, whenever she asks him. His preparations for the trip baffle his daughter. He buys an ancient Volkswagen bus, modified so that she can practice her cello on the way without jarring it, and duffle bags to replace their nice luggage. On the trip he tries in various other ways to give her an idea of the sixties, hoping to prepare her to understand and not hate the mother who cavalierly gave her away. He stops at a record store to select old discs of the period, which she finds musically offensive and he finds wildly overpriced, acquires a guitar, which, to her astonishment, he plays very well, visits an activist friend, Gwen, in Des Moines, only to discover that she has become a lesbian, and works his way back into the feel of the earlier time, with Sib composing a cello expression of all as he gives the explanation. Gradually, Sibilance reveals to the reader the real reason for the trip. From journalists who cover the European musical competitions that she has consistently won, she has learned of a Russian cello genius named Dzyga who, as a thirteen-year-old, won all the same competitions some thirty-six years earlier, then disappeared. She finds an old wire recording of his very distinctive playing and single-mindedly searches for other clues, finally discovering a contraband disc from Poland with the unmistakable style on cello in a string quartet. She writes the recording company, saying that she admires the venture and would like to be part of it if they plan future recordings, enclosing an audition tape, knowing that her own musical fame will at least get her a hearing. Some time later she gets a letter from a new school in San Francisco, asking her to come for an audition and play the concerto that she has never played except for the audition tape she sent to Poland. Her mother's place, to their surprise, is a handsome Victorian house in an affluent neighborhood. Connie has gone into real estate and become a stylish, very successful businesswoman. She sends Sib off with her secretary, Martin Meriweather, a handsome young dilettante and failed architectural student, to buy new clothes and see the town, shows Sib off to her arty friends at a cocktail party, and takes her to the run-down neighborhood where she finally swore off being a hippie. They spar verbally and, to her surprise, Sib likes her mother. At the audition, which Taxi has stayed to attend, Sibilance performs brilliantly, then for an encore, plays the sixties music they composed in the bus. The reaction is outraged, but because Dzyga insists, the board decides to accept her. When no one can find her, Connie hunts up Taxi, who never stays for the encores, tells him about it, and he leaves, believing that she has chosen her mother but told him goodbye with the music. After he pulls away, he discovers that she is in the back of the bus, with her cello, having rejected her mother's life and the marvelous school to return with him and go to Julliard as they had planned. The story is essentially a record of discovery. Since Taxi has always been non-directive, Sib thinks that her success has been her own making, and only through the trip and her San Francisco experience does she realize what her father has done for her all her life. Characterization of the three main figures is memorable. With his gentleness, honesty, and refusal to make himself look good at the expense of his ex-wife, Taxi exemplifies the genuine idealism of the sixties, while Connie has rejected her past and ironically become a successful 1980s figure. Dialogue is sharp and often witty. The structure, with frequent flashbacks and essential information withheld, creates suspense, and Sibilance's smart, rather thorny personality keeps her voice interesting and convincing. Fanfare; SLJ.

**MIGUEL MALDONADO** (*The Honorable Prison\**), Marta's father, whose outspoken articles about the country's tyrannical regime result in his and his family's imprisonment. Miguel came from the peasant class, managed to go to law school, met and married Margarita\*, of the moneyed class, and became a champion of peasants' rights. Although he is a kind and caring father, he is completely dedicated to his cause. Because he felt that the General would be a better ruler than the previous one, he supported him. When he, too, turned out to be extremely repressive, Miguel felt even more compelled to speak out against the ruler's policies. The several passages in which atrocities to the peasants are described gain the reader's sympathies for Miguel's efforts for reform.

**MISS MICHAELS** (*Tancy\**), white worker at the Freedmen's Bureau in Knoxford. She helps Tancy to find jobs, locate a place to live, and care for Jemmy. She also has a great influence on the girl's thinking, for example, urging her to save her money and not spend it on frivolous things, as many ex-slaves do. Miss Michaels is often angry and frustrated about the corruption and ineptness of the system that is supposed to help the freed slaves but only seems to compound their problems. She represents the idealistic and honest northern social worker.

**MISS PUDDIN GAITHER** (*Tancy\**), Cornelia Gaither, Tancy's mistress, wife of Mas Gaither, the owner of Gaither plantation and mill, and mother of Billy, Tancy's half-brother. A vain, pampered woman, seemingly almost simple but really very clever and all-seeing, she has a strong social awareness, is very conscious of appearances, and insists on good labor and proper behavior from her slaves, although on the whole she is fair and kind to them, considering the system. Upset by the departure of the slaves, whom she continues to consider hers, and the death of her son in the war, she has a strong survival instinct and internal resources that enable her to get by. Tancy notes with some surprise that Miss Puddin really does know how to keep house. When Tancy returns from Knoxford, Miss Puddin sees an opportunity to keep her at Gaithers' plantation and urges her to marry Stud, but Tancy has developed internal resources of her own and makes up her own mind about her life. When last seen, Miss Puddin tells Tancy, "I'll have you back yet."

**MOM MCALLISTER** (*December Stillness*\*), Kelly McAllister's commercial artist mother, who has developed a popular line of cards featuring unicorns, dragons, and similar fantasy figures. Kelly looks down on her work, asserting that she will do proper art when she grows up. Great-Aunt Eliza helps Kelly see that being a wife and mother limited her Mom's options. A kind of sandwich, Mom often intercedes for her husband (Dad\*) with her daughter and vice versa.

**THE MOONLIGHT MAN** (Fox\*, Paula, Bradbury, 1986), realistic novel of contemporary family life set for a month in Nova Scotia about a girl's growing understanding of her father. Catherine Ames, 15, a student at an exclusive girls' boarding school in Montreal, hardly knows her father, Harry, a novelist and travel-book writer, since her parents were divorced when she was three. Thus she is elated by the prospect of spending the summer vacation with him. When at year's end, June 7, he does not appear for her as agreed and sends no message, she manages to stay on, determined not to lose this chance to be with him. Three weeks later he calls her in high spirits, giving no explanation for his tardiness, just vague excuses, and tells her to come to Nova Scotia where he has taken a "funny little house" on the edge of a cliff. Although Catherine is not aware of it at the time, this is typical behavior for Harry. There, two nights later, she is shocked, disappointed, and angered to see still another side of him. He and two local men, a farmer and a bus driver, carouse at the Ames cottage all night to near insensibility. At five in the morning he tells her to drive the men home. This is a terrifying experience for her since the roads are dark, narrow, and winding. Long ago words of her mother ring in her ear, that wherever they lived, Harry always managed to "find all the local rats." She realizes now why he had not picked her up from school. He had been on a binge, drinking to escape "reason and obligation." As July moves along, Catherine becomes better acquainted with her father, seeing aspects of his character that both repel and attract her. After using an old shed in the countryside for target practice, he blithely lies to the young investigating Royal Mounted policeman, Alistair\* Macbeth, then takes her along with him and the Mountie to buy moonshine from local farmers, imbibing the product en route until he can barely move. Though he has married again, he brings a neighbor's wife home with him from town one afternoon, obviously intent on seducing her, Catherine notes when she stumbles upon them. Offsetting such episodes are memorably good ones, idyllic walks through the fields, restful and soul-searching talks, trips to the sea, tasty meals he prepares for her, and his generously buying a tricycle for the housekeeper's son. Well read, he shares his love of literature with her, often reading to her in his mellifluous voice, tells her of his many travels, and promises to take her to certain places, promises she now knows he means but will never keep, and, while sometimes he scorns or patronizes her, he validates her often as pretty, intelligent, and capable. Frustrated with his irresponsibility and deceit, she flies up at him once, calling him a "bastard." Yet she feels deep love and a curious kind of admiration for him and even finds herself wanting to take care of him.

He can be so charming and articulate that he easily talks himself out of situations, adapting his words and demeanor to the audience, a manipulative and opportunistic man. Catherine thinks that living with him is like living with a "crowd of people," he is so changeable. At the end, she returns to her mother with relief and joy. Yet she has respect and love for her father, too, a "moonlight man," the opposite of her normal, responsible, serious "daylight" mother, Beatrice. She tells Beatrice that she can see why her mother fell in love with Harry and also why she could not live with this chameleon of a man. The plot ambles, events serve characterization rather than action, and most episodes could easily be interchanged. Suspense is minimal, and what there is arises partly from the author's style, which employs understatement and sets of short, simple sentences for action scenes, later relieving the tension by more complex sentence structure. Suspense also comes from whether or not Catherine will make good her promise to herself to walk out because Harry is so disgusting. While the reader sympathizes with Catherine, especially in such places as once when she sees her father so drunk among the local people that he is on his knees crawling around and barking like a dog, and another time when he is so drunk that she must call on Reverend* Ross for help. The book is Harry's, however; he captures the reader's attention just as he takes over Catherine's life while she is with him, the skillfully drawn portrait of an aging, potbellied, dissipated alcoholic who cannot control the problems he knows he has but helps his daughter to acquire a great gift, to see that forgiveness and acceptance are qualities that keep the wheels of life oiled. ALA; SLJ.

**MOORE, LILIAN** (1909–      ), born in New York City; teacher, reading specialist, editor, poet. Moore is a graduate of Hunter College and studied further at Columbia University. She taught elementary school in New York City and for many years was a staff member of the Bureau of Educational Research. In 1957 she started the Arrow Book Club for Scholastic Book Services and for eight years she wrote monthly stories for *Humpty Dumpty* magazine. She worked as editor of an easy reader series for Grosset and Dunlap and wrote eleven "Wonder Books" in this series. She was also an editor for Thomas Y. Crowell Company. Over the years she has written many books for children, mostly picture books, easy readers, and poems. Two of her books of poems are *Sam's Place: Poems from the Country* (Atheneum, 1973), inspired by her husband's farm in upstate New York, and *Something New Begins* (Atheneum, 1982), an American Library Association Notable Book. In 1985 she was honored with the National Council of Teachers of English Award for Poetry for Children. An anthology she compiled, *To See the World Afresh* (Atheneum, 1974), was also an ALA Notable Book. Her poetic animal fantasy, *I'll Meet You at the Cucumbers** (Atheneum, 1988), was named to the *School Library Journal* Best Books list.

***MORE STORIES JULIAN TELLS*** (Cameron*, Ann, ill. Ann Strugnell, Knopf, 1986), five separate realistic episodes of family life set in a contemporary middle-class residential neighborhood and told by Julian, a child of about eight first met in *The Stories Julian Tells*. Julian's adventures revolve around his spunky little brother, Huey, and his best friend, clever, fun-loving Gloria, who lives a couple of houses away. They have to do with everyday matters, and sometimes feature his father as peacemaker or problem solver. One hot summer day, the children are bored, and Huey suggests that they visit Dad at his auto repair shop, a dangerous idea, Julian thinks, because Dad believes the world offers so many possibilities no one should ever get bored. They go anyway, impulsive, indiscreet Huey cautioned not to mention being bored, but he blurts it out anyway. Surprisingly, Dad says he gets bored, too, particularly on days so hot "frogs wear shoes." At his suggestion, they help him finish work early, and then he drives them to the river, where after they have dunked a while, they discover that frogs have hopped into their shoes left lying on the bank. Another day, Julian and Gloria bet on jumps, Julian winning every time. Then Gloria bets a movie ticket that she can make him see the setting sun from his eastern-exposure bedroom window. She wins by reflecting the sun on his wall with a mirror. Two episodes grow out of Julian calling Huey names. After Julian calls Huey a scaredy-cat for not jumping out of the moving swing onto a pile of sand, Huey practices from the top bedroom bunk and cuts himself badly. He eventually succeeds after eating broccoli and wearing his lucky T-shirt. Another time, Julian calls Huey "bean sprout," and Dad seems angry, brings a cardboard box, which he makes them open, and they discover two baby rabbits inside for pets. In the last episode, Dad solves the problem, too. Julian's bottle with a message in it gets caught on a bend in the river, and Gloria retrieves it, to Julian's great disappointment. Then, after Dad says that he must make a trip downriver, giving Julian another try at a bottle deposit, Julian suggests that all three make up bottle messages. Dad drives them to the bridge beyond the bend, where they throw the message-bottles in, with wishes. The book is aimed at children of about Julian's age, who are just beyond primers, to read to themselves, but never sounds primerish. It is almost all dialogue, vocabulary is easy, and sentences are short and uncomplicated but strongly composed and often pithy. Julian and his friends are typical in the things they do and the way they speak. Julian has a strongly developed sense of right and wrong and displays the usual over-dramatizing attitude of his age. He wonders why he has so many problems: "Really, I don't understand how I get into it [trouble] so often when I hate it so much." Afraid his father will be angry and punish him for thoughtlessly calling Huey bean sprout, he notes that his father has "cobra eyes" and smiles "like a tiger." The humor is gentle, growing naturally out of domestic situations, and often ironic. The view of life is affectionate and upbeat, interpersonal relationships are warm and respectful, and adults are supportive and natural and require good behavior but do not belabor it. The book is a consistently amusing, wholesome but never sentimental, instructive, or inspirational view of middle-class family life from the point of view of a loved, well-brought up, active child. Though the text does not specify, the illustrations show the characters as black. ALA; SLJ.

**MORTON BRIGGS** (*M. E. and Morton*\*), M. E.'s pleasant, shy brother of fourteen, whose learning disability and school retentions embarrass M. E. She even lies that she does not know him but gradually comes to see that, while the other children tease him for his awkwardness and take advantage of his slowness, they really like him because he is genuinely nice, a quality she sees that she herself lacks. She realizes that he even finds satisfaction in the children's perverse pleasure at teasing him. At the end she is able to value him for his good qualities, no longer is jealous of him, and expresses her love for him. When last seen, Morton is on his way to school, tagging behind the children but happy, proudly calling their attention to the skillful somersaults M. E. is turning. She shows off a little more then, just to please him.

***THE MOST BEAUTIFUL PLACE IN THE WORLD*** (Cameron\*, Ann, ill. Thomas B. Allen, Knopf, 1988), short, realistic, contemporary account of a few years in the life of young Juan in a poor family in the mountain village of San Pablo, Guatemala. Juan looks back on his early years with appreciation for the area's natural beauty and objectivity about his family's meager and difficult circumstances. After his father, a caretaker, runs out on his seventeen-year-old wife, she takes her baby and returns to her mother's house, which is already crammed with a dozen other members of the large extended family. The grandmother, who is a woman of means compared to most people because she owns her little house, sells *arroz con leche* (rice with milk) for a living in the local market. When Juan's mother remarries and his stepfather does not want Juan, Juan stays on with his grandmother, sleeping on the floor on rice bags. Juan is fairly happy, but he resents his little half-brother who has parents when he does not. One day his grandmother decides that he is old enough to work and sets him up on a likely corner as a shoeshine boy. He is careful and does well, soon earning a dollar a day, half as much as a grown man. He yearns, however, to go to school and wonders whether maybe his grandmother has not enrolled him because she wants his earnings. He sets about teaching himself to read, using signs and newspapers and soon is quite adept. When he brings up the matter of school to his grandmother, she apologizes for not having thought of sending him, saying she did not realize that he was already seven years old, and tells him that he must always stand up for what he wants. She promptly enrolls him, and when he is commended for his work and advanced to second grade, his grandmother confides that she too had wanted an education but was kept home by parents who wanted her wages. She tells him that she does not expect him to be a paragon, but she urges him always to do his best. The story ends with a discussion between them about the most beautiful place in the world, which is, perhaps, San Pablo. Then grandmother says that the most beautiful place in the world is "Anyplace you can hold your head up. Anyplace you can be proud of who you are." Juan thinks to himself: "where you love somebody a whole lot, and you know that person loves you, that's the most beautiful place in the world." The plot seems fragmented and some places are sentimental, like the ending. Juan, however, is a charming, plucky little fellow with an upbeat view of life in spite of his unfortunate circumstances, and the grandmother is a strong, sensible, courageous woman. There is some humor of irony, and the grandmother's words are often moralistic but suit their situations. The warm relationship between the grandmother and the boy, the upbeat tone, the picture of the poor in the mountain village, though limited, and the author's ability to elicit sympathy for them without overt statement are the book's best features. Language is simple enough for beginning readers but never primerish, and the sentence structure is uncomplicated. Child Study.

*MOTOWN AND DIDI* (Myers*, Walter Dean, Viking Kestrel, 1984), realistic novel subtitled "A Love Story," about two young people in Harlem who find each other despite the threatening drug culture of the 1980s. Raised in a series of foster homes, Motown (Frank Williams), 17, is now living in an abandoned building, working when he can, trying to save enough to get a place of his own. Having been emotionally hurt too often, he steers clear of people, except for Tutmose Rogers, a simple-minded fellow who runs a news stand, and the Professor, an old bookseller who befriends him and loans him books. Didi Johnson is an ambitious girl, determined to go to college despite her mother, Darlene, who has occasional mental lapses during which she wanders off, to return sometimes days later often battered and drunk, and her younger brother, Tony, who is in with a bad crowd led by a drug pusher, Touchy Jenkins. When she discovers that Tony is on drugs, Didi is so furious that she goes to the police, demanding that they arrest Touchy. This information is quickly relayed back to Touchy, who details a couple of underlings to beat her up and rape her. By chance, Motown sees them dragging her into a building. He rescues her, and later she finds him and thanks him. Although he is reluctant to let himself love anyone and she is determined not to care for someone with as few prospects as Motown, they feel a strong attraction to each other. Touchy sets Tony up to be arrested. He pretends that he is asking Tony to deliver some dope but knowing that he will first use a portion of it gets word to the police where he will be. Motown stumbles onto the situation, follows Tony to a roof, takes the drugs from him, and throws them away in time to save him from the police. Hearing that Touchy is going to get even with Motown, Didi goes to warn him, finds him a cheap apartment, and helps him fix it up. Didi is offered a partial scholarship from the University of Wisconsin, but before she accepts her mother has a stroke. She applies to City College instead. Although she fights against her feelings for Motown, she continues to see him. Touchy sends his subordinate, Reggie, with a gun to get Motown, but, knowing that Reggie is afraid to shoot him, Motown beats him up and throws the gun down a sewer. Touchy is warned by the major drug dealer who supplies him that he has failed three times to get rid of his "problem" and that maybe he is not big enough to hold his territory. Tony, finally realizing that he cannot handle the drugs, asks Didi to help him, and she agrees to go with him to see a social worker. First, however, he finds Touchy, who gives him some dope, saying that it is weak when actually it is almost pure. Tony overdoses and dies. Hysterical, Didi rushes to Motown and tells him to kill Touchy or she will do it herself. Motown buys a knife and sets off. The Professor finds Didi, who has misgivings, and they take a cab to try to intercept Motown. They come on the scene as Carlos, another of Touchy's punks, hearing the police siren approaching, refuses to shoot Motown. Touchy grabs the gun himself. Didi rushes between and is shot in the arm. She intervenes as Motown almost knifes Touchy, gets the gun away, and they watch as Touchy is arrested. The Professor decides to give his life's savings to Motown to get him a good start. Presumably Didi will go to City College, and together they will make something of their lives. Despite the gritty street scenes and details of poverty and misery in Harlem, the novel has a sentimental tone, probably because the reader is told, at length, about the emotions of both Motown and Didi rather than being shown by their actions. Motown is a stock self-made superman, righting wrongs, gentle by nature but implacable to evildoers, and the Professor is the *deus ex machina* by which the happy ending is achieved. There is a good deal of discussion about being a black warrior and standing by the tribe, which fails to ring true. C. S. King Winner.

**THE MOVES MAKE THE MAN** (Brooks*, Bruce, Harper, 1984), realistic sports novel focusing on an unusual friendship between a confident young black basketball whiz and a troubled white boy, set in Wilmington, N.C., evidently in the early 1960s. Although fatherless Jerome Foxworthy, 13, is bored with baseball, he recognizes the athletic skill of the shortstop on the white team playing an exhibition match. He is impressed by the strangeness of the well-dressed, attractive woman, obviously the boy's mother, who cheers and calls, "Bix! Bix!," from the sidelines. As the one black in the newly integrated junior high the next fall, Jerome has little trouble, although a prejudiced coach denies him the right to try out for the basketball team. When his mother is ill and he takes over the cooking, Jerome enters a Home Ec class and discovers that the only other boy, Braxton Rivers the Third, is Bix, the shortstop. Together they wage a revolt against the mock apple pie made of Ritz crackers. Jerome considers it a joke while Bix becomes very upset at the dishonesty of the fake apples and of the pretense that it is delicious. Bix drops the class, and Jerome loses track of him. As Jerome's mother recovers, he is able to slip out after dinner to pursue his great love, solo basketball practice. His favorite isolated court, deep in the woods, is too dark by this time, but he finds one near the railway tracks, and he practices his moves and trick shots every night. Once when a passenger train is stalled there, a black railroad worker bets that Jerome cannot beat his assistant in a little one on one, putting up his railroad lantern against Jerome's ball and taking side bets from the passengers. Jerome wins the lantern. The next night he goes back to the little court in the woods and, to his astonishment, finds Bix there, although he does not know how to play basketball. For the next six or eight weeks, Jerome teaches him, finding him remarkably adept, until they get to the stage to learn moves, the fakes and tricks that Jerome loves in the game. Bix refuses to try any of them. They quarrel, but two months later Bix shows up again and asks Jerome to provide the light and to referee in a game between him and his stepfather, who was a good college basketball player. If Bix wins, he will get to see his mother, now in a mental hospital in Durham; if he loses, he will stop needling his stepfather and begging to see her. Bix is determined to play it "pure and honest," with no fakes or tricky moves. The stepfather soon is ahead eight to two. Their underlying quarrel wells up, and the man tells Jerome how Bix, always determined to be honest, set his unstable mother into a wild suicide attempt when he told her, truthfully, that, no, he did not love her, meaning at that moment. Infuriated at the story, Bix starts to play with all the fakes he has seen Jerome use and soon wins. When Bix comes to dinner so that Jerome's mother can meet the boy before allowing her son to go to Durham with him, Bix puts on a false charm and, to rub in the insult, brings a mock apple pie. Nevertheless, Jerome goes to the hospital with Bix and his stepfather. When Bix goes into the ward, his mother does not recognize him. He pretends he is visiting the woman on the next bed, throws himself on her, and sobs. Then he gets up, clearly says, "Goodbye, Mother," and walks out the other end of the ward. After he is out of sight, his mother suddenly realizes who he is and screams, "Biixxx!". Later Jerome gets a postcard from Washington, D.C., with no message. He is not sure whether Bix, who has disappeared, is reaching out to keep in contact or trying another fake, a technique he picked up very quickly. Jerome wonders if he caused the change from honesty to trickery in Bix. The story is narrated by Jerome, a cocky but bright and likeable boy from a solid and loving family. There are strong scenes, but Bix's sudden ability at basketball moves is implausible, and the ending leaves unanswered questions. The theme seems to be that the nature of honesty is ambiguous. Is Bix's self-righteous honesty worthier than Jerome's frank fakes? Was Bix better telling his mother the truth than being the tricky character he becomes? How is the boy of thirteen surviving on his own? ALA; Boston Globe Winner; Newbery Honor; SLJ.

**MR. BLACKPOOL** (*The Secret Life of Dilly McBean**), the man-of-all-work at Dilly's house in Hennessey Depot. His wife is cook-housekeeper. Mr. Blackpool is big, tall, and dark: "his shock of inky hair was the blackest Dilly had ever seen." Mr. Blackpool has a habit of appearing and disappearing silently and, it seems, coincidentally wherever Dilly is, often in a black car. His behavior makes him appear sinister to both Dilly and the reader. Later Dilly learns that Mr. Blackpool has been instructed to guard Dilly. Mr. Blackpool fights magnificently with his great strength in the battle against Dr. Keenwit.

**MR. BOB WEEMS** (*December Stillness**), homeless Vietnam veteran, known as the bagman, whom Kelly McAllister befriends and who changes her outlook on life. In the only passage where he talks much, he describes himself as a "dumb kid and I wanted to do something for my country, you know, for Uncle

Sam, so I joined the army . . . [and was] sent to 'Nam. . . . It was like dying and going to hell.'' He spends his days in the public library looking at books of war dead, his black bags of possessions always beside him, and lives by scrounging from garbage bins. He refuses help from everyone, keeping people at bay, among other ways, by looking at them through a "telescope" fashioned of his hands. He is a memorable if stereotypical figure.

**MR. HENRY WHEATLEY** (*Quentin Corn**), small-town handyman who befriends Quentin Corn, assuming that the pig is a runaway boy but respectfully never asking questions. He appears to be gruff and hurrying at first but proves unexpectedly congenial and caring. For no reward except personal satisfaction, he has taken the large, poor Mears family under his wing, especially Andy*, the only boy. He remembers Andy's birthday with a bird-shaped whistle that he has whittled purposely for him. For years Mr. Wheatley has sought the hand of Mrs.* Ada Benway in marriage. When Pete, her runaway son, returns and sauces his mother, Mr. Wheatley proposes once more, and, this time accepted, lays down the law to Pete, telling him "to shape up or ship out." The reader is left to guess what course Pete will follow. In his youth, Mr. Wheatley was with the railroad, ambitious to become an engineer, but was blackballed for some trouble. Now reformed, he enjoys an excellent reputation in town for industry, decency, and community spirit. He is an engaging type, appropriate for the plot.

**MR. HOMER ORBED** (*The Secret Life of Dilly McBean**), the bouncy round man with ginger hair who is Dilly's solicitous guardian. He is some sort of scientist and was a professional friend of Dilly's father. Dilly has not heard of him until he shows up one day and asks Dilly's opinion about living in a house of his own and going to public school. It comes out later that Mr. Orbed has known all along about Dilly's gift of magnetism, has decided that Dilly's gift be developed, and has persuaded Dr. McEvoy to come to Hennessey Depot to do it. In the battle with Dr. Keenwit, he fences with a sword hidden inside the gold-headed cane he always carries. He is a sinister, comic, and heroic figure all in one.

**MR. HUNTER** (*Cracker Jackson**), Jackson Hunter's easygoing, always joking father. Mr. and Mrs.* Hunter got divorced because he refused to get serious, apparently a problem in his interpersonal relationships because this was his third marriage. Jackson discovers that his father can sometimes be very serious, however. Mr. Hunter turns off the silly chatter when Jackson tells him that Alma* Alton is being abused by her husband. Mr. Hunter insists that Jackson inform Mrs. Hunter, who then attempts to intervene on Alma's behalf. Mr. Hunter also helps take Alma to the safe house.

**MR. NAIDO** (*So Far from the Bamboo Grove**), janitor at the girls' school where Yoko* is enrolled. A stutterer, he has been unable to get another job, and he is mimicked cruelly by the snobbish girls. He is kind and helpful to

Yoko, letting her go through the trash for usable paper and other supplies that she cannot possibly buy, and he sells the cans she finds along with the ones he collects and gives her the money. When she wins the essay contest and must have a male guardian to attend the banquet, she asks him, and he is pleased. When she speaks slowly to him, his speech improves and she thinks that he might be curable.

**MR. PRATT** (*The Facts and Fictions of Minna Pratt**), Minna Pratt's father, a psychologist. Instead of using words like "deviant" or "obsessive," he says that Minna's mother is in "the land of La." Minna realizes that he loves her mother's erratic ways and is more than a little different and obsessive himself. He fails at teaching McGrew* to play baseball, just getting aches and pains, conducts recorded symphonies (which Lucas* Ellerby enjoys watching), and sings arias to records in his office. He spends a lot of time on his books and patients, is often immersed in thought, and is much in love with Mrs.* Pratt. They write notes to each other, signed "luv," and kiss with great passion anywhere in the house and even in the yard, leaning against a tree. All this fascinates Minna.

**MRS. ADA BENWAY** (*Quentin Corn**), talkative, warmhearted owner of the rooming house at which Quentin lodges. She mothers all her boarders, feeding them and coddling them, and insofar as possible running their lives. She takes to Quentin, who is mannerly, perhaps because her own son, Pete, was insolent and has run away, and gives Quentin Pete's room and some of his clothes. She has consistently refused Mr.* Henry Wheatley's proposals of marriage because she says he "has a dark disposition." Confronted by the return of her thieving son, she gives in and agrees to marry her patient suitor. She discovers Quentin's "beautiful" soprano and arranges for him to join the church choir. Sentimental Mrs. Benway is a familiar type who promotes and suits the plot.

**MRS. BLACKPOOL** (*The Secret Life of Dilly McBean**), Dilly's cook and housekeeper, wife of Mr.* Blackpool. Dilly's hound-like dog, Contrary*, takes a liking to her. His affection troubles her because she does not like dogs and provides some comedy. She is a fine cook and likes to feed Dilly. In the battle with Dr. Keenwit, she karate chops opponents in a magnificent manner. Her ability amazes Dilly because she is a small, seemingly meek woman.

**MRS. BRIGGS** (*M. E. and Morton**), M. E.'s worried mother, who works in a hospital. Her husband runs a bookstore. She has ambivalent feelings about both M. E. and Morton*. She seems proud of M. E.'s intellectual achievements, though the girl does not feel that they are sufficiently acknowledged, but constantly pushes her socially. She spends much time with Morton on arithmetic and also urges him to bring home friends. She seems, quite understandably, to have trouble coping with two such diverse children. She does not want to make

Morton feel inferior by praising M. E. too much; yet M. E. misses the attention. Mrs. Briggs often talks to an invisible "listener" about her problems. Much of the book's action takes place while the children are home and she is at work. At the end, she seems to appreciate both more for what they are.

**MRS. CONNORS** (*The Third Eye**), Karen Connors's very socially conscious mother. She urges Karen to submerge her psychic gift because she says that it provoked so much notoriety when Karen was little that they had to move. She is also afraid that the gift will prevent Karen from being popular. She very much wants Karen to be as strong a social leader as she says she was in her youth. All this proves to be lies, as she admits in private conversation to Karen in the end. She also admits that the incident that aroused so much attention and that she attributed to Karen was really the result of her own psychic gift. A troubled woman, she is both likeable and unsympathetic.

**MR. SCULLY** (*One-Eyed Cat**), a small, stooped old man who always dresses in a green and black plaid wool shirt and black trousers. He lives in an old house that is cluttered with a lifetime's accumulation of possessions. Ned does chores for him, like cutting wood and carrying out trash, for a few cents a week. It is at his place that Ned first sees the one-eyed cat. Mr. Scully says that it is one of the several feral cats that frequent the woods and his back yard. The cat sleeps on an old quilt on top of an abandoned icebox near the decrepit shed. Ned and Mr. Scully become friends through their common concern for the handicapped creature, and, after Mr. Scully suffers a stroke, Ned visits him regularly at the nursing home. There he tells Mr. Scully that he wounded the cat. By this point in the story, Ned is convinced that he really did maim the animal.

**MRS. HUNTER** (*Cracker Jackson**), Jackson Hunter's decisive, well-organized, serious mother. She has never been particularly friendly with Alma* Alton, regarding Alma's relationship as baby-sitter for Jackson purely a business arrangement. She does not like Alma to call Jackson Cracker because she detests nicknames, disapproves of Alma's easygoing ways, and worries a lot. She also dislikes Mr.* Hunter's joking. She is responsible for getting Alma to the hospital and eventually to the safe house in Avondale.

**MRS. MOORE** (*Sweet Creek Holler**), hateful neighbor of the Shortts, who spreads lies about them and other neighbors and causes trouble for Mama* Shortt. Mrs. Moore gossips that Nit* Purvis "takes advantage" of little girls, especially the Shortt girls, and even spreads the rumor that he is the father of the baby of Lou* Jean, his daughter. Mama sensibly cautions her daughters about reacting to Mrs. Moore, reminding them that because somebody says something does not make it so. Mrs. Moore is the stereotypical small-town troublemaker.

**MRS. PRATT** (*The Facts and Fictions of Minna Pratt**), Minna Pratt's mother, who writes novels for children and whose letters from fans provide humor. She is casual about housework, cannot keep the wash straight, and hates to cook, but she is compulsive about answering every fan letter promptly and getting facts straight for her readers in her books and in her replies to their letters. Instead of asking questions mothers normally ask, she is inclined to query Minna about such things as whether or not she thinks of love and if she has been in love with an older man. When Minna, however, having fallen in love with Lucas* Ellerby, longs for such a discussion, her mother ironically does not ask. Mrs. Pratt allows Lucas's frogs to be housed temporarily in her writing room and says that they love her stories. She and Mr.* Pratt are much in love, and the scene in which they kiss, described as the children view them, is one of the book's funniest.

**MRS. SCALLOP** (*One-Eyed Cat**), housekeeper for the Wallis family, whose voice is "as sharp and grinding as a woodcutter's saw," in Ned's opinion. She often insults him and is so contradictory in her speech and behavior that he thinks she is very silly. She tries to compensate for her feelings of insecurity by dominating the Wallises, even Mrs.* Wallis, who often feels compelled to speak up to her. Mrs. Scallop enjoys cooking and immodestly praises her ability. Reverend* Wallis gets her a position in a local nursing home, where she seems quite happily in control of things. Ned sees her there when he visits Mr.* Scully, and she is no less disrespectful to the boy then. A flat figure, almost a type, she is a foil for Reverend Wallis as well as Mrs. Wallis.

**MRS. WALLIS** (*One-Eyed Cat**), Ned Wallis's Mama, wife of the Reverend* James Wallis. She has suffered from arthritis for several years, so much so that she is largely confined to her room. Although removed from events by her illness, she knows what is going on in the house and does not let Mrs.* Scallop dominate her. She has an alert and perceptive mind and is, Ned observes, as much interested in what he is thinking as in what he does. Relieved of much of her pain by a new treatment, at the end of the story she is able to walk outside by herself and thus meets Ned at the Makepeace mansion. There she confides that she saw him on the night he fired the rifle and that years before she had run out on her family because she felt intimidated by her husband's goodness. More than any other character, she helps Ned come to terms with what he has done. She also points out to him that he cannot be sure he is the one who maimed the cat.

**MYERS†, WALTER DEAN** (1937–        ), born in Martinsburg, W. Va.; editor, novelist. He grew up in New York City and attended Empire State College, N.Y. From 1955 to 1958 he served in the United States Army and from 1970 to 1977 worked as a senior editor for Bobbs Merrill publishers, also teaching part time creative writing and black history during this period. Since 1977 he has been a free-lance writer. All of his more than thirty books either take place in Harlem or have some strong element of black experience in the incidents or language. Some of his novels for middle-grade readers are lighthearted, like *Fast Sam, Cool Clyde, and Stuff†* (Viking, 1975) and *Me, Mop, and the Moondance Kid\** (Delacorte, 1988). *Scorpions\** (Harper, 1988) has a protagonist of about the same age but draws a much darker picture of city life, of gangs and shootings. It was a Newbery Award Honor book and was named to both the American Library Association Young Adult and Notable Books lists. In both *Hoops†* (Delacorte, 1981) and its sequel, *The Outside Shot* (Delacorte, 1984), a basketball star fights off underworld efforts to get him to fix a game. Three of his novels have won the Coretta Scott King Award: *The Young Landlords* (Viking, 1979), a story of Harlem neighborhood buddies, *Motown and Didi\** (Viking, 1984), a novel of young love under very difficult circumstances, and *Fallen Angels\** (Scholastic, 1988), a Vietnam War story with a protagonist from Harlem. *Fallen Angels* was also named to the American Library Association Young Adult list and the *School Library Journal* Best Books list. He has also written as Walter M. Myers.

# N

**NANCY** (*Dogsong**), the Eskimo girl-woman Russel Susskit saves late in the novel. Out on the tundra "because the missionaries had told her it [to be pregnant and unmarried] was a sin she had been driven by her mind . . . out . . . to die on the snowmachine," but she became afraid, tried to go back, had run out of gas, walked, and has fallen in the cold when Russel finds her. She is very young, not much older than he, and provides the means technically in a series of scenes that somewhat parallel those of his running dreams for him to do a heroic deed on behalf of someone else. She is further undeveloped as a character.

**NAYLOR†, PHYLLIS REYNOLDS** (1933–     ), born in Anderson, Ind.; educator, prolific writer. She attended Joliet Junior College and received her B.A. degree in psychology from American University, Washington, D.C. She has taught in elementary school in Illinois, was executive secretary to the Montgomery County Education Association in Rockville, Md., and editorial assistant on the *NEA Journal* before deciding, in 1960, to devote her full professional time to writing. Some of her novels are problem stories, like *The Solomon System†* (Atheneum, 1983), about a family in the process of divorce, which won the Child Study Award, and *The Keeper** (Atheneum, 1986), about a boy struggling with his father's mental illness, which was named to both the American Library Association Young Adult and Notable Books lists. Some of them are mysteries, like *Night Cry** (Atheneum, 1984), a story of suspense and kidnapping which won the Edgar Allan Poe Award. Some are lighter, like *The Agony of Alice** (Atheneum, 1985), an ALA Notable Book, and *Alice in Rapture, Sort Of* (Atheneum, 1989), amusing but still sensitive growing-up stories. Naylor has also written two novels for adults and nonfiction for both adults and children.

**NELSON, THERESA** (1948–     ), born in Beaumont, Tex.; novelist for middle-grade and young adult readers. Her book, *Devil Storm* (Orchard, 1987), is a story of the Great Storm of 1900 on the Bolivar Peninsula between Galveston Bay and the Gulf of Mexico, a region near where she grew up in a family of eleven children. In *The 25¢ Miracle** (Bradbury, 1986), also set in Texas, a girl's attempts to beautify the gritty trailer court where she and her father live eventually lead to a greater understanding and hope for a better life for both of them. It was named to the *School Library Journal* list of Best Books for Children. Nelson lives with her husband and family in Kolanah, N.Y.

**NICHOLAS PINKERTON** (*Unclaimed Treasures**), Willa's twin brother, whom she always introduces as her younger brother because he followed her by seven minutes, a statement he never bridles at simply, Willa says, because that's the way Nicky is. Nicholas likes to experiment with language and often comes up with well-turned phrases. He is a realist, occasionally a cynic, but on the whole is easygoing and sensitive. He warns Willa of trouble if she maintains her infatuation for Matthew. He and Willa get on very well and share confidences. Usually mature in behavior, he acts like a very pleased little boy when Matthew Morris takes an interest in his drawings. Likeable and well depicted as a character, a fine foil for Willa and Horace* Morris, Nicholas grows up to become a successful painter.

*NIGHT CRY* (Naylor*, Phyllis Reynolds, Atheneum, 1984), novel of mystery and suspense, set at Crow's Point in Mississippi hill country in the contemporary period, involving a kidnapping and a daring rescue. Since her younger brother died after being thrown by his horse, Sleet, a year earlier, motherless Ellen April Stump, 13, has feared the animal, although she used to enjoy riding him. She is relieved when her father, Joe*, hires Jimmy-Clyde*, 14, the retarded boy who delivers their groceries on his bicycle, to tend to Sleet and clean his stall while he is off on his new job, which involves traveling. Still, she is uneasy being left alone in their isolated mountain farm with only the big yellow dog, Turbo, for companionship. Her disquiet is increased by Granny* Bo, an old woman whose cabin is a forty-minute walk over the hill trail from their house. Every few days Ellen visits her, to see that she is all right, and listens to her tales of how the devil from old man Keat went into Sleet, how "haints" roam the hills, and how a night cry sounds a warning for the hearer. Alone at night, Ellen is startled by a man coming from the barn, and when he approaches the window she threatens to set the dog on him. He tells her that he has his sick wife in a derelict cabin on the other side of the ridge, and he needs food for her. Ellen sets a bag of food on the porch, which he takes, but the next morning he is back, insisting on working for food until his wife is better and he can move on. Joe, suspicious at finding him working in the garden, softens when the man tells him that his wife is mentally ill and he is trying to get her to her sister in Biloxi. By the time Joe goes off again, Gerald is a fixture at the Stump farm, taciturn but hard working. Ellen goes with a friend to a celebration in nearby Millville, where a local man, now a film producer in California, has donated an auditorium and returned with his wife and four-year-old son, Jason, to dedicate it. A couple of days later Ellen hears the news: Jason Cory is missing, evidently kidnapped. The party line is alive with rumors, most of them about Granny Bo, who is locally distrusted. Ellen also overhears gossip implicating her father. She catches Gerald in a couple of lies, and while she conceals her knowledge, she is terrified, not knowing whom she can trust. At night she hears the cry of a child, cut off in the middle. She hikes up to the ridge and climbs to a lookout her brother fixed in a tree, from which she can see the deserted cabin where Gerald is staying. After more than an hour of waiting, she sees a woman take a small boy to the outhouse, her hand over his mouth. Ellen sneaks around the far side of the old cabin and lights a rubbish pile afire. As Gerald and the woman rush to put it out, Ellen ducks into the cabin and gets Jason. Back at her own house she looks frantically for a hiding place, then pops Jason into the oven. Gerald appears a minute later, having cut the phone wires, and sees her trying to make a call. She tells him that Granny Bo has broken her hip, and that she is trying to call Dr. George. Only half believing her, Gerald searches the house. They are interrupted by Jimmy-Clyde delivering groceries. Ellen, sticking to her story, tells him to ride his bike for Dr. George and ask him to get an ambulance to Granny Bo's cabin. When Gerald leaves briefly, Ellen moves Jason from the oven to Sleet's stall, her fear of the man overcoming her terror of the horse. They crouch among bales of hay while Gerald searches. Then Ellen takes Jason in front of her on Sleet, plunges out of the barn past the woman, and rides desperately for Granny Bo's cabin, where Dr. George, the ambulance driver, and the sheriff are all talking to the old woman, puzzled by the false summons. The story builds to a breathtaking climax, exploiting Ellen's feeling of isolation and growing suspicion of everyone around her, and while a reader early knows that Gerald is not what he claims to be, the suspense does not depend on identifying the kidnapper but on escaping him. The mountain and small-town people are well drawn, and even Gerald is not a standard villain but a complex and interesting character. Poe Winner.

**NIT PURVIS** (*Sweet Creek Holler**), town drunk and father of pretty Lou* Jean Purvis. Christine Ratliff calls him a "card" because he tells such funny jokes and is so jolly when he has been drinking. He often swears to quit but never does. He tries to comfort Lou Jean when she tells him that she is pregnant and to keep her mother, his wife, from berating her, even swearing on his coming grandbaby to stop drinking, but he reneges this time, too. After he saves the Shortt girls from the snakes at Copperhead Bridge (the snakes miss him and strike his liquor bottle), Mrs.* Moore spreads stories of sexual misconduct about him and young girls. He knows that Lou Jean has been setting fires and tries to get her to own up about it but fails. He is a likeable and decent man and a foil to his increasingly hateful, vengeful, and emotionally unstable wife.

**NIXON†, JOAN LOWERY** (1927–      ), born in Los Angeles, Calif.; teacher and author best known for her many mystery and suspense novels for children and adolescents. She received her bachelor's degree from the University of South

California in journalism and her teaching certificate from California State College, married Hershell Nixon, a petroleum geologist, and made her home in Texas. Of her more than four dozen books of fiction for young readers, three for adolescents have won the Edgar Allan Poe Award, *The Kidnapping of Christina Lattimore*† (Harcourt, 1979), which improvises on the Patty Hearst case; *The Seance*† (Harcourt, 1980), a murder-mystery set in an East Texas town; and *The Other Side of Dark** (Delacorte, 1986), in which a high school girl who awakens from a long coma is in danger from the man who injured her and killed her mother because she is able to identify him. Two books have been nominated for the Edgar Allan Poe Award, *The Mysterious Red Tape Gang*† (Putnam, 1974), for elementary readers, and *The Ghosts of Now** (Delacorte, 1984), a story for teenagers about a high school girl's harrowing attempt to bring to justice the hit-and-run driver who injured her younger brother. Nixon's stories, particularly those for older readers, are tense thrillers, fast moving, well paced, and stylistically superior to most of this genre.

# O

**O'DELL†, SCOTT** (1903–1989), born in Los Angeles, Calif.; author of novels widely accepted as among the strongest American historical fiction in the last half of the twentieth century. Active well into his ninth decade, he donated the Scott O'Dell Award for the best historical novel dealing with the western hemisphere and won it for *Streams to the River, River to the Sea** (Houghton, 1987), a story of the Indian woman, Sacagawea, who accompanied the Lewis and Clark expedition to explore the Northwest Territory. Another novel, *My Name Is Not Angelica* (Houghton, 1989), was also highly honored. O'Dell's best known book was published almost thirty years earlier and remains highly popular: *Island of the Blue Dolphins*† (Houghton, 1960). A survival story of a girl stranded on a Pacific island, it was a Newbery Award winner, named to the Fanfare, *Choice*, and Lewis Carroll lists, and chosen by the Children's Literature Association as one of the Top Ten American Books of all time. *The Black Pearl*† (Houghton, 1967), a story of pearl divers in Baja California, *Sing Down the Moon*† (Houghton, 1970), about the disastrous relocation of the Navaho Indians in the late nineteenth century, and *The King's Fifth*† (Houghton, 1966), a novel of the Spanish conquistadors seeking gold, were all Newbery Award Honor books. His trilogy, *The Captive* (Houghton, 1979), *The Feathered Serpent* (Houghton, 1981), and *The Amethyst Ring* (Houghton, 1983), concerns the Spanish conquest and destruction of the Maya culture. Typically, he employed an emotionally restrained first-person narrator, a device that works well in situations where understatement adds to the sense of endurance but sometimes causes underdeveloped characterization.

**OLD PEPPER** (*Unclaimed Treasures**), great-grandfather of Porky Atwater, neighbor boy of Willa Pinkerton. Old Pepper is an ancient, "dried apple" of a man who often speaks in run-on sentences, keeps an old parrot called Bella-Marie who also speaks in run-on sentences, is pushed around the near-neighborhood by Porky in a wheelbarrow, sometimes wanders naked in his backyard, and hunts for birds. Although usually a comic figure, he can be shrewd and witty. He maintains that ordinary and extraordinary are the same thing, meaning that it is not the nature of the thing itself that determines its nature but the observer's point of view. In a wild, slapstick scene, he manages to get Horace* Morris and Willa to the hospital. He manipulates the steering wheel while Horace manages the pedals. Once there, he gets them inside where the action is by stoutly asserting that he is *Dr*. Pepper, a stunt he pulls off with aplomb.

**OLIVE JOHNSON** (*Come Sing, Jimmy Jo*\*), mother of James and wife of Jerry* Lee. When she became pregnant at fifteen or younger and her boy friend took off for the Navy rather than face her father, she ran away and joined the Johnson Family singers, marrying Jerry Lee and leaving her baby for Grandma to bring up. A shallow woman, she has never appreciated her mother-in-law, considering her an old-fashioned country hillbilly, and she has never taken much interest in her son. When the manager they hire at her insistence wants James to join the group, she has mixed feelings, being ambitious to play at better places than their usual tent meetings but also jealous of her own son's success. She changes her name to Keri Sue, renames James Jimmy Jo, and speaks for him in interviews, even knocking a year off his age so he will seem cuter, but she resents losing some of her star status. Whether she and Uncle* Earl, Jerry Lee's younger brother, are already lovers is not explicit, but it is clear that they hope to leave the others behind and make a success in Nashville.

**ONEAL†, ZIBBY (ELIZABETH BISGARD ONEAL)** (1934–      ), born in Omaha, Nebr.; best known as the author of sensitive novels for young adults. She attended Stanford University and received her B.A. degree from the University of Michigan, where she later served as a lecturer in English. Although she wrote *War Work* (Viking, 1971), a mystery story set during World War II, for middle-grade readers and several books for younger children, her reputation rests mainly on three novels for older readers: *The Language of Goldfish* (Viking, 1980), in which a troubled girl attempts suicide and gradually works her way back to mental health, *A Formal Feeling*† (Viking, 1982), of a teenaged girl's struggles to resolve her ambivalent feelings about her deceased mother and her new stepmother, and *In Summer Light*\* (Viking, 1985), in which a talented girl struggles to free herself artistically and emotionally from the domination of her father. *A Formal Feeling* won the Christopher Award, and *In Summer Light* was highly honored as winner of the *Boston Globe-Horn Book* Award. It was named to both the American Library Association Notable Books and Young Adult lists, to the *School Library Journal* Best Books list, and to the *Horn Book* Fanfare list. All three novels are meticulously crafted, dealing with intense but restrained emotion, full of sensory detail that brings the setting to life, never exploiting the situation for sensational effect. Oneal is married to a surgeon, has two children, and lives in Ann Arbor, Mich.

***ONE-EYED CAT*** (Fox*, Paula, Bradbury, 1984), realistic novel of family life set from September to April in 1935 in a semi-rural area in New York State overlooking the Hudson River. For his eleventh birthday, only child Ned Wallis receives a coveted Daisy air rifle from his Uncle* Hilary, the brother of his mother, Mrs.* Wallis, who has been invalided by arthritis. Ned's elation over the gift is soon dispelled by his father, the Reverend* Mr. James Wallis, a Congregational minister, who orders him to put the gun aside until he is fourteen. That night, Ned steals to the attic of their big, old family home, removes the gun from its box, and takes it outside, where he playfully sights and aims with it, then, attention caught by a shadowy shape by the old shed, involuntarily presses the trigger and fires at it. For weeks thereafter, Ned is haunted by the conviction that he has harmed a living being. He becomes convinced that his victim is a one-eyed cat "gray as a mole with matted fur," one of several feral cats that frequent the surrounding woods and the yard of old Mr.* Scully, who lives down the road and for whom Ned does small chores, and by the fear that his deed is known. After firing the shot, Ned had glanced upward toward the attic where he thought he detected the outline of a person's head against the window. Was it his father who saw? or his mother? or sharp-tongued Mrs.* Scallop, the bullying housekeeper? Ned diligently sneaks scraps of food for the cat, lies to his parents about his abstracted manner and lowering grades, especially as cold weather intensifies his fears for the cat. He refuses Uncle Hilary's invitation to spend Christmas vacation in the Carolinas because of his obligation to the cat. Then Mr. Scully suffers a stroke and must enter a nursing home, his daughter sells the house, and Ned falls ill and is unable to continue caring for the animal. When recovered, he takes to tramping the hills and woods, sometimes stopping by the empty old Makepeace mansion whose grounds abut those of the Wallises, where on one occasion he sees what he thinks is the one-eyed cat. He visits the nursing home, where he confides his guilty secret to the old man and senses in the press of the dying fingers understanding and forgiveness. A new treatment gives Mrs. Wallis greater mobility, and one night in mid-April, she follows Ned on a night walk to the Makepeace verandah. The two watch the one-eyed cat and his family play in the moonlight, Ned confesses, his mother informs him that hers was the face at the window, and conversation between the mother and son leads Ned to the relieved understanding that everyone makes mistakes and that it is all right to be less than perfect. Although the plot is thin and its resolution somewhat abrupt and puzzling and the book has a static air, characters are boldly sketched, and it is easy to sympathize with Ned, whose fears and uncertainties seem appropriate for a youth of his religious and moral upbringing. Much of the book's appeal comes from the small details of Ned's reflections and observations of life with mother, father, and community, which seem seen at a distance, as though through a mirror, and create the impression of memoir rather than lived experience. Style is vivid with imagery: the family home is a "big, ailing old house," the parsonage appears as a "mean, small house," after treatments his mother "feels like silk," and his father sometimes speaks "in a cemetery voice." Some phrases, however, strike false notes. Ned was "pretty sure he'd never seen her [a neighbor woman] without an infant clinging to some part of her body" and a school chum Ned's age describes her friend as a "skinny little beetle," turns of expression that seem to voice the author's observations rather than those of the characters. ALA; Child Study; Fanfare; Newbery Honor.


*ON MY HONOR* (Bauer*, Marion Dane, Clarion, 1986), brief realistic novel of a drowning in the Vermilion River near Starved Rock State Park, Illinois, in the 1980s. Neighbors and best friends, Joel Bates and Tony Zabrinsky, both twelve, start out to bike to the state park, Joel first having asked and received permission, to his dismay, from his father, who reminds him that he is on his honor. Joel knows that Tony wants to climb the dangerous bluffs, and he has been counting on his cautious father to decide that the ride is too far. Typically, Tony says that his mother agrees, though he has not asked her, and claims Joel's ten-speed Schwinn instead of his own clunker. When they reach the bridge, Tony suggests a swim and taunts Joel, who knows that the river is dangerous. Unwilling to seem cowardly, Joel agrees and, to show Tony that he is not afraid, dares him to swim out to a sandbar. It proves more difficult than Joel has expected, and when he makes it, he discovers that Tony is nowhere in sight. At first he thinks that his friend has turned back and is hiding to tease him, but he remembers that Tony has never done much swimming in the city pool, preferring to play in the shallow end, and he realizes that the boy swims very poorly. Desperately, he dives in the muddy water, searching for Tony, then runs to the road and flags down the car of a teenaged couple. The older boy dives in repeatedly with no success. Reluctant to get involved further because his girl friend has faked illness to leave work, he accepts Joel's assurance that he will notify the police. As he heads home, Joel invents a story about refusing to swim with Tony and riding on toward Starved Rock, then finding it too far and coming back alone. When his father questions him, he forgets the story and says just that he got tired and came back while Tony rode on. He takes his little brother, Bobby, 4, on his paper route but feels disoriented, unreal. That evening he cannot seem to wash the smell of the river off in the shower. After blaming everyone else, including his father for giving him permission, Joel finally blames himself and tells the truth to his father, Tony's parents, and the police, who bring back Tony's bike and clothes. His sympathetic father sits by his bed and points out that Tony's death will be a hard thing to live with, but that there is nothing else to do. The single incident story is contrived to teach a middle-grade audience about responsibility and the betrayal of trust. Characters are functional, with Tony and Joel the only developed figures, painted with broad strokes in the early chapters. Joel's panic, fear, grief, and self-blame are well handled, however, and convincing, and there is no attempt to soften the conclusion or to sugarcoat the moral implications. ALA; Newbery Honor; SLJ.

**OOGRUK** (*Dogsong**), blind old Eskimo friend and mentor of Russel Susskit. Oogruk has lived alone for many years, and, until Russel moves in, has been dependent upon the villagers' generosity for meat. He especially enjoys caribou eyes, which he considers a great delicacy. He senses Russel's need for stability and tells old stories to Russel in a voice "like strong music." One of the founders of their village many years ago, he says that the people have forgotten the old ways because of the missionaries. When the people gave up the old songs they gave up themselves, he says, because people *are* the songs. He thinks that maybe the songs will come back if people live in the old way. Russel then decides that he wants to become a song by learning the old ways, and Oogruk instructs him orally as was the custom. Oogruk dies, in the old fashion, out in the snow alone when he feels the time has come. He is the novel's most compelling figure.

**OOM KOOS** (*Waiting for the Rain**), owner of the farm in the South African veld on which Tengo lives and which Frikkie expects to inherit. Oom Koos, Frikkie's uncle, is kind but demanding. He assumes white supremacy is a God-given right and says that he will fight the blacks' desire to have a share in ruling "with the last drop of my blood." He thinks liberals overseas are stirring up the blacks (whose minds he regards as deficient) and giving them ideas that they are the whites' equals. He believes that the Dutch descendants of the Boers should have the land because they won it from the blacks. Oom Koos represents the traditional white attitude in South Africa.

**ORSON** (*The Facts and Fictions of Minna Pratt**), Minna Pratt's co-musician in the chamber group that rehearses at concert hall. He has tight black curls and a sly smile, appreciates big, unusual words and like Imelda* enjoys strange facts, and drops a new stunner, like "rebarbative," at almost every rehearsal. He refers to Mozart as "WA" and plays second violin "with a sloppy serenity, rolling his eyes and sticking out his tongue, his bowing long and sweeping and beautiful even when out of tune," which is usually.

***THE OTHER SIDE OF DARK*** (Nixon*, Joan Lowery, Delacorte, 1986), realistic mystery-detective novel, set in Houston, Texas, in the mid–1980s. Stacy McAdams, 17, tells of her shock upon awakening from a four-year coma and finding that she is no longer a little girl, that her mother is dead, and that her life may be in danger from the same man who murdered her mother. When the newspapers publicize the story of the "Sleeping Beauty" awakened who knows who killed her mother and shot her but cannot recall his face or name, Stacy's shock turns to fear for her own life and then to hatred for the man who has caused her family so much trouble. Such problems as getting caught up in school and on the latest fashions in makeup and clothes take a back seat when such disturbing events occur as seeing a prowler in her backyard while she is next door babysitting, spotting a mysterious car cruising up and down her street, and receiving threatening phone calls. Even the pleasure of a new boy friend, handsome, charming Jeff* Clinton, whose interest makes her the envy of other high school girls, does not diminish her concern about her overriding personal problem. Trouble intensifies at a welcome-back party at the home of an old school friend. When Jarrod Tucker, a guest who is just beyond high school age, invites her out to see his car, having plied her with vodka, she suddenly realizes his is the face with the yellowish eyes that haunts the edges of her memory. Just before he can harm her, Jeff happens on the scene. There follow typical police procedures. She must identify Jarrod in a lineup as the man who broke into her house and wounded her, and she is interrogated by the assistant district attorney, a tough-minded woman who upsets her. There is also an unsettling visit from Mrs. Tucker, who pleads with her and threatens her on Jarrod's behalf. At the hearing, Jarrod suddenly collapses and is taken to the hospital emergency room. That night he evades his hospital guard and makes his way to Stacy's house. Alone at home, she takes refuge in her old dilapidated tree house. In the ensuing scuffle, she grabs Jarrod's gun and almost shoots him when Jeff Clinton suddenly arrives, intervenes, and takes Jarrod prisoner. Jeff reveals that he is an undercover narcotics detective who has been working on the problem of drugs in the schools, where Jarrod has been a suspect, and has been assigned to protect Stacy. Although attracted to each other, Stacy and Jeff decide to put their romance on hold for the time being. Blending a murder mystery and modern medical advances to keep comatose people alive and exploring the personal problems that develop from their being out of touch for so long keep this from turning into just another amnesia story. Characters and situations are conventional—the cliffhangers, the tight climax, the timely rescues, the spoiled youth into drugs and in trouble with the law, the phoned threats, the sweet, mysterious boy friend who turns out to be an agent, and the numerous red herrings, of which Jeff is one. The pace is fast, and the book is almost all conversation. Police are presented sympathetically, and the representatives of the media are pushy and more concerned about getting stories than the effect on the people involved. Poe Winner.

**OUT FROM THIS PLACE** (Hansen*, Joyce, Walker, 1988), historical novel of freed blacks on the Sea Islands off South Carolina from May 1862, to March 1866, sequel to *Which Way Freedom?**. Slave girl Easter (so named because she was an Easter gift to her mistress), about fourteen, escapes from the Jennings farm near Charleston, S.C., but near the coast she is captured by Confederate soldiers. When the army is near Charleston, she runs away from home, hoping to find little Jason*, 8, whom she raised from a baby, and then to leave with Jason and to search for Obi, her sweetheart and fellow fugitive from whom she had become separated. When she arrives at the Phillips plantation, next door to the Jennings farm, she finds Jason now the dandified special house servant of Mistress Phillips. She takes him and joins her friends, Rose, the cook, and Rayford*, the plantation manager, and some others, who, armed, flee to the coastal islands and freedom. Along the way they have a close encounter with Rebels, probably runaway soldiers, who challenge them, but eventually they all reach the coast, where they are ferried across to Santa Elena Island by the Freedom Man on his Freedom Boat. They are assigned to work the Williams plantation, which has been appropriated by the Union, along with some forty other ex-slaves, and believe the government has promised them that they will eventually own the land they work, as well as receive wages. Easter is disappointed because Obi is not there. She resolves to leave and search for him as soon as possible. Over the next several years she retains this goal, but one responsibility after another prevents her from leaving. Rose and Rayford also advise against it, urging her to acquire land since she has the chance. They are treated rudely by soldiers and other Union officials, the field work is very hard, they must fear attack from runaway Rebel soldiers, "buckras," who hide in the woods, and they must fix up the rude huts to make them habitable. They develop a kind of council made up of "elected" slaves, Rayford, and Brother Thomas, the kind, heavyset preacher, among others, who address problems and mediate with the plantation administrator. As soon as she can, Easter persuades the women to pay her for taking care of the young children, thus freeing the women from that burden and rescuing Easter from the field labor she detests. Shortly after they arrive, Rayford starts to teach her and some others to read and write, and later a white teacher arrives, Miss Grantley. Easter progresses so rapidly that Miss Grantley urges her to enroll in a freed slaves school in Philadelphia. But she has Jason to care for and fears missing Obi, if he should trace her to the Williams place. Her own efforts to find him through the Freedmen's Bureau come to nothing. The most joyful event is the wedding of Rose and Rayford, over which a judge officiates, because Rayford does not want a "slave wedding," but one with real authority, and which is the occasion of a big party. The tensest scene occurs when the federal government decides to return the land to the Williams family. Rayford is killed and Brother Thomas wounded and struck dumb in a clash of arms. Easter takes the lead in working for a compromise that enables the ex-slaves to own the land they have been working and purchase more on certain terms. After Miss Grantley leaves for another school, Easter takes her place until a black teacher, Miss Fortune, arrives. When Jason, now twelve, decides to join a traveling medicine peddler as a song and dance attraction, Easter refuses the offer of marriage of Julius, another Phillips ex-slave, and decides to go to the Philadelphia school. Rose has given her two acres, in return for her help after Rayford's death, so Easter has land of her own. She will return to the couple who befriended her at the Rebel army camp because she feels that if Obi tries to find her he will go there as well as to the Freedmen's Bureau, and then she will go on to Philadelphia. In an epilogue, the reader sees Obi as a soldier on board a Union ship planning to trace her through the Bureau and the Confederate camp, as she suspected he would. Thus the reader is left to believe that the two will eventually find each other again. Since the author fails to exploit opportunities for tension and few scenes are fleshed, the book ambles along to a conclusion that comes too quickly and seems rushed. The depiction of the hopes, fears, and problems of the slaves, though not as developed as it might be considering the span of time, is the best part of the book, especially the horrible change in Union policy, to return to the previous owners the land the freed slaves felt would be theirs by right of hard labor. Most characters are functional types, and Easter's decision is predictable. ALA.

**THE OUTLAWS OF SHERWOOD** (McKinley*, Robin, Greenwillow, 1988), highly fictionalized retelling of the stories of Robin Hood, with character development, motivations, and details of action and setting typical of realistic novels. In this version Robin is a junior forester, an indifferent marksman, and a reluctant outlaw, fleeing to the depths of Sherwood Forest only after he has slain a fellow forester in self-defense. The motivating force behind the band is Much, son of the owner of Whitestone Mill, a friend of Robin from childhood, who has organized a small group of revolutionaries to defy the regent, John, while King Richard the Lionhearted is at the Crusades. Marian, also a childhood friend, is the daughter of a Saxon noble who plans to marry her to a Norman, thereby achieving security in the politically unstable country. Seeing Robin as a symbol to rally those unhappy with present conditions, Much hides him out and persuades him to head the band, which will live in the forest and prey on rich Normans. Although he lacks political fervor, Robin is a good organizer and a practical leader, and it is he who starts helping out the poor who are suffering under unjust taxes and the harassment of the Sheriff of Nottingham, a fat toady to the Norman lords. A great deal of the story concerns romances between Robin and Marian, who continues to sneak into the forest and participate in the group's activities against the wishes of Robin, and between Little John and Cecily Norwell, sister of Will Scarlet, who has run away from home disguised as a boy rather than marry the Norman her father has chosen for her. Hiding her identity as a woman, she puts up with the rough tutelage of Little John at first to prove herself worthy of a place in the band and later because she has fallen in love with the huge yeoman. Among the other outlaws are several familiar from earlier retellings, including Alan-a-dale and Friar Tuck, and a number evidently invented for this novel, including several women who are prominent characters. The story ends with the coming of King Richard, not to the outlaw hideout in Sherwood, but to the castle of Sir Richard of the Lea, whose lands the outlaws have saved by paying off his usurious creditor and who has taken them in after a desperate battle with Guy of Guisborne and his brutal followers. King Richard metes out justice by enlisting most of the remnants of the band into his force for a new Crusade, taking Much and Alan-a-dale, who have both been wounded, and Alan's wife, Marjorie, as scribes, and Friar Tuck as a healer for the sick and injured. While there is no central source for the Robin Hood tales, the book departs widely from the early ballads, on which most retellings are based. There are plenty of swashbuckling scenes and exciting incidents, but the effort to make details of life in the forest realistic is less successful than McKinley's works that frankly include fantasy elements. The number and prominence of women in the

Sherwood band is a twentieth-century element imposed on the late twelfth-century story. ALA; Fanfare.

**OWEN PEARCE** (*Rear-View Mirrors\**), rural New Hampshire high school boy who has been recruited by Hannibal\* Tate to substitute for his younger brother as yard boy to impress Hannibal's daughter, Olivia. Once the girl realizes the ruse, she insists that the younger boy get his job back, but Owen continues to turn up, bringing vegetables and with various other excuses. Suspicious Olivia believes that his visits are still at her father's motivation, even the trip to the county fair, until Owen, a boy of almost no words, tells her that he likes to carve things and gives her a departure present. When she discovers that it is a silhouette of her face, she is very touched, realizing that Owen, at least, has found her attractive, and even though she is not in love with him, she is grateful. The next summer she meets him working at the local gas station and thanks him, although she is not able to tell him how much the carving boosted her self-image.

# P

**PARK, BARBARA** (1947–      ), born in Mount Holly, N.J.; author of popular, amusing novels for middle-grade readers. She received her B.S. in education from the University of Alabama and has made her home in Phoenix, Ariz., with her husband and two sons. Among the awards her books have won are the IRA/ CBC Children's Choice Award, the Texas Bluebonnet Award, and the Georgia Children's Book Award. *The Kid in the Red Jacket\** (Knopf, 1987), a story of a boy's difficulties when the family moves to a new city, was named to the *School Library Journal* Best Books list. *Operation: Dump the Chump* (Knopf, 1982), a story of how an eleven-year-old boy's attempt to get rid of his younger brother for the summer backfires, and *Buddies* (Knopf, 1985), a summer camp story, are among Park's most popular books. Other titles include *Don't Make Me Smile* (Knopf, 1981), *The Beanpole* (Knopf, 1983), *Skinnybones* (Knopf, 1982) and its sequel, *Almost Starring Skinnybones* (Knopf, 1988).

*PARK'S QUEST* (Paterson\*, Katherine, Dutton, 1988), realistic problem novel of family relationships set in Washington, D.C., and rural southwest Virginia in the 1980s. Parkington Waddell Broughton V, known to his friends as Park, is a dreamy eleven-year-old whose favorite books are Arthurian tales and who imagines events in his own life as if they took place in the era of knights and noble deeds. He lives with his mother in a scruffy apartment where he sleeps on the living room couch. The newly built Vietnam War memorial reawakens questions he has long puzzled about concerning his father, who died in Vietnam, a man he knows only by name and a snapshot that he found in a book of poems. His mother, Randy, has avoided any mention of his father and, when Park quizzes her, puts him off, seeming to suffer so much at the mention that he does not persist. After he goes to the memorial by himself and finds his father's name, she agrees to arrange that he visit the family near Strathaven, Virginia. He assumes that Frank\*, the man who meets him, is hired help only to learn that he is an uncle Park has never heard of. Reality is almost a parody of Park's romantic imaginings. Although the farm house is very large, it is old-fashioned and run down. Park's grandfather, whom they call the Colonel, is a stroke victim, and the boy is not allowed into his sick room. The housekeeper, Mrs. Sada Davenport, is a dumpy woman who speaks in the first-person plural, and Frank leaves Park to explore by himself. Worst of all, he is challenged by a little Oriental girl who turns out to be Thanh\*, Frank's Vietnamese stepdaughter, just a few months younger than Park. Thanh is much more agile than Park, skilled at farm chores, and scornful of his city-boy clumsiness. She is also sassy, with a prickly temper, and seems cowed only by Frank's quiet firmness. From Mrs. Davenport, Park learns that Frank's wife is expecting a baby. Frank agrees to teach Park to shoot, and the boy is thrilled that they use the same twenty-two rifle and the same target his father used. When Frank inadvertently mentions that the Colonel's first stroke came right after the divorce, Park learns with a shock that Randy divorced his father. The next day, although Park has decided to go home, Frank quietly insists that he meet his grandfather, and leaves them together on the porch, the old man, evidently unable to comprehend or talk, in his wheelchair. While Park dozes, Thanh, upset because Frank is rushing her mother to the hospital, wheels the chair into the yard. Park wakes to see her pushing it in a wild ride down the hill. Panicky, Park chases them to the spring-house, where Thanh insists that the grandfather has loved it and gets him a cold drink, then lets Park push the chair, with great effort, back up the hill. In Frank's absence, Park finds the keys to the gun case and takes the twenty-two to the far pasture, where he is sighting on some crows when Thanh jumps on him. The gun goes off, and one crow falls. Hysterically, Thanh pummels Park, calling him a murderer. When he discovers that the bird is still alive, Park seeks her help. He sees a picture on her bedside table of an airman, whom he recognizes as his father. Together, they care for the bird, and he figures out that Frank married his father's widow. He explains to Thanh that they must be brother and sister. That night, after learning that the newborn is a boy, they sneak out to care for the bird. Hearing the Colonel crying, they get him into his wheelchair, and Park pushes him carefully to the springhouse, where Thanh leaves them while she runs to the pasture to feed the bird and retrieve the gun. In her absence the old man attempts to speak. The boy realizes that he is trying to say "Park," motioning to both of them, then wailing the name again to indicate the son he lost. Together they weep until Thanh returns, calling that the bird has recovered and flown. She then brings them a coconut shell of spring water, which they share in the moonlight, like wine from the Grail. It is difficult to believe that a mother as caring as Randy would allow a young boy to go into such a strained household without telling him the vital facts that he needs to understand the relationships and what has happened. Given the situation, however, the psychology of the major characters is convincing and all of them, particularly Thanh, are well drawn. Park's daydreaming, couched in medieval language and images, is interspersed throughout the text in indented passages until the very end, where it merges with reality. Fanfare.

**PATERSON†, KATHERINE (WOMELDORF)** (1932–      ), born in Tsing-Tsiang, China; missionary, teacher, author. The daughter of a clergyman, she spent her childhood in both China and the United States, received her B.A. degree from King College in Bristol, Tenn., her M.A. degree from Presbyterian School of Christian Education in Richmond, Va., and her M.R.E. degree from Union Theological Seminary in New York. She also studied at Kobe School of the Japanese Language in Japan. She has taught in public and private schools in New Jersey and Virginia and served as a missionary in Japan. Her first three novels are set in ancient Japan: *Sign of the Chrysanthemum* (Crowell, 1973), *Of Nightingales That Weep*† (Crowell, 1974), and *The Master Puppeteer*† (Crowell, 1975), which was a National Book Award winner. *Bridge to Terebithia*† (Crowell, 1977) was a Newbery Medal winner and *The Great Gilly Hopkins*† (Crowell, 1978) was a National Book finalist and a Newbery Award Honor book. Paterson became one of the rare authors to win the Newbery Medal twice with *Jacob Have I Loved*† (Crowell, 1980), a novel set on an island in Chesapeake Bay in the World War II period. *Come Sing, Jimmy Jo*\* (Dutton, 1985) a story of a family of country music performers, was named to the American Library Association Notable Books list and to the *School Library Journal* List of Best Books. *Park's Quest*\* (Dutton, 1988), a *Horn Book* Fanfare book, is about a boy whose father was killed in Vietnam and his discovery of long-hidden secrets in his family. It has been pointed out that the search for a father or mother is a recurrent theme in these stories. Whatever the setting, her novels have a strong sense of the cultural patterns and ways of thinking of the period and locale, and exciting action is subordinate to interesting characters.

**PATTY OSBORNE** (*Incident at Loring Groves*\*), best friend of Cassidy Keaton. Although the two girls have been very close since third grade, Cassidy has hardly noticed the changes in Patty's personality and behavior because they have both been busy with school activities and excuses come easy. Patty has been spending more time with kids Cassidy does not know and has been increasingly irritable and unpredictable in personality. Patty confides to Cassidy that she has been taking diet pills secured from her older sister, and Cassidy knows that Patty occasionally smokes marijuana, but it is not until the night of the dance that Cassidy discovers drugs and liquor have become a way of life for Patty. Because she realizes that she did not help Patty when she might have, out of mistaken loyalty, Cassidy decides to go to the police with what she knows about Wayne\* Wagger. Patty is a classic teenaged drug case.

**PAULSEN, GARY** (1939–      ), born in Minneapolis, Minn.; educated at Bemidji State University in Minnesota and the University of Colorado at Boulder; prolific author of nonfiction on sports and outdoor subjects and of novels for adults and children with nature settings. In children's literature he is best known for his survival stories, including *Dogsong*\* (Bradbury, 1985) and *Hatchet*\*

(Bradbury, 1987), which are both American Library Association Best Books for Children and Newbery Honor books. *Dogsong*, about a modern Eskimo youth's long journey by dogsled to prove himself and recapture his heritage was also a Best Book of the *School Library Journal*. *Hatchet* is the exciting story of a boy surviving alone after his plane crashes in the Canadian wilds. Its sequel is *The River* (Delacorte, 1991). Other titles of particular note are *Dancing Carl* (Bradbury, 1983), *Tracker* (Bradbury, 1984), *The Crossing* (Orchard, 1987), and *The Island* (Orchard, 1988), all American Library Association Best Books for Young Adults. An outdoorsman himself, Paulsen lives in Minnesota and has taken part in the Iditarod, the 1,049-mile dogsled race across Alaska.

**PECK†, RICHARD** (1934–      ), born in Decatur, Ill.; highly popular writer best known for his contemporary problem novels for young adults, although he has also written mysteries, thrillers, melodramas, fantasy, humor, and poetry. He attended Exeter University in England and received his bachelor's degree from DePauw University and his master's from Southern Illinois University and studied further at Washington University. He taught English in high school and at Southern Illinois University and at Hunter College in New York City and was an editor with Scott, Foresman and Company. His most critically acclaimed books include *Are You in the House Alone?†* (Viking, 1976), a thriller that won the Edgar Allan Poe Award; *Dreamland Lake†* (Holt, 1973), a murder-mystery that was nominated for the Edgar Allan Poe Award; *Remembering the Good Times** (Delacorte, 1985), a contemporary problem novel about teenage suicide that was a Best Book of both the American Library Association and *School Library Journal*; *Blossom Culp and the Sleep of Death** (Delacorte, 1986), a humorous fantasy involving extrasensory perception and time travel, which was an American Library Association Best Book for Children; and *Princess Ashley** (Delacorte, 1987), a sociological problem novel about contemporary teenagers gone out of control that is also on the SLJ list. He has written several other books about Blossom Culp and her friend Alexander Armsworth, among them *The Ghost Belonged to Me* (Viking, 1975), *Ghosts I Have Been* (Viking, 1977), and *The Dreadful Future of Blossom Culp* (Delacorte, 1983). The Bluff City in which these books are set is drawn from Peck's memories of his home town as it was years ago. His other publications include several well-received anthologies of modern poetry, novels for adults, and collections of essays.

**PEDRO** (*The Honorable Prison**), young campesino (peasant) soldier who becomes the unofficial protector of the Maldonado family, bringing them food on the sly, most of which Ricardo gets because they have formed a friendship. Pedro first appears, half-drunk, at their door, carrying the bad news of the death of his godfather, Honorio, because Honorio had brought a bouquet of herbs as medicine for Miguel* Maldonado. At the end, Pedro is shot by the base soldiers as a deserter.

**PERMANENT CONNECTIONS** (Bridgers*, Sue Ellen, Harper, 1987), novel set in the 1980s about a troubled boy who grows up and learns to appreciate his family when he is forced to take responsibility for an injured uncle in the southern Appalachian Mountains. Surly, unhappy Rob Dickson, 17, is on the outs with his parents, doing poorly in school, and dependent on alcohol and marijuana for his only relief from a sensation of sinking and being boxed in by life. When his father, Davis*, insists that Rob accompany him to his home town of Tyler Mills, where Davis's older brother, Fairlee*, has just suffered a broken hip, the boy is angry and resentful, determined to be as uncooperative as possible. They find Fairlee cheerful in the little hospital of Tyler Mills, but at the rundown farm six miles from town Rob's grandfather is cantankerous, and Aunt Coralee* is a victim of agoraphobia, unable to leave the house. Aunt Rosalie visits the next day from town, bossy and self-righteous but harassed and too busy to be of much practical help. When Davis is unable to find anyone to live in and help care for Fairlee, he decides that Rob will stay, attending high school at Tyler Mills, until Fairlee recovers. Rob, feeling trapped and betrayed, is appalled by this solution, but for once Davis is firm. Despite the isolation, Rob meets three young people: Rosalie's daughter, Leanna, who tries to be friendly but reminds Rob of her domineering mother; Leanna's boy friend, Travis Williams, a good-natured football star; and Ellery Collier, whose parents' divorce has torn her from her home and friends in Charlotte and landed her in a rustic house on the mountain above the Dickson farm with her mother, Ginny*, who weaves and, according to Ellery, plays at being a forty-year-old hippie. Their mutual discontent with Tyler Mills throws Rob and Ellery together, but both are so touchy that their potential romance is more a series of fights. After one quarrel Rob gets drunk. The next time, he pressures Travis, who has confided that his older brothers grow marijuana in the tradition of their moonshining grandfather, to provide him with two joints. Unused to the potency of the local product, Rob gets very high and runs Fairlee's truck off the road. He starts to walk to town for a wrecker, decides against it, and plods back through the rain to the truck, where the local patrolman waits, having discovered the marijuana butts on the truck floor. Fairlee gets him a lawyer and suggests that they handle it without telling Davis. In the three weeks before his trial, Rob is hounded by a deputy to tell where he got the marijuana and is shocked when he hears that the Williams farm has been raided, fearing that he has inadvertently given it away and, although nothing incriminating was found, that the older brothers will come after him with guns. Worried and tense, he reacts to his grandfather's irascible harping by storming off in the truck. When he returns late that night, Fairlee is standing with his walker, gazing anxiously out into the storm where Grandpa has gone looking for Rob. The boy finds him fallen in a gully, soaked and nearly drowned by the swollen stream. Coralee bravely faces the outside world to hold her father on the way to the hospital. Phoned by Rob, Davis comes to Tyler Mills and, understanding his son's real contrition and need, stays for the trial, where the judge dismisses the charges for lack of evidence but reads Rob a stern lecture.

Realizing what his family means to him and with Ellery admitting that she loves him, Rob decides to stay on the Appalachian farm. The novel is a moving study in parent-child conflicts and love, as exemplified not only by Rob and Davis and by Ellery and Ginny Collier, but also by Davis and his father. There is also a theme of women's need for independence in the stories of Ginny's divorce, Coralee's memory of her mother, and Leanna's ambivalent love for Travis. Family dependence and closeness dominate the relationships, despite misunderstandings and antagonisms. All the major characters are developed believably. Though not initially likeable, Rob and Ellery are so well drawn that eventually sympathy for them is strong. The aging farmhouse, with its ingrained cooking odors and rotting drainboard, and Ginny's bright new house, with its raw wood floors and unpainted rooms full of looms and soft wools are described in sensory detail. Southern mountain dialect, never overdone, adds to the sense of place. SLJ.

**PFEFFER, SUSAN BETH** (1948–      ), born in New York City; prolific author for both middle-grade readers and young adults. She received her B.A. degree from New York University with a major in television, motion pictures, and radio, and since 1972 has been an instructor in English at Orange County Community College in Middleton, N.Y. Between 1970 and 1989, she produced thirty-six books, only one of them, *Awful Evelina* (Whitman, 1979), a picture book. Typically they have realistic contemporary settings, those for younger readers dealing with concerns like being popular or earning money, as in *Kid Power* (Watts, 1977), a story of a youthful business ("no job too big or too small"), and its sequel, *Kid Power Strikes Back* (Watts, 1984), both noted for witty dialogue. In her young adult books, she deals with more controversial subjects like suicide, divorce, and censorship. In *About David* (Dell, 1982) the focus is on a girl whose closest friend kills his adopted parents and himself; it won the South Carolina Young Adult Book Award. *The Year Without Michael\** (Bantam, 1987) deals with the family trauma caused when one child disappears. It traces the various stages of anguish, anger, and acceptance, resisting the easy solutions of having him return or his absence explained. It was named to the American Library Association Young Adult and the *School Library Journal* Best Books lists. Pfeffer's novels have been praised for well-crafted, swiftly paced narratives and criticized for sometimes superficial characterizations.

*A PLACE TO COME BACK TO* (Bond\*, Nancy, Atheneum, 1984), realistic novel of family life, companion to *The Best of Enemies*, set for about a week in January 1980, in Concord, Massachusetts, in which characters, interpersonal relationships, and setting have more impact than plot. Charlotte Paige, 15, much the youngest in a large, close family, and Oliver Shattuck, 16, have been friends since junior high. An only child of divorced parents, Oliver attended boarding schools until he moved in with his great uncle, retired naval officer Commodore Samuel Shattuck, 82. Although at best he is moody and self-contained, Charlotte notes that since he returned from Washington, D.C., for his annual Christmas visit with his divorced mother, a career woman, and her husband, television news personality Eric Preston, Oliver has been even more abstracted and remote. Meeting her at her locker one day after school, he invites her for a milkshake at the local student hangout, Friendlys', where he tells her that Uncle Sam died in his bed the evening before. Oliver is reluctant to tell anyone else because he knows that he will no longer be able to control his life as he has since he arrived at Uncle Sam's. Charlotte listens patiently, goes with him to take care of Amos, his dog, and then brings them both home, where Oliver remains until after the memorial service the following Tuesday. At dinner, Oliver informs the Paiges, who, as he predicted, take over the many details necessary for the circumstances. Charlotte is amazed at how ordinary things continue to be, since meals, work, and the like go on in the midst of the extraordinary, and she increasingly wonders what will happen to Oliver. She knows that he did not want to live with either parent. She makes other discoveries, too—that Kath Schuyler, their long-time mutual friend, is in love with Oliver, and that Kath's twin, Andy*, becomes just as emotional over the death as Oliver is stoic. The Friday before the interment, Oliver cooks the Paiges a fine dinner, completely at ease, if bossy, about this normal responsibility. On Monday he gets permission to drive Uncle Sam's old Ford to school, but he heads for the ocean, offering to drop Charlotte off if she wants, but she declines, realizing that he has something important in mind. They drive to Newburyport and Plum Island National Wildlife Refuge, where they spend most of the day. He asks her to commit herself to him. Not sure that she loves him that way, she refuses, aware that she is hurting him but realizing that she must be true to herself. He reveals that he has learned that his stepfather has taken a position in London, and now he knows that he will be enrolled in school there. Scolded for the escapade, they get through the memorial service on Tuesday, Oliver's parents having arrived. That night, bothered by their relationship, Charlotte gets up and goes down the hall to Oliver's room, where she embraces him and offers to keep Amos, so that Oliver will have some place and someone to come back to. Bothersome about the plot is the lack of exploration of Kath Schuyler's suggestion that Oliver could stay in town, perhaps with the Paiges, to finish his secondary schooling, a possible solution that, given Oliver's stubborn temperament as presented, makes his acquiescence disturbing. The Prestons seem decent, if career driven, but their coolness offsets the warm closeness of the Paiges: Mrs. Paige, a decorator, Mr. Paige, the administrator of the local museum, and Deb, Charlotte's older sister, who runs a natural food store in Concord. If Charlotte seems slow at grasping Oliver's sexual need, it can be attributed to her circle of nondating friends and her "tailender" family status. The Concord setting exudes a sense of intellectual and social timelessness. Conversations and interpersonal relationships seem authentic. Although Charlotte is the protagonist, since things are seen from her viewpoint, Oliver dominates the book, a not always likeable but consistently interesting and sympathetic figure. Fanfare.

***PLAYING MURDER*** (Scoppettone\*, Sandra, Harper, 1985), mystery novel set
on an island off the Maine coast in the 1980s, in which a game played by the
local young people turns into deadly actuality. Dismayed that she must leave
her boy friend and her high school before her senior year, first-person narrator
Anna Parker is more concerned with her own losses than with the plight of her
twin brother, Bill, who has stolen money belonging to the football team, of
which he is the manager. Both of them realize that the decision of their father,
who teaches at the high school, to relocate to Maine is mainly to save him and
their mother embarrassment, but they are powerless to change the plan to buy
an outdoor clambake restaurant in which all the family, including Kate, 11, will
work. On their first evening on Blue Haven Island they visit the Cunninghams,
former owners of the restaurant, who have sold it because the father has an
inoperable brain tumor. The Cunningham young people, handsome college student Kirk, Larry, a computer addict the age of the twins, Nicki, 16, and April,
12, will all continue to work at the restaurant. At first sight of Kirk, Anna decides
that the move may not be all bad, and after a short time they are making secret
trysts, although he is officially going with Charlotte Coombs, who also works
at the restaurant and whom Kirk says he cannot break up with because it could
cause a recurrence of her mental breakdown. Anna and Bill are soon part of the
group, which includes the Cunninghams, Kirk's best friend and college buddy,
Dick Beal, and Watson Hayden, 18, lobsterman for the restaurant, who has
college ambitions. After work they play an elaborate game called Murder, in
which they draw slips of paper designating one of them as the detective, who
announces his position immediately, and one as the murderer, who keeps his
choice secret. They then scatter in the darkness for three minutes, the detective
blows his whistle, and during the next three minutes the murderer must find a
victim, who screams appropriately, then "dies" on the spot. The others, including the murderer, return to home base and the detective, by questioning
them and using deduction, must find the victim and discover who murdered him.
On the night when Anna is the murderer, she smooches with Kirk, then "kills"
him, only to be filled with horror when he is found actually dead, with his own
knife plunged into his back. To complicate matters for Anna, her old boy friend,
Tony Nardone, is hiding in her room when she returns, having, he says, just
hitchhiked to the island. She is torn between trying to protect him, knowing that
any off-islander will be suspected, and telling the truth to the detective, Harvard
Smolley. When Bill is arrested for the murder because his finger prints are found
on the knife, Anna decides that she must solve the case in the manner of the
amateur sleuth in the novels her mother writes. As she investigates, she learns
that Kirk was not the sensitive, kind young man that she thought and that almost
everyone present that night had a good reason for wanting him dead. Her suspicions shift from Charlotte, who has never had mental problems, to Nicki, who
was abused by her older brother, to Larry, who was forced to sell drugs by Kirk,
to Tony, who was actually on the island several hours earlier than he has said,
and finally to Watson Hayden, from whom Kirk took Charlotte. As she waits

for Watson in his lobster shack, she is confronted by Dick, who admits that he killed Kirk, sick of playing sidekick to a young man growing more and more depraved. Fortunately, Tony, who has been following Anna, and Harvard Smolley arrive before Dick can strangle her. The story also includes scenes of the clambake, for which groups make reservations long ahead, descriptions of the behind-the-scenes hard work involved, a late-night search for evidence by Anna and Bill in which they are separated in dense fog and Anna is knocked out by an assailant she cannot see, and views of the beach and the tourists. Bill's motivation for taking the money—because he is only five feet four inches tall and craves attention—is weak, and Tony is too well set up as a possible villain, selfish and quick-tempered, to be acceptable as the hero at the end. Action, however, is exciting and the reader's suspicions manipulated skillfully. The style is complex, with many flashbacks. Poe Nominee.

**POD JOHNSON** (*Princess Ashley\**), high school youth Chelsea Olinger's age, who becomes her boy friend and who attempts to help her see the falseness of Ashley* Packard. He gets a job helping Chelsea's father with the dogs, and the two also spend hours tinkering with Pod's car. Pod is more serious about school and life than he seems at first, when he affects a "cowpoke" attitude. A "closet student," he makes the honor role and later gets a job at Western Auto to "support his Mercury habit." Under the pen name of Phillip Ogden Davies (his actual first and middle names and hence his nickname of Pod), he writes a series of exposés of student life for the school paper that rock the school community. During their junior year, Chelsea discovers (late, it seems) that he lives in a big house, his father and mother are ex-hippies, and his father teaches political science at the community college. Pod is a foil for Craig* Kettering.

**POLARIS** (*A Good Courage\**), man from the Home Place, a rural commune where Ty and his mother once lived. A real father figure to Ty, he included Ty with his own son, Moonman, to make a family, the happiest period in Ty's memory. When Ty finally reaches him by phone, he does not hesitate to promise to come for him and welcomes Sam* as well. Unconventional but loving, he represents the best in the hippie culture.

**POLESE, CAROLYN** (1947–      ), born in Berkeley, Calif.; free-lance writer and college teacher. She received her B.A. degree from the University of California in Berkeley, later attended the University of California in Los Angeles, and earned her M.A. degree from Simmons College in Boston. Besides being a lecturer at Deep Springs College, Deep Springs, Calif., she has been the founding librarian at Gateway Community School, Arcata, Calif., Artist in Residence at Gateway School, and the Mary Tinkham-Broughton Fellow at Bread Loaf Writers' Conference, Bread Loaf School of English, Vt. She has also worked for *Horn Book Magazine* and the Joy Street Press. Her novel for middle-grade readers, *Promise Not to Tell\** (Human Sciences, 1985), about an attempt at sexual abuse of a child, won the Christopher Award. An earlier book is *Something about a Mermaid* (Dutton, 1977). She is married to a professor, has two sons, and has made her home in Arcata.

**POLLY** (*M. E. and Morton\**), new girl with whom M. E. becomes friends and who changes her life. Polly is ironically much like M. E. in behavior and personality: headstrong, domineering, highly imaginative, and proud. She lives with her grandmother because her mother does not have the money to care for her. She dresses in her grandmother's clothes, which M. E. takes as eccentricity, until she visits the grandmother's tiny apartment and deduces their economic situation. One of the book's funniest and most revealing scenes is that in which Polly visits M. E. and insists that they play with the paint pots that M. E. has been using as dolls to play school. Polly wins out; they paint over M. E.'s protests. Eventually M. E. realizes that Polly prefers Morton\* simply because he is nicer. Polly and M. E. are foil characters.

**POLO BELTRÁN** (*The Honorable Prison\**), young soldier of the peasant class assigned to guard the Maldonado family and escort Marta and Ricardo to market on Saturday mornings. Although he is always conscious of his responsibility toward the Maldonados since they are political prisoners, he grows to like them and becomes protective of them. He identifies Ricardo's boils as the result of lack of proper food, informing Marta that the peasants suffer the same disease for the same reason. He runs away when the General's regime topples.

**POPPY SHORTT** (*Sweet Creek Holler\**), paternal grandfather of Ginny and Junie\* Shortt. He makes it possible for them and their Mama\* to buy the tiny, ramshackle house in Sweet Creek Holler. He usually goes back on his promises to visit them and on his offers to help. He does show up with lots of gifts at their first Christmas, saving the day, since Mama does not have enough money from her Social Security check to give the girls a Christmas and has grown despondent about it. When Ginny falls ill from malnutrition, he brings them a refrigerator. Most of the time he seems loving and well intentioned but too busy with other things to give them the attention he should.

**PORCH** (*The Facts and Fictions of Minna Pratt\**), Minna Pratt's music teacher, whom McGrew\* calls Old Back. Porch scuttles sideways like a crab between music stands with his arms full of music for Minna's chamber group, what he calls "mass assembled sound." Astute and patient, he puts up with the children's idiosyncrasies, prodding them into practicing and often calling their bluffs. To keep the group serious about rehearsal, he has them play back to back, facing outward in four directions. He informs Minna that Willie\*, whom she had considered just a street player, plays in the symphony chamber group and that getting a vibrato is "like a light going on over your head." Minna likes him.

***PRAIRIE SONGS*** (Conrad*, Pam, ill. Darryl S. Zudeck, Harper, 1985), realistic
novel set for about a year among pioneers in Nebraska not far from Grand Island
in the late nineteenth century. Louisa Downing, about ten, and her family have
adapted to and even enjoy their isolated and demanding prairie life. Hardworking,
even-tempered Poppa spends long hours in the fields. Gentle, serious Momma
keeps the house going, worries because Lester, perhaps seven, is shy and fearful,
is pleased that Louisa expresses herself so articulately although she has had no
formal schooling, and still mourns baby Delilah, who died without a doctor's
care. In late spring, Louisa and Lester are out gathering cow chips for fuel when
the neighbors who will live three miles down the wagon track arrive, young Dr.
William Berryman and his wife, Emmeline, of New York. Wanting a doctor,
the neighbors banded together to build a sod house for them, and the arrival is
a major event. The doctor seems capable, Louisa, the narrator, thinks, if peremptory, and Emmeline is strikingly beautiful with dark hair and a violet dress.
She seems faint and gray, but like the doctor the Downings attribute her appearance to the trip west and her pregnancy. Although the doctor seems satisfied
with circumstances, Emmeline is unhappy right from the start. The vast, expansive prairie, which Louisa thinks free and open and Momma thinks peaceful,
she regards as lonely, barren, and intimidating with coyotes and Indians. She
dislikes the rude sod hut, abhors gathering cow chips, and misses the busyness
of the city, and the social life, household conveniences, and servants she had.
Louisa admires her genteel ways, as well as her physical beauty, and she especially longs to read the many books Emmeline has brought with her. To ease
Emmeline's nerves, Doc asks Momma to teach her to shoot, and the Downings
invite the Berrymans to dinner, Momma making the best of their rude appoint-
ments. Momma arranges for Emmeline to teach Louisa and Lester in return for
doing Emmeline's laundry and other chores for her. Doc occasionally reacts to
Emmeline's complaining, sharply telling her not to be a child. After the elegant
imported baby crib arrives too crushed to use, Emmeline gets "a wild kind of
look in her eye," as Poppa puts it, but Momma says that they must give her
time. Then rebellious, undisciplined, headstrong Paulie Whitfield, Louisa's age,
grabs the Berryman gun when his mother wants him to go to school to Emmeline,
too, and threatens his mother with it, shocking Emmeline into a faint and the
baby to come early and die. Even after lessons resume, at Doc's request, Emmeline behaves oddly, and tension builds. When the men are called to Grand Island
to help with a train wreck, Momma urges Emmeline to stay with the Downings,
but curiously she refuses. Indians come, Momma feeds them, and they leave,
heading in the direction of the Berrymans. The next morning, Momma and the
children rush over and find Emmeline, outdoors in the cold, frozen in a sitting
position by the side of the soddy, where she evidently fled, a look of horror on
her face. Much later, at the Fourth of July celebration at Central City, Louisa
recites part of Tennyson's poem, "The Eagle," which Emmeline had shared
with her, and seeing a portrait of her sturdy family taken the previous summer
by an itinerant photographer is prouder than ever of them, even though they are

not elegant like the Berrymans. Home again, in bed, she reassures shy Lester that he, too, will some day also achieve, when he is ready, for everything has its time and place. She understands that the prairie was not for Emmeline. Louisa's uncomplicated, understated narrative supports the stark, naturalistic picture of pioneer life. The fragile, pampered young wife, dutifully following her husband, contrasts well with resilient Momma, also loyal and dutiful but more mature and adaptable, and with the idealistic, determined young doctor. Incidents are drawn with clarity, the tragic climax adequately foreshadowed, and the pace rapid. The Indians are presented as foul-smelling savages, "grunting and tearing [their food] like dogs with meaty bones." Boston Globe Honor; IRA; Spur; Western Heritage.

**PRINCESS ASHLEY** (Peck*, Richard, Delacorte, 1987), realistic school novel with sociological problem story aspects set in a town called Crestwood in a hilly area of the United States in the late 1980s. Of modest circumstances, her mother the high school counselor, her father a Vietnam veteran who trains dogs for a living, pretty, fifteen-year-old Chelsea Olinger tells in retrospect how her friendship with beautiful, influential, affluent Ashley* Packard leads her to review her values. New in town, entering tenth grade, headstrong, and rebellious toward her mother, Chelsea is determined to go her own way. She ignores her mother's warnings about getting involved with over-advantaged students and is thrilled and elated when socially prominent Ashley invites her to join her select little group, not realizing until much later that she has become simply, for Ashley, just another girl in Ashley's stable. She visits Ashley at her home, which is well appointed with such amenities as pool and maid, and is flattered when Ashley asks her to model with her for a charity. Impressed by what she feels are Ashley's sophistication and maturity, she becomes her willing clone, adopting Ashley's hair color and hairstyle and insisting on earrings like Ashley's even though they are more than her family can afford. She even lets Ashley dictate her clothes. She imitates Ashley's behavior and attitudes, too, becoming manipulative, selfish, and saucy. Pod* Johnson, a boy she met at sophomore registration who becomes her boy friend, warns her about Ashley. He says that Ashley will let her down if it suits Ashley's purpose and also tells her that the poems Ashley presented as her own in creative writing and that Chelsea admired were really written by another girl from whom Ashley bought them. In spite of more disquieting episodes, Chelsea remains loyal to Ashley and her crowd even when Ashley dumps Chelsea for another model, giving as an excuse Chelsea's mother's hospitalization after a student assaulted her with a wastebasket. Chelsea later learns that Ashley has gone on a trip abroad with the other girl and her family. Craig* Kettering, Ashley's boy friend and a big man on campus, gets in trouble in school and is sent to in-school detention, where the counselor (Chelsea's mother) finds him with drugs; he comes drunk to Ashley's New Year's Eve party and vomits into the swimming pool; Ashley slaps her stepmother, Celia*, at the same party; and Craig is arrested for selling liquor to minors. Although she is uneasy about it, Chelsea does not blow the whistle even when Ashley and Craig decide without permission to hold the end-of-the-year junior class party at the old Pforzheimer mansion on the property on which the Olingers are tenants. The party gets wild, with droves of cars blocking the streets, and Craig doing good business selling liquor. Inebriated, on the way to replenish his sales supply, he crashes his car and is left brain damaged and paralyzed. Mrs. Olinger quits her job, insisting that she and the school have failed their students, Chelsea included, since such an event could go on without any student having the moral stamina to inform the authorities. Later, a soberer Chelsea discovers Ashley, as self-centered as ever, leaving for boarding school. Ashley says that Celia is "getting impossible" and that Crestwood has become boring. Although characters are types and the plot is predictable, the book is consistently interesting because Chelsea, looking back and having learned some truths, is honest about herself and can drop hints about coming events. The book is a thought-provoking indictment of the contemporary school scene, showing kids out of control because parents and teachers either do not care enough to discipline them or are afraid to do so. The ending, with Mrs. Olinger's resignation, while understandable, is unsatisfying since the school appears to be left without anyone to continue the good fight. SLJ.

**PROBABLY STILL NICK SWANSEN** (Wolff*, Virginia Euwer, Holt, 1988), realistic sociological problem novel set in Portland, Oregon, in the late 1980s. Only child Nick Swansen, 16, is "Special Ed.," one of about ten learning disabled students in Mr. Norton's Room 19. The book opens with a joyful occasion: Shana* Kirby's "Going Up" celebration, the send-off party Nick's class gives her when she is mainstreamed into high school. Nick loses his heart to the delighted, glowing, pretty blond and invites her to the high school prom. For days he works hard at odd jobs, particularly at the local greenhouse, to pay for such expenses as a tuxedo, tickets, etc., and for hours he practices dancing in front of the mirror in his room. He learns the dress, which she is making, is lavender and orders a pink rose corsage, which he delivers to her house on his bike. All these preparations comprise no simple feat for a boy who thinks slowly and is easily disoriented. His parents (dentist father, mother a volunteer for Free Lunch) are supportive and check all the arrangements with the Kirbys. Nick is devastated when Shana stands him up. He waits all evening outside the hotel ballroom for her parents to drop her off, but they never arrive. His sympathetic parents try to soften the blow by praising his courage and enterprise, but he is not consoled. On Monday he refuses to go to school. He isolates himself in his room, and during the day when his parents are gone he gets drunk on his father's whiskey. He is upset partly because Shana lied to her parents, saying that he called to say that he was sick and would not be going to the prom, and partly because at the prom, while waiting outside for her to arrive, he overheard a couple of father-chaperones discussing the "droolers" in Room 19. He is sure that Shana "trashed" him because he is still in Special Ed. and she is not. Still at home on Wednesday, he discovers that Patsy, his beloved dog, has been struck by a car, somehow having strayed from the yard. He takes his mother's car, which he does not know how to drive, and heads for the veterinarian's office with the dog but en route is involved in an accident. Eventually all this is straightened out, and Patsy is treated for her injuries. He returns to school on Thursday, since his parents insist, and is pleased when the class claps to welcome him back. While he is running at the school track after classes, he encounters Shana. She is contrite and almost pathetic in her eagerness to make up. When she asks if she may run with him on Friday, he is cool but accepts her company the next day anyway. She explains that because the dress she was sewing turned out badly, she lied to her parents, and when they found out she was grounded. She also tells him that she is not happy in regular school, finding the demands and competition very stressful. At home afterward, Nick realizes that he has come to a kind of peace with himself and the world. Although life is full of uncertainties and nothing is sure, he is probably still his old self; at least he is not "jagged" any more over what happened with Shana. He has learned that he has to play the cards life deals him the best he can. Scenes are strong: Nick's recurring dream about the drowning death of his older sister, Dianne, whom he wishes he could question about "girl things"; the warm family times with his caring parents, who want to help but are wary of being overprotective, uncertain about how to handle him but always loving and concerned; school scenes with Nick's fundamentalist classmate and astute, clever teacher; the passages where Nick thinks about amphibians, about which he is an expert; the funny-terrible episode on the way to the veterinarian; and in particular the devastating evening at the prom where he lurks outside the building, afraid to go in before Shana comes and growing steadily colder and angrier. The point of view is so carefully restricted to Nick, although the book is not in first person, that it almost seems to be narrated by him. The passages in which Nick ruminates about his parents and the feelings of those around him have great power and reveal him to be a very well-brought up and lovable boy. Although the book exploits a handicapped child's problems, the author avoids a didactic tone. IRA; SLJ.

*PROMISE NOT TO TELL* (Polese*, Carolyn, ill. Jennifer Barrett, Human Sciences Press, 1985), novel for middle-grade readers concerning the threat of sexual abuse. Meegan, a pre-adolescent girl of perhaps ten or eleven, on a camping trip with her parents and her little sister, Suzette, three or four, is getting her heart's desire, riding lessons at the nearby stables. Her one difficulty is opening and shutting gates on horseback, and the handsome young cowboy instructor, Walt, has promised to give her secret extra lessons before the Trail Trials. When she helps Walt saddle the horses, she is surprised that he holds her hand briefly. That evening, he intercepts her on the way to the camp restroom and suggests that they go see Charlotte, the horse Meegan rides at the stables. Instead he leads her down toward the lake, hugs her, and slides his hands inside her clothes. Meegan, though flattered, is also confused and frightened. When she sees a flashlight bobbing in the trees, she cries out that it is her father looking for her, and she manages to get away, though not before Walt has warned her that he will "get her good" if she tells anyone. The flashlight bearer is a boy named Daniel from her riding class who casually walks her back to her family's tent, unaware of her fright. Her parents are playing cards with their friends, Mr. and Mrs. Lindley, an older couple who are neighbors from home and who are camping in a trailer nearby. They put off her attempts to get them alone so she can talk to them. The next morning she refuses to go to her riding lesson, much to the annoyance of her father, who has spent good money on the course. Instead she plays in the sand with Suzette and Suzette's pet newt, Clifford. Later that day, at the store with Suzette and Mrs. Lindley, Meegan runs into Walt, and when Mrs. Lindley gets into conversation with him and volunteers that she and the girls are neighbors in San Luis and is about to tell their street, Meegan pushes over the bookrack to create a diversion. Walt seizes the opportunity to warn her again and to suggest that harm might also come to Suzette if she says anything. Meegan tries to tell Mrs. Lindley her problem and is shocked when the older woman does not believe her and chides her for making up things that could get an innocent man into trouble. That evening, when Suzette suddenly misses her newt, Meegan takes her back to the lakeshore to hunt for it and hears someone in the trees near them. Terrified, she clamps her hand over Suzette's mouth and pulls her down to hide in the bushes. When she thinks that the person is gone, she pushes and drags Suzette through the bushes and then runs with her back to the campsite. Thoroughly shaken, she insists on getting her mother's attention and telling her the whole story. At first, relieved to be no longer alone with her secret, she does not want to let anyone else know, even her father, but two things change her mind. Her mother has learned from the owner of the stables that Charlotte is always shy of gates unless they are approached from her left side, and Meegan realizes that Walt has withheld this information from her to trick her into secret "lessons." Then a younger girl in the restroom confides that she is going to start riding lessons, and Meegan realizes that Walt could trap another victim. She announces that she wants to tell her father and the stable owner and the sheriff. The story does not go on to detail the confrontation or the difficulties that might arise from such a charge. The whole situation is simplified and moderated for a young audience, with Meegan fortuitously escaping after Walt has done only a little feeling instead of a rape, but her fear and conflicting emotions are convincing, as is the adults' failure to sense her difficulties. The novel is obviously written to express a thesis, however, and does little to develop character or style. Christopher.

# Q

QUENTIN CORN (Stolz*, Mary, ill. Pamela Johnson, Godine, 1985), amusing talking animal fantasy set in a small Maine community "a long time ago" in the days of buggies, crank-up trucks, and Model A cars. The uncomplicated plot follows one week in the life of a modest, earnest barnyard pig. Having learned that he is to be barrowed (neutered) and eventually barbecued, Farmer Quigley's big, brown boar runs away to become a man, since it appears to him that men are the only creatures that can control their lives. He steals a checkered shirt, pants, and painter's hat from the Quigley clothesline, dons them, and as he does so, acquires human speech, the ability to walk upright, and some other human attributes like using a knife and fork. Handyman Mr.* Henry Wheatley, a gruff but genial sort who has a soft heart for children and unfortunates, assumes that he is a runaway boy. Having seen how hard and conscientiously Quentin works unloading sacks of grain, Mr. Wheatley offers him three dollars a week to be his helper and secures him room and board with matronly widow Mrs.* Ada Benway (Mr. Wheatley's reluctant sweetheart) for two dollars a week and chores. Thinking quickly, the pig gives his name as Quentin Corn, after a Quigley horse and the local grain, "Q" for short. Since Mr. Wheatley is painting the rectory for the Reverend Mr. Wendell Emerson, Quentin becomes friends with the rector's daughter, precocious Emily*, about six, who recognizes his true nature but keeps mum, instructs him in how to behave (e.g., sleep *on* not *by* the bed), starts to teach him to read and write, and reads him stories (he likes them all except "The Emperor's New Clothes," which strikes too close to home). As she helps him gain insights into the ways and attitudes of humans, the two often laugh together, and Quentin concludes that laughing is the best part of being human. Little Andy* Mears, the three-year-old son of the local constable, whose large and poor family Mr. Wheatley befriends, recognizes Quentin's pigness, too, but like Emily he agrees to keep quiet. Quentin's seventh day in town, a Sunday, brings the book's climax. After church, where the choirmaster invites Quentin to join the choir because he has a clear, true soprano (albeit with a squeak like a pig's in the upper register), he has dinner at the Emersons, during which Josephine, the rector's horse, sticks her nose through the parlor window, breaking the glass and chewing Mrs. Emerson's cherished Spanish shawl. The same day, Mrs. Benway's runaway, ne'er-do-well, son, Pete, 16, returns and recognizes Quentin as a pig. When Pete asserts that he will use Q to make his fortune at carnivals, Quentin runs away, leaving Mrs. Benway a drawing of a red heart with a purple Q inside as a parting token of appreciation but bidding farewell to no one else. In the woods, he meets a "little wild pig . . . in Quentin's eyes, wildly pretty," whose group he joins. While the wild pigs' existence has dangers, at least they are free. The book's attraction comes from its warm, congenial, intimate tone, the winking wit with which the writer invites the reader to play along with the patently flimsy device of "clothes making the man," and the effectiveness with which she creates the small town atmosphere and elicits sympathy for Quentin, so sensitive, dutiful, and respectful, yet always in danger of being found out, if ever the adults stop seeing only what they want to see. The similarities to *Charlotte's Web* do not detract: the friendship between the pig and a keen, realistic girl; the threat to the pig's life that initiates the plot; the pig's naiveté; the sensory descriptions of settings; the kindly, gullible adults easily deceived by appearances; and the heavy reliance on irony as well as situation for humor. For example, Quentin feels "jolts" at such disparaging human idioms as "being brought up in a pigsty" because he tries hard to keep himself clean and neat. He declares himself a vegetarian to avoid eating the pork and beef of which the humans seem fond and often takes remarks literally, such as assuming that the "drummer" who "travels in ladies' corsets" really does both. Some scenes are very funny: Quentin taking a Saturday night bath in a wash tub while singing "Shenandoah," and Quentin clad in a choir robe to demonstrate his vocal ability for the choirmaster, among others. SLJ.

# R

RABBLE STARKEY (Lowry*, Lois, Houghton, 1987), girl's growing-up novel set in Highriver, West Virginia, presumably in the 1980s. Rabble (Parable Ann) Starkey and Sweet-Ho (Sweet Hosanna), who became her mother when she was just fourteen, live in two rooms over the garage at the Bigelows, where Sweet-Ho is housekeeper. This suits Rabble, the twelve-year-old narrator, just fine, since Veronica Bigelow, also twelve, is her best friend and they are both very fond of Veronica's four-year-old brother, skinny, homely little Gunther, and her father, Philip. The girls also share an understanding about Veronica's mother, who suffers from depression, evidently a condition brought on by Gunther's birth, the occasion for Mr. Bigelow's hiring Sweet-Ho and of Rabble's joining her mother after being farmed out to, first her grandmother and, at her death, to other relatives. Much of this information is brought out as the girls work on their sixth grade assignment to construct family trees, and Sweet-Ho tells them about running off when she was thirteen to marry red-haired Ginger Starkey, who disappeared from her life before Rabble was born. Mrs. Bigelow's condition, which has worsened over the past four years, comes to a crisis when she follows the children down to the stream and almost drowns Gunther, attempting to "baptise" him. After she is taken to a mental hospital, Sweet-Ho and Rabble move into the guest room, so that Sweet-Ho can care for Gunther more easily, and gradually they seem to form a family, with the two girls feeling like sisters and kindly Mr. Bigelow treating Rabble and Sweet-Ho with affection and generosity. At Christmas Rabble even sees Mr. Bigelow kissing Sweet-Ho in a far from brotherly fashion. He also encourages Sweet-Ho to take classes at the community college and supports her interest in literature by bringing home books and reading aloud. In the spring it comes as a shock to Rabble that Veronica's mother is improving, but she envisions them all still living together. Sweet-Ho, however, realistically makes other plans, and before Mrs. Bigelow returns in June, she is off to Clarksburg with Rabble, where she will work in an insurance office and attend the university, planning to become a teacher. This basic story is rounded out with much small-town and schoolroom action. Norman Cox, the minister's bratty son, at first terrorizes the neighborhood children and on Halloween even throws a stone that hits ninety-three-year-old Millie Bellows over the eye. The girls, detailed by Sweet-Ho to drop in on cranky Millie to see that she is all right, are slowly drawn into her life and find themselves doing her housework. Veronica, who knows that Norman is sweet on her, even gets him to help, an activity that reforms him. The girls attend their first boy-girl party in new dresses Mr. Bigelow has bought them. Millie dies, and another family moves into her house. Rabble realizes that they have all changed, that time moves on, and that much as she loved the family feeling, it is time for them to leave. All this is related in Rabble's "country" dialect, which she begins to correct at the end. Her fascination with words makes the first-person narrative plausible. She is a spunky, perceptive character, but her mother is the most interesting figure, a warm-hearted woman who has raised little Gunther and loves him, but is willing to give him back to his own mother and who, at twenty-six, has already supported herself for a dozen years and is not afraid to reach out for a better life. Boston Globe Winner; Child Study; Fanfare.

**RAGS O'LEARY** (*Angel's Mother's Wedding**), Angel's brother, barely five years old. At the end, he is adopted by Rudy* Pappadopolis. Rags is an earnest little fellow, a child who embraces projects with single-minded vigor. He digs out an entire city under the back porch and paints Rudy's car with red stripes for a surprise wedding present. He often speaks in rhymes, to Angel's embarrassment and Rudy's amusement.

*RAMONA FOREVER* (Cleary*, Beverly, ill. Alan Tiegreen, Morrow, 1984), mostly episodic novel of realistic domestic adventures, starring Ramona Quimby, now a third grader, who first appeared in the Henry Huggins series and then in several books where she is the protagonist. She and her sister, Beezus (Beatrice), now in junior high, are tired of going to the Kemp's house after school while their mother works and where Mrs. Kemp, grandmother of Howie and Willa Jean, does not really like them. They are able to make the break when Howie's rich Uncle Hobart comes back from Saudi Arabia. Ramona does not like him because he teases, looks like a bearded hippie instead of a romantic sheik, and mostly because she gets blamed when Willa Jean breaks the accordian he brought her. With the excuse that Mrs. Kemp wants more time with her son, the Quimbys let Beezus take care of Ramona after school, an arrangement that causes some difficulties until the two have to cooperate to bury the old cat, Picky-picky, which they find dead in the basement. Their father has warned them not to upset their mother, and their suspicions are confirmed when she admits that she is pregnant. Ramona has mixed feelings about the coming baby. It is fun to look up names and their meanings, but she realizes that she will lose her place as family youngest. Their father, who has been studying to be a teacher, gets his credentials but is offered no job except in southwestern Oregon. They contemplate moving, but he takes a job as a manager of a Shop-Rite market instead.

When Willa Jean says that Uncle Hobart has a girl friend, Ramona suspects that it is her Aunt Bea and is depressed to learn that she is right and that they plan to marry and move to Alaska. Aunt Bea, a teacher busy with the end of the term, wants to be married at City Hall, but Uncle Hobart insists that he will manage a real wedding and sweeps all objections aside, marshalling all the children in a shopping trip to buy new clothes, ordering flowers for everyone with a grand flourish, stocking up on heavy clothes for Alaska, and ending with double-scoop chocolate mandarin-orange ice cream cones with nuts for everyone. Although there are a few things Uncle Hobart forgets, the only real glitch in the wedding is that Mrs. Kemp has sewn the ring to its cushion so that reluctant ringbearer Howie will not drop it, and as the best man tugs it off it is dropped. Only Ramona sees that it is encircling Aunt Bea's heel, and she dives down to retrieve it, thereby saving the day. Shortly afterward, their mother goes to the hospital and a sister, Roberta, is born. Ramona is humiliated that she must wait in the lobby while Beezus and her father see the baby. A passing doctor examines her, says that she has acute siblingitis, and prescribes plenty of attention, which her understanding father supplies. When they can finally bring Roberta home, Ramona is astonished that her mother says that the funny red-faced baby looks just like her as an infant, and she is relieved that she has grown up. Ramona is the same spunky, outspoken child as in earlier books of the series, now matured enough to look at Willa Jean and recognize herself at an earlier stage and to be glad that she is older and wiser. The expected baby and Aunt Bea's wedding hold the various episodes together, but each is amusing and resolved in itself. The book's strength is in the point of view, seeing adult concerns through the eyes of a child. ALA; SLJ.

**RAYFORD** (*Out From This Place**), stalwart leader of the slaves who escape from the Phillips plantation and to the Sea Islands off South Carolina. He is their "boss man" on the Williams plantation. The slaves respect and like him, though he gets bossy sometimes, and trust his judgment. He saves Easter and Jason* from being sent north as orphans by saying that they are related to him. Literate because he taught himself to read, he teaches Easter and some of the others, and lacking books for them to practice with, he hunts for newspapers to help them develop their skills. He and Rose marry before a judge because he does not want them to have a wedding that is not bound by law like those of slaves who were then sold apart. He is killed in the clash between the slaves and the Union officials over the ownership of the Williams plantation land. The author fails to exploit the impact that his death must have had on the ex-slaves.

**REAR-VIEW MIRRORS** (Fleischman*, Paul, Harper, 1986), girl's growing-up novel in which a California teenager, having just graduated from high school, returns physically and in memory to the New Hampshire house where she spent her previous summer and comes at last to resolve her relationship with her father. In a series of flashbacks Olivia Tate tells of the strange message that she received from her father, the first communication from him since her mother left him, taking eight-month-old Olivia with her: "Olivia. Remarkable opportunity. Return trip paid. Come if you can. Your father." Goaded by her mother's curiosity, she uses the enclosed tickets for a plane and bus to North Hooten, where her father, Hannibal*, has forgotten to meet her. In the next weeks, she is continually surprised by this man about whom she has known virtually nothing, except that he writes mystery novels that she has deliberately not read. A bald man with a massive frame and large hands and feet, he has the unlikely passions of gardening, Red Sox baseball, collecting butterflies, and listening to classical music. He has summoned her because he has discovered that he has heart palpitations and desires an heir, someone who will love his house and land and who will carry on his series about Virgil Stark, detective. He proposes that she try out for the role for a month. Determined not to be easily wooed after having been ignored for more than sixteen years, Olivia is prickly, sniping back at his jibes about her mother, in particular her social activism, which Olivia has shared, and her tendency to write pretentious articles. She is annoyed that he has arranged for Owen* Pearce, a boy her own age, to substitute for his younger brother as his yard helper, obviously to increase her interest in the place. She is amused by his near panic when they meet Flora Gill, a middle-aged neighbor and unsuccessful artist who is pursuing him relentlessly with marriage in mind. Instead of a month, she spends the whole summer, gradually coming to know her father better. When her Uncle Leo (Napoleon), a professor from Boston, visits and they explore an old graveyard and crumbling foundation of a house, Olivia realizes that she has developed a passion for discovering the past, an interest connected to her attraction to rocks, which she has always collected. Her uncle supplies some of the tenderness and acknowledgement of her attractiveness that she has unconsciously hoped for from her father. Although the rural life is new to her and not altogether appealing, Olivia comes to understand its charms and at the end of the summer, although they make no show of affection when they part, she promises that she will try to come back and her father remarks that she has the inside track for the job of heir. Sometime between the two summers, he has been killed by lightning while replacing shingles on his roof. Now Olivia has returned for a brief stop on her way to an archeological dig in Maine. She is determined to repeat the annual seventy-mile bike ride her father always made from North Hooten to Lake Kissadee and back, the challenge being to return before sundown. She performs this rite of passage with some difficulties, taking spills twice on his old bike, the second time so damaging the front wheel that she has to forage through mounds of bike parts in a junk yard, finally finding and taking a wheel from a cart as a replacement, and arriving back at the house just as the sun sinks. The next morning she sets off for Maine and, ultimately, for college, feeling that she has proved herself to her mother by graduating with high marks and to her father with this less conventional ritual. In structure the novel is demanding, skipping back and forth in time repeatedly as Olivia looks back on the previous summer and struggles to complete her self-imposed task.

What could be a conventional plot is made unusual and interesting by the characterization of Olivia, a bright, strong-willed girl with a sharp tongue, outwardly competent and sarcastic but inwardly craving affection, and Hannibal, a mixture of eccentric passions and prejudices, scared by the realization of his own mortality. Despite her resistance, she comes to recognize and describe vividly the beauty of the New Hampshire countryside. Setting is presumably in the 1980s. SLJ.

**REEDER, CAROLYN,** author of one of the more unusual novels of the American Civil War and its aftermath. *Shades of Gray\** (Macmillan, 1988) explores the problems of the conscientious objector in a story of a boy who must go to live with an uncle who has refused to join the Confederate Army, despite having no sympathy with the Union cause. Gradually he comes to understand that in facing the hard life on his marginal farm and the hostility of his neighbors, his uncle shows a deeper sort of bravery than the flamboyant soldiers that he has admired. The novel is the outgrowth of visits to battlefields and the reading of firsthand accounts of the war's effect on citizens of rural Virginia. It is winner of the Child Study Award. Reeder lives in Washington, D.C., with her husband, with whom she has co-authored three books about the Shenandoah Valley.

*REMEMBERING THE GOOD TIMES* (Peck\*, Richard, Delacorte, 1985), realistic sociological problem novel set in a developing rural area somewhere south of Cleveland, Ohio, at the time of publication. Buck Mendenhall, 16, looks back to when he is twelve, thirteen, and fourteen and he and classmates Kate Lucas and Trav Kirby form a threesome. Buck traces the events that lead up to Trav's suicide at the beginning of their sophomore year. Buck lives with his divorced father, a construction worker, in a cramped trailer behind a gas station. Kate lives nearby with her mother, who dates frequently, and her great-grandmother, Polly Prior, the third oldest woman in Slocum township, in Polly's old farmhouse. Buck and Kate meet Trav, son of a lawyer in the adjacent fancy new Greenbriar subdivision, when he stands up to bully Skeeter Collins on behalf of vulnerable young English teacher Sherrie Slater. The three hang out together, usually at Kate's, often playing cards with Polly, for whom Kate, a take-charge sort, has assumed responsibility. Trav, an extraordinarily good student, deplores what he feels are deteriorating world conditions, the scholastic apathy of the students, and the ineffectual teachers. He tends to overreact and worry. During the summer before ninth grade, Trav and Kate ''pair up'' while Buck is visiting his mother in Cleveland, causing him some jealousy. In reaction, he goes out for football, from which they ''rescue'' him, at mostly Kate's instigation. When someone leaves an anonymous note on Sherrie Slater's desk, threatening sexual assault, and then her car is stolen and the tires slashed, the three are sure that Skeeter is at fault. Kate arranges for Mr. Slater to beat Skeeter up on Halloween, an act that she feels is justified but which horrifies Trav. Later Kate wins the part of Laura in *The Glass Menagerie*, and on the night of the big performance at the school year's end, Buck learns that Trav has been arrested for shoplifting. In the fall, Buck learns that Mr. Kirby, a lawyer, had arranged for Trav to spend the summer on a relative's farm in Iowa. Just before school starts, Trav turns up tanned and husky, with gifts of perfume for Polly, his favorite pocket calculator for Buck, and his beloved Paddington Bear for Kate. During sophomore registration, for which Trav does not appear, Kate and Buck are surprised to be called home. They learn that Trav has hanged himself in the tiny clearing in Polly's orchard where he and Kate had spent many happy hours together. Since his suicide rocks the community, the school administration calls a public meeting so people can air their grief. In a long speech the assistant principal blames Trav's home for the incident, and Mr. Kirby responds by blaming the school and resigning his post as school board president. Old Polly, speaking from her wheelchair, asserts that what happened to Trav is a community responsibility, advises acceptance, and says that "remembering the good times" is what is important now. Her words enable Buck and Kate to vent their grief in tears. While there are hints here and there that Trav is maladjusted, his problems are not sufficiently explored to prepare the reader for his suicide. The novel appears to suggest that there is no easy answer to the terrible late twentieth-century phenomenon of teen age suicide. Characters exist for the plot and are recognizable types. Suspense grows after the shoplifting episode; before that the book ambles along, presenting the youths as interesting if obvious foils. Some humor relieves the seriousness. ALA; SLJ.

*THE RETURN* (Levitin*, Sonia, Atheneum, 1987), novel of the actual contemporary exodus of black Ethiopian Jews, known as Falashas (strangers), to Israel, as told by Desta*, about fourteen, a young girl who might have participated in it. Since their parents died, Desta, her older brother, Joas*, and their younger sister, Almaz*, 9, have been living with their loving Aunt* Kibret and staunch Uncle* Tekle, a blacksmith, a difficult but content existence in a mountain village with their Falasha neighbors. Since early childhood, Desta has been betrothed to Dan*, the serious son of the priest of a nearby village, an arrangement about which she has mixed emotions. Blighting their otherwise happy lives is the constant fear of religious persecution, especially from Christians. They are denied schooling, blamed for famine and disease, and occasionally beaten, tortured, or harassed by other religious elements. Two warring factions, the Dergue (Communist) government and the rebel Liberation Army, raid villages for food and carry off inhabitants to uncertain fates and youths for their armies. The Falashas have long yearned to emigrate to Israel, but, although intensely scorned, they have been denied permission to leave. When it appears that Joas will be impressed into the army, he plans to escape to Israel, even though Aunt Kibret and Uncle Tekle strongly object. Even Desta opposes him, for the chances of success are slim. Then Dan's aged grandmother, Weizero* Channa, has a dream that they feel portends freedom, the famine worsens, and a village is burned. The three children, Dan, and Dan's family, including the grandmother, decide to try for freedom by walking to the Sudan, from where they can get to Israel. Separated from the group at the very beginning by a misunderstanding, the three siblings plod along for several days, held together by Joas's wit and determination. When Joas is shot by bandits, the girls stifle their grief, laboriously bury him in the rocks, and continue their tortuous, fearful journey alone through the mountains in the general direction of the Sudan. They are saved from starvation by a famine-ravaged Muslim family to whom Desta gives some of her precious jewelry to buy food for them all. In a village market, to their surprise they encounter a cousin of Dan, Melake, who has bravely come to the town on the chance prospect of finding them. Together with Dan and the grandmother and led by a disdainful, opportunistic, greedy guide, they continue for several weeks an incredibly hard journey to the border. By cover of night they cross the barbed wire barricade into the Sudan, their passage made possible by a diversion that Dan creates and which results in his capture. They cross the desert and arrive emaciated, ill, and dispirited at the Sudanese Red Cross camp of ten thousand other starving refugees. After a long wait, they are taken by bus with other Falashas to an airport, whose officials have been bribed by persons unknown, and are flown to Israel, where their health is gradually built up and the children enrolled in school. One day an official announces that Operation Moses, the airlift smuggling of black Ethiopian Jews that rescued them, has been halted. On a visit to the grandmother, they joyfully discover Dan, who escaped from his captors. Desta and Dan decide not to marry right away as custom would require, and the book ends with a visit to the Western Wall in Jerusalem to pray for their friends and relatives back in Ethiopia. Although characters are well drawn and the principal ones are dynamic, emphasis falls on political, social, and economic realities, especially the religious discrimination. The early part of the book, in which Desta describes their way of life and tells why they are always afraid, is vivid with pictures of everyday activity from the girl's point of view but slow moving. The pace accelerates with the departure, which has many tense scenes, and the journey's hardships and terrors sustain the reader's attention well. Desta grows up believably, and her introduction to twentieth-century technology in Jerusalem is skillfully presented with some humor as it is seen through her wondering eyes. ALA; SLJ.

*RETURN TO BITTER CREEK* (Smith\*, Doris Buchanan, Viking, 1986), realistic novel of the gradual reuniting of an estranged family, set in the Appalachian Mountains of North Carolina in the late twentieth century. When Lacey Bittner, 12, returns with her mother, Campbell\*, and Campbell's lover, Iranian-born David\* Habib (pronounced Dah-veed Ha-beeb) to Bitter Creek, she only partly understands her mother's reluctance to see the parents from whom she fled when Lacey was two years old. David, who has engineered the move by accepting a position as the new blacksmith at the Mountain Crafts School, is determined to "melt them," but ten years has made little change in attitudes at Bitter Creek, especially in Grandmom\* Eva Bittner's narrow-minded morality, possessiveness, and need to dominate. She expects Lacey to live with her, rather than in the house David has rented a couple of miles away and is annoyed when Lacey, who knows that her grandmother tried to get legal custody of her ten years earlier, refuses. Campbell's brother, Kenny, who runs the garage across from Grandpop's store (the two business buildings of Bitter Creek), is glad to see them and immediately wants them to join in all the family doings. His daughter Tam, 12, who like her two little sisters is a blond, wispy duplicate of their mother, Marlene, says that she has waited all her life to meet Lacey and tries to tell her cousin what to do and think. Grandmom starts the war of wills with Campbell by coming, with Tam and her sisters, to drive Lacey to school. When David genially says that they plan to take Lacey the first day to register her, then let her ride the school bus, Grandmom goes off in a huff. She also insists on calling Campbell "Ann" and refuses to pronounce David's name correctly or to sit next to him at the regular Sunday family dinners. At Lacey's suggestion, Tam meets her halfway between the two houses, and they find a special spot at the creek to call their own. One day Lacey walks home with Tam, and they visit Grandmom, the first time Lacey has been in her house, where they seem to find a common interest in wildflowers. Then Grandmom abruptly sends Tam away and tries to pump Lacey about the "living arrange-ments" of Campbell and David. The incident leaves Tam jealous and resentful, and the new congeniality between Lacey and her grandmother is destroyed. David, who has rented a barn for his blacksmithing work, invites the family there for Sunday dinner. Neither Campbell nor Grandmom comes. Slowly, how-ever, David's goodwill and cheerfulness smooth the troubled relations. He starts building an A-frame cabin on land he buys at the barn site and gets a mare in foal to own with Lacey, equal shares. Harris, a bearded man who makes stained glass, helps with the cabin. Everything seems to be going perfectly for Lacey when David is killed in a traffic accident. Campbell is devastated and for more than two months does nothing but cry, not even working on her leather tooling. When their rent runs out, she and Lacey move to the barn, where they construct a lean-to between the horse's stall and the forge. Harris comes to the barn, and he and Lacey start work on the cabin again. Needing more help with the heavy siding, Harris tentatively suggests that Wally Palmer would like to help. Lacey knows that Wally is her father, now married with a family living in a nearby town. Although she has no curiosity about him and is reluctant even to see him, she agrees, since no one else has volunteered. They work together until the heavy siding is up, but Wally and Lacey tacitly agree that there is no emotional relationship between them. Gradually, Campbell picks up the pieces of her life, finishing the wrought-iron railing with trillium, oak leaves, and other mountain motifs for a new resort which David's death had left half-done and working on tooled leather saddles and other leather goods for sale. In a showdown at a family dinner, Tam sides with Campbell and forces Grandmom to stop calling her daughter "Potato, Cream of Mushroom" and other soup names that she has been using scornfully. When the foal is born, Lacey changes her mind about naming it "Starfire," as she has planned. Noting the shape of the blaze on the colt's forehead, she calls him Trillium in honor of David, who loved the early spring flowers. Campbell invites the family to see the foal and have Sunday dinner at their new cabin, and even Grandmom comes. She brings a quilt that she has made with a square for each member of the family, including one for David, with a hammer, anvil, and flames of the forge. Although events are seen from Lacey's point of view, Campbell and Grandmom are the main antagonists in the plot with their love/hate relationship, and their prickly reconciliation forms the denouement. Characters are sharply drawn, even minor figures like Marlene and Grandpop, and the attitudes of the mountain community as well as the physical beauty of the area form a compelling setting. ALA; SLJ.

**REVEREND MR. JAMES WALLIS** (*One-Eyed Cat**), Ned Wallis's father, a Congregational minister. He is highly thought of by his parishioners, whose ladies lavish food and attention upon him and his family. They appear to feel sorry for him because his wife, Mrs.* Wallis, has been invalided by arthritis. He is a kind and gentle man, solicitous of his wife and son, for whose feelings he shows an unusual awareness. He is so considerate that he even finds another position for Mrs.* Scallop, the housekeeper, instead of just firing her. Not perfect, he can become irritable about small things, like the condition of the road and the roof, and his quick and stern command that Ned not use the Daisy air rifle leads to the story's central problem. He insists to Uncle* Hilary and to Ned, "What is there to imagine with a gun? . . . Something dead." He is a kind, decent man, a foil to Mrs. Scallop, who self-righteously wears her goodness on her sleeve.

**REVEREND ROSS** (*The Moonlight Man**), minister in the part of Nova Scotia where Harry and Catherine Ames are vacationing. When he and Harry go fly fishing, at Harry's invitation, on the way in the car he gives them "what Catherine suspected was the entire history, with footnotes, of the maritime Provinces." An elderly man "with weatherbeaten face and a large jaw" and a "deep baying voice," he soon catches four trout to Harry's none (to Harry's chagrin), gives three to Harry, eats a sparing lunch for fear of indigestion, comments astutely and uncharitably on his parishioners' communion habits, and impresses Harry as lacking in "the warmth of Christian love." When, after imbibing the boot-leggers' moonshine, Harry has a convulsion, Catherine seeks help from Reverend Ross. Ross comes without question or complaint, cares tenderly for Harry most of the night, sympathizes with her, saying that he is sorry that she has to see her father like this, and advises her to remember that drinking is a "terrible misfortune." He tells her that he had Harry's "trouble" when he was a young man. His loving words and solicitous behavior help to lift the load of shame she feels.

**RICK WINN** (*Invincible Summer**), leukemia patient of nineteen, with whom Robin Gregory falls in love. Rick is an ideal sweetheart for a "nice" girl like Robin, good looking, intelligent, high-minded, fun-loving but serious when necessary, respectful, a thoroughly decent sort. He gets financial support from his parents, which provides for the best treatment possible for his disease, but he gets very little emotional undergirding from them. His mother is seen weeping most of the time, and his father, a wealthy farmer, appears to take the disease as an affront, only near the end finding it possible to stay near his son.

**ROBERTS†, WILLO DAVIS** (1928–     ), born in Grand Rapids, Mich.; author of many books for both adults and young people, notably novels of mystery and suspense. She attended schools in Pontiac, Mich., and worked in hospitals and doctors' offices as a paramedic. Her first book for young people, *The View from the Cherry Tree* (Atheneum, 1975), is a mystery of a child who sees a murder but cannot convince adults. *Don't Hurt Laurie* (Atheneum, 1977), a story of a young girl physically abused by her mother, won the Young Hoosier Award and other honors, including one from Australia. In a lighter vein, two books about a family propensity to precipitate exciting events, *The Minden Curse* (Atheneum, 1978) and *More Minden Curses*† (Atheneum, 1980), are mysteries more humorous than spine tingling. *Megan's Island** (Atheneum, 1988), winner of the Edgar Allan Poe Award, fuses mystery and fantasy. Of a different sort is *Sugar Isn't Everything* (Atheneum, 1987), about a young diabetic. Her novels cover a wide range of types—Gothic, historical fiction, and nurse stories as well as mysteries—and she has also written nonfiction, more often for adults than for children.

**ROBIN KELLY** (*Sons From Afar**), dark and skinny, shy new boy in school about Sammy* Tillerman's age but much less capable and self-assured because he has been overprotected by his fearful mother. Sammy invites him to join his crabbing business, and after talking things over with his parents and trying the activity out, Robin accepts. Robin has recently moved to Crisfield because his divorced mother has married Mr. Norton, the French teacher at the high school. Robin's father, an army colonel, does not keep in touch. Robin makes excuses for him, saying that he is busy and has an important job, and thinks of him as his father, but he calls Mr. Norton Dad and knows that Mr. Norton cares about him and wants to adopt him. He has opportunities and material things that Sammy has never had, but Sammy is more capable in a practical way and better able to handle himself. The scenes at the Norton house point up the differences in their characters and home situations. Sammy takes uncomfortable pleasure in discovering that Robin's father is irresponsible, too. The boys are foils for each other and also for James* Tillerman.

**RON WILSON** (*The Third Eye**), nervous, very blue-eyed, rookie policeman who enlists the help of Karen Connors in the missing children cases through which the two fall in love. When his nephew, Matt, is abducted, he is certain that this case is connected to one involving baby snatching in Dallas on which his former English teacher, Anne Summers, also a psychic, is working. He introduces Karen and Anne in the hospital where Anne lies near death with a gunshot wound. Anne helps Karen appreciate her gift and gives Ron and Karen clues from visions. Through this case Ron also solves a personal problem. He has been in conflict with Matt's father since childhood, feeling overshadowed by his brilliant older brother. He does not feel cut out for police work, however, and with Karen's encouragement he decides to return to college to study law, an area he had not gone into simply because his older brother did.

**ROSAMUNDE WEBBER** (*Izzy, Willy-Nilly*\*), the schoolmate of Izzy Lingard, who does the most to ease Izzy over the hurdles presented by the amputation of her right leg. When previously Rosamunde tried to join Izzy's set, her overtures of friendship were scorned by the girls since she is socially inept, plain, poor, and the daughter of a policeman. Rosamunde, who never holds grudges, befriends Izzy in various ways while she is in the hospital and after she gets home and is back in school. She brings a wall hanging and a vase her mother, a talented potter, made to brighten up the institutionally drab room as well as books and games. After her first visit, Izzy's mother sees her by the elevator, crying over what has happened to Izzy. After a while, Izzy realizes that Rosamunde is a truer friend than Izzy's "best friends." In school, on one occasion, Rosamunde even tries to take the blame when Izzy falls and they are both late to Latin class. Izzy's mother is not pleased with their relationship, however, since Rosamunde is not pretty and her parents are not of the Lingards' social set. She hopes to make Rosamunde over, for example, suggesting that she have her hair cut in a more pleasing and fashionable style. She is also afraid that Rosamunde will become a "clinger" and do Izzy severe social harm. Izzy realizes that this could be possible and that Rosamunde needs to build social confidence. At a party she suggests that Rosamunde circulate on her own as well as with Izzy. Rosamunde is a convincing figure, not just a foil for Suzy\*, Lisa, and Lauren, Izzy's "best friends," as well as for Izzy herself.

**ROSTKOWSKI, MARGARET I.** (1945–      ), born in Little Rock, Ark.; teacher, author of novels for young adults. She received her B.A. degree from Middlebury College, Vt., and her M.A.T. degree from the University of Kansas. She taught English, French, and reading in middle schools in Ogden, Utah, from 1974 to 1984, and since 1984 has taught English and writing in Ogden High School. Her first novel, *After the Dancing Days*\* (Harper, 1986), about the sometimes hostile reception for the handicapped soldiers who returned from World War I, has been highly honored by winning the International Reading Association Award and the Jefferson Cup Award for historical fiction, and being named to both the American Library Association Young Adult and Notable Book lists. Her second novel, *The Best of Friends* (Harper, 1989), is about the Vietnam War period.

**RUDY PAPPADOPOLIS** (*Angel's Mother's Wedding\**), the thoroughly nice young man Angel O'Leary's mother marries. He is a television clown by occupation, whose show has become so popular that it needed a larger studio. He has a warm, outgoing disposition and is a perpetual optimist, looking on the bright side of everything. An ideal father figure, he has the talent of focusing on motives rather than outcomes and thus smooths over potential problem situations before they become troublesome. A group of his clown friends come to the wedding, in street clothes, Angel is relieved to note, because she was afraid that they might come in their work clothes, which, she thinks, would not be appropriate. Rudy, ironically, is married in clown clothes because his suit did not come back from the cleaner's. Lack of a suit does not faze him at all. As usual, he concentrates on basics, delivering his "love speech" to Mrs. O'Leary from the heart and giving presents to them all as tokens of his deep affection.

**RUFUS** (*A Fine White Dust\**), Pete Cassidy's realistic best friend. Pete says that in fifth grade, Rufus declared himself a "CONFIRMED ATHEIST" and wonders why they remain best friends, since they have such different ideas about God and religion. Pete concludes that Rufus admires his spirituality and that he needs Rufus's solid hold on reality. Because Rufus can read situations and gets around town to see the way things go, he is able to accompany Pete home the night that the Preacher Man stands Pete up. Rufus avoids Pete after Pete blows up at him, but one day while Pete is mowing the lawn, he curses, Rufus overhears, and they make up. To thank Rufus for sticking by him, Pete gives him a guitar. At the very end, Rufus concedes that maybe someday he will believe in God, but both know he is quite satisfied with himself as he is for now. Rufus and Pete are foil characters.

*A RUMOUR OF OTTERS* (Savage\*, Deborah, Collins, 1984; Houghton, 1986), realistic adventure novel of the survival type, with girl's growing-up story elements, set in the early 1980s on New Zealand's rugged South Island. Problems plague Alexa, 14. She is angry and resentful because her father, Jim, who owns a hardscrabble sheep station, is not allowing her to join the annual autumn sheep muster (roundup) although he is taking her brother, Tod, 16, and she knows that she is as good a rider as Tod. Moreover, Tod is being allowed to take her pet horse, Nelson, and her father is threatening to get rid of Max, her beloved pet dog, proved useless for herding. Her correspondence school research paper is due, too, and, since she wants something "different" to write about, she has not yet come up with a topic that satisfies both her and her teacher. Her apparent destiny in life also bothers her; she is dissatisfied with her mother's kitchen work and with helping with the baby. She is not quite ready to cope with her developing sexuality either; she is uncomfortable with the looks the hands give her, particularly young Clive, about twenty. Perplexed and troubled, she decides to run off to a lake in the remote, demanding mountains overlooking the station to hunt for otters that Billy Turoa, old Maori tribesman and her father's sometime hand, has told her about, although otters are not otherwise known to inhabit the region. She gathers food, blankets, a knife, twine, matches, and her notebook (she will sketch and write on the otters for her paper), the area map from Jim's study, Hobo, the old horse not taken on the muster, and Max, the dog. Without telling her mother, she heads off in the direction of the secluded lake. Although the going is consistently treacherous, her first great test comes when crossing the rapid Waiau River, where she loses her food sack but gains a new sense of purpose and inner direction—she is running *to*, not away. Once at the lake, the story interest focuses on the details of her search for food and need for warmth and shelter and less than the reader might expect on the hunt for the otters. She gathers berries, catches crawfish, and, the otters having found her, the male otter brings her an eel, prompting her to fish for eels herself. Because she needs the blankets for old Hobo after the snow starts, she kills and skins an injured goat that she encounters and wears the pelt for protection. Max finds a little crevice or overhang she fixes up for a shelter. Somewhat later, the otter throws stones on her while she dozes in the snow, awakening her before she becomes somnolent with cold. While Alexa is showing that girls can be tough and independent, Tod attempts to prove himself a man on the muster. Assigned to Billy's contingent, the boy stubbornly decides to try to round up sheep that Billy says are in a spot too dangerous to search and almost loses Rose, their best dog. Having presumably learned a lesson, Tod goes off to hunt for his sister, for whom a massive search is now underway, but he does it with Billy's advice. Tod gets caught in an avalanche and must shoot his wounded packhorse, although he is able to proceed with Rose the dog and Nelson the riding horse. Otters lead Alexa to a saddle out of the valley, where she spies Tod, plants the red scarf Billy had given her (to be used when she is ready to tell the world "Here I am!"), makes her way to Tod, who has barely survived the river crossing, and revives him. After a quiet but joyful reunion with Tod, Alexa says goodbye to her otter, which lets her pet him, gives an otter stone to Tod as a memento, and the two ascend to a peak where they are picked up by the rescue helicopter. Alexa feels better about her girl's lot in life, having proved her mettle, and even accepts a date with Clive, though she knows now that she does not want to spend her life on a station. Except for Tod and Alexa, the characters are minimally developed, and all, even the principals, are types necessary for events. It is easy to identify with both Alexa and Tod, each of whom wants to be seen as an individual and as important by the adults. Although Tod concludes that he wants to remain on the station, following his father, Alexa still feels that her mother's life is too restrictive. Thus the resolution of Alexa's situation is left ambivalent. Since the author did not make more of interpersonal relationships, the emphasis is on the adventure, which is conventional in its incidents. Most interesting are the descriptions of the terrain, which are vivid and colorful, and of the survival details. Billy is too mystical and "all-wise" to be convincing, and the otters too fortuitously helpful. ALA; SLJ.

**RYLANT, CYNTHIA** (1954–      ), born in Hopewell, Va.; writer of short stories, poetry, and novels for elementary and middle-school children. Most of her writings draw on her childhood in a coal-mining area of West Virginia. She has published about twenty books, most of them short stories put out in picture book form, like her first book, *When I Was Young in the Mountains* (Dutton, 1982) and *The Relatives Came* (Bradbury, 1985), both Caldecott Honor books. She has also published a collection of her own verse, *Waiting to Waltz: A Childhood* (Bradbury, 1984); books of short stories, *Every Living Thing* (Bradbury, 1985) and *Children of Christmas* (Orchard, 1987); the popular Henry and Mudge easy reader series (Bradbury, 1987–1989); the story of her childhood in a small West Virginia town, *But I'll Be Back Again: An Album* (Orchard, 1989); and *Appalachia: The Voices of Sleeping Birds* (Harcourt, 1991), a book of description and personal experience handsomely illustrated by Barry Moser. Her novels include *A Blue-Eyed Daisy** (Bradbury, 1985), the episodic story of a girl and her father that is an American Library Association Best Book; *A Fine White Dust** (Bradbury, 1986), about a traumatic relationship between an impressionable youth and a revival preacher that is a Newbery Honor book, a Fanfare selection, and a Best Book of both the American Library Association and the *School Library Journal*; and *A Kindness** (Orchard, 1989), concerning a teenage youth and his unmarried, pregnant mother, and the new baby, that is an SLJ Best Book. Although the plots tend to be weak, Rylant's novels stand out for their settings and their ability to evoke emotion. Rylant received her B.A. in English from the University of Charleston, W. Va., her M.A. in English from Marshall University, Huntington, W. Va., and her M.L.S. from Kent State University in Kent, Ohio, where she has made her home.

# S

**SACHS†, MARILYN (STICKLE)** (1927–     ), born in New York City; author of popular novels about contemporary urban children in family and neighborhood situations. She grew up in the Bronx, graduated from Hunter College, and received her degree in library science from Columbia University. She was a children's librarian for the Brooklyn Public Library, and in 1961 she moved to San Francisco, where she held a similar position in the San Francisco Public Library. Since 1964, she has written more than two dozen books for later elementary readers, some amusing, some serious. Acclaimed books include *Veronica Ganz†* (Doubleday, 1968), a realistic story about a girl who is the neighborhood bully, *A Pocket Full of Seeds†* (Doubleday, 1973), a historical novel about Jews in World War II France, and *The Bears' House†* (Doubleday, 1971), about a family whose single mother is mentally ill, which was a National Book Award Nominee. The story of Fran Ellen, her siblings, her mother, and the make-believe bears of *The Bears' House* continues in *Fran Ellen's House\** (Dutton, 1987) and was written in response to inquiries from her readers about what happened to Fran Ellen. It is an American Library Association Best Book for Children and won the George G. Stone Award. Other titles include the novels *Underdog\** (Doubleday, 1985), which is the Christopher Award-winning book about a girl's search for her lost dog, *The Fat Girl* (Dutton, 1984), and *Baby Sister* (Dutton, 1986), and picture book stories like the baseball fantasy *Matt's Mitt* (Doubleday, 1975).

**SAM** (*A Good Courage\**), Samarah, girl whose parents defected, leaving her behind at the Kingdom of Yahweh, where she is called a devil's child and treated like a leper. She has sustained herself by getting away to her cave when she can sneak out at night and by planning to run away as soon as she is old enough to pass without being brought back by the police. A very bright girl, she is the source of much of Ty's knowledge of the real workings of the Kingdom. She warns him, futilely, not to get too attached to the rabbit, Ophelia, having once made a pet of a young goat, only to have Brother\* Daniel slit its throat as a punishment for her. While Ty is teaching Noah to read, she is teaching one of the little girls, but they are not present when the boys are caught. Ty does not know her last name or her real first name.

**SAMMY TILLERMAN** (*Sons From Afar\**), tall, athletic, active boy of twelve, younger brother of James* Tillerman, of whom he seems the exact opposite, and sibling also of sisters Dicey* and Maybeth, adopted son of Gram Tillerman. He is a practical boy with plenty of common sense, is well liked in school, and is usually very confident. Unlike James, he does not care much about grades and thinks that he does not have the mind James does, but in the report he gives in class on Phaeton, he shows that he thinks clearly and can express himself well. Although the class does not think much of the report, the teacher compliments him, and he feels very good as a result. He comes up with sensible solutions most of the time to the problems they confront in searching for their father. In the bar, however, he goes beyond common sense in asking questions of the Chief and in telling the Chief that Verricker is his father, thus sparking the brawl and inviting the physical punishment that the boys endure. He makes friends with Robin* Kelly, a new boy, and invites him to join his crabbing business. At the end, he realizes that all along Maybeth had wanted to be part of the enterprise and invites her, too. Like James, Sammy is a well-drawn, rounded, and dynamic character.

**THE SAMURAI'S TALE** (Haugaard*, Erik Christian, Houghton, 1984), historical novel of the bloody rivalries of warlords to become ruler of Japan in the sixteenth century, set mostly in the province of Kai (now Yananashi). The warlord to whom his samurai father belongs having been defeated and his father slain, the narrator, not yet five, is dressed in rough peasant clothes and hidden with a servant in a chest in a storehouse. When they are discovered and brought before the commander, the boy seizes his bamboo sword to defend himself, an action that so amuses Lord Takeda Shingen that he spares the boy, although his mother and brothers have been slain and his disguise is transparent. The warlord gives him to Lord Akiyama* Nobutomo, who renames him Taro and makes him a helper in the cookhouse that prepares meals for his lowest servants. There the cook, Togan*, is kind to the boy until, at a wrestling match in a bad part of town, he is killed by a ruffian. Akiyama makes Taro one of his stable boys. There he rises slowly in status and is given some duties of more importance. When he is fourteen Akiyama makes him a messenger and the next year gives him a new name, Murakami Harutomo, a rise in status both real and symbolic. Among the messengers he gains a true friend, Yoshitoki, a warm, generous lad who sees the ironic humor in life. When Taro is eighteen, Lord Shingen makes a bid to control Japan, and Akiyama, as his follower, gathers some two thousand warriors to take Iwamura Castle in Mino. Taro, to his disappointment, is made assistant to Wade* Kansuke, the old samurai in charge of the stores, but he soon finds that it is a position of some importance and Kansuke is a good master. On the march to Iwamura, Taro acquires a devoted servant, Yoichi*. At one point he rides back along the trail to look for stragglers and encounters a ronin, a masterless samurai, who has just stolen a packhorse and slain its leader. By good fortune, Taro wounds the ronin so badly that the man commits hari-kari, and Taro's status rises again. Akiyama lays siege to the castle, which is over-crowded and its occupants soon hungry. Then, pretending to retreat, he withdraws most of his army, leaving only a token force, which he hopes will draw out an attack from the defenders. The trap works. By clever tactics, Taro saves the doomed men under his charge. Akiyama woos and wins the widow of the governor of the castle, a young aunt of their chief enemy, Oda Nobunaga, who has forced her into three unwelcome marriages. Taro falls in love with Aki-hime, daughter of Lord* Zakoji, one of Akiyama's retainers. The courtship, carried on mostly through an exchange of poems, seems hopeless since Taro has no land or wealthy parents, but it progresses nonetheless. This happy period comes to an end with the death of Takeda Shingen, since his son shares his ambition but has neither his charisma nor his good sense. Eventually, Akiyama and some of his men find themselves besieged in Iwamura Castle, while most of his army is slaughtered in a hopeless battle ordered by the new overlord. Taro is sent to take a message asking for reinforcements. He goes through the lines dressed as a charcoal burner, but despite the aid of Akiyama's father, he gets no help from Shingen's son. He returns, again dressed as a charcoal burner, to find that almost all the people of the castle have been killed. Desolate, Taro wanders around the scene of carnage until he is found by Yoichi, who takes him to a dilapidated shack. There he finds Aki-hime, dressed rudely as the poorest of peasants, and the three make their way back to Kofucha in Kai. The complicated history of the period is made comprehensible by a map, a preface, and a list of characters at the opening of the novel. Nevertheless, the book is demanding because of the abundance of unfamiliar and similar names. As the story of the rise of a bright but penniless orphan, it makes use of good char-acterization and, even more importantly, a strong underpinning in the social customs and elaborate system of Japanese manners of the period. ALA.

*THE SANDMAN'S EYES* (Windsor*, Patricia, Delacorte, 1985), mystery set in Kornhill, an American town, presumably in the 1980s, uncovering the truth about events that happened two years earlier. When Michael Thorn, 18, returns from the school, evidently a psychiatric reformatory, where he was sent when he was sixteen, he realizes bitterly that almost everyone is afraid of him: Rosie, his grandfather's second wife who raised him from the age of three, Iraleen Johnson, mother of Lindsay, the girl who has been his friend since early child-hood, even irascible Grandpop, with whom he shared a house most of his life but never a real conversation. Although they do not say it, they seem to assume that he was guilty of pushing a woman off a high wall in Monrovia Park to her death, a murder he witnessed and reported. He was sent away, however, for compulsively entering strangers' houses, not stealing but walking through, oc-

casionally sitting for some time in the living room or lying on the bed, and for
being seized with trauma and unable to talk when he was caught. Not wanting
to risk seeing Lindsay until he knows why she did not write to him in two years,
Michael goes to her Aunt Neva, whose husband is caretaker of the cemetery.
Aunt Neva warns him not to go near the Johnson house, but she gets him a job
as a gravedigger and quietly arranges a meeting for him with Lindsay in one of
the tombs where they used to play. Lindsay, however, now sixteen, has grown
up in the two years and wants to make love, a change that he is not ready for.
She accuses him of not answering the many letters she wrote to him and will
not believe his protest that he never received even one. A newspaperman, Gary
Longman, rents a room in Michael's grandfather's house where he plans to write
a book about the case, and Michael willingly talks to him, even going with him
for long walks at night, although he is put off by Gary's bragging manner. At
his request, Gary finds out that the school never confiscated any letters from
Lindsay. Michael makes a date with Mary Ann Hlavadic, a girl from his high
school class who now works in a beauty shop, and to his surprise he has a very
nice time. Two occurrences scare him, however. After he is hit on the head and
knocked into a grave that he has been digging, he realizes that Aunt Neva, who
was bringing him a cool drink, must have seen his attacker but said nothing.
Later, when they are parked, Mary Ann sees someone creeping up to the car.
When Gary hypnotizes him, bringing back many memories of his mother, and
then tells him that his mother is still alive, now released after some time in a
mental hospital, Michael suspects everyone of lying. He rummages in Gary's
room, discovers that the book research has been subsidized by one of the psychiatrists no longer at the school who wants to prove that Michael became a
murderer because he lacked a father, and that Gary is attempting to write about
a teenage murderer, not to find the real story. Enraged, he tells Gary to move
out. A few days later Gary, repentant, calls and gives Michael his mother's
address. Michael takes Grandpop's old Mercedes, which has been kept up on
blocks, and drives to the farm where his mother is now house-sitting, calling
herself Allison Jones. Their meeting is strange, but he stays several days until
Gary shows up. His mother is disturbed when it comes out that Lindsay was
Michael's girl, and she asks that they tell no one in Kornkill where she is. Gary
has learned that Iraleen was probably the one who hit Michael on the head and
that a taxi driver dropped a slightly built man off at Monrovia Park the night
that Michael saw the murder. Against his better judgment, Michael follows the
suggestion in a cryptic note saying that he will find out the truth at the wall at
midnight. He meets Iraleen dressed as a man and wielding a knife. She rants
about her husband's girl friends and how Michael and Lindsay must not be
lovers. Realizing that she is mentally unbalanced, he grabs the knife, cutting
his hand badly, and throws it away. She runs off, and he understands that her
husband is his father, that she intercepted the letters from Lindsay, and that she
pushed the woman, another of her husband's girl friends, off the wall two years
earlier. The final outcome is predictable well before the end, but the main interest

is in Michael's confusion and worry and in the apparent threats to his life. Grandpop, who stays mostly in his room upstairs studying insects, and Rosie, who stays mostly in the kitchen, are eccentric but believable characters. The tone is tense and the pace lively. Poe Winner.

**SARAH, PLAIN AND TALL** (MacLachlan*, Patricia, Harper, 1985), short novel of family life set on the American prairie during the pioneer period, in which two children fear that a potential stepmother will choose not to marry their father. Young Anna tells how she and her younger brother, Caleb, half-orphaned when Caleb was born, are happy on their farm with Papa, their dogs, and their horses. Papa, however, does not sing as he did when Mama was alive, and when Caleb asks why, Papa says that he has forgotten the old songs. Then he tells the children that he has put an advertisement in the newspaper for a wife and has received a reply from a Sarah Elisabeth Wheaton of Maine. They all write answers to her and receive replies in turn. They like what she says but are afraid that she will not come because she loves the sea and is used to a big house and their house is small, far inland, and remote. Then Papa says that Sarah has agreed to visit for a month "to see how it is. Just to see." Sarah says that she will come by train, wear a yellow bonnet, is "plain and tall," and, most important to the children, sings. Sarah comes in the spring. While Papa fetches her with the wagon, the children take care of the animals and clean. Caleb worries about whether Sarah will like them, but Anna reassures him. Sarah arrives, "plain and tall," with her cat, Seal, and a collection of shells. She gives one to Caleb and a sea stone to Anna. Although they all like her right away, Papa and Anna are quiet and shy with her, but Caleb chatters away, quite at ease. Anna apprehensively senses that Sarah misses the sea. Sarah dries the flowers they gather "for winter," a hopeful sign they think, cuts Caleb's hair and then Papa's, and brushes Anna's, and she sings. She talks to the sheep, names the lambs after her aunts and cries over a dead one, draws pictures with charcoal to send home, slides down the haystack, helps with the plowing, teaches the children to float in the cow pond—she joins willingly and happily in everyday tasks and activities. Every sign that she likes them raises their hopes. Whenever she talks about Maine, though, they get scared. The neighbor woman to the south, Maggie*, visits, with a gift of chickens, which Sarah likes right away and names, and flowers for a garden by the porch. Sarah helps fix the house roof, gets the animals in during a sudden storm, and when Papa puts his arm around her, the children take that as another good sign. When Papa teaches Sarah to drive the horses and wagon because she wants to go to town by herself, the children worry. Caleb is troublesome the whole day that she is gone and bursts into tears of relief when she returns at dusk. When they tell her that they were afraid that she would not come back, she says that she misses her old home but would miss them more and has brought them a gift, three colored pencils so that she can put the sea colors she misses into her charcoal drawings. Although the story is slight, the book's power comes from its clever conversion of the familiar wicked stepmother pattern, from the way the family and Sarah find satisfaction in simple pleasures and in everyday work, and from the love and consideration they show to one another. All the characters have dimension—patient, understanding Papa; loving, kind, helpful Anna; volatile, urgent Caleb, whose heart is always on his tongue; and especially Sarah, the lean, practical, individualistic, compassionate down-easter who is the story's focus. The understated and economical style requires close reading for maximum effect. ALA; Christopher; Fanfare; Jefferson; Newbery Winner; O'Dell; SLJ.

**SAVAGE, DEBORAH,** novelist for young adults whose books are set in New Zealand, where Savage and her husband lived for two years on the Great Barrier Island and in Auckland. *A Rumour of Otters** (Collins, 1984; Houghton, 1986), named a Best Book by both *School Library Journal* and the American Library Association, is an unevenly plotted but exciting adventure and survival novel of how a teenaged girl goes by herself in search of otters said to exist in the rugged New Zealand wilds. *Flight of the Albatross* (Houghton, 1989) concerns a girl whose discovery of an injured albatross leads to conflict and then friendship with a Maori boy, and *A Stranger Calls Me Home* (Houghton, 1992) tells of the efforts of three teenagers to unravel the secrets of their interlocking pasts. A native of Pennsylvania, Savage has also lived in New England.

**SCOPPETTONE, SANDRA** (1936–     ), born in Morristown, N.J.; playwright, author of novels dealing with young adult problems. Several of her plays have been CBS Playhouse productions, among them *Thanks for Everything, Malloy*. With Louise Fitzhugh† she co-authored *Suzuki Beane* (Doubleday, 1961) and *Bang, Bang, You're Dead* (Harper, 1969). *Playing Murder** (Harper, 1985), which was a nominee for the Edgar Allan Poe Award, is about a group of young people on a resort island whose game of simulating a murder and playing detective turns to deadly reality. Most of her books have contemporary subjects, like *Trying Hard to Hear You* (Harper, 1974), which deals with homosexuality, and *The Late Great Me* (Putnam, 1976), about a sixteen-year-old alcoholic.

*SCORPIONS* (Myers*, Walter Dean, Harper, 1988), sociological problem novel set in Harlem in the 1980s. When his older brother, Randy, 18, who is in prison for killing a man in a holdup, sends word that Jamal Hicks, 12, should look up Mack, his warlord in the Scorpions gang, Jamal is hesitant. He does not want to end up like Randy; yet he feels vulnerable, in need of protection from Dwayne, an older boy who torments him at school and beats him up. With his best friend, Puerto Rican-born Tito* Cruz, Jamal hunts Mack up in a crack house. They both know that Mack is a little off in the head, maybe slightly retarded, maybe brain damaged by drugs, and when he suggests that Jamal, backed by Randy's directive and Mack as warlord, take over the Scorpions and raise money for Randy's appeal, they put him off for a couple of days. After seeing his mother's great worry over Randy and having further trouble with Dwayne, Jamal takes the pistol Mack brings him and goes to the deserted fire station that the Scorpions use as a clubhouse. Some of the gang members, all fourteen or fifteen, are doubtful about Jamal as the new leader, particularly Indian and Angel, but the gun stops their objections. The gun causes Jamal continued worry and trouble. Dwayne insists on fighting out their quarrel in the school storeroom. Jamal knows that he cannot win and is determined to take a beating and call it quits, but when Dwayne seems determined to maim or kill him, he pulls the gun that Tito previously stashed on a shelf and scares the bully into stopping. Angel and Indian come into the grocery store where Jamal works part time, making trouble and causing him to lose his job there. Tito, who is scared of the gun and urges Jamal to throw it away, loyally keeps it for him after the storeroom incident. When Tito's grandmother finds it, she kicks him out, and he is devastated. Jamal promises to get rid of the gun, but he keeps it, knowing he will have a con-frontation with Indian and Angel. After Randy is knifed in prison and Mama visits him in the hospital, she tries to borrow money for an appeal from her employer and is refused. Jamal sends word to the Scorpions that Randy wants Indian to take over the gang and raise the appeal money. Indian insists on meeting Jamal late at night in an isolated park. Although Jamal is sure that he will be beaten by the older boy and thinks that the best plan is to take it and get out of the gang, he gets Tito to accompany him, carrying the gun. With Angel backing him, Indian beats Jamal viciously. When Angel pulls a switch-blade knife, Tito shoots both of the older boys. Jamal and Tito run, throwing the gun into a garbage dumpster on the way. Jamal is terrified because some of the Scorpions know where he lives. Mack waylays him on the way to church and says that he has killed Angel and seriously wounded Indian, who has been arrested for possession of narcotics, claims that in his screwed-up mind he seems to believe. Jamal is relieved, but he worries about Tito, who is ill and whose grandmother will not let Jamal see him, although he waits on the doorstep for hours. When at last Tito comes out, he admits to Jamal that he confessed to his grandmother and to the police, although he left Jamal out of the story, and that he is being sent to Puerto Rico to live with his father. As a going-away present, Jamal wraps up a drawing of Tito that he made, a gift Tito at first rejects and then accepts. Interspersed with the main plot are Jamal's troubles in school, his ambivalent feelings toward Randy and his mostly absent father, his squabbling with his little sister, Sassy, his anxiety about Mama, who has aged with Randy's troubles, and scenes of street life in Harlem. The odds are so against Jamal that the novel has a depressing tone, yet he seems to be pictured as a survivor and, not very believably, as a talented artist. Except for Tito, the other figures are stock characters and the situations, while plausible, are ones that have been dealt with frequently in earlier novels. ALA; Newbery Honor.

**SECOND FIDDLE: A SIZZLE & SPLAT MYSTERY** (Kidd*, Ronald, Lode-star, 1988), lighthearted realistic detective novel, set in Los Angeles at the time of publication, sequel to *Sizzle & Splat*. Sizzle* (Prudence Szyznowski), seventeen and five feet, seven inches tall, is a junk food addict and trumpet player in the Pirelli Youth Orchestra that meets regularly in the music building on the UCLA campus. She tells how she and Splat* (Arthur Hadley Reavis Pauling III), a scrawny, acned, tuba player partial to T-shirts with punny mottos like "Haydn go seek," discover who is behind the unnerving pranks that disrupt the orchestra, leaving doggerel notes signed Merry Prankster. Overhead sprinklers suddenly drench the orchestra, four dozen pigeons clutter up Mr. Pirelli's office and orchestra hall, fish jam Splat's tuba, and firecrackers demolish the $250,000 Stradivarius in concertmaster Kevin Lim's case, each of these to the accompaniment of appropriate music, like Handel's *Water Music* for the sprinkler trick. Although discouraged by trench-coated, Bogart-sounding police detective Niles Denton, who maintains that these are all just coincidences, the two amateur detectives follow leads and gradually eliminate suspects in good sleuthing style, among them, Myron Mann, the orchestra practical joker and the most obvious suspect; Arnie Klingmeyer, music librarian; Buffy Dupree, second violin who lost out as concertmaster to Kevin Lim; and Harvey Bitner, malcontented oboe player. The game turns deadly when bees are released while they are driving along in Splat's classic Packard, an arrow is shot at them while they are eating in Splat's house, and a cannonball just misses them in the park. Simultaneously, Sizzle pursues a personal problem, the identity of the beautiful blond her father tells her he saw Splat with at the fancy Chez Pierre restaurant on Friday night. Although her conscience bothers her since Splat says that he only goes out with his mother, she tails him and discovers that the blond is indeed his mother, tiny, shy Gwendolyn. After further adventures and mix-ups, they learn that Kevin Lim was responsible for the early Merry Prankster tricks, having snapped because his famous violinist father, Bradford, denigrates him at every turn. They also learn that the destroyed violin was a reproduction, not a real Stradivarius, and that Bradford was responsible for the deadly tricks because he wanted the insurance money from the supposedly destroyed Stradivarius to buy a second one and was afraid that Sizzle and Splat would trip him up. After the rousing climax involving a showdown with the murderous Bradford and Denton luckily on the spot, the quiet conclusion finds Sizzle and Splat contemplating the blossoming romance between their parents, a quiet mailman and accomplished amateur chef and the beautiful blond. Characters are distorted for comic effect and are differentiated in broad outline by usually one very obvious trait: Vidor Pirelli, kindly maestro who fractures the English language; Buffy Dupree, sullen second violin given to buffing her nails; Gwendolyn Pauling, tiny fairy-tale princess; Bradford Lim, arrogant genius; and so on throughout the large cast. The book is almost all dialogue, contemporary, snappy, and witty, with many one-liners and one-ups. Other humor comes from insult, wordplay, situation, coincidence, literal misunderstandings, and names (Lucinda Lust, Myron Mann, "my man"). Although events carry an important lesson in the need for trust in human relationships, this theme is never obtrusive, and the abundant humor, sparkling style, fast-moving plot with numerous if typical complications, and attractive main characters make for splendid light entertainment with a consistently late twentieth-century tone. Poe Nominee.

*THE SECRET LIFE OF DILLY MCBEAN* (Haas*, Dorothy, Bradbury, 1986), humorous mystery-fantasy set in the 1980s in a rural area somewhere in the United States. After the death of his parents—a load of hay toppled on their car—Dilly (Dilloway) McBean is raised by the directors of the Commercial Chemical & Corn Trust & Savings Bank, who send him to a series of boarding schools and summer camps. When he is about twelve or thirteen, his guardian, portly Mr.* Homer Orbed, who has been at the South Pole, turns up. He decides, with Dilly's agreement, that Dilly needs a more settled existence. He buys a rambling old house for the boy in the country town of Hennessey Depot, furnishes it with Dilly's family's possessions, engages a couple, Mr.* and Mrs.* Blackpool, to care for him, and enrolls him in public school. Dilly arrives in Hennessey Depot sometime before school starts, buys a bike and a pleasant but independent dog that he names Contrary*, and roams the countryside, soon logging over 350 miles on his odometer. At school he soon makes close friends with two boys, Matt and Bryan, and a girl, Jessica, who is the envy of the two boys because she received a bulldozer of her very own for her birthday. Odd things soon happen. Dilly notices that one or the other of the Blackpools seems to turn up whenever he is in the town, and an eminent woman scientist, Dr. McEvoy, who visits his general science class, takes an unusually strong interest in him and his magnetism project. He learns, to his surprise, that Dr. McEvoy has been encouraged to take a sabbatical year in Hennessey Depot to help Dilly develop and learn to control the marvelous gift with which he was born, magnetism in his hands, a talent that Dilly has suppressed lest he become an object of curiosity. While this is going on, unknown to them all, a Dr. Keenwit has made other plans for Dilly with the connivance of Jepson Whirtby, the helper assigned to Mr. Orbed by the bank. Dr. Keenwit's plans gradually unravel in short italicized chapters interspersed at irregular intervals throughout the main narrative. Keenwit, Whirtby, and other "operatives" in service to Keenwit, plot to kidnap Dilly for ransom to finance a scientific project in which Keenwit is engaged. Whirtby lures Dilly on a walk, in a funny episode that reveals Whirtby as a consummate bungler and in which Dilly and Whirtby are accompanied by Dilly's three school friends, to Whirtby's chagrin. Dilly is carried off in a van to Dr. Keenwit's underground laboratory inside a hill. The other three children see the kidnapping, race home, get Jessica's bulldozer, and with it burst into Keenwit's underground laboratory, soon followed by Orbed, McEvoy, and the Blackpools. A terrific fight ensues, during which Dilly sends forth a tremendous charge of magnetism and destroys Dr. Keenwit's diabolical Great Harmonizer machine, with which he planned to control the world. Back in Hennessey Depot, Dr. McEvoy decides to move in with Dilly to teach him more conveniently, start investigating his father's scientific papers, and serve as his surrogate mother. Although coincidence and hyperbole figure strongly in the plot and Dilly himself is a bland figure, the magnetism concept is inventive and intriguing, and the story is consistently lively. New twists keep the pot boiling, and tension runs high. The climax seems rushed, but everything comes to rights satisfactorily in the end. Whirtby is too much of a bumbler to be a proper villain, and his amateurishness prompts one of Keenwit's operatives to defect and inform Dr. McEvoy, and thus the adults appear just in the nick of time to follow up on the children's flamboyant rescue. Poe Nominee.

**SELINA** (*Waiting for the Rain**), Tengo's mother, who is cook for Frikkie's Tant* Sannie on the farm in the South African veld that belongs to Tant Sannie and Oom* Koos. Selina works from dawn until late in the evening for a subsistence wage to supplement the subsistence wage of her husband, Timothy, who is "boss-boy" (foreman), then goes home to her mud hut in the kraal (black sector) to take care of her family there. Selina has lost two children, one while the girl was staying with relatives in order to attend school. Selina also has a sickly little girl younger than Tengo. Although Selina can read and write, having been taught by a missionary, and desires her children to be educated, she is reluctant to let Tengo go away to school. Her reasons are partly emotional and partly practical. She knows that she will need someone to care for her in her old age. If the little one, who has tuberculosis, dies, Tengo will be all that she has left. Selina represents blacks who know that they are exploited and abused and who yearn for a better life, especially for their children, but feel hopeless to achieve it. Tant Sannie is her foil.

**SEX EDUCATION** (Davis*, Jenny, Orchard, 1988), realistic novel of young love that ends in tragedy, told as a record of her ninth-grade year by a patient in a mental hospital, presumably in the 1980s. When Livvie (Olivia) Sinclair, 14, starts biology class in the town to which her family has just moved, she is surprised that their unconventional teacher, Mrs. Fulton, begins with a semester of sex education. The class soon becomes her favorite, not only because David Kindler, the boy who has been helpful to her the first day and to whom she is attracted, sits next to her, but also because of the lively discussion and the unusual assignments. For instance, for one week the homework is to stand alone and naked in front of a full-length mirror for five minutes a day, which sounds easy but proves to be intensely embarrassing. The big project for the semester is to care about someone to whom they have not previously had a close attachment. David and Livvie, who both live in the High Ridge subdivision, decide to work together by caring for a new couple, Maggie and Dean Parker, who have just moved into the only older home in the neighborhood, a former farmhouse set high on the ridge, up from the street two and a half flights of steep concrete steps. Their arrival is dramatic, with Maggie stepping out of the truck and collapsing in the street. When both Parkers leave in the ambulance, the neighbors unpack their U-Haul and carry all its contents up to the house, but that is the last time most of them have any contact with the new couple. Dean Parker puts up a large "No Trespassing" sign and ignores questions about his wife's health. Word spreads that she was pregnant but has lost the baby. Meeting her at the supermarket, however, Livvie learns that although Maggie is occasionally hemorrhaging and experiencing an unusual amount of sickness, she is still pregnant. She is also very lonely and welcomes visits from Livvie and David in the afternoons. They soon realize that something is odd about her relationship with her husband and avoid the Parker house when he might be home. David, whose fourteen-year-old unmarried mother abandoned him and who has been brought up by Marie, the midwife who delivered him, has been hoping for a father figure and is disturbed that the man is so remote. Maggie seems overwrought and upset by the blasting for a new road nearby and is horribly frightened by snakes in the yard and the basement. Livvie and David, pleased to be offering her friendship, do not seek advice from their parents. At Christmas time, they are surprised when Maggie invites them to "a little get-together," mostly for people from the radio station where Dean works. They feel a bit awkward but stay until they see Dean holding a blond from the station on his lap and nuzzling her breasts. They realize that Maggie, too, has seen, and they leave the house unnoticed and worried. Because Livvie suffers a severe case of flu, they do not see Maggie again for some time and are shocked to find her thin and disoriented, with an injured arm. Partly because their own romance has reached a boiling point, they neglect their project of caring, but they see the Parkers going off to the hospital and learn that Maggie has a boy. A week later, when they do visit, they are shocked to find the baby crying and neglected and Maggie lying soiled and bloody, in pain and feverish. As David changes the baby and Livvie cleans up Maggie, they realize that she has been beaten. Livvie gets Maggie dressed, planning to take her to her home, but Dean arrives before they can leave. David sends them out the back way and goes to distract Dean until they can get down to the street. Livvie hears Dean's angry voice and sees him push David backward down the steep steps. David's neck snaps, and he dies instantly. Livvie is in shock for months, unable to speak or to recognize anyone. She later learns that Dean is convicted of negligent homicide, sentenced to one year, and paroled after four months. She does not know what has happened to Maggie and the baby. In the epilogue, closing the frame story, Mrs. Fulton visits the hospital and says that she is terribly sorry that she gave the assignment and let them get into the dangerous situation. With sudden insight, Livvie tells her that it is not her fault, that neither of them is responsible for David's death, and for the first time she is able to cry and to want to go on living. The treatment of young love is sympathetic, with the main characters well developed. Some of the school scenes are very funny, handled without sensationalism and with believable voices of young teenagers. Although Livvie and David never have intercourse, their desire is strong and realistic, and the book is nonjudgmental on the subject, except to come out strongly for birth control. SLJ.

**SHADES OF GRAY** (Reeder*, Carolyn, Macmillan, 1989), historical novel of a boy's adjustment when the Civil War has destroyed his family and he must go to live with relatives he has never known. After his father dies fighting for the Confederacy, his little sisters die of typhoid spread from the Yankee camp, his older brother is shot by a Yankee sentry, and his mother gives up and dies, Will Page, 11, is taken to the Virginia Piedmont to live with his Aunt Ella Jones, his mother's sister. The rough country house is very different from his carpeted Winchester home that employed three slaves. Food is scarce, and he is unaccustomed to the work that he is expected to do, but Will adjusts to these changes and soon loves his aunt and is fond of his cousin Meg, 10. However, he cannot bring himself to call his Uncle Jed by name or feel anything but contempt for the man who fought for neither side in the war. He is also appalled that there has been no school in the district since the beginning of the war. His twin cousins, 16, have gone to Ohio to work for wages, so Will tries to take their place in doing the farm work, although Meg often does more than he can. The local boys, led by Hank Riley, son of the storekeeper, are antagonistic and mock him for his city manners and his uncle's pacificist posture. One of the boys reports that his older brother saw a Charlie Page in Winchester shot when he was taunting the Yankees by hiding behind a tree and showing a coat on a stick to make the sentry nervous. Will is grateful when Meg denies that this was his brother. Later, Will admits to Meg that he could not stand the pity of his Winchester neighbors and wants to forget the way his brother died. At first it seems as if Hank may become a friend, but showing him the collection of buttons he found on the battlefield, Will slips and mentions Charlie, and wins back Hank's scorn. Later, Hank goads Will into a fight and beats him badly. Men in the neighborhood decide to repair the mill, and Uncle Jed takes Will along. Tom Riley, Hank's older brother, rudely says that they do not need Uncle Jed's help, but that they could use Will's. Angry at this rejection, Will opts to go home with his uncle. Later, one of the men approaches Will and suggests that he ask his uncle to come back to help them get the mill started. Will says that they better send Tom Riley with the message. Eventually Tom comes to the farm and curtly delivers the request. Warning Will to pretend that there has been no unpleasantness, Uncle Jed takes him to the mill and, being experienced, makes adjustments to the millworks. They both get the best meal in years from the miller's wife, a basket of food to take home, and the first sack of flour ground in the repaired mill. Uncle Jed regains some of the respect of his neighbors. A letter from Doc Martin, back in Winchester, saying that his sister has come to keep house for him, suggests that he would be glad to have Will return and be raised as his son. To his own surprise, Will does not jump at the chance. Without telling the family of the offer, he mulls it over until Uncle Jed takes in a sick Yankee soldier, Jim Woodley, trying to make his way back to Pennsylvania and lets him stay until he is well enough to move on. Will holds himself aloof and is uncomfortable that Jim leaves him a copy of *Moby Dick* when he moves on. To his astonishment, Will discovers that Meg cannot read, so he starts reading the book aloud and plans to teach his cousin to read before he returns to Winchester. Although he expects to take Doc Martin's offer, two things change his mind. The school is to be reopened, and Meg's twin brothers decide to stay in Ohio. When Will realizes that both his aunt and Meg are devastated and turn to him to fill the gap and that his uncle really needs his help, he sees that his place is with this family. For the first time he uses the term, Uncle Jed, and they all rejoice when Jim sends them enough money to buy a cow and perhaps a horse to restock the farm. Will's prejudice and gradual understanding of his uncle's position make a good story, with a likeable protagonist, but it is handled heavily, and the themes of standing up for one's own convictions and the devastation of war for both winner and loser are enunciated too often by both the characters and the author. Details of the farm work and of the hard rural life in the postwar period are interesting and add conviction. Child Study.

**SHANA KIRBY** (*Probably Still Nick Swansen\**), the Special Ed. classmate Nick Swansen invites to the prom and who stands him up. Shana explains that because the dress she was making for the dance was ruined she did not want to go to the dance and so lied to her parents that he phoned to say that he was ill. Nick listens to her explanation but privately thinks that it is flimsy. He feels that she could have found some other pretty dress to wear. He is too polite to belabor the point with her, however. Shana's hair has been specially done for the occasion, and afterward in anger and shame she chops it off. She tells Nick that she and he have "minimal brain dysfunction," a term he has difficulty catching, and that they are less disabled than the Down's syndrome children in their room. She also tells him that he is a "savant," since he knows so much, more than anyone else in school, about amphibians. She suggests that perhaps he likes amphibians so much because if his sister Dianne had been an amphibian she would not have drowned. Nick thinks that maybe she is right. Like Nick's, her behavior seems typical of many who are learning disabled because of moderate retardation.

**SHREVE, SUSAN (RICHARDS)** (1939–      ), born in Toledo, Ohio; educator and novelist for adults and young people. She received her B.A. with honors from the University of Pennsylvania and her M.A. from the University of Virginia, has taught English in private schools in Cheshire, England, and in Pennsylvania and Washington, D.C., has been on the literature faculty of George Mason University, Fairfax, Va., since 1976, and has been a visiting professor at Columbia. She was well established as an adult novelist before she began writing for children. Of her mostly lighthearted books of home and school life for a young audience, *Family Secrets: Five Very Important Stories* (Knopf, 1979) was an American Library Association Best Book, and *The Flunking of Joshua T. Bates* (Knopf, 1984) was a Junior Literary Guild Selection. *Lucy Forever & Miss Rosetree, Shrinks\** (Holt, 1987), in which two schoolgirls playing at being psychiatrists solve a mystery about a little mute girl, was nominated for the

Edgar Allan Poe Award. It is strongly plotted, has dialogue that sounds like contemporary speech, and deals perceptively but nondidactically with the current social problem of child abuse. A recipient of a Guggenheim Fellowship for writing, Shreve lives with her husband, a literary agent, in Washington, D.C. Her adult novels include *A Woman Like That* (Atheneum, 1977), *Queen of Hearts* (Linden, 1986) and *Daughters of the New World* (Doubleday, 1991).

**SHURA (CRAIG), MARY FRANCES** (1923–1991), born in Pratt, Kans., died as the result of injuries suffered in a fire in Maywood, Illinois; prolific novelist for both adults and young people. She spent her early years in the Pacific Northwest, with summers at Twin Lakes, Ida. After her father's death, the family moved to Missouri, where she later attended Maryville College. Her first book was *Simple Spigott* (Knopf, 1960), and in the next twenty years she published seventy books for both adults and children as Mary Francis Shura and under several pseudonyms: M. F. Craig, M. S. Craig, Mary Craig, Mary Shura, Alexis Hill, and Meredith Hill. She also taught and held administrative posts with Mystery Writers of America. Among her novels for teenagers is *The Josie Gambit** (Dodd, 1986), a story about high school chess players with mystery story aspects, which was named an American Library Association Notable Book. Other novels for young adults are *Jessica* (Scholastic, 1984), *Marilee* (Scholastic, 1985), and *Gabrielle* (Scholastic, 1987). For younger children her companion books, *Chester* (Dodd, 1979), *Eleanor* (Dodd, 1983), and *Jefferson* (Dodd, 1984) are well known. Among her books for adults are *The Third Blond* (Dodd, 1985) and *Flash Point* (Dodd, 1987), both published under the name M. S. Craig.

**SILAS GORMAN** (*Charley Skedaddle**), sixteen-year-old Union drummer boy who teaches Charley Quinn drumming and then himself becomes a soldier. Through him, since Silas must always attend the officers, Charley (and the reader) becomes privy to news about the war. Silas is wounded (and probably dies) at the Wilderness. When Charley last sees him, he is trying to tend to his shot leg and apparently calls to Charley for help, though Charley cannot hear what he says because of the din of battle. Though ashamed, Charley flees anyway. Silas and Charley are foil characters.

**SIN** (*Tancy**), Lucinda, Tancy's mother, also known as Lulu and Lucy. Tancy runs into her at Shantytown, where the ex-slaves are her tenants. After being sold off the Gaither plantation by Mas Gaither, who had taken her as his mistress, she was soon sold off the Shuford plantation, where Mrs. Shuford regarded her as a "bad woman." Sin became a favorite of her new master, Hub Rankin, who settled the Shantytown property on her and still visits her regularly, a circumstance that the other ex-slaves resent. Eccentric in dress and behavior, belligerent, loud, Sin is far from the ideal mother that Tancy seeks, and the girl is very disappointed. Her acceptance of her mother as she is represents another step in

Tancy's maturing. Sin is the foil of Julia*, Miss* Puddin, and Miss Michaels*, as well as some other less important women in the book.


**SIRENS AND SPIES** (Lisle*, Janet Taylor, Bradbury, 1985), psychological mystery set in Millport, Connecticut, in contemporary times but harking back to incidents during the German occupation of France in World War II. When Miss Fitch, exotic and flamboyant violin teacher, is the victim of an assault, Elsie* Potter, 14, once her favorite and most promising student, refuses to visit her in the hospital. Mary* Potter, 15, a violin student without Elsie's talent, cannot understand her strange, independent sister, who isolates herself in the room she keeps in fanatic order amid the general chaos of their home. A softhearted, unsuspicious girl, Mary is shocked when Elsie finally tells her that Miss Fitch is a fraud with a series of nighttime men visitors, one of whom, Elsie is sure, must be the assaulter. The actual attacker, however, is a homeless alcoholic named Jimmy Dee, who has been attracted to Miss Fitch's nightly violin playing, has watched and listened repeatedly from a concealing clump of laurel bushes, and on a night when she does not play, has blundered into her house in a drunken attempt to get his concert started and knocked her down, with her head hitting a piece of furniture. An extraordinarily organized girl, Elsie has watched outside Miss Fitch's house, carefully recorded her visitors, and in the library researched the wartime period of Miss Fitch's youth in France. It is there that she runs into a picture, which she tears from the book, taken after the Liberation of Miss Fitch with her head shaved as a collaborator, a baby in her arms. When Elsie shows her the picture, Mary insists on confronting the teacher directly and letting her tell her side of the story. Miss Fitch, obviously shaken when Elsie abruptly produces the picture, tells them about the war and how as Renée Fichet, daughter of a shoemaker, she fell in love with Hans, a young German junior officer, and of their brief, idyllic romance. She also tells how Hans was shot as they emerged from the forest where they met and, briefly, how she was treated by her neighbors, escaped to Paris where her child died, and made a new life for herself in the United States. In the end, Elsie has softened a bit to understand, if not forgive, her former teacher and also her own distracted mother. Mary, who has always defended Miss Fitch against Elsie's critical suspicions, admits that the dramatic woman is something of a fraud. Point of view switches mostly between Mary and Elsie, although some passages are seen through the eyes of Jimmy Dee and the long story of Miss Fitch's youth is a flashback of her memories. The two sisters are in most ways opposites; yet both are idealistic and moral, each in her own way. Characterization of both of them and of Miss Fitch is strong, as, to a lesser degree, is that of gentle young Hans, Mrs. Potter, and the two younger sisters, Heide and Roo. The ethical questions raised are explored but not resolved. The reader, like the girls, is left with questions of how much of Miss Fitch's story is true, of why, with her great musical talent, she settled in run-down Millport, and of whether her male visitors are really old bachelor friends come for a good home-cooked meal, as she says. The novel is compelling and in some ways disturbing. ALA; SLJ.

**SIZZLE** (*Second Fiddle\**), Prudence Szyznowski, close friend, music colleague, and would-be sweetheart of Splat\*. She lives with her divorced father, Raymond, a thirty-six-year-old ex-hippie mailman and talented amateur chef, her mother having run off when Sizzle was a child to pursue a law career and a six-figure salary. The two are very close and enjoy a casual relationship for the most part, though Sizzle is somewhat protective of her father. When Raymond fails with the Salmon Szyznowski he prepares for dinner with Gwendolyn Pauling, Sizzle realizes that Kevin Lim is the Merry Prankster because, like making good Salmon Szyznowski, playing a Stradivarius takes practice. She realizes that the violin Kevin practices on when they are at his house sounds bad because Kevin is playing the real Strad. Thus she knows what really happened in the firecracker episode: Kevin destroyed with firecrackers a reproduction of his father's violin.

**THE SKELETON MAN** (Bennett\*, Jay, Watts, 1986), novel of mystery and suspense set in Kent, a town half an hour from Atlantic City, presumably in the 1980s. Although he knows little about his uncle, Edward Bond, and sees him seldom, Raymond Bond, 18, feels close to this brother of his father, a gambler who died in jail. The day after Ray's birthday, his uncle takes him to rent a safety deposit box in the local bank, puts in it thirty thousand dollars in cash, says that it is for Ray's college education, and makes him promise to tell no one about it. The next day Uncle Ed is found dead outside his hotel, evidently having jumped from the twelfth floor window. When Ray goes with his girl friend, Laurie, to Atlantic City and waits outside while she plays the slot machines, he is approached by a down-and-out gambler who trades him a Congressional Medal of Honor for nine dollars to get his car out of the parking lot. Haunted by his memory of the man, Ray adds the medal to the money in the safety deposit box. Shortly afterward, a man arranges to meet Ray in the park, introduces himself as Albert Dawson, and, with threats on Ray's life, demands the thirty thousand dollars, which he says he loaned Uncle Ed. A woman named Alice Cobb makes an appointment to meet Ray at a hotel in the next town. On the bus there Ray talks to a friendly man named Pete Wilson, whom he suspects of following him. Obviously afraid of Dawson, Alice Cobb tells Ray that she lived with Uncle Ed, that he cared deeply for Ray, and that she is sure that he was pushed from the window. She urges Ray to stall Dawson since she needs just a little time to get the proof. Harassed by both Dawson and Pete Wilson, who warns him against going to the police, Ray considers just giving back the money. He quarrels with Laurie, trying to protect her by distancing himself from her. Dawson tells him that Alice Cobb was a mental patient and cannot be believed. As an object lesson, he shoots a cat lounging near their park bench. Alice calls again, saying that she has the proof, but when Ray goes to her room he finds her dead body in the closet. Afraid and unable to sleep, Ray gets the money from the bank and tries to give it to Dawson but is forced into Dawson's car and driven to a beachfront hotel, closed for the winter. There Dawson says that he is reluctant to kill Ray, but those above him insist. Just as he is about to fire his gun, a shot rings out, his hand streams with blood, and Pete Wilson, identifying himself as a man from the Treasury Department, arrests him. Later, talking with Ray and Laurie, who are together again, Wilson says that the money, evidently loaned through Dawson to Ray's uncle by underworld figures, will probably end up as Ray's. The title comes from Uncle Ed's description of himself as a "skeleton man," drained of his humanity by his compulsion to gamble. The plot is simple and predictable. The novel's strongest element is its tone of mounting terror, enhanced by the bleak winter setting, the terse style, and the sense of impotence against dehumanized criminals. Only Ray is developed as a character, with the others drawn, perhaps deliberately, as stereotypes of evil or helplessness. Poe Nominee.

**SKURZYNSKI†, GLORIA (JEAN FLISTER)** (1930–     ), born in Duquesne, Pa.; author of a wide variety of books for young people. She attended Mt. Mary College in Pittsburgh, married an aerospace engineer, and has five daughters, one of whom is a doctor, a profession which has influenced three of her mother's books: *Bionic Parts for People: The Real Story of Artificial Organs and Replacement Parts* (Four Winds, 1978), *What Happened in Hamlin†* (Four Winds, 1979), in which a mold on grain that produces a psychedelic condition is presented as an explanation for the children's dancing, and *Manwolf* (Houghton, 1981), about a boy affected with an obscure disease that causes its victims to become like werewolves in appearance. She is also the author of several brief, illustrated books of folk tales and of the Mountain West Adventure series, one of which is *Trapped in the Slickrock Canyon** (Lothrop, 1984), winner of the Spur Award from the Western Writers of America. An earlier novel in the series is *Lost in the Devil's Desert* (Lothrop, 1982), which is set in Utah where Skurzynski makes her home.

**SLEATOR, WILLIAM (WARNER, III)** (1945–     ), born in Havre de Grace, Md.; pianist, author best known for novels of science fiction and fantasy. He received his B.A. degree from Harvard University and served as accompanist for ballet classes at the Royal Ballet School, London, in 1967 and 1968 and as rehearsal pianist for the Boston Ballet Company from 1974 to 1983. Besides writing picture books illustrated by Blair Lent, Trina Schart Hyman, Ruth Sanderson, and Steven Kellogg, he has produced a number of imaginative and intricately plotted novels of science fantasy, among them *Interstellar Pig** (Dutton, 1984), in which a space-age board game is revealed to be a conflict to the death between cosmic forces. It was named to both the American Library Association Notable Books and Best Books for Young Adults lists, to the *School Library Journal* Best Books list, and to the *Horn Book* Fanfare list. *The Boy Who Reversed Himself** (Dutton, 1986) also deals with cosmic forces, these involved with various dimensions of space and the beings who protect our dimension from incursions from others. It was named an ALA Young Adult book and an SLJ Best Book, as was *The Duplicate\** (Dutton, 1988), a story of a more localized but still chilling situation, in which a boy finds a way to make a clone of himself and discovers that having two, and eventually three, of himself more than triples his problems. Sleator's novels are noted for their ingenuity but sometimes criticized for their undeveloped characters.

**SMITH†, DORIS BUCHANAN** (1934–      ), born in Washington, D.C.; author of books for children and young adults on contemporary problems. She has lived in the South, mostly Georgia, since she was nine, attended South Georgia College in Douglas, and has been a free-lance writer since 1971. In addition to their own four children and one permanent foster child, she and her husband have been foster parents to more than twenty children. Her novel, *Tough Chauncey†* (Morrow, 1974), reflects this experience, being about a boy abused by his grandfather and neglected by his mother who seeks help as a foster child. Probably her best-known book, *A Taste of Blackberries†* (Crowell, 1973) is credited with breaking a prohibition in modern children's books against dealing with death. Among her other novels are *Salted Lemons* (Four Winds, 1980), set in Atlanta during World War II, about a friendship between a Yankee girl and a Japanese-American girl, both outsiders; *Last Was Lloyd* (Viking, 1981), about a coddled, overweight boy in Georgia; and *The First Hard Times* (Viking, 1983), its companion novel about Lloyd's friend, Ancil. *Return to Bitter Creek\** (Viking, 1986), set in the Appalachian Mountains, is strong in subtle and convincing characterization. It was named to both the American Library Association Notable Books list and the *School Library Journal* list of Best Books for Children.

**SNOWY COBB** (*Through the Hidden Door\**), weak, spindly, half-blind sixth grader in Winchester Boy's School who discovers an extensive cave containing steps, a road, a village, tombs, and a temple, all scaled for people six to eight inches tall. Snowy's father was a career army officer, reported dead seven years before but believed by the boy to be still alive, working for the CIA. He pours over *Soldier of Fortune* magazine, circling faces that resemble his father and ordering eavesdropping devices and other spy gear. Because his father evidently told him of marines who landed on a Pacific island inhabited by a race of pygmies, an island afterward bombed to extinction by the Japanese, Snowy believes from the first that what he finds in the cave are artifacts of an ancient miniature race. He is jealously possessive of his cave, not letting even Barney\* Pennimen see the entrance and only reluctantly allowing him to enlist the help of the Finneys.

*SO FAR FROM THE BAMBOO GROVE* (Watkins\*, Yoko Kawashima, Lothrop, 1986), autobiographical novel set in Korea and Japan in the last days and directly after World War II. When Yoko\* Kawashima, a Japanese who has never seen her homeland, is eleven, her family lives in Nanam, Korea, less than fifty miles from the border of Manchuria, where her father is a government official, and equally close to Russian Pacific ports. Since she takes dancing lessons, as well as lessons in calligraphy and The Way of Tea, she goes with her sister, Ko*, 16, and other children to entertain in the military hospital nearby. After the performance, she is asked to go to the room of a badly wounded soldier, Corporal* Matsumura, whose eyes are bandaged but who feels her face and her kimono and talks with her. As he recovers, he visits the family often. Her brother, Hideyo*, is sent to work in an ammunition factory twenty miles away. They learn that Tokyo has been demolished, and they prepare for air raids, but they are still surprised when Corporal Matsumura pounds on their door one night and says that the Russians are landing and that they must leave at once, since they will be specially sought out as the family of a Japanese official. Although their mother is reluctant to leave without Hideyo, she, Ko, and Yoko squeeze into a boxcar of a crowded hospital train on which the corporal has obtained permission for them to travel to Seoul and begin a nightmare journey. There is little water and almost no food; a woman next to them gives birth; another's baby dies and, when its body is flung from the train, jumps after it; Korean Communist soldiers search specifically for the three, but, with blood rubbed on them by the medics, they pass for wounded. When the train is bombed, forty-five miles from Seoul, they start down the tracks, walking by night and hiding in brush when they hear anyone approaching. They are discovered by Korean soldiers, who are just about to rape Ko when a plane flies over, strafing and killing the soldiers, wounding Yoko in the chest, and deafening her. Their mother shaves the girls' heads so that they will pass for boys, they all dress in the uniforms of the dead soldiers, and go on, although Yoko can scarcely manage the big uniform and suffers from pain in her chest and ear. They reach Seoul after about a dozen days of walking. There the Japanese are in charge, and a doctor who knows their father treats Yoko's wound and ear, both of which are infected. For weeks they live in the train station, hoping that Hideyo will arrive. Ko teaches Yoko how to scrounge food from garbage pails, but when they see girls being dragged away and raped, they board an open flatcar on a freight train to Pusan. There the mistreatment of Japanese women is even worse, but eventually they are able to board a cargo ship for Japan, imagining that all will be well when they arrive at their grandparents' home in northern Honshu. The devastation at Fukuoka, where they dock, disillusions them, and after living in a refugee camp for a month, they are forced to move on. Their mother decides that the girls must go to school in Kyoto, the only city to escape bombing. There she arranges for Yoko to attend a girls' school, and Ko starts at the university, though they live in the train station and eat garbage, while their mother travels north to find her parents. The girls at Yoko's school, who have mostly been spared the hardships of war, are very snobbish and ridicule her ragged clothes and short hair, but she makes a friend of the janitor, Mr.* Naido. After a week, Yoko's mother returns, looking terribly worn and having the sad news that both her parents and her husband's parents were killed in the bombing. Before Ko arrives, the mother dies. A woman keeps the funeral men from cheating them, goes with them to the crematorium, and offers them space to live above a warehouse that her husband owns. The next morning Yoko investigates the wrapping cloth, in which her mother carried all their small belongings, and discovers secret pockets sewn into it, one containing about a hundred dollars, and the savings books of all three children, emptied and canceled two weeks before they left Nanam. Every Saturday they go to the port at Maizuru, looking for Hideyo and pasting up posters, which Yoko makes of newspaper, giving his name and their address. In the spring, as Yoko is cooking supper outside as they have all winter, a young man approaches and she discovers that it is Hideyo. The story alternates between Yoko's adventures and those of her brother, who journeys on foot from Nanam, experiencing great hardship and many narrow escapes, so many that if the book were not based closely on real experience, they would strain credulity. The girls squabble realistically. Japanese formal customs are preserved even among the horrors of refugee life, and the importance of education, although they wear rags and live in the station, is not questioned. ALA; SLJ.

*SOMETHING UPSTAIRS* (Avi*, Orchard, 1988), mystery-fantasy involving time travel to a historical dimension, set in Providence, Rhode Island, in 1988 and almost two hundred years earlier. In an italicized frame story, frightened, nervous Kenny Huldorf, compulsively clutching a key chain, tells the author a terrifying story, which Avi sets down for the reader. On the day Kenny's family moves into the 1789 Daniel Stillwell House on Sheldon Street in Providence, Kenny senses that there is something special about the two little rooms that open off his attic bedroom. A few nights later, he awakens to the sense of a strange presence, investigates the rooms, and in the smaller one watches the ghostly figure of a teenaged boy laboriously emerge from a broad stain on the floor. Curious about the house's history, Kenny compiles a list of previous residents from a scrapbook that came with the house; reads about the history of Providence in the library; has the stained wood analyzed and learns that it is human blood; and consults a reference librarian at the Historical Library, a strange, enigmatic man called Pardon Willinghast. Willinghast seems to know about him and the house, but offers nothing in the way of help on this or later occasions, only vague warnings, behavior that foreshadows his villainy to come. Subsequently awakened again, Kenny learns that the ghost's name is Caleb, that, a slave, he was killed in the little room for protesting against the illegal slave trade, and that he wants Kenny to find and deal with his murderer. Once, after Kenny leaves Caleb's room, Kenny finds that his attic has reverted to the earlier period. He follows a dark-caped man through the night streets and finds himself in Providence of 1800 and in the midst of a bitter dispute over enforcement of the slave-import laws. Later, Kenny reads in an 1800 newspaper that Caleb took his own life in his room, a fact Caleb hotly insists is a lie. When next Kenny goes back in time, Caleb accompanies him. Kenny is taken prisoner by a slave trader, who, to his surprise, is Pardon Willinghast, but Caleb escapes. Willinghast seizes Kenny's key chain, evidently the boy's time-travel token, and says that he will return it when Kenny kills Caleb. Kenny realizes that he is caught between conflicting bitter memories, each trying to make the past what he wants it to be. Home again, Caleb suggests that Kenny pretend to shoot him, thus luring Willinghast to the attic, and then shoot Willinghast, the man who murdered him. Although reluctant and suspicious, Kenny conforms. Willinghast comes, summoned by the shot, but he detects the hoax and tries to force Kenny into shooting Caleb. Thus cornered, Kenny fires at Willinghast as planned, apparently the only one of several people Caleb had enlisted over the years in his cause to do so. When Kenny checks the 1800 newspaper again, he finds no mention of Caleb's death, just a notice about the mysterious suicide of one Pardon Willinghast. In the frame story conclusion, Kenny shows Avi Willinghast's gravestone, asserting that the "hand" by which Willinghast died was his, not Willinghast's, as the news story says. Now obsessed with his experience, he also wonders where Caleb is and whether or not he is out trying to erase other bitter memories. Although some plot details, such as the power of the key chain and Willinghast (or Caleb) to take Kenny back in time, are unexplained, the author's skill at creating tension and mystery make matters seem real and credible until looked at in retrospect. The plot premise is not new (what if history could be changed? would things be better?), but Avi's adroit handling of it and conventional Gothic elements gives it freshness and universality. The young slave's anger, frustration, and lack of confidence in Kenny, since Kenny is white, and his skill at playing on Kenny's emotions and sense of justice are convincing. Just enough background is given of the Providence slave trade, made illegal by a 1744 law that was not enforced, along with scenes of the slave merchants' greed and of local unrest to win Caleb sympathy and play up Kenny's dilemma. Artfully arranged events, judicious revelation of history, some prefiguring, and a style made quick by the many short, simple sentences and uncomplicated, concrete language result in a top-notch thriller. Poe Nominee.

**SONS FROM AFAR** (Voigt*, Cynthia, Atheneum, 1987), contemporary realistic boy's growing-up novel, set during the school winter semester in Crisfield, Maryland, and continuing the story of the Tillermans, first met in *The Homecoming* and *Dicey's Song†*. Dicey* is away at college, and Maybeth, about thirteen, a fine musician but academically slow, and her two brothers, pragmatic, active Sammy*, 12, and introverted, academically advanced James*, 15, still live with sturdy, redoutable Gram Tillerman, who has adopted all four of them. A story in which character is more important than plot, the book follows the efforts of the two boys to locate their father, whom neither can remember and who abandoned their now-deceased mother when they were very young. The enterprise is sparked by James's sense that he is different, being dark-haired, intellectual, and, he thinks, "wimpish," whereas Sammy is popular, outspoken, and athletic. Although at first he is not much interested, Sammy gradually gets caught up in the search, and the two brothers prod each other on, putting together details and clues until they get as near to the truth as they need to and grow closer as a result. They learn from Dicey that their father was Francis Verricker, a merchant seaman, once sought by the police when they still lived in Massachusetts. Sammy asks Gram for his birth certificate, and from it they learn that Verricker was born in Cambridge, Maryland. When the Reverend Mr. Smiths takes them with him on a business trip there, they talk to their father's third grade teacher, Mrs. Rottman, now an old woman. She recalls Francis as a bright, angelically handsome, curly-haired, big-eyed mischief-maker, a natural leader. She also remembers that he stole money from her, was a liar, was always in trouble, and was expelled from high school. When they contact the high school principal, he remembers Francis with loathing, calls him a ''creep,'' and says that he was expelled for gambling in school. On his own, James decides to try the Hall of Records in Annapolis, hoping to find information about the Verricker family, and he takes a job doing clerical work with two local doctors to earn the money for a school field trip there. Although he has no luck in Annapolis, James realizes that what he really wants to know is why Verricker behaved as he did, ''running off on responsibility and looking for the quick easy way'' because ''then he'd have some idea of how to be a man'' himself. He realizes that since Verricker was intelligent, he must consciously have taken the route that led to trouble. Interspersed among the quest scenes are episodes of home and school life that reveal the boys' gradually changing attitudes. Since James has his job with the doctors, Sammy enlists the help of Robin* Kelly, a new boy whose mother is divorced, to help with crabbing in James's place. Under pressure, James gives notes for a French paper to corner-cutting, cheater Andy Walker, an action he immediately regrets. The desire for information about Verricker nags the boys, however, and Sammy finally gets the idea of investigating the merchant seamen's union in Baltimore. Mr. Lingerle, Maybeth's music teacher, helps them get there. At the office they are directed to Al's Bar and Grill, in a still seamier section on the harbor, where a man called the Chief may be willing to talk to them. They cool their heels in the bar for some hours, frightened and uncomfortable, and when the Chief, a tough, brutish man, arrives, from a back room where he has been gambling, he informs them heatedly that Verricker owes him twelve hundred dollars. They learn from another sailor that Verricker jumped ship at Fiji a few years ago. This man thinks Verricker was smart enough to advance professionally but instead spent all his time figuring out how to beat the system. Although James longs to leave, Sammy persists with questions, and when the Chief learns that the boys are Verricker's sons, he attacks them, and in the ensuing brawl both boys are beaten and injured. James manages to get them home, with Mr. Lingerle's help. They have bravely survived this ordeal but have learned little they did not already know about their father. Back in school, James owns up to Mr. Norton about his part in Andy Walker's French report, earning a failing grade for the marking period but feeling better about his own morality. He has faced up to himself, unlike his father, and, to boot, he wins the respect of the girl he has a crush on. Sammy also has a moral problem. He takes Robin crabbing and loses the anchor, but he recognizes that the loss happened because he was irresponsible and unthinking. Both boys realize that the Verricker business is over. They have gotten along well without a father and know that they can continue to make good lives for themselves. They conclude that not having a father is exciting rather than frightening. Although knowing the companion Tillerman books, of which there are several, adds facets of understanding to this one, *Sons From Afar* can stand on its own. The characters are firmly and credibly drawn, and the book is richly detailed and allows plenty of space for the brothers to discuss openly and ruminate inwardly, to grow and develop, so that the reader gets to know them well. The pace is unhurried but never plodding, and, while the reader is mostly interested in how the boys gnaw away at their problem and appreciates the inevitable changes in their characters as a result, the father, though never met, emerges as a significant figure, making this an unusual father-son story. Adding texture are such other matters as James's crush on Celie Anderson, who he happily learns has integrity as well as beauty, his growing desire to become a doctor rather than a lawyer, his discovery that her husband ran out on one of the doctors for whom he works, Sammy's relationship with Robin and his growing appreciation of Maybeth's needs, and Sammy's school report, which is on Phaeton and Apollo, another father-son story. Characters and situations are neatly foiled, and some humor relieves the seriousness. This substantial slice of life makes a worthy contribution to the Tillerman series. SLJ.

**SPLAT** (*Second Fiddle**), Albert Hadley Reavis Pauling III, close friend and music colleague of Sizzle*, whom she tacitly regards as her sweetheart. Though otherwise seemingly of modest means, Splat drives and cherishes a classic Packard and is very protective of his mother, tiny, blond, shy Gwendolyn. His wealthy father simply dropped them to pursue other matters, but they receive a good allowance from the Pauling family and thus their overgrown, unkempt house in Topanga Canyon is well appointed inside and they have money for fancy restaurants. Splat takes his mother to one every Friday or Saturday, the only place she will go because of her shyness. There they enjoy lavish meals in a private room. Gwendolyn likes Sizzle immediately, invites her to her house, and accepts Sizzle's invitation to dinner at Sizzle's house, unusual behavior for her. Thus Sizzle gets the idea that Kevin Lim was behind the Merry Prankster tricks, and the romance starts between Raymond Szyznowski and Gwendolyn.

**STAY AWAY FROM SIMON!** (Carrick*, Carol, ill. Donald Carrick, Clarion, 1985), brief story of a retarded boy set in West Tisbury on Martha's Vineyard in Nantucket Sound in the 1830s. Lucy, 11, and her little brother Josiah, who have walked a long distance to school, are frightened when Simon, the miller's big, slow-witted son, joins in the schoolyard snow fight even though he no longer is one of the pupils. Lucy's friend, Desire, tells her scary stories of Simon, repeated from her brother who works in the village store. With a storm approaching, school is dismissed early. Lucy tries to encourage Josiah on the long walk home by repeating the counting song, "One, two, buckle my shoe. . . . " When she hears Simon echoing the words, she realizes that he is following them, and she cautions Josiah to hurry and pay no attention. Hoping to shake the older boy from their trail, she takes Josiah on a shortcut through the woods and soon is thoroughly confused as landmarks are hidden by the snow. Just as she is beginning to panic, Simon appears beside them, takes Josiah piggyback under his woolen smock, and lumbers off. Lucy clings to the back of his smock and, to keep her little brother from being terrified, starts the counting verse again, repeating it over and over to assure him that she is nearby. Finally, just as she is sinking exhausted into the snow and not responding to Simon's urging that she get up, her father arrives on horseback. As he takes both children up on the horse and Simon follows on foot, Lucy realizes that the miller's boy had been taking them home all along. Her parents insist that he eat dinner with them and stay the night, though they respect his wish to sleep in the barn. Lucy tells her fears to her father, who explains the unkindness of Desire's stories. Her mother sends her to the barn with a cup of hot cider for Simon. Before he will drink it, he detains her and repeats, in his halting speech but with both pride and pleasure, the verse all the way to "Nine ten big fat hen." The story is written in simple language for early readers, obviously designed to illustrate the unfair treatment of the mentally handicapped and to show the dangers of jumping to stereotyped conclusions. The basic plot is filled out with period details, especially in the scene of the schoolroom under the severe teacher, Master Hume, and the whole is pleasantly illustrated. SLJ.

**STAY PUT, ROBBIE MCAMIS** (Tunbo*, Frances G., ill. Charles Shaw, Texas Christian Univ., 1988), historical novel of pioneer hardships set from early spring to midsummer probably after the Civil War by a river along a wagon train route. The story starts tensely with Robbie McAmis, 12, bruised, battered, bloody from a wound to the head among others, awakening on the ground near Mr. Bradley's wrecked covered wagon, having been unable to control the horses during a river crossing when a terrible rainstorm struck. The only other survivors of Robbie's extended family seem to be aged, hard-to-please, fuzzy-headed, frail Grammie (Elza McAmis); Robbie's cousin Jamie, 10, ill apparently with consumption; Robbie's sister, Cynthy, 6; and three other younger cousins, two lively little girls and a baby in arms. The wagons were on their way to join Barth, Robbie's father, and Tim McAmis, Jamie's father and Robbie's uncle, on their homestead Out West. Before the crossing, Uncle Adan McAmis ordered Robbie to "stay put and watch out for Grammie and the younguns" if anything happened during the crossing, and throughout the book Robbie stubbornly does so, although sometimes he is tempted to leave to look for the rest of the family. His efforts, under Grammie's prodding and occasional directions, insure their survival in potentially hostile territory over the next weeks. Although they are fortunate to have food from the wrecked wagons with which they can supplement what they gather, like wild parsnips, and Robbie's game, tools that were intended for homesteading, like axes and a plow, a sturdy team of horses, cows, chickens, guns, good dogs, and seed, among other supplies and materials, their time is almost entirely devoted to making a living. Major efforts include building a lookout in a tall tree, which Jamie mans; fashioning a pen for the cows, one of whom has a calf the girls name Sugar, and a small chicken house; and plowing and planting a garden and eventually plowing for and putting in a corn crop. The biggest task is building a large and roomy cabin because Grammie insists that she must have a decent roof over her head. A brush fire poses a temporary problem, as do a landslide and a wildcat, which Grammie douses with hot water and Robbie shoots. They find a bee tree from which they gather honey, and they can wild plums. Robbie hunts, usually for rabbits, but he also bags a deer. Robbie sets snares for small game, and Jamie fashions a fish trap. Robbie is bothered by the morality of using Mr. Bradley's things, a matter that does not concern pragmatic Grammie at all. Altogether they are doing very well, Grammie having become more hale, hearty, and clear headed than she has been in years and Jamie no longer needing to remain in bed, when Barth and Tim McAmis and Tilson Bradley (Mr. Bradley's grown son) find them. The men have left Out West for home, when their families do not arrive as expected and also because they have become disillusioned about the wisdom of farming such "inhospitable" land. Finding their families not at home and no word about them either, they trace the wagon train route over some days. After encountering, almost by chance, Robbie's little group, Barth and Tilson leave in search of the others, locating them, lucky survivors of the storm and flood in which Robbie was injured, with a wagon train shunned because it was thought to carry cholera. A joyful reunion concludes the book. The question of what happened to the lost McAmises and Mr. Bradley is never satisfactorily answered, and the little group's efforts seem implausibly successful. Except for almost constantly grumbling Grammie and sturdy, very hardworking, never complaining Robbie, characters are undeveloped, faceless, and indistinguishable. Suspense revolves around what happened to the rest of the train and why it happened rather than around how Robbie's group will survive. Most of the interest arises from the numerous, careful details of wilderness survival, which except for the immense amount of work Robbie accomplishes almost single-handedly in so short a time, seem entirely plausible. Dialogue is "country," and tone for the most part is serious. Western Heritage.

**STOLZ‡ †, MARY SLATTERY** (1920–     ), born in Boston, Mass.; for forty years a prolific and popular author of novels of romance, growing up, family and neighborhood life, easy-to-reads, fantasy, and other realistic fiction. She attended Birch Walthen School, Columbia University, and Katherine Gibbs School, working as a bookseller at Macy's and as a secretary at Columbia Teachers' College before becoming a writer. Since the publication of *To Tell*

*Your Love‡* (Harper, 1950), a teenage romance that is the first of her some five dozen published books, she has received many honors for such animal fantasies as *Belling the Tiger†* (Harper, 1961) and *Quentin Corn** (Godine, 1985), an amusing, inventive story about an unusual pig, which was a *School Library Journal* Best Book for Children; stories of family and neighborhood life, like *The Noonday Friends†* (Harper, 1965), *A Dog on Barkham Street†* (Harper, 1960), its companion, *The Bully of Barkham Street†* (Harper, 1963), and *A Wonderful, Terrible Time†* (Harper, 1967); *The Edge of Next Year†* (Harper, 1974), a sociological problem novel concerning a death in the family and alcoholism; *Cat in the Mirror†* (Harper, 1975), a time travel fantasy; and realistic school novels like *Because of Madeline†* (Harper, 1957) and *In a Mirror†* (Harper, 195ɔ). For younger children she has written, among others, the popular reader *Emmett's Pig* (Harper, 1959) and *Zekmet, The Stone Carver: A Tale of Ancient Egypt* (Harcourt, 1988), a story published in picture book form. Some of her books have been translated into foreign languages and issued in Braille. She received the Recognition of Merit Award from the George C. Stone Center for Children's Books in honor of her total writing for the young.

**STONE FOX** (Gardiner*, John Reynolds, ill. Marcia Sewall, Crowell, 1980), brief novel for early middle readers set in Jackson, Wyoming, evidently in the very early twentieth century, telling how a young boy and his dog save the family farm from being sold and his grandfather from mental and physical collapse. Little Willy, 10, lives on a small potato farm not far from town with Grandfather, a cheerful, fun-loving man, and Searchlight, a big black dog with a white spot on her forehead the size of a silver dollar. One morning when Grandfather will not get out of bed or answer him, Willy is so worried that he goes for Doc Smith, a woman doctor who lives not far away. She says that there is nothing physically wrong with the old man and suggests that they arrange for a woman in town who takes care of the old and sick to take him in, find a home on a farm for Searchlight, and have Willy come stay with her. Willy refuses, determined to run the farm himself and make his Grandfather want to live again. He makes two important discoveries: that Grandfather can communicate "Yes" and "No" by hand motions, and that the money box is empty except for some letters. When Willy suggests using his fifty dollars saved for college to rent a horse for the potato harvest, Grandfather signals, "No." Willy solves the problem by hitching Searchlight to the plow and sells the harvest, but Grandfather is still troubled. During the winter Willy and Searchlight practice racing home from town with the dog pulling a lightweight wooden sled. One day a man waiting for them at the farm turns out to be a tax collector, and Willy learns that the letters in the money box are ten years of tax bills and that they owe five hundred dollars. Willy talks to Doc Smith, to the banker, to his teacher, and to all the rest of his friends in town, and they all advise him to sell the farm. Then Willy sees a poster about the National Dogsled Races in February, with a cash prize of five hundred dollars. Confidently, Willy takes his fifty dollars from the bank for the entrance fee, although he is warned that a Shoshone Indian named Stone Fox, who has won many races, is also entered. The week before the race he sees the Indian, a giant who will speak to no white man and who drives a team of beautiful Samoyeds. The night before the race, Willy, coming home late from town with medicine for Grandfather, hears barking coming from an old barn and, investigating, sees the white Samoyeds in the dark barn. Then a great fist crashes into his face, knocking him over backward. Although Stone Fox does not speak to him, Willy explains why he needs the money and insists that he will win. The next morning, with his right eye swollen shut, Willy lines up at the race start with Searchlight, the only single dog and the only boy among nine entries. His lightness and Searchlight's familiarity with the route give Willy an early head start, and as they pass the farmhouse he sees Grandfather in the window, the first time the old man has left his bed in months. Gradually, Stone Fox catches up until, just a hundred feet from the finish line, Searchlight puts forth a tremendous effort and her heart bursts. Stone Fox pulls his sled up alongside, then draws a line across the road, fires his rifle in the air, and speaks for the first time to white men, "Anyone crosses this line—I shoot." He holds all the other racers until Willy picks up Searchlight and carries the dead dog across the finish line. Though predictable, the story is pleasantly written, and little Willy is an appealing hero. The win of a single dog against trained teams and the characterization of Stone Fox might not bear close scrutiny, but in context for the intended audience both are believable. Stone.

**STRASSER, TODD** (1950–      ), born in New York City; journalist, author of novels for teenagers. He received his B.A. degree from Beloit College and worked as a reporter for the *Times Herald Record* in Middleton, N.Y., as a copywriter for an advertising firm, and as a researcher for *Esquire* magazine. He is also the owner of a fortune cookie company. His first novel, *Angel Dust Blues* (Coward, 1979), about young people and drugs, set his pattern of dealing with contemporary and often controversial subjects. *Friends Till the End* (Delacorte, 1981) features a boy whose friend has leukemia. It was named to the American Library Association Best Books for Young Adults list, as was *Rock 'n' Roll Nights* (Delacorte, 1982), about a young rock band. Its sequel is *Turn It Up!* (Delacorte, 1984). *A Very Touchy Subject* (Delacorte, 1985) is about sex. His mystery story, *The Accident\** (Delacorte, 1988), was a nominee for the Edgar Allan Poe Award. Using the pseudonym of Morton Rhue he wrote *The Wave* (Delacorte, 1981), a novelization of a teleplay by Johnny Dawkins.

***STREAMS TO THE RIVER, RIVER TO THE SEA*** (O'Dell\*, Scott, Houghton, 1986), biographical novel of Sacagawea, the young Indian woman who accompanied the Lewis and Clark expedition to the Pacific Coast in the first decade of the nineteenth century. At thirteen, the narrator, Sacagawea, which means Bird Woman, and her cousin, Running Deer, of the nomadic Agaiduka Shoshone people, are captured and enslaved by the Minnetarees from the east. They are taken from what is now Three Forks, Montana, to the village of Metaharta, near what is now Mandan, North Dakota. There Sacagawea's captor, Tall Rock, is overruled by the chief, Black Moccasin, who wants Sacagawea as a wife for his son, Red Hawk. She is kidnapped by Tall Rock and taken to Hidatsa, a nearby but hostile Minnetaree village, where the one-eyed chief, known as Le Borgne, wants the girl for himself. Afraid of both men, Sacagawea slips away and takes a bull boat, which wrecks on an island in the Missouri River. There she stays alone through the fall and early winter until a man and an Indian girl, paddling upstream, pick her up and take her to Metaharta, where the man, a half-French, half-Sioux trader named Toussaint Charbonneau, claims her, as do also Red Hawk and Le Borgne, who is visiting to trade. The three men play the Game of Hands, a variant of the shell game, for her, and the Frenchman wins. Sacagawea must marry him. He and his first wife, Otter Woman, go off trading, and Sacagawea discovers that she is pregnant. Before she delivers, the Lewis and Clark expedition, sent in 1804 by President Thomas Jefferson to explore the newly purchased Louisiana Territory, arrives at Metaharta. Captain William Clark, whose friendliness and copper-colored hair attract Sacagawea from the first, hires Charbonneau as a guide, partly because his Shoshone wife may be useful in helping them acquire horses when they reach the mountains. They wait until Sacagawea's baby is born, a boy she calls Meeko, meaning Little Brown Squirrel, Charbonneau calls Jean Baptiste, and Clark calls Pompey. They encounter numerous hardships going up river. Charbonneau proves to be uncouth, brutal, and, Sacagawea suspects, treacherous to the expedition. Near the headwaters of the Missouri, they find the Shoshones, led now by Sacagawea's brother, Cameahwait. Although she and the baby could stay with them, Sacagawea opts to continue, mostly because she deeply loves Captain Clark, who calls her Janey, teaches her English, and seems to return her affection. Surviving extreme difficulties, they finally reach the Pacific Ocean and return over the mountains to Fort Mandan. On the eastern slope of the Rockies, Sacagawea hopes to lose Charbonneau to the third wife he has acquired, a Flathead chief's daughter, but he returns to the expedition. On the Yellowstone, Clark carves his name on a high rock, which he names Pompey's Pillar for the baby. Before they leave Fort Mandan, Meriweather Lewis gives Sacagawea his Newfoundland dog, Scannon, and Clark proposes that he take both her and the baby to St. Louis to school. She remembers the warning of Clark's black servant, Ben York, that a white man who marries an Indian is called a Squawman and is looked down upon. Sacagawea takes the baby and starts back westward, giving up her hope of a life with Clark and planning to return to her Shoshone people. The novel follows the journals of the Lewis and Clark expedition closely, departing from them mainly to omit those things that Sacagawea could not know and adding her own emotional reactions to events and especially to Captain Clark. Whether he fully returns this love or whether he considers her only a charming and beautiful Indian child is left unresolved. O'Dell.

**STRIEBER, WHITLEY** (1945–      ), born in San Antonio, Tex.; advertising executive, novelist, writer of screenplays, known in children's literature for his controversial novel *Wolf of Shadows\** (Knopf, 1985). A Best Book for Children of the *School Library Journal*, it tells how, after a nuclear holocaust devastates the United States, a resourceful leader wolf and a strong human woman unite in an effort to survive. The story is especially vivid in its delineation of the stricken terrain and the ways of wolves, which Strieber has tracked and studied in northern Minnesota, the area of lakes and woods that is the novel's initial setting. Strieber first gained attention for his adult novels of the occult and the supernatural, *The Wolfen* (Morrow, 1978) and *The Hunger* (Morrow, 1981), both of which were adapted for the screen. His concern with nuclear war also appears in his adult books like *Black Magic* (Morrow, 1982) and *Warday: And the Journey Onward* (Holt, 1984). He was graduated from the University of Texas with a B.A. degree, received a certificate from the London School of Economics and Political Science, and has made his home in New York City.

**SUZY** (*Izzy, Willy-Nilly\**), Izzy Lingard's best friend until after the auto accident that claims Izzy's right leg. Suzy is bright, articulate, fashionable, and popular. For years the two, along with Lisa and Lauren, have formed a foursome that everyone knows is very close, a social clique. Izzy knows that Suzy is not always on the up and up with her friends and is very good at dissembling and evading, even lying, especially to her mother, but has always made allowances for her. After the accident Izzy knows that something is wrong with their friendship when Suzy is slow about visiting her in the hospital and then calls her and emotionally asks her not to tell anyone that Marco Griggers was driving the car. Later when she realizes that Suzy and Marco are dating, she concludes that the two deserve each other. Eventually Suzy drops Marco for a college man she meets in a mall. She represents the superficial teenaged girl who chooses her friends because they are socially important to her and values looks above almost everything. She is a foil for Rosamunde\* Webber.

***SWEET CREEK HOLLER*** (White\*, Ruth, Farrar, 1988), substantial realistic novel of family and neighborhood life set from 1948 to 1954 in Sweet Creek Holler, a pocket in a coal-mining region of the Virginia Appalachians. Ginny (Virginia Carol) Shortt, six when the story begins, tells how she and her family, her shy, attractive Mama\* and her sister, spunky Junie\*, 9, move to a four-room shack in the Holler after her coal miner father is shot to death, concentrating on the first and last years of this six-year span. Two main aspects unify the episodic plot: Ginny's friendship with pretty, sparkly Lou\* Jean Purvis, a neighbor girl five years her senior, and her family's relationship with the Clancys, the wealthy owners of the local mine. On the day the Shortts arrive in Sweet Creek Holler, Ginny and Junie acquire a puppy, Buddy, who becomes special to Ginny, and meet chattery Christine Ratliff, 11, who lives next door and enjoys sharing information about neighbors and school and likes to organize them. Lou Jean Purvis soon invites them to a candy party, and, in spite of the age difference, she and Ginny grow very close. The girls have good times over the years, playing pretend games, swinging on the vine that extends out over the often smoldering slag heap behind the Clancy house until Josh* Clancy, who runs the local mines, has to rescue Lou Jean from falling into it, and attending a revival, among many other activities. After sixth grade, Lou Jean goes to Coaltown to school, and at sixteen she acquires a boy friend, by whom she becomes pregnant. Her religious, termagant mother berates her constantly for shaming the family. When her mother's verbal abuse continues after the baby is born, Lou Jean commits suicide by setting herself on fire, an act that shocks the little community. On arrival, the Shortt girls also learn about and much later become acquainted with the Clancys, who live in the biggest house around. Christine early informs them that the Clancys are "strange," that Mrs. Clancy, Josh's mother, is a witch, and that the elder Mr. Clancy went mad and shot his two little girls to death. On the way home from Lou Jean's candy party, in the dark, Junie sees the two Clancy girls sitting on the Clancy porch. Several other sightings follow as the years pass. The Shortt girls meet Mrs. Clancy for the first time when they go to her house to borrow catalogs so that Junie may find a new hair style for a party and are greeted courteously if distantly. Later, Josh accidentally drives over Buddy the dog, takes distraught Ginny into his house, and fetches Mama and Junie. Soon Mama becomes the Clancys' housekeeper and a friendship develops between the two families and a low-keyed romance between Mama and Josh. The girls learn that local gossip is wrong and that the Clancy girls died of typhoid. After their death old Mr. Clancy, stricken with grief, shot himself and Mrs. Clancy became a recluse. Associating with the Shortts brings Mrs. Clancy out, but the Clancys have decided to sell their mines and move back to Pennsylvania. Mrs. Clancy finds a job for Mama with her sister, who owns a bookstore there, and the Shortts plan to move, too. The girls look forward to their new life and to a possible marriage between Mama and Josh. The very large cast of characters also includes Mrs.* Moore, the vicious hollow gossip and Lou Jean's often inebriated father, Nit* Purvis. Episodes are constructed with skill, among them Buddy following Ginny to school and winning the regard of her at first highly disapproving teacher when he bites the room bad boy; the Sweet Creek Star Club excluding Ginny because she has grown bossy and they disagree with her about mounting a play that she wrote; Poppy* (grandfather) Shortt appearing at Christmas laden with gifts. The fantasy scenes—the sightings of the dead girls and especially the one in which they speak to each other about Ginny—seem unnecessarily concocted for suspense and pathos. The book has plenty of action and human interest to hold the attention without them, and the mystery about the Clancys does not need such bolstering. Some colloquial speech spices the style and contributes to setting and characterization. Ginny seems to be an observant and honest narrator but lacks definition and functions more as a window on events rather than as someone with whom the reader can identify.

The other main characters are individualized and rounded, but except for Lou Jean, the most interesting figures are the adults. Best are the pictures of coal-mining life in the small, secluded, claustrophobic, economically marginal area where everyone knows everyone else and feels justified in helping them run their lives and of the Shortts' austere but warm domestic situation. The fairy-tale ending is satisfactory given the characters of Mama and Josh as presented. ALA.

# T

**TAMER SHIPP** (*Come a Stranger**), young Harlem minister who takes the Reverend Mr. Amos Smiths's place with the Crisfield black congregation for the summer, so Mr. Smiths may serve a more needy congregation and Mr. Shipp can get a rest from the difficult parish he serves in New York City. Tamer is handsome, capable, very outgoing and people oriented, devoted to his calling, astute, and well liked in the community. He delivers his sermons in a voice "low and rich, like a bassoon" and is indulgent to a fault with his fluttery, clinging wife, Alice*. He shares his doubts about his faith with Mina, saying that something is wrong with a world in which there is so much suffering and injustice, a world in which someone as stirring as Bullet Tillerman can be killed in a senseless war. Mina eventually finds a way to help him see that the Tillermans have survived this hard knock along with others. At the end Tamer takes a job with a college, where he will be able to stretch a little both intellectually and religiously. Tamer Shipp earlier appeared in *The Runner*, a companion book to the Tillerman series.

*TANCY* (Hurmence*, Bertha, Clarion, 1984), substantial historical novel that takes place in the North Carolina Piedmont near the town of Knoxford for two years beginning at Christmas in 1864. Shortly after the death of Mas Gaither, on whose plantation Tancy, 16, is a favored slave, being maid to the mistress, the inquisitive girl makes an important discovery. She reads in his daybook the entry recording her birth and another indicating that her mother, Lulu, was sold while Tancy was still a baby to Thad Shuford of the neighboring plantation. She makes another important discovery when Miss* Puddin, her mistress, catches her son, Billy, trying to rape Tancy and blurts out that Tancy is his sister. Tancy realizes that Mas Gaither was kind to her because she was his daughter and becomes determined to find her mother. Billy is killed in the war, leaving Miss Puddin in sole charge of the plantation, and times become very hard, especially after the war ends. Most of the slaves leave then, including Julia*, the regal cook, and Stud, formerly Billy's body slave and now in charge of the Gaither mill. Although still curious about her mother, Tancy stays on for some weeks, not yet self-possessed enough to leave, sincerely attached to Miss Puddin, who very much needs her, and drawn to little Jemmy, three or four, whose mother, Mary, had also been sold off the plantation. Finally realizing that Miss Puddin will never willingly let her go, Tancy takes little Jemmy, who remains her responsibility for most of the rest of the book, and leaves early one summer morning. She makes what for her, inexperienced as she is, seems a frightening journey to Knoxford and the Freedmen's Bureau. There a white woman in a mobcap, Miss* Michaels, who authorizes meals for hungry people and detects that Tancy is literate, gets her a job in her office. Tancy continues to inquire about her mother, while holding several other positions, including teaching both adults and children in the little bureau school. Mrs. Shuford, who shows up intending to reclaim her "niggers," tells her that Lulu was sold off Shufords' because she was a "bad woman." Tancy also encounters Stud, who informs her that Jemmy's mother is in Shantytown, the ragtag cluster of shacks occupied by ex-slaves not far from Knoxford. Torn between emotion and morality, for months Tancy delays investigating Shantytown. She works diligently and saves her money, depositing it in the bank at Miss Michaels's suggestion. Stud proposes to her, but she refuses, not yet ready for such a commitment. Christmas comes, and then spring, when nightmares over her dilemma and Jemmy's questions about his mother so bother her conscience that she is motivated to action. In Shantytown, she soon encounters Mary (Jemmy's mother) and meets Mary's younger brother, Henry*. Henry proudly shows her the school that he has started in Shantytown and introduces her to the woman landlord of Shantytown, coarse, blowsy Sin*, who ironically turns out to be Tancy's mother. Though Sin is far from Tancy's romantic notion of what her mother would be like, Tancy stays with her for several days, but, when Henry presses her to teach at his school, she leaves. Finding the bureau closed and Miss Michaels gone, she decides to return to the Gaithers' plantation. There she soon realizes that if she stays Miss Puddin will run her life again, returns to Knoxford, to be near to but not to live with her mother, and takes a job at the bank. She looks forward to the position as an adventure in finding out what she is suited for in life. The first half of the book presents a strong sense of slave life, particularly from the woman's point of view, and the second half looks at the turmoil of Reconstruction, from both the slaves' vantage point and that of a deeply concerned and sympathetic white woman. Generous details flesh out the picture of plantation life during that turbulent period, in both the big house and the slave quarters, and Tancy's term at the bureau and in Shantytown have a strongly ironic twist as the hopes of helpful and idealistic northerners and southerners are dashed by circumstances beyond their control. Tancy grows believably from a simpering, manipulative, sly, barely likeable girl into a strong, assertive young woman able to take charge of her destiny. Other characters, if stereotyped, are skillfully foiled, and while the plot seems predictable and tailored for instruction, it is sufficient to hold the reader's interest. SLJ.

**TANT SANNIE** (*Waiting for the Rain**), Frikkie's aunt, wife of Oom* Koos. Tant Sannie represents white South African women, particularly those of Dutch descent, who assume that they are naturally superior to the blacks who work for them, have a right to their labor, and feel contempt for them. Tengo wonders why, when Tant Sannie is a big, husky woman who can do for herself, she should take it for granted that his overworked and tired mother, Selina*, should work such long hours for her. He feels that it is unreasonable, but typical of the whites, for Tant Sannie to require that Selina stay extra hours doing things that only make life more comfortable for Tant Sannie and Oom Koos but are not really necessary.

**TAYLOR†, MILDRED D.,** born in Jackson, Miss.; teacher and author of realistic stories for children, most noted for her several novels about Cassie Logan and her relatives, the black family in Depression Mississippi about whom the Newbery Award-winning *Roll of Thunder, Hear My Cry†* (Dial, 1976) revolves. Taylor grew up in Toledo, Ohio, received her degree from the University of Toledo, and did graduate work in journalism at the University of Colorado. She helped organize a black studies program while she was at Colorado, served in the Peace Corps in Ethiopia teaching English and history, and later recruited for the corps. Her books evolved from the stories her father told about the history of the blacks and his own family and carry the conviction of actual experience. Her other books about the Logans include *Song of the Trees* (Dial, 1975), *Let the Circle Be Unbroken* (Dial, 1981), *The Friendship** (Dial, 1987), which was a *Boston Globe-Horn Book* Award Winner and winner of the Coretta Scott King Award, as well as being named a Best Book by the American Library Association, and *The Road to Memphis* (Dial, 1990). A companion novel is *Mississippi Bridge* (Dial, 1990). *The Gold Cadillac** (Dial, 1987), a brief story of a black Toledo family's disturbing trip south based on Taylor's own experiences, received the Christopher Award.

**THANH BROUGHTON** (*Park's Quest**), wild, cheeky Vietnamese half-sister of Park, now stepdaughter to Park's Uncle Frank*. Having survived the war, boat life, and years in a refugee camp, Thanh has an externally tough independence, but with the baby on the way she displays her vulnerability in her fears that Frank, whom she obviously adores, will no longer want her when he has his own child. Although she is exasperatingly cocksure and makes fun of Park, she accepts stoically his statement that their father is dead and seems to feel a genuine bond with him after they care for both the injured crow and their handicapped grandfather together.

**THEO** (*The Beggar Queen**), hero of a series of three novels by Lloyd Alexander* set in the fictitious kingdom of Westmark*. In *Westmark*, Theo is a lowly printer's devil who gets caught up in events that restore Augusta, the lost princess of the realm also known as Mickle*, to her rightful position. In *The Kestrel*, while Mickle is ruling as Queen Augusta, dissident aristocrats conspire to over-throw her, and Theo becomes the war leader known as Captain Kestrel for his bold and daring raids against the enemy. In the last book, *The Beggar Queen*, Theo must help Mickle recover her kingdom after a coup by the notorious Cabbarus, former prime minister, and at the end becomes her husband.

*THE THIRD EYE* (Duncan*, Lois, Little, 1984), psychic thriller set for a few weeks in the period of publication mostly in Albuquerque, New Mexico. Serious-minded, pretty, blond high school senior, Karen Connors has always been a little different. Her unusualness becomes a matter of public record when she locates through a brief vision little lost Bobby Zenner, a boy that she has been baby-sitting and who has climbed inside the trunk of Karen's boy friend's car. The policeman on that case, young, strikingly blue-eyed Officer Ron* Wilson, convinced that she has psychic powers, asks her to help find another missing child, Carla Sanchez. She does, although the child is dead, having been drowned in the river. When the publicity about these cases gets out, Karen is besieged by requests for help, which pour in by phone and mail. Mrs.* Connors is highly disapproving, fearing that the family will be ostracized. Then Karen's boy friend, Tim Dietz, big man around school, urges her to discover the questions on their American literature exam, but Karen refuses and they break up. On graduation night, she dreams that a little blond girl is in danger and awakens in fear. This buildup leads to the book's big problem: Karen is kidnapped on the way to her summer job in the nursery at Heights Day Care Center. Her kidnappers are a red-haired woman, who says that she is Betty Smith, and a bearded man called Jed. Outside the apartment in which they confine her Karen sees a laundry truck. Having escaped by activating the smoke alarm, to which she is attracted by the visionary blond girl, Karen learns that twelve babies have been kidnapped from the center, borne off in a laundry truck. Officer Wilson persuades her to accom-pany him, one of the children being his strikingly blue-eyed nephew, Matthew, and they drive north into the mountains. Another psychic, Anne Summers, Ron's tenth grade high school teacher, who has been working on a similar case in Dallas and has been shot, has had a premonition that the kidnappers are heading for mountains. Karen's own psychic "third eye" view of a scene among red rocks and a snow-covered mountain and a chance discovery of a post card with scenes from that vision lead them to the Garden of the Gods near Colorado Springs and then toward Denver. Her psychic powers have also determined that Betty and Jed are running an adoption black market, selling kidnapped babies. The rousing climax comes at a remote mountain cabin where the dozen babies are held. Ron gets shot, and Karen is captured trying to help him. Suddenly, when all seems lost, police break in and rescue them, having been alerted to their whereabouts by a mysterious phone call from a woman. Karen later learns that it was her mother who called and that Mrs. Connors also has psychic powers which hitherto she has denied. Karen also learns that the little girl of her vision is her daughter-to-be by Ron, the two by now having fallen in love. The story is realistic except for the visions, which are made to seem possible, but the little blond girl is overly melodramatic. Coincidence plays a strong role in resolving the carefully constructed plot, but characters, except for the faceless villains, have more depth than usual for the form, and the reader has been prepared for the outcome by small hints about Mrs. Connors. The atmosphere of tension starts early and holds to the very end. Poe Nominee.

**THROUGH THE HIDDEN DOOR** (Wells*, Rosemary, Dial, 1987), novel of two boarding school boys who discover the remains of an ancient miniature civilization in a cave in Massachusetts, presumably in the 1980s. Because as an outsider from Colorado he is lonely, the narrator, Barney* Pennimen, 13, has allied himself with the worst element in Winchester Boys' Academy, led by Rudy Sader. He has helped them cheat and pull mean tricks, but he is genuinely shocked when they stone the collie belonging to the headmaster, Mr. Finney, which is acting strange. While Barney protests ineffectually, half-blind Snowy* Cobb, a strange little sixth grader, rushes up and discovers a bone caught between the dog's teeth, and the older boys flee. Although he smashes his glasses and cannot recognize the other boys, Snowy identifies Barney by his lisp, which recurs when he is upset, and Mr. Finney pressures him to name the others, who are then expelled. Because the publicity will be bad for the school and one of the wealthy fathers offers to donate a new indoor pool to hush up matters, the board of directors reverses Mr. Finney's decision, and the boys are reinstated with full pardons. Mr. Finney resigns in protest, Mr. Silks, the martinet science teacher, is named head, Barney is severely punished, and Rudy's gang starts to terrorize him. Because part of his punishment is to write long research papers and because Rudy's gang cannot get at him in the library, Barney spends all his free time there, where Snowy also puts in long hours researching the bone pulled from the collie's teeth, which appears to be a tiny human leg bone and has been carbon-dated at one hundred thousand years old. Snowy enlists Barney as an aide, blindfolds him to ensure his keeping the place secret, and leads him into a cave where the dog discovered the bone. There he has uncovered a set of miniature marble steps leading down to an underground river. Although Barney resists the idea, Snowy is convinced that these were built by an ancient pygmy race. Partly because the cave is a place to hide out from Rudy and his friends, Barney joins Snowy in clearing away deep sand to hunt for further artifacts. Gradually they uncover a miniature village, a fire pit, and a temple with columns wound with carved snakes. Snowy continues to insist on the blindfold, and the only people taken into the boys' confidence are the Finneys. Mr. Finney, examining Barney's drawings of their find, thinks that it is the work of some mad hermit or a group of snake worshipers who passed through the area years before. Dr. Dorothy Finney, his scientist wife, is more open to their suggestion of a pygmy race because she notes that no individual fireplaces or cooking facilities are provided in the little homes and points out that fire cannot be miniaturized, though scale-model replicas would make provisions for individual fires. They also find tiny gold faces, like death masks, surrounded by what looks like delicate ivory spears. Inadvertently Barney brushes one with his hand and is in a coma for more than four weeks, evidently bitten, the doctors think, by a snake. Trouble with Rudy's gang erupts again, when they think that he has reported them cheating and vow revenge, breaking one of his fingers as a reminder. They follow Snowy and blindfolded Barney into the cave and vandalize the little village. Snowy tries to shoot them with a pistol that Barney's father gave him. Barney takes the weapon, shoots out the lanterns, and Snowy leads him out, blindfolded as usual, leaving Rudy and his gang in the cave. At the graduation celebration that night, Mr. Silks, who previously has sabotaged Barney's efforts to get into his father's prep school, offers to fake perfect grades on Barney's application if he will tell the boys' whereabouts. Barney rejects the bribe. Mr. Finney, however, persuades Barney to try to find the way back to the cave and save the boys. He does, taking the collie with him for protection. When they are out, the dog gets away and the boys attack Barney. He scares them off with a cobra's tooth he took from the cave. Leaving further exploration of the cave to Snowy, Barney goes to Exeter, where Mr. Finney has become dean of students. The boarding school milieu provides an interesting, if exaggerated, setting for the story, which is treated as entirely realistic, although the idea of a miniature race will be considered fantasy by most readers. Barney's doubts, which gradually decrease, help to establish credibility. Characters are somewhat overdrawn but effective in the context. The school assignments, described in detail, sound too advanced for eighth grade, even in a demanding school. Poe Nominee.

**TITO CRUZ** (*Scorpions**), best friend of Jamal Hicks, different in personality but devoted to the more assertive boy. Tito is round-faced and pretty, timid, and a devout Catholic. He is always uneasy with Jamal's gun and urges him to throw it away or give it back to Mack, yet ironically his grandmother finds it when he is keeping it for Jamal and it is he who shoots both Angel and Indian. His guilt so preys on his mind that he becomes ill, and, by the time he starts back to Puerto Rico, he has become pale and gaunt.

**TOGAN** (*The Samurai's Tale**), cook for the lowest servants in Lord Akiyama's* mansion. His nickname, meaning melon, refers to his unusually large head which, combined with very short legs, gives him an almost deformed appearance. Togan is educated, a musician, and something of a philosopher, attempting to make Taro contented with his position in life. Although he is unsuccessful in this, he does teach the boy many things and is always a kind, if firm, master, a father figure of importance to him. He dies defending Taro from a renegade soldier at a wrestling match.

**TOLAN, STEPHANIE S.** (1942–      ), born in Canton, Ohio; college teacher, playwright, novelist. She received her B.A. and M.A. degrees from Purdue University and was an instructor in continuing education at the Purdue University campus in Fort Wayne, Ind. In addition to teaching speech, theater, and English at the State University of New York at Buffalo, at Franklin and Marshall College in Lancaster, Pa., and at Indiana University, she was an actress with Curtain Call Company in the early 1970s. Since 1976 she has been a full-time writer and in 1981 was a fellow at Breadloaf Writers Conference in Vermont. Most of her novels for young people have teenaged characters, an exception being *A Time to Fly Free* (Scribner's, 1983), in which a ten-year-old, a misfit in school, learns about himself and life by helping a retiree who rescues wounded birds. Among her other novels are *The Last of Eden* (Warne, 1980), a story of a girls' boarding school, *The Liberation of Tansy Warner* (Scribner's, 1980), about a girl's conflict with her father after her mother leaves the family, and *A Good Courage** (Morrow, 1988), in which a boy is trapped in an abusive religious sect. Tolan has also written poems, several plays, nonfiction, and adult novels.

**TONI DOUGLAS** (*Circle of Gold**), Mattie* Mae Benson's best friend, "a bouncy, cheerful girl with bright black eyes and thick black hair that she wore in braids," "a chocolate bubble floating through life." A clever shopper, she takes Mattie to Stern's department store, where she helps Mattie make her clothes money go much farther than Mattie could have and where Mattie spies the beautiful gold and pearl pin that she sets her heart on for her mother. Toni is a staunch and loyal sidekick.

**TONY MARCEL** (*Izzy, Willy-Nilly**), handsome, intelligent, serious-minded senior at Izzy Lingard's high school, editor of the school paper. At the post-game party, he offers to drive Izzy home when it is obvious that Marco Griggers has had too much to drink but does not push the offer when Marco takes offense. After the accident that claims Izzy's right leg, he feels guilty because of the drinking and his lack of assertiveness. To help her and to ease his conscience, he explains, he asks Izzy to work on the paper. When Deborah, his dark, pretty, smart girl friend, also on the paper staff, gets accepted to Stanford, Tony mopes, knowing that she will grow away from him because he will be attending state college. Because Izzy has put extra time in on the paper, other staff members having devoted themselves to exams, listens sympathetically, and advises him to make the most of the life he has, he takes her seriously, perks up, and says that he hopes that she and he will always be friends. When at the end he walks away from their conversation, leaving Izzy to get her crutches for herself, the first time that he has forgotten to help her, she realizes that he likes her and accepts her for herself alone and not because she is a cripple. If Tony is too good and an obvious foil for Marco, he is still an interesting character who does more than advance the plot.

***TRAPPED IN THE SLICKROCK CANYON*** (Skurzyznski*, Gloria, ill. Daniel San Souci, Lothrop, 1984), adventure novel set in Arizona in modern times, in which two cousins through a harrowing experience overcome their mutual antagonism and learn to appreciate each other. In alternating chapters, first-person narrators Justin Farrell and his cousin, Gina Farrell, both twelve, tell of twenty-four hours starting when they accompany their fathers on a rock-climbing picnic. Gina's father, Dylan, is a surgeon from Denver, with elaborate and expensive climbing gear, while his identical twin brother, Bill, is a hard-working rancher. Both are skillful climbers. Gina, whose mother recently left the family to become a potter in San Francisco, becomes almost hysterical watching the men climb, and, to get her out of the way, Bill tells Justin to take her for a walk to see a petroglyph that he found earlier. Annoyed at having to share his discovery with Gina, whom he considers a spoiled rich brat, Justin sets an extremely fast pace, and Gina, rather than admit that she can barely keep up, grits her teeth between their exchanged insults and says nothing about the blisters that her new hiking boots are rubbing on her heels. As they reach the ridge, they hear the whine of a power rock saw, and, peering over the edge, they see two vandals cutting the petroglyph from the cliffside. They also see that the men have a high-powered rifle and that a Bureau of Land Management man is climbing the steep slope, taking pictures of the vandalism as he approaches. Spotting this BLM man, the vandals give him a push, sending him backward down into the chasm. Gina screams, attracting the attention of the vandal named Jaggers, who seizes the rifle and climbs toward them. Chased by Jaggers, the two youngsters run down the path that they just climbed, then detour into a side canyon rather than cross an open space. Gina jumps from a pile of boulders onto a muddy spot and is almost sucked down by quick sand. Justin has just saved her when he notices clouds and hears the sound of a flash flood. He nearly panics, since the canyon sides are slick and vertical. Gina discovers a series of small holes, Moki steps, carved by ancient Indians to get to a storage ledge. Gina climbs ahead, but the water rises before Justin can reach the ledge, and a log swept by the rushing waters hits and breaks his foot. Gina, who wants to be a surgeon and knows a good deal about medicine, cuts off Justin's boot with the edge of her broken mirror, diagnoses the break, and binds the foot with strips torn from her shirt. The two spend a cold, wet, and hungry night, huddled together for warmth, confessing to each other their hurt, Gina from her mother's abandonment, and Justin from the death of a friend in a motorcycle accident just after they quarreled. In the morning, despite her sore heels and her fear that Jaggers might still be seeking them, Gina starts out, hoping that she can follow the directions Justin gives her to reach the highway. Toward late afternoon Justin hears voices from above. Gina has met their fathers, who are searching on horses, and they have ridden over the top of the mesa. Dylan rappels down to the ledge, examines and rebandages Justin's foot, and fastens him into a harness so that he can pull himself up to the cliff top. Rescuers have found the BLM man, who has fallen on a ledge, badly injured but alive, and the body of Jaggers, drowned in the flash flood. The other vandal has been caught and the petroglyph saved for a museum. Gina's mother, alerted when the youngsters were missed, has flown from San Francisco, and it is arranged that Gina will spend some vacations with her, some on the ranch with Justin. The adventures are action packed and absorbing, with a good sense of the physical setting. The youngsters' personal problems are less compelling, with Justin's guilt about his motorcycling friend dragged in unnecessarily. Spur.

**TROUBLE'S CHILD** (Walter*, Mildred Pitts, Lothrop, 1985), girl's growing-up novel set for a year and a half in the early 1980s among the black fisherfolk of tiny Blue Isle off the coast of Louisiana. Pretty Martha Dumas, 14, must choose between the pattern of life for women on the island and her intense desire for more education. The island women, and particularly her grandmother, Titay, who has raised her, expect her to declare her quilt pattern, that is, indicate that she is ready to marry, follow in her grandmother's footsteps, and become the next midwife, caretaker, and wise woman for the island's 250 inhabitants. But Martha, who enjoys helping her grandmother gather herbs and cure, feels that she simply does not know enough and yearns to go to high school, an impossibility since the nearest one is fifty miles away and they have little money. Since the islanders believe that one born in a storm as Martha was is destined for trouble, Martha has doubts about the rightness of her ambition. Miss Boudreaux, her former teacher, encourages her, however, and even tutors her in high school subjects so that by book's end Martha is ready for tenth grade. Tee, the intended of her old school friend, Ocie, also tells her to try for further schooling. After Ocie and Tee are married, Tee is lost at sea in a terrible storm, and Titay heals of a fever a young stranger, naturalist Hal Saunders, who has been washed ashore by the storm. Two people cause trouble for Martha. Ocie claims Martha is stuck up for wanting to go away and for questioning island assumptions like the evilness of mirrors. Cora LaRue, who wants to be the island midwife, casts aspersions on Martha's name after Martha is seen returning from Hal's boat, where she has taken refuge during a sudden squall. The book's climax comes with Ocie's death. Although Ocie's health has deteriorated dangerously during her pregnancy, Ocie has refused Titay's help. She clings to Cora, who lacks Titay's skill and knowledge and shamefully neglects the girl. After Ocie is in hard labor more than two days, her father intervenes and asks Titay to come. With Martha's help, Titay saves the baby but Ocie dies. Martha "cleans up" afterward so efficiently that she gains her grandmother's admiration and gratitude, as well as those of the islanders. Hal asks Martha to marry him and go to Florida with him, where he intends to return to college, but she refuses although she finds him attractive. She has written to Miss Boudreaux, who after some time answers that Martha can live with a physician in New Orleans and attend school there free. Martha cannot bring herself to tell Titay until the very night the women are to gather for the announcement of Martha's quilt pattern. Titay, indomitable as ever, surmounts her disappointment and announces that Martha is leaving to go to school with her blessing. Characters are familiar types, the resentful school friend, the handsome stranger who represents an intellectually and technologically advanced world, the acid-tongued gossip. Martha (the two-minded adolescent) and her grandmother (the wise woman) have more dimension but are conventional for the form. Most memorable is the picture of island life. Scenes in the only store, in church, at the fish festival with dancing and singing, the constantly present sea, and especially the beliefs and values system create the physical and psychological atmosphere in such strength that the setting almost functions as a character. Island dialect and the grandmother's pithy and proverbial expressions add stylistic dimension. C. S. King Honor.

**TUNBO, FRANCES G.**, author of *Stay Put, Robbie McAmis*\* (Texas Christian, 1988), the story of a pioneer boy's efforts to "stay put and watch out for Grammie and the younguns" when his wagon train is scattered and wrecked while crossing a river during a torrential rainstorm. The novel received the Western Heritage Award.

*THE 25¢ MIRACLE* (Nelson\*, Theresa, Bradbury, 1986), realistic novel of a girl's efforts to stay with her widowed father, despite a life that is far from ideal, set in Calder, Texas, in the 1980s. Elvira Trumbull, 11, lives with her father, Hank, in the Happy Trails Trailer Park, the latest of a series of temporary homes as he restlessly moves from one place of work to another. Having lost his latest job, he decides to have Elvira go to live with his older sister, Darla, a domineering woman with a hen-pecked husband and teenage son in Sulphur Springs, but he cannot bring himself to tell his daughter of his decision. Longing for permanence and beauty in her life, Elvira spends the grocery money on a yellow rose bush, a Davidica, and plants it at their trailer door, despite her father's annoyance. Fearing that it is not thriving, she goes to the public library, where she meets Miss Ivy Alexander, director of the children's room, who helps her find books on rose care and, sensing the girl's loneliness, invites her to come to tea at her home and see her garden of roses. Elvira finds that Miss Ivy is a divorcee with two boys, Curtis, about nine, and John David, several years younger. Though extremely nervous at first, Elvira has a marvelous time. She agrees to weed Miss Ivy's garden in exchange for good soil, fertilizer, and other necessities for making her rose thrive. Miss Ivy helps her replant her rose and adds other flowers that she has thinned from her garden. Elvira is stunned when Hank tells her that Aunt Darla will be coming in a few weeks to take her to Sulphur Springs. She makes a list of possible ways to avoid the fate, including dying, and then hits on the perfect solution: she will get Hank to marry Miss Ivy! As a first step, she invites Miss Ivy to dinner and carefully plans a meal of spaghetti, with candles on the table, to be concluded with a lemon pie that she has seen in an advertisement labeled "the ultimate dessert." The pie almost defeats her, and when it is done and a success, there is so little time left that she panics. Hank, to her astonishment, helps her clean up and even goes out to buy wine. He is suitably impressed by Miss Ivy, but time is getting short. Elvira seizes every opportunity to get them together, volunteering her father to fix Miss Ivy's television set and to take them on an all-day fishing expedition. With a fish fry planned for the next night, she thinks that her plan may work, but they return to the trailer to find that Aunt Darla has arrived early, is spending the night in a motel, and plans to take Elvira to Sulphur Springs in the morning. When Hank, not too happy with the arrangement, goes out to drink, Elvira runs all the way to Miss Ivy's house and asks her to marry Hank. Gently, Miss Ivy explains that while she likes Hank and appreciates his helpfulness, she does not know him well enough to marry him and, anyway, does not plan to marry again. Because it is raining hard, she drives Elvira home and watches her enter the trailer, assuming that Hank is there. Elvira digs up her rose bush and sets off toward Houston, thinking that she will somehow lose herself in the big city. Finding her gone, Hank rushes to Miss Ivy's house. She calls the police, who are not much concerned until they find Elvira's notebook with the list, which they interpret as a suggestion of suicide. Elvira has slogged through the rain and mud as far as the Old and Lost River, where the bridge has no room for pedestrians and she dares not cross. A black man and his children find her in the morning lying under a live oak, weak and feverish, and bring her back to the trailer, still carrying her rose bush. When she wakes, she learns that Hank has decided to keep her. He even replants her rose bush. The title refers to Elvira's confidence in a guarantee of your money back if a breakfast cereal fails to please. Hank has told her that she should not waste a stamp writing to the company, that it will be a miracle if she gets an answer. After she gets well, she receives a money order from the cereal company for $1.49. The plot is predictable and Miss Ivy is a too fortuitous good fairy, but strong characterizations of tough, beauty-loving Elvira and her feckless father keep the story interesting. The Texas dialect and physical setting of the sunbaked, gritty trailer park establish credibility. SLJ.

**TWIG** (*The Facts and Fictions of Minna Pratt\**), maid at Lucas\* Ellerby's house, "tall, thin, with pale straight hair and large eyes . . . like a fish on its feet" and dressed in white like a nurse. She does housekeeping for money for art school. A terrible driver, she transports Minna Pratt and Lucas in the Ellerby car, creating havoc in the streets and yelling near-obscenities at drivers who offend her. She and Willie\* are in love.

**THE TWISTED WINDOW** (Duncan\*, Lois, Delacorte, 1987), realistic novel of mystery and suspense set for about one week mostly in the contemporary Texas town of Winfield. Half-orphaned New Yorker Tracy Lloyd, 16, feels deeply the loss of her mother, dead from a mugger's knife, and resents her actor father's putting her with her childless but well-meaning aunt and uncle in Winfield while he is on location in Europe. One Tuesday lunch hour at school a handsome youth, who says that his name is Brad Johnson, strikes up a conversation with her. Brad, too, is angry and unhappy, furious at his ex-stepfather for, Brad says, "child snatching" his two-year-old half-sister, Mindy. Brad has traced Gavin Brummer to Winfield, where Gavin lives in a singles complex and has a married sister. Tracy's unhappy personal life and strong sense of justice move her to accept Brad's plea for help. Tracy cleverly manages to find the Carvers' house, where peering surreptitiously one night through a window with a warped pane, Brad identifies for Tracy a beautiful, blond, dimpled toddler as his beloved Mindy. On Friday night, Tracy baby-sitting, they are in the process of snatching Mindy when Mr. Carver unexpectedly returns. Brad threatens him with a rifle that Tracy did not know he had, and they take Mindy, jump into Brad's car, and head for his home in Albuquerque. Not long out, while changing Mindy, who insists on being called Cricket, Tracy notices that the child lacks a scar that Brad says Mindy has on her stomach and suspects that they have kidnapped the wrong child. A little later at breakfast, Tracy secretly calls Laura Brummer, Brad's mother, and is horrified to learn that Mindy was struck and killed by a car four months earlier. Laura says that she will send Jamie Hanson, Brad's closest friend, to help Tracy. When Tracy returns to their table, she discovers that Brad has taken off with Mindy/Cricket (obviously the Carvers' child). When Jamie (to Tracy's surprise she is a girl) arrives, she informs Tracy that Brad has been emotionally disturbed since his father's sudden death and his mother's remarriage. They deduce that Brad will take Cricket to the Johnson cabin in the Pecos Mountains and head there in Jamie's car. When the girls attempt to retrieve Cricket, Brad's gun goes off accidentally. The sound shocks him into admitting the terrible truth that he has up to now denied: he himself killed his little sister, unwittingly reversing his car and running her over during an argument with Gavin. In his guilt-induced dementia he has imagined that Cricket is his lost Mindy. The youths' view through the twisted window pane had also been distorted by their own warped attitudes. They saw what they wanted to see. The characters are types, from Tracy's well-meaning relatives through her boy-crazy girl friend to Jamie (the liberated girl who works on cars) to the protagonists themselves. Brad's personality is so winning, however, his story so plausible, that it takes in the reader as readily as it does vulnerable Tracy. The narrative is in third person, but the point of view shifts between the two young people, and thus their motives and feelings become apparent, although, like Tracy, the reader does not discover that Brad killed Mindy until the very end. Short passages here and there from the vantage point of other characters alert the reader that Brad's and Tracy's perceptions may not be accurate. The plot is the main item. Constructed with precision, it moves evenly with steadily mounting tension to the horrifying climax on the second to last page and leaves the reader with all questions answered and also with a sense of sorrow and sympathy for unfortunate, self-deluded Brad. Poe Nominee.

# U

**THE UNCLAIMED TREASURES** (*Unclaimed Treasures**), the three maiden great-aunts who live next door to Willa Pinkerton's family. When Mab dies, Willa meets Matthew Morris for whom she immediately develops an infatuation. Vigorous and sharp in spite of their age, Aunt Crystal, once an eminent violinist, and Aunt Lulu run the house since Winnie, Matthew's wife, left. They often go for bird walks and picnics and generally lead full, rich lives, though their actions and speech are tinged with the eccentric. They have a musical ensemble, in which Winnie also performed. When she returns, they immediately include her in their group. Though caricatures, they are handled with sympathy and provide some comic interest in the story.

*UNCLAIMED TREASURES* (MacLachlan*, Patricia, Harper, 1984), amusing realistic novel of family and neighborhood life set one summer not long ago and seen from the viewpoint of fierce, independent, romantic Willa Pinkerton, almost twelve, who longs for extraordinary happenings and watches constantly for her true love. She, her father, Ted, a writing professor, her pregnant mother, and her twin, Nicholas*, an aspiring painter, have just moved next door to the Morrises, Matthew, a painter, whose wife, Winnie, has "gone to seek her fortune," their son, Horace*, about Willa's age and a perpetual eater of apples, and their three musical, cat-loving, eccentric maiden aunts, called the Unclaimed* Treasures. When Great-Aunt Mab dies, Willa meets Matthew, in her opinion an extraordinary figure and the true love for whom she has been seeking. Her intense but controlled passion, kept secret from all but perceptive Nicholas, works itself out in a series of understated scenes in which dialogue carries the details of the story and principals are subtly revealed, and there is abundant humor of situation, language, understatement, and character, much of it overt and some even slapstick. Sitting for Matthew to finish the portrait of his wife proves less joyous than Willa anticipates as she comes to see that she is merely the means by which he can express on canvas his enduring love for absent Winnie. Other events also claim her attention. She learns that her mother had once aspired to be a dancer, an ambition that she gave up when Willa and Nicholas were born, and grapples with mixed emotions about the baby-to-be. She practices kissing on her bedpost; happens upon a love story about two characters named Ted and Wanda written by one of her father's students, and reads it while she is supposed to be vacuuming the study; accompanies her mother on a visit to the obstetrician; has discussions about the ordinary and extraordinary with Matthew, Nicholas, Horace, and Old* Pepper, who lives nearby, speaks in run-on sentences, and is pushed about in a wheelbarrow by his great-grandson; and observes that the Unclaimed Treasures go on picnics and bird walks. Her mother's remark that there are "some things you can't do just for yourself, Willa. You have to consider others," gives her food for thought. Willa resorts to extraordinary measures after two strangers enter her life, one a young woman named Wanda, who turns up at the door. Willa soon connects her with the story, realizes that she is a student infatuated with Ted, and gets rid of her by saying that Ted has a "grand array" of children. Then Winnie pops up, and after pondering Winnie's obscure remark about everyone being an unclaimed treasure, Willa makes more connections and then cleverly manipulates Winnie into returning to Matthew by affixing to the finished portrait her own love note signed with a W. This accomplished, she realizes that calm, steady, ordinary Horace is her true love after all. Near summer's end, the book reaches a climax of emotion and action when an unexplained fire breaks out in the Morris house. Nicholas breaks his leg rescuing the painting and is taken to the hospital in the same ambulance that takes their mother to obstetrics. Old Pepper drives Horace and Willa on a wild ride to the hospital after them, Willa's mother gives birth to a little girl, and Willa happily welcomes an ordinary little unclaimed treasure named Jane, having learned that everyday life holds plenty of excitement and that everyone is important in his or her own way. An italicized frame story with unnamed characters occasionally reverted to piques the curiosity and helps to unify the fragmented story. At the end the reader learns that they are Willa and Nicholas a dozen years later, Nicholas now a painter, Willa now married to Horace and pregnant with her first child, and young Jane now the age of Willa in the story and much like her elder sister in early adolescent temperament and inclination. It seems that the story may repeat itself. The plot is weak, but the characters are consistently interesting, if a too fortuitous mix of ordinary and extraordinary, and it is easy to like intelligent, life-loving Willa, an early adolescent who yields to her common sense. Unerringly accurate point of view and dialogue add much to the interest and credibility, and even if much of the humor is best appreciated by adults, the themes are labored, continuity is questionable, and the elderly are caricatured, the total effect is pleasing, a girl's growing-up story related with flair in which parents and children like each other and are treated with sympathy and respect. ALA; Boston Globe Honor; Fanfare.

**UNCLE CRISPIN** (*The Village by the Sea*\*), Aunt\* Bea's husband and Emma's uncle by marriage. A gentle, sweet-tempered, white-haired man, English by birth, he makes a modest living teaching music in school during the year and giving private violin lessons during the summer. At the outset, Emma is aware that he does not really want her to stay with him and Bea, but he is unfailingly considerate and caring, both of her and of Aunt Bea. At the end, Emma realizes that life with Aunt Bea is peaceful for him only when the two are alone. Emma overhears part of the conversation in which Crispin charges Aunt Bea with drinking again, but not the one about the wrecked village. He can be assertive but apparently loves his misanthropic and eccentric wife and usually treats her tenderly. He met Bea through Emma's father, whose violin teacher he was. He is a sympathetic and not pathetic figure, who apparently gains psychic satisfaction from his seemingly difficult situation.

**UNCLE EARL JOHNSON** (*Come Sing, Jimmy Jo\**), younger brother of Jerry* Lee. He plays guitar and sings bass in the Johnson Family singing group. A big, crude man, he quarrels with Olive* and his father, resents the addition of James to the group, and is jealous that his brother is deservedly their mother's favorite. He and Olive seem to be having an affair and are trying to break away from the family, dreaming of success in Nashville, but they actually depend on Jerry Lee for the songs he writes and his better grasp of the true country music that the group plays.

**UNCLE HILARY** (*One-Eyed Cat\**), Ned's uncle, Mrs.* Wallis's brother. A writer, he travels a great deal. He visits the family on Ned's eleventh birthday, bringing with him as a gift for Ned the Daisy air rifle that contributes to the story's central problem. He is a warm, outgoing man, affable and affectionate, and Ned and the family enjoy his company. Ned wants very much to accept his invitation to spend Christmas in the Carolinas but refuses because he feels that he must take care of the cat that he is sure he has unwittingly maimed. Uncle Hilary's engaging letters to the family only increase Ned's feelings of guilt. Although Uncle Hilary makes only one appearance in the novel, he greatly influences the action.

**UNCLE PAUL MACLEOD** (*After the Dancing Days\**), dashing, musical uncle of Annie Metcalf, who died in France in World War I. He was very close to his sister, Annie's mother, who shared his musical interests, and he brought his friends from the music school to her house rather than to his home across the street. Annie remembers him with devotion because he really listened to her and considered her an important individual. When he bought his motorcycle, he took her on a secret thrilling nighttime ride. He also took her to her first opera, treating her, she reports to her mother, like a lady. The young lieutenant who comes to see the family after his death leads them to believe that he died in battle, whereas actually he died of untreated measles.

**UNCLE ROGER CUMMINGS** (*Underdog\**), Izzy's kind, often abstracted, affluent lawyer uncle, her dead father's brother. Uncle Roger's mind is usually on his work, but he genuinely cares about Izzy. He is very angry when he learns that Izzy lied about going to school and spent her time hunting for Gus the dog instead. He says that she must live with them, dog or not, because she is his brother's child. He tells her the story of how her mother died, and along with that, the story of how he and her father fell out, a little mystery that unifies the first part of the novel and holds the reader's attention until Izzy launches her search for the dog. Roger is likeable, and the adult reader, at least, can sympathize with him and his wife, Aunt* Alice, who suddenly become responsible for a child at this stage in life and career. Like Alice and some other adults in the novel, he is a type, distorted for effect.

**UNCLE TEKLE** (*The Return**), Desta's* uncle, a blacksmith. He is a patient, caring, and sensible man, who understands the children's desire to go to Jerusalem. Also Falasha, he has suffered greatly from religious persecution, having been lamed "from what those devils did to him," as Desta puts it. He is not bitter, however, and enjoys much respect in the village for his winning personality, patient suffering, and great skill at his work. His fate is unknown at the end of the story.

*UNDERDOG* (Sachs*, Marilyn, Doubleday, 1985), realistic contemporary novel set mostly in San Francisco for about a week during which a timid girl learns to assert herself and changes the direction of her life. After her father, Mark, a lawyer noted for championing the unfortunate, is killed in an auto accident, Izzy (Isabelle) Cummings, 11, feels disappointed and rejected when both her ex-stepmothers refuse to take her and she must go to live with her Uncle* Roger Cummings, an affluent lawyer who was on the outs with her father, and his wife, Aunt* Alice, an associate in an art gallery. Although she does not know them and is uncomfortable in their almost entirely white apartment decorated in what to her seems grotesque modern art, Izzy is obsequious and compliant even to the point of agreeing to go to boarding school because she is afraid that they will not want her either. Things change abruptly one night, however. While she and Aunt Alice are looking through old family photos, they come upon one of Izzy's mother (who died when Izzy was four), her father, Roger, and Alice on a picnic, along with a little black dog. Izzy is ecstatic; memories of happy times with Gus the dog flood over her, and she wants the animal with all her heart. Uncle Roger says that, after Izzy's mother died, he took Gus to Mrs. Firestone, their next-door neighbor on 126 Mimosa Street. On what should be her first day in regular school (to finish out the year), Izzy skips, finds Mrs. Firestone, a half-senile old woman with an odd assortment of pets, who says that she gave the dog to her grocer. Over the next several days, Izzy surreptitiously and painstakingly traces leads, until finally she retrieves the dog from the S.P.C.A., where he has been treated for a broken leg, and brings him home, well aware that a storm will follow, since she has lied about attending school. When Aunt Alice insists that the dog cannot stay, Izzy bursts into tears, her pent-up frustrations and fears pouring out. She identifies with Gus; it seems both are being shunted from pillar to post. When Roger proves to her that this black dog is not really the Gus of her early childhood, since Gus had cocker ears and this one's are pointed, she says that she will go to live with Mrs. Firestone, who agrees to take her and the dog. It is the dog, not the ears, that matters. Uncle Roger says that she is like her father: stubborn and "for the underdog," but he also says that since she is a member of the family he is determined that she will continue to live with them. Aunt Alice gives in when Izzy says that this Gus is housebroken. Izzy realizes that she will not be sent to boarding school now but will have to adjust to a room with a painting in it that looks like "pigeon droppings." It seems that life consists of give and take, one adjustment after another. Izzy's first-person account speeds along in lively fashion and is completely engrossing, even though she gets about the unfamiliar city while tracing the dog with too much ease. The adults she meets are distorted, particularly Mrs. Firestone, whose personality borders on the absurd with her assortment of cats, dogs, and geese, all of whom she has invested with distinctive personalities and tastes. The little mystery about the brothers' falling out holds the attention and unifies the story, but it seems overdone when the reader along with Izzy learns from Roger that Izzy's mother fell and broke her neck while chasing the dog. When Izzy's father wanted the dog killed, Roger intervened, and the brothers argued. Izzy's ironic attempts to fashion herself to her stepmothers' and relatives' specifications are both funny and poignant, and the end seems forced and overly compressed. Though the effect may be true to a child's point of view, the distortion and melodrama bring the book closer to the style of the 1960s and 1970s than to its contemporaries of the mid–1980s. Christopher.

*UP FROM JERICHO TEL* (Konigsburg*, E. L., Atheneum, 1986), lighthearted fantasy-mystery set for several weeks in the mid-1980s mostly in Empire States Mobile Home Park on Long Island, New York. Although their personalities differ, Jeanmarie Troxell (who tells the story) being overly dramatic and imaginative and Malcolm Soo being almost fanatically neat and organized, the two children have much in common. Each is eleven and in the sixth grade at Singer Grove Middle School, lives with one parent (Jeanmarie her mother and Malcolm his father), is a latchkey child, likes to dominate, and aspires to fame, she as an actress and he for the Nobel Prize in physics or chemistry. While digging to bury a Dalmatian in the small clearing behind their trailer park, where they have placed other small creatures they have found and that they call Jericho Tel, they fall through the ground into a shaft at the bottom of which is a room bathed in an amber-rose light. There they meet the aging spirit of a dead actress named Tallulah (in speech and manner the replica of historical Tallulah Bankhead), who smokes incessantly, speaks of herself in third person, and calls them darling. She sets them to a number of tasks to prove their worthiness for the ultimate quest, which is to find her valuable lost necklace whose centerpiece is the Regina Stone. Tallulah's current dwelling place is called Rahab Station, and the Dalmatian is Spot, her "Now" dog, she having had a number of other

Dalmatians also called Spot. As the children fall into the shaft, they pass through the Epigene, which makes it possible for them to see the incorporeal, and when they leave on quests, they acquire invisibility by passing through the Orgone. They also learn that they can only enter Rahab when Spot is at Jericho Tel, that is, when Tallulah wants them, and while on trips for her they can terminate the adventure by saying Papillon (butterfly). Their "test" journeys include finding a Mr. Carl A. Vogel, who turns out to be a charlatan faith healer whom they unmask, and failed playwright Horace Livermore and his fiancée, Isobel Wooten, whom they observe cheat a fancy restaurant out of a meal. After these adventures, since they return with desired cigarettes and matches for her, Tallulah sends them on the big quest. She is certain that one of her street-performer friends, who were guests at her apartment when she died, or one of her servants took the necklace from her dead body. After a hilarious episode in the Long Island Internal Revenue Service Center to get the guests' current addresses (where they invisibly work the computers), the children visit the former friends in succession. They discover that Fiona and Edgar Widdup (Tallulah's former maid and butler) now run a successful nursery called Smarty Plants, which they started with money from the apartment that she left them in her will. Her friend Nicolai Ion Simonescu now has a successful business making puppets, one he built up through luck and hard work. Patrick Henry Mermelstein, erstwhile magician, now runs a music shop, a spinoff from a family business. Jeanmarie chances to find the remaining performer, Emmagene Krebs, a singer, in a park, and at a get-together of all the performers during which the children are visible, they learn that Emmagene took the necklace, believing that it might be a good-luck piece. It did her no good, however, as Malcolm points out, since she failed as a singer because she was so stingy with her talent, even keeping meticulous track in a record book of all the songs she sang, positive that only 18,000 were allotted to her. At the end, the children have gained self-assurance, and Jeanmarie decides to try out for the school play, certain that she will be wonderful in it. It is not clear what themes drive the plot, characters have no depth, the plot is overextended, and events are not always logical. For example, Malcolm just seems to know that Carl Vogel is a charlatan who should be unmasked. Jeanmarie tells her story in a vigorous, contemporary tone, including much social comment, like her remarks about her "clone" schoolmates, faith healers, and opportunistic celebrities. Fast action, rapid scene shifts, minimal description, and abundant dialogue produce an effect like comic television. Best are the details that recreate pre-adolescent thinking and behavior, like preparations and ceremonies for burying dead animals and the animosities between groups of youth their age, and the arresting turns of phrase, quips, wordplay, and one-liners. Malcolm says that he cannot skip school because "Immigrants are always overachievers" (Malcolm is from Korea). When Malcolm attempts to explain chlorophyll and photosynthesis to Tallulah, she replies, "let's not get carried away. Good explanations are like bathing suits, darling; they are meant to reveal everything by covering only what is necessary." ALA.

# V

**VERNON MALCOLM** (*Edith Herself\**), Edith Ostermann's nephew, her age of about six, with whose family she comes to live after her mother, his grandmother, dies. At first he "glared at Edith. He thrust out his lower lip and drew his brows together. Edith saw his fists clench at his sides." He resents having her in his family at first, but later he comes to respect and like her. At first he refuses to let her play with his dog and is generally disagreeable toward her. He is astonished at her seizures, saying, "You was a-twitchin' to beat the band, and your eyes looked funny . . . it surely was somethin' to see." He is grateful when she covers for him after he wets his pants in school (the action that really cements their friendship) and helps him wash them out so that he will not get a spanking. By book's end, after he sticks up for her when she has a seizure in school, she tells him that he is a "nice boy" and thanks him. He responds with a grin, saying, "And you're my *aunt*." Their developing friendship is one of the book's most pleasing aspects.

*THE VILLAGE BY THE SEA* (Fox\*, Paula, Orchard, 1988), realistic novel of family life set in the late 1900s, in which character revelation and interpersonal relationships are more important than plot. While her violin teacher father has a heart bypass operation, Emma, perhaps ten, is sent to stay with relatives she barely knows, her father's much older half-sister, Aunt\* Bea, and her husband, Uncle\* Crispin, at their bayside home on Peconic Bay, Long Island, New York. She arrives with apprehension because of worry about her father and because her father has described Aunt Bea as a "terror," but she soon finds Uncle Crispin, also a violin teacher, kind and gentle and a welcome buffer between her and her acerbic, embittered, shapeless aunt, whom she later discovers has alcoholism. To get away from the woman's uncomfortable jibes and probes and almost constant put-downs, Emma spends most of the two weeks with lively, imaginative Bertie (Alberta), who is visiting with her grandmother next door. The two collect shells, seaweed, driftwood, and other beach leavings and use them to construct a miniature village, one part of which consists of a small forest with a tiny plastic deer that Emma found. The girls proudly take pictures of the completed village. While Uncle Crispin admires and praises, Aunt Bea refuses to go to look at it with the others. On Emma's last evening, however, the woman sneaks out in the middle of the night and wrecks it. Uncle Crispin sympathizes and persuades Emma not to seek revenge by destroying Aunt Bea's favorite poster, a reproduction of "The Cliffs at Etretat" by Monet. Back home in her New York apartment, Emma discovers that Aunt Bea has written in Emma's almost blank diary, describing herself as "a bad sad old woman," an indication that she realizes that she causes her own problems. The economical style gives the book the flavor of a short story, and the reader is left to ponder why Emma's parents, who dislike denigrating, resentful Aunt Bea and have had little to do with her, could not have found other accommodations for their daughter for these two weeks. Certainly this slice of real family life has opened her eyes to a side of her family that she could probably have done without. The reader also is never enlightened about why Aunt Bea is so bitter toward her father's second wife, Emma's father's mother, now dead. Events are presented from Emma's point of view, although not in first person, but Aunt Bea holds the focal position, and thus the thrust of the book appears to involve how people must adjust to and cope with the vagaries and demands of an eccentric alcoholic, even a non-practicing one. ALA; Boston Globe Winner; Fanfare; SLJ.

**VOIGT†, CYNTHIA** (1942–     ), born in Boston, Mass.; teacher and highly regarded writer of contemporary novels for children and young adults. The most acclaimed of these are her several generously detailed, strongly characterized stories about the Tillerman family and their friends, the first two of which are *The Homecoming* (Atheneum, 1981) and the Newbery Award-winning *Dicey's Song†* (Atheneum, 1982). Sammy* and James* Tillerman search for the father they have never known in *Sons from Afar** (Atheneum, 1987), a *School Library Journal* Best Book for Children, and Dicey's* friend Mina Smiths is the focus of *Come a Stranger** (Atheneum, 1986), a companion novel that is also an SLJ Best Book. Other related books are *A Solitary Blue†* (Atheneum, 1983), about Jeff, a youth introduced in *Dicey's Song*, who subsequently becomes her sweetheart, and *The Runner* (Atheneum, 1985), while *Seventeen Against the Dealer* (Atheneum, 1989) continues Dicey's own story. Voigt also wrote *The Callender Papers†* (Atheneum, 1983), a novel of suspense that won the Edgar Allan Poe Award; the SLJ Best Book *Building Blocks** (Atheneum, 1984), a time-slip fantasy in which a boy travels backward in time and befriends his father as a boy; and *Izzy, Willy-Nilly** (Atheneum, 1986), the story of a girl who loses a leg in an automobile accident, which was chosen for Fanfare by the editors of *Horn Book*. *The Vandemark Mummy* (Atheneum, 1991) is also a mystery. Voigt received the 1989 Assembly on Literature for the Adolescent of the National Council of Teachers of English (ALAN) Award for significant contribution to adolescent literature.

# W

**WADE KANSUKE** (*The Samurai's Tale**), elderly samurai in charge of the Konidatai, the baggage train. Although considered a hard master, he is fair to Taro and becomes a father figure to him. He has a rigid code of propriety and interprets many of the samurais' actions for Taro. His life seems fulfilled by having someone to serve with devotion, Lord Akiyama*, and someone to care for, Taro. He is killed in the hopeless battle to take Nagashino Castle.

*WAITING FOR THE RAIN* (Gordon*, Sheila, Orchard, 1987), substantial, serious realistic novel about South African racial strife in the 1980s. The story covers nine years in the lives of white Frikkie (Frederiek) and black Tengo, starting when both boys are ten years old. Frikkie's uncle, Oom* Koos, owns a large farm in the veld. Tengo's father is Oom Koos's farm "boss-boy," and his mother, Selina*, is cook for Frikkie's Tant* (Aunt) Sannie. Frikkie hates school and thinks that the farm is the best place in the world, thrilling to both its geography and the work. He spends all his holidays there, helping Oom Koos and playing with Tengo on the increasingly few occasions that Tengo is free from work, and he looks forward to running the place one day with Tengo as his "boss-boy." Tengo, on the other hand, yearns to go to school, his head filled with questions about the world and life whose answers he is sure lie in books. He is also a talented sculptor and thinks that he may study art. The nearest school for blacks, however, is fifty miles away, and his family simply does not have the money, since they just manage to get food and clothing as it is. Oom Koos is a kind if patronizing and demanding master, and life on the farm is hard for the blacks though still less threatening than conditions in the township near Johannesburg where Tengo's cousin Joseph* lives. Tengo has been taught to read and write by his mother, who writes to her sister, cook for a liberal doctor in Johannesburg, asking her to ask her madam to send used books for Tengo. Tengo plunges into them, studies hard, and begins to wonder about the vast differences between his and Frikkie's way of life and about the rightness of the traditional white assumption of God-given superiority over blacks. Oom Koos notices Tengo's cleverness and occasional sullenness and grows disapproving and suspicious. More and more aware of slights and disparaging remarks, Tengo once loses control and rages at one of Frikkie's cousins for ordering around the local black patriarch and calling the respected old man "boy." At fourteen, Tengo's parents finally permit him to go to Johannesburg, although Oom Koos disapproves. There Tengo lives with his aunt's family and goes to school in the township. School is extremely hard because Tengo is behind, but he works diligently and single-mindedly, is tutored by kind, white Reverend Gilbert, and soon shows great promise. He is determined to win a scholarship to the university and maybe even study in the United States. Revolution has begun, however, and the township is a hotbed of resentment and insurrection. When the students boycott the school because they know that the education they receive is inferior and slanted toward menial occupations, rioting ensues, the school is closed, and Tengo's hope of taking the matriculation exams is dashed. Despairing, he learns from Joseph, who has secretly been working with the African National Congress, that youth are being smuggled to Zambia to train as freedom fighters, and some are educated there. Tengo plans to join the fighters, until one night at the funeral of seven people shot by police, four of them children, more rioting occurs. In an attempt to get away from a situation for which he has had no responsibility and of which he wants no part, Tengo hides in an abandoned shed, shortly to be found by a blond white soldier searching for rioters. Tengo bashes the soldier with a crowbar and takes his gun. Then he discovers that the soldier is Frikkie. When Frikkie regains consciousness, the two ruminate on old times and discuss freely the changing conditions, in an honest if didactic discourse contrasting black and white attitudes toward social, political, and economic issues. The youths part agreeably, but the incident has made up Tengo's mind for him. He will leave for Zambia with Joseph but to get an education, not to fight. The first and last thirds of the novel are the most powerful, the first part because it shows the demeaning and exploitive treatment of blacks and the last because it explores the issues surrounding the blacks' civil disobedience. Although patently didactic, the book has great power because both boys are likeable, the issues are personalized through them, and the reader knows that the friendship is doomed by the tragic circumstances. Many scenes contrast the white and black ways of life. Most telling of these are the lavish birthday party for Oom Koos, while thin, tattered, black farm children stare wide-eyed through the fence; that in which Tengo overhears Tant Sannie tell her niece that she must *never* let a black boy in her room for any reason; the one where Frikkie gives his sister a prized marble instead of the red clay bull Tengo made and she covets in order to buy her silence about Tengo's outburst over the old black, what he regards as the ultimate evidence of his friendship; and episodes at the Millers' house, the white liberals in Johannesburg who have a mansion and wide green grounds with all the amenities, a setting used by blacks to substantiate the blacks' arguments that the liberals shed crocodile tears and are not much different from the reactionary whites. The title has a double meaning. For the whites it is literal, for blacks metaphorical of the hope for a better future. Addams; ALA.

**WALTER, MILDRED PITTS** (1922–     ), grew up in Louisiana; received her B.A. from Southern University, La., and studied further at the University of California at Los Angeles, California State College, and the University of Southern California at Los Angeles; educator and writer for children and young people of picture book stories and novels of the black experience. She began writing for children while she was teaching in Los Angeles and has since published some one dozen books. Her first ones, for younger readers, like *Lillie of Watts: A Birthday Discovery* (Ward Ritchie, 1969) and *Lillie of Watts Takes a Giant Step* (Doubleday, 1971), were followed by books for young adults, including the Coretta Scott King Honor Book *Trouble's Child\** (Lothrop, 1985), a growing-up novel set in the Louisiana bayou about a girl shackled by tradition who yearns for a high school education, and *The Girl on the Outside* (Lothrop, 1982), a re-creation of the 1957 integration of Little Rock High School. Walter won the Coretta Scott King Award for *Justin and the Best Biscuits in the World\** (Lothrop, 1986), a short novel for younger readers of how a boy becomes aware of his racial heritage through his rancher grandfather's stories about black cowboys.

**WATKINS, YOKO KAWASHIMA,** Japanese-American born in Nanam, Korea, whose autobiographical novel, *So Far from the Bamboo Grove\** (Lothrop, 1986), tells of her harrowing escape across Korea to Japan in the last days of World War II with her mother and older sister and the tenacious survival of the two girls after their mother's death. It was named to both the American Library Association Notable Books list and the *School Library Journal* list of Best Books for Children. After attending an experimental English Village program at Kyoto University, she began working as a translator at a U.S. Air Force base where she met her husband, Donald. They moved to the United States and lived in Minnesota, Wisconsin, and Oregon before settling down in Brewster, Mass. The Watkinses have four children.

**WAYNE WAGGER** (*Incident at Loring Groves\**), handsome, curly-haired high school junior, son of a lawyer. He supplies marijuana to the school kids, even growing some in his back yard. Although very intelligent and articulate, Wayne disdains classwork, choosing to get along by using others' notes and assignments. The students think that he is a fraud but harmless. Ken discovers that he is an egomaniac who enjoys exerting power over people. Wayne boasts to Ken about breaking rules and being his own authority and about how he always takes some token from the girls he goes out with, about whom he then speaks disparagingly. He shows no remorse over killing Mary Lou. Wayne is a typical pathological killer.

**WEIZERO CHANNA** (*The Return\**), Dan's\* aged grandmother, highly respected because she is the mother of a *kess* (priest) and has prediction dreams. Although Desta\* fears her at first and dislikes the idea of having to take orders from her if she marries Dan, during the journey she discovers that the old woman is kind and caring. Weizero Channa is so old and frail that she must be carried, at first on a kind of litter and later on someone's back. During the last part of the trip, she becomes confused, but in Jerusalem she recovers her health and some of her senses. She is a well-drawn figure.

**WELLS†, ROSEMARY** (1943–      ), born in New York City; illustrator, author of picture books and novels. She attended Boston Museum School and started her career as a book designer. Her first book was made of her illustrations for a Gilbert and Sullivan song, *A Song to Sing, O!* (Macmillan, 1968). In the next twenty years she published nearly forty books, many of them self-illustrated picture books, but a number of them novels for young adults. *When No One Was Looking†* (Dial, 1980) is a mystery story of the junior tennis circuit, which was a nominee for the Edgar Allan Poe Award. Also a Poe nominee was *Through the Hidden Door\** (Dial, 1987), a story of two boys who discover the remains of a miniature culture in a cave near their boarding school. Both books have intriguing mysteries and better characterization than most novels of the genre.

**WESTMARK** (*The Beggar Queen\**), the fictitious kingdom of the Westmark trilogy by Lloyd Alexander\*. In the first book, *Westmark*, the land is ruled by the villainous prime minister, Cabbarus, because King Augustine is despondent over the loss of his daughter, Princess Augusta. In *The Kestrel*, Augusta, also known as Mickle\*, has been discovered and restored to her rightful position, but in the war with the Regians, Dr. Torrens, her prime minister, uses similar dictatorial tactics to maintain order. The last book, *The Beggar Queen*, has Augusta giving up her throne and marrying Theo\*, after another attempt by Cabbarus to secure power has been thwarted.

**WHICH WAY FREEDOM?** (Hansen\*, Joyce, Walker, 1986), historical novel of the black regiments in the Civil War, set from July 1861, to April 1964, in South Carolina and Tennessee. Obi, sixteen or seventeen, slave of John Jennings, has been worked hard but not otherwise badly treated on the small tobacco farm until Jennings's brother, Wilson, returns and begins to drive the three slaves, Obi, Easter, 13, and little Jason, 7, unmercifully. Obi can hardly remember his mother, a slave on a Sea Island plantation, but the sound of her screams as he was taken from her at six or seven haunts his dreams. From Buka, a slave so old that he has been discarded and lives in a shack down by the stream, he has learned that her name was Lorena. Obi has long planned to run away, find her, and head for Mexico, though he has no idea of the direction or distance. When their mistress tells them secretly that John and Wilson plan to sell them and head west to avoid the war, Obi consults Buka and, with Easter dressed like a boy, they start off by night, although Easter is reluctant to leave Jason behind. They head through the woods and swamp toward the river, where Buka has a friend on an island farm who will help them. Easter, grieving at leaving Jason, is sullen and hostile, and Buka gets weaker until Obi must carry him. Before they reach the river, they are intercepted by Confederate soldiers, to whom Obi says he and his younger brother, Ezra, are trying to take their grandfather to die on his home island. Obi is impressed into the building of defenses, and Easter, who volunteers that she can cook, works in the officer's kitchen. Buka, who is told to get out of camp, is taken in by some of the island slaves, also impressed for camp labor, including Gabriel, from whom he had hoped to get help for Obi and Easter. Watching the women weave baskets, Obi thinks of making a basket boat to get to the island, and they work secretly by night. When the Yankees attack the camp, Gabriel, his wife, and Easter refuse to come, but Obi and Daniel, a slave who has left a wife and child on the island, attempt the crossing. Halfway across, the reed boat overturns and Obi is nearly drowned before they are pulled out by soldiers on a Yankee gunboat. The Union soldiers declare that they are the property of the Treasury Department, and Obi is put to work in the fields. Daniel, who knows the territory and becomes a spy and guide for Union forces, is able to see Easter and promises to bring her to the island, but she is moved before he can do so. When word comes that blacks are being allowed to join the Union army, Daniel signs up, but Obi is deeply suspicious. It is not until he learns that Daniel has been killed that he tries to join, only to learn that the regiment is being disbanded. The next year, when an officer tells the island workers of the Emancipation Proclamation, it is also announced that blacks can join the army and Obi signs up. Because he has no last name, he is listed as Obidiah Jennings, much to his disgust. A northern black named Thomas West befriends him, and together they train on a sea island, where Obi becomes an artillery expert, and Thomas starts to teach him to read. Eventually they get to Fort Pillow, Tennessee, where they are among the few who live through the terrible massacre by the Rebel troops. Though wounded, Obi saves Thomas, and they end up in a hospital. Since his papers as well as his money were stolen by a Confederate, Obi decides to change his last name to Buka, or, as Thomas spells it, Booker. Although he has given up finding his mother, he wants to find Easter and Jason, then head north. Much of the book is given to the original escape, a dramatic story but similar to many told before. The more original material of the black regiment and the life of former slaves as soldiers is compressed into the last few pages and is not highly developed. An interesting aspect is the variety of fates of slaves who ran away to the Union army. Some became soldiers like Obi, some were impressed into slave labor for the military, some were paid wages, and some were even returned to their owners. C. S. King Honor.

**THE WHIPPING BOY** (Fleischman*, Sid, ill. Peter Sis, Greenwillow, 1986), comic realistic period novel set in an unnamed kingdom at the time of knights and moated castles. Irrepressible Prince Horace, about ten, is so naughty and disagreeable that "not even black cats would cross his path" and hence has come to be known throughout the kingdom as Prince Brat. Jemmy, the orphaned son of a rat-catcher who serves him as whipping boy, is sometimes beaten several times a day for Brat's misdeeds, especially when the prince, who has not yet learned to read and write, refuses to do his lessons. Jemmy, on the other hand, has heard the lessons so often that he has become adept at reading, writing, and sums. When Prince Brat decides to run away because he is bored, he orders Jemmy to go along, since he has no friend to enlist in this prank. Before Jemmy can slip away in the night fog, they are apprehended by two cutthroats, big, raw, red-haired Hold-Your-Nose Billy, who smells "like a ton of garlic" and whose anti-social exploits have become the material for widely sung ballads, and bony, cleaver-nosed Cutwater, his sidekick. Having found Prince Brat's gold crown in the picnic basket he brought along, they decide to hold the boys for ransom, and, when Prince Brat cannot write the note and Jemmy can, they assume that Jemmy is the prince. Jemmy plays along with this idea, hoping to enable the prince to escape, but Prince Brat proves to be so thickheaded that the plan fails. When they do manage to break away, Prince Brat refuses to identify himself to soldiers searching for him, since he so much enjoys being free of palace restraints. Jemmy, ironically, yearns for life in the palace and especially for his shelf of books. The thugs capture them again while they are riding in the coach of Capt. Harry Nips, the Hot-Potato Man. Billy whips the prince, thinking that he is beating the whipping boy, but Prince Brat, who had hated it when Jemmy refused to bawl or even whimper when beaten, now emulates Jemmy's control and refuses to howl, having come to admire Jemmy's courage. A girl of about fifteen, Betsy, sets her tame bear named Petunia on the ruffians, and the two boys continue with Nips and Betsy to the city fairgrounds. Prince Brat first catches on to what people in his kingdom really think of him when a woman who sells milk says that she has heard the prince was "abducticated" but wonders why the king should cry since Prince Brat is so bad. Jemmy leads Prince Brat for safety into the main sewer, whose opening is off the river, a place with which he is familiar from life with his father, the cutthroats in pursuit. Just as the cutthroats are about to apprehend them, Prince Brat creates a diversion by tossing an old birdcage in the direction of a riverside brewery. Believing that the boys are over there, the thugs head that way and are set upon by rats. Now more mature than he was, for his first act of kindness as royalty, Prince Brat orders Nips and Betsy to turn Jemmy in for the reward posted for him because he knows that they can use the cash, and all go off to the palace. The king thanks Jemmy for bringing Prince Brat back. Jemmy realizes that, although Prince Brat had no friend with whom to run away and hence chose Jemmy to go along, Prince Brat now knows that he has a friend in Jemmy. Proof of this is that, to keep Jemmy with him, Prince Brat promises his father that he will do his lessons and behave. As for the two thugs, they are last seen stowing aboard a ship, which, unknown to them, is a convict bark headed for a penal island. This fast-moving farce, a hilarious remake of *The Prince and the Pauper*††, roars along in comedy-of-errors fashion, with lots of deliberately contrived dialogue and situational humor. Most characters are distorted for humorous effect, and the setting is delineated only in the most necessary terms. The only serious element is the theme of friendship and loyalty, as evidenced by Jemmy's decision to stay with the prince because of the principle of the matter. Prince Brat grows up sufficiently to recognize Jemmy's worth, the first sign of which is his calling Jemmy by his name instead of the disparaging one that he had been using, Jemmy-From-The-Streets. An author's note at the end informs the reader that some royal households did keep whipping boys to answer for princely offenses. ALA; Newbery Winner; SLJ.

**WHITE, RUTH C. (RUTH WHITE MILLER)** (1942–      ), born in White-wood, Va.; teacher of English, librarian, and writer for early adolescents. The fourth daughter of a miner who died when she was six, White grew up in the poverty-stricken mining area in which her novels are set. She attended the mountain college of Montreat-Anderson, from which she received her A.A. degree, Pfeiffer College for her A.B., and Queens College in Charlotte for her library media specialist degree. She has taught English in middle school and high school in North and South Carolina and been a school librarian in South Carolina and Georgia. Her previous novel, *The City Rose* (McGraw, 1977), published under the name of Ruth White Miller, was cited as the best children's book by a North Carolinian by the North Carolina chapter of the American Association of University Women in 1977. *Sweet Creek Holler** (Farrar, 1988), her second novel, concerns six years in a family's hardscrabble existence in an Appalachian coal-mining region and is based on White's own youth. Named a Best Book for Children by the American Library Association, it is a detailed slice of mid-twentieth century mountain life.

**WILL GREGORY** (*Invincible Summer**), Robin Gregory's undemonstrative, very quiet father, who is hit hard when Robin is diagnosed with leukemia. He gradually accepts the situation, however, and sits by her bedside, though he can hardly bear to look at the ravages of the chemotherapy. He is quite different from Tad Winn, Rick's* father, who only after three years of Rick's fight with the illness finds it possible to hold his son's hand during treatment. At Rick's urging, Will plans to do some organic farming, a clear symbol of Rick's intel-lectual legacy.

**WILLIE** (*The Facts and Fictions of Minna Pratt**), William Gray, the young violinist that Minna Pratt thinks of as just a street musician but who is really an accomplished symphony player. Minna always gives him a quarter, which he always graciously gives back. She envies him his vibrato, wondering why a street player has it and she does not. Next to his violin case sleeps a small brown dog, which Willie simply calls Dog and says loves Mozart. Willie poetically tells Minna that the vibrato "will creep up on you, like moonlight." When he plays, which is almost constantly, he becomes totally engrossed and can produce an "arpeggio so bright that it seemed to call out the sun." He and Twig* fall in love and at the end, with the $200 from Minna and Lucas* Ellerby, leave for Iowa, where his mother lives and where, he says, the "corn stalks are like an audience of music lovers."

**WINDSOR, PATRICIA** (1938–      ), born in New York City; editor, educator, novelist. She attended Bennington College and Westchester Community college and worked for some time in England for the Family Planning Association and the National Council of Social Services. This experience is reflected in her novel, *Mad Martin* (Harper, 1976), in which a young English boy goes to a foster home after his grandfather, with whom he lives, breaks his hip. Since 1973 she has been a senior editor at Harper & Row and has also taught at the University of Maryland, Open University in Washington, D.C., and the Institute of Children's Literature in Redding, Conn. Among her other novels are *Home Is Where Your Feet Are Standing* (Harper, 1975), a story of a boy with learning disabilities, and *Killing Time* (Harper, 1980), a mystery concerning modern-day Druids in New York State, descendants of ancient Celtic settlers. Windsor's chilling murder novel, *The Sandman's Eyes** (Delacorte, 1985), won the Edgar Allan Poe Award. She has also contributed stories and articles to periodicals and written lyrics for popular songs.

**WITH WESTIE AND THE TIN MAN** (Adler*, C. S., Macmillan, 1985), realistic novel of a teenager whose life in his first months after release from reform school is complicated and finally salvaged by his mother's lover, a recovering alcoholic. After serving eleven months for habitual shoplifting, Greg Wightman, 15, finds the outside world strange, and he also has to cope with the move of his mother, Ellie, from New York City to Englewood Cliffs, where she is sharing a house and a picture-framing business with Manny Horowitz, whom she met at Alcoholics Anonymous. Mutual tension and distrust mark their first meeting and persist as Greg explores the house and the neighborhood, the only redeeming feature being the West Highland terrier that Manny recently inherited from an aunt. Westie, as Greg calls her, has been spoiled and not well house trained, and after she tears up a sampler left for framing, Manny vows to take her to the animal shelter, relenting conditionally when Greg, backed by Ellie, pleads. If Greg can train Westie, Manny agrees to sell her to him for fifty dollars, as long as he earns the money himself. Greg meets a girl his age, Annabelle Waks, who has a paper route and whom he likes immediately, but the acquaintance adds to his financial problems, since dates cost money. He tries mooching from his mother, as was his previous habit, but Ellie is not the soft touch she once was. Training Westie is not an easy task either. Greg resents Manny's realistic but tactless reminders that Greg had better carry his own weight, and he resents Ellie's frequent attendance at the AA meetings, since he has never admitted to himself that she is alcoholic, although he was often embarrassed and worried when she appeared drunk in public or passed out in their apartment. Annabelle, too, has problems. Her father wants a divorce, and her mother, a school principal, is devastated and leans on her in a new and disturbing way. On impulse, Greg takes some of his mother's paintings, which are marked for sale in the shop, to an art fair, where he sells several of them for fifty dollars more than the marked price. He plans to use the extra money to buy Westie, but when his mother, delighted, gives him fifty dollars commission and Manny says that taking the pictures without permission is the same as stealing, Greg keeps quiet about the extra money he made. The truth comes out, however, when the purchaser brings the pictures into the shop for framing. At first Greg lies, damaging what little trust was building between him and Manny. When Westie gets away, however, Manny helps Greg hunt for her, and, when they eventually find her and have to pay for some damage she has done, he loans Greg the money. Although he wants to spend full time on the shop, Manny takes an evening job to make ends meet. Through the rest of the summer, their relationship gradually improves, as do also Westie's manners and Greg's friendship with Annabelle. A woman who met Greg at the art fair hires him for yard work, after Annabelle vouches for him. His mother, Manny, and mostly Greg himself worry because he has never told Annabelle about the reform school. Finally, he gets up nerve to confess, and she is deeply disturbed. Greg thinks that their friendship is over and finds unexpected sympathy from Manny. Greg realizes that he has changed greatly since leaving the school and welcomes Manny's support. When Annabelle calls and apologizes, the future looks bright. Although the novel is obviously written to show how the AA approach can apply to other problems based on self-deception, like Greg's shoplifting, it is not oppressively didactic because the characters are believable and appealing, particularly Manny and Ellie. The parallel between Westie and Greg, both troublemakers capable of reform, is explicit. The setting is used with some skill, especially in a couple of trips the youngsters take into the city. Child Study.

**WOLFF, VIRGINIA EUWER** (1937–     ), born in Portland, Ore.; novelist and teacher of English in public and private schools in New York, Pennsylvania, and Oregon. A graduate of Smith College with an A.B. in 1959, she studied further at Long Island University and Warren Wilson College. Her first novel, for adults, *Rated PG* (St. Martin's, 1981), revolves around the romantic relationship between a naive young woman and an Ivy League college student. Her second book, for adolescents, *Probably Still Nick Swansen** (Holt, 1988), a sensitive, nondidactic story about a learning disabled boy, won the International Reading Association Award and appears on the *School Library Journal* Best Books for Children list. Wolff has also published *The Mozart Season* (Holt, 1991), about a talented girl violinist, and has contributed stories and poems to magazines.

*WOLF OF SHADOWS* (Strieber*, Whitley, Knopf, 1985), fantasy set in the future after a nuclear war, which begins northwest of Lake Superior and ends in the Ozark Mountains. A pack of wild wolves and two humans unite to survive the environmental and social devastation and the terrible cold of the nuclear winter. Because he is unusually large, has a black coat and pale eyes, and therefore has become a lone wolf, Wolf of Shadows learns something of the ways of humans and is more self-sufficient and attuned to the physical environment than the gray pack leader. One June, as night falls, he sees a series of brilliant white flashes in the sky, followed by the glare of fires from the human lands, and realizes great danger is imminent. Soon a plane lands on the lake nearby, carrying three humans, a mother and two daughters, one so severely burned that she soon dies. The mother recognizes the wolf from an earlier research expedition (the reader later learns that she is an animal ethologist from the University of Minnesota), and he recognizes her as one not hostile to wolves. From the humans' conversations the reader learns that there has been a nuclear war of many sudden strikes, one at Minneapolis forty miles from where the woman lived. The little family erects a tent against the increasingly hostile weather of rainstorm and sleet, and hunters arrive from across the lake. One of them shoots at the watching wolves over the woman's protests. After the hunters and the woman bury the dead girl, the hunters steal the plane, but they crash it into the lake during a storm. The storm continues for days, temperatures steadily dropping. Food becomes scarce, the cubs are especially at risk, and Wolf of Shadows becomes certain that he must lead the group south in search of the sun, fights the gray for leadership, and begins the journey. The woman and remaining daughter, about twelve, follow first at a distance and later as increasingly respectful and docile members of the pack. The land is like a depopulated desert. The travelers come upon abandoned dwellings, the places looted and the people dead, even murdered, and strings of cars with the people inside dead. The humans share canned goods with the increasingly hungry wolves, and the wolves share their few kills with the people. At Minneapolis, the woman saves the wolves by driving them away from ground zero. The wanderers plough their way steadily southward, deteriorating physically, cold, hungry, paws and skins scraped and tender from sleet and the terrain. The wolves slay a cow in defiance of the woman, who wants it for milk, but Wolf of Shadows does not slay or punish her because he interprets certain behavior as submissive. After crossing the Missouri River by a bridge that she shows them, they reach the Ozark plateau, where two hunters become so threatening that the wolves drive them away. So close do the woman and Wolf of Shadows become that he thinks of her as the "mate of his heart." At one point, the pack rejects his leadership, and Wolf of Shadows, the gray, a female, and the humans constitute the pack. So cold and hungry they can barely move, they manage to kill a deer. Another bad sleet storm and then rain afflict them, but the refugees trudge steadily southward, hoping for warmer weather ahead. This is a gripping story in which the horrors of nuclear holocaust are made palpable by personalizing the survival effort. It becomes increasingly obvious that only those who are unusually able and intelligent, like the wolf, or possess special knowledge of nature, like the woman, as well as true grit and some luck, will survive. Character is less important than plot, setting, and atmosphere, and the story moves relentlessly from explosion to open-ended conclusion. The wolves are never anthropomorphized or sentimentalized, and their behavior is described as from the standpoint of an intelligent, knowledgeable observer of wolf ways. The humans are mostly seen from the vantage point of Wolf of Shadows; thus, for example, they have long forepaws that they fold over themselves in front and speak in growls that vary in intensity depending upon whether the conversation is casual or heated. An endpaper map contributes information about the route of the journey and the size and location of the nuclear strikes, which to judge by the megatonage and number have almost annihilated the United States. In an afterword, the author says, ''The true end of the story comes when we decide, as a species, to dismantle the machine and use our great intelligence on behalf of the earth that bears us, instead of against her.'' SLJ.

# Y

**YARBRO, CHELSEA QUINN** (1942–      ), born in Berkeley, Calif.; author of novels of many types—fantasy, Gothic, science fiction, suspense, and westerns—under the name of Yarbro and the pseudonyms Terry Nelsen Bonner and Vanessa Pryor. She attended San Francisco College and has made her home in Berkeley. Her best-known novels for adults are a series about the Count de Saint-Germain, an immortal vampire, a figure more tragic than horror inspiring, each title set in a different historical period. For four years she worked at the Magic Cellar in San Francisco, an experience that is reflected in her novel for young people, *Floating Illusions** (Harper, 1986), which involves a stage magician on an ocean liner. It was a nominee for the Edgar Allan Poe Award. Other books for young people by Yarbro are *Lacadio's Apprentice* (Harper, 1984) and *Four Horses for Tishtry* (Harper, 1986). She is also a composer of serious music.

***THE YEAR WITHOUT MICHAEL*** (Pfeffer*, Susan Beth, Bantam, 1987), psychological novel of a family's problems after the disappearance of the middle child, a boy not quite fourteen. Jody Chapman, 16, through whom most of the action is viewed, is the last to see Michael, on the first day of September, when they discuss, inconclusively, whether their father's weekend at the cabin to "think things out" means that their parents are contemplating divorce. As Michael starts out to play softball with a friend, Jody reminds him to be home for supper. When he does not return, Jody's mother, Linda, calls his friends, gets his uncle to drive to the cabin, thinking that Michael might have gone to talk with his father, Tom, and eventually calls the police. Officer Dino questions Jody and her younger sister, Kay*, a seventh grader, and the next day they are taken to the police station to look at mug shots of known child molesters. Jody's two best friends, flighty Maris* and steady Lauren, try to be helpful, but school is a nightmare for both Jody and Kay, with the curious asking tactless questions. As the days and weeks pass, the tension in the family becomes worse instead of lessening. Linda insists on making and decorating Michael's favorite cake for his birthday, having convinced herself that he will show up for the occasion.

Jody, whose birthday is next, refuses to let her mother plan anything and is genuinely astonished and touched when her friends give her a surprise party. Kay, however, lets her mother plan a party and invite a few of her close friends, none of whom come, some having their mothers call with fake excuses and some just not showing up. Both girls visit their wealthy paternal grandparents in Florida for Thanksgiving. They find the visit difficult, with their grandmother saying alternately that Michael ran away because Linda smothered him with affection or that she was too harsh with him, and the other old people in the apartment complex refer to them as "oh, you poor children." Their grandparents hire a detective, who questions both girls and their parents and gives them brief hope. At Christmas Linda insists that everyone buy and wrap presents for Michael as usual, and she accuses the girls of being selfish when they protest. On New Year's Day, Jody, waking early, quietly collects Michael's gifts still unopened under the tree and stores them in his closet. Her determination to start her own life going again in the new year is helped by the class play, "You Can't Take It With You," in which she has the lead. She starts dating her co-star, Jim Adams. Her parents, too, make an effort to return to normal life, venturing out to a movie together. Her mother looks for a job again. In March, the parents fly to Cleveland to identify a body of a boy, but it is not Michael. Depressed, Jody lets her grades slip and her romance drift away. The detective, having found nothing, resigns from the case. In May, the tensions erupt when Kay puts an advertisement in the newspaper asking Michael to call home. Furious, her mother attacks her physically, then insists that she live with her grandparents through the summer and go to boarding school in the fall. Although her father thinks that this is irrational, he goes along with the plan, to Jody's distress. In August, Jody makes one last effort to find Michael. Enlisting Maris to cover for her, she takes a bus to New York, planning to interview street kids who might know Michael. Almost immediately, she sees that it is a mistake. She does talk to a young male prostitute, who warns her that if Michael did run away to the city, she will not want to know him now; however, he takes the picture of Michael that she offers and says that he will ask around. Unable to take a bus home until morning, Jody wanders into a church, where the minister is understanding and lets her spend the night in his office. He also makes her see that she is not responsible for her mother's crazy actions, or her father's weakness, or Kay's anger. She returns to find that her parents have discovered her lie about being with Maris, but her trip was perhaps not in vain. It has shocked her father into deciding to send for Kay, get the whole family into therapy, and try to start a rational life again. The third-person story is bracketed by a brief, first-person frame in Jody's voice. Although the possibility of a divorce with which the book opens seems extraneous, the year-long ordeal is movingly told, with the ups and downs of hope and disappointments, the anger that Linda and Kay take out mostly on each other, the times when Jody seems to be the only normal one left in the family, and the periods in which she withdraws in emotional numbness all well evoked. The end is hopeful only in that the family is trying to pull itself together, not in any new information about Michael's disappearance. SLJ.

**YOICHI** (*The Samurai's Tale**), toothless, uneducated, devoted servant to Taro. Originally, Yoichi is one of the peasants who leads an army pack horse, carrying at the same time a heavy load of rice on his own back. On the march to Iwamura Castle, he reports to Taro that some rice has been stolen from his pack. Because Taro believes him and sets him to watch, they catch the thief. Although Taro has been told to kill anyone stealing rice, he instead beats the man and makes him carry Yoichi's load as well as his own. This earns him the undying loyalty of Yoichi, who later acts as go-between, through a female servant, to take Taro's love poems to Aki-hime. When Iwamura Castle falls, Yoichi somehow rescues Aki-hime from the dreadful carnage and hides her in a poor hut until Taro returns, and all three escape to Kofucha.

**YOKO KAWASHIMA** (*So Far from the Bamboo Grove**), Japanese girl born and raised in Korea, who is caught in the crossfires of World War II and must flee her home in the bamboo grove and become a refugee. Very small for her age, she is called by her family "Little One," and she is pampered and a bit spoiled before the horrible experiences she endures. At school in Kyoto, she suffers more from the scorn and ridicule of the other girls than she does from her lack of shoes and sufficient food, and she nurses her hatred of them, vowing to get perfect grades to shame them, which she does. Her essay, which wins the big newspaper contest for her age group, is called "Understanding" and is critical of the girls. After it wins, they shun her and no teacher in the school mentions the essay, but the prize money supplies food for some time.

**YOLEN, JANE (HYATT)** (1939–     ), born in New York City; editor, columnist, lecturer in education at Smith College (1979–1984), and author of more than one hundred books for children and young people, many of them literary fairy tales as well as novels. Her books often utilize folklore themes and motifs. She has also published nonfiction, books of her own verse, several novels for adults, and a book on writing for children, and has edited a dozen collections that range from books of musical rounds to spooky tales to science fiction and folk tales. Her *Owl Moon* (Philomel, 1987), illustrated by John Schoenherr, received the Caldecott Award. *The Seeing Stick* (Crowell, 1977), illustrated by Remy Charlip and Demetra Marsalis, won the Christopher Award. *Heart's Blood** (Delacorte, 1984), an exciting futuristic adventure novel set on a planet in space with an economy based on dragons, is the second in her Pit Dragon series, which began with *Dragon's Blood* (Delacorte, 1982), and includes *A Sending of Dragons* (Delacorte, 1987). *Heart's Blood* was chosen by the American Library Association as a Best Book for Children.

# LIST OF BOOKS BY AWARDS

The following novels have been cited for the awards indicated and appear in this dictionary. Non-fiction books are not included.

## JANE ADDAMS PEACE ASSOCIATION CHILDREN'S BOOK AWARD

Waiting for the Rain

## AMERICAN LIBRARY ASSOCIATION BEST BOOKS FOR CHILDREN

After the Dancing Days

After the Rain

The Agony of Alice

Amy's Eyes

Blossom Culp and the Sleep of Death

The Blossoms and the Green Phantom

A Blue-Eyed Daisy

Come Sing, Jimmy Jo

Cracker Jackson

Dogsong

The Facts and Fiction of Minna Pratt

The Fighting Ground

A Fine White Dust

Fran Ellen's House

The Friendship

The Goats

Hatchet

Heart's Blood

The Illyrian Adventure

In Summer Light

Interstellar Pig

In the Year of the Boar and Jackie Robinson

The Josie Gambit

The Keeper

M. E. and Morton

Me, Mop, and the Moondance Kid

The Moonlight Man

More Stories Julian Tells

The Moves Make the Man

One-Eyed Cat

On My Honor

Out From This Place

The Outlaws of Sherwood

Ramona Forever

Remembering the Good Times

The Return

Return to Bitter Creek

A Rumour of Otters

The Samurai's Tale

Sarah, Plain and Tall

Scorpions

Sirens and Spies

So Far from the Bamboo Grove

Sweet Creek Holler

Unclaimed Treasures

Up from Jericho Tel

The Village by the Sea

Waiting for the Rain

The Whipping Boy

## *BOSTON GLOBE-HORN BOOK* AWARD HONOR BOOKS

Prairie Songs

Unclaimed Treasures

## *BOSTON GLOBE-HORN BOOK* AWARD HONOR BOOKS

The Friendship
In Summer Light
The Moves Make the Man
Rabble Starkey
The Village by the Sea

## CHILD STUDY CHILDREN'S BOOK COMMITTEE AT BANK STREET COLLEGE AWARD

December Stillness
The Most Beautiful Place in the World
One-Eyed Cat
Rabble Starkey
Shades of Gray
With Westie and the Tin Man

## CHRISTOPHER AWARD

Borrowed Summer
The Gold Cadillac
Promise Not to Tell
Sarah, Plain and Tall
Underdog

## CORETTA SCOTT KING HONORABLE MENTION

Circle of Gold
Junius Over Far
A Little Love
Trouble's Child
Which Way Freedom?

## CORETTA SCOTT KING AWARD WINNER

Fallen Angels
The Friendship
Justin and the Best Biscuits in the World
Motown and Didi

## THE *HORN BOOK MAGAZINE* FANFARE LIST

After the Rain

The Beggar Queen

Beyond the Chocolate War

Cracker Jackson

The Facts and Fictions of Minna Pratt

A Fine White Dust

The Goats

The Hero and the Crown

In Summer Light

Interstellar Pig

Izzy, Willy-Nilly

Junius Over Far

A Little Love

Midnight Hour Encores

One-Eyed Cat

The Outlaws of Sherwood

Park's Quest

A Place to Come Back to

Rabble Starkey

Sarah, Plain and Tall

Unclaimed Treasures

The Village by the Sea


## INTERNATIONAL READING ASSOCIATION CHILDREN'S BOOK AWARD

After the Dancing Days

Prairie Songs

Probably Still Nick Swansen


## JEFFERSON CUP AWARD FOR HISTORICAL FICTION

After the Dancing Days

In the Year of the Boar and Jackie Robinson

Sarah, Plain and Tall

## JOHN NEWBERRY MEDAL HONOR BOOKS

After the Rain
Dogsong
A Fine White Dust
Hatchet
The Moves Make the Man
One-Eyed Cat
On My Honor
Scorpions

## JOHN NEWBERRY MEDAL WINNERS

The Hero and the Crown
Sarah, Plain and Tall
The Whipping Boy

## SCOTT O'DELL AWARD FOR HISTORICAL FICTION

Charley Skedaddle
The Fighting Ground
The Honorable Prison
Sarah, Plain and Tall
Streams to the River, River to the Sea

## NOMINEE FOR THE EDGAR ALLAN POE AWARD BEST JUVENILE MYSTERY CATEGORY

The Accident
The Falcon Sting
Floating Illusions
Following the Mystery Man
The Ghosts of Now
Is Anybody There?
The Lamp from the Warlock's Tomb
Locked in Time
Playing Murder
Second Fiddle: A Sizzle & Splat Mystery
The Secret Life of Dilly McBean
The Skeleton Man

Something Upstairs
The Third Eye
Through the Hidden Door
The Twisted Window

## WINNER OF THE EDGAR ALLAN POE AWARD BEST JUVENILE MYSTERY

Incident at Loring Groves
Lucy Forever & Miss Rosetree, Shrinks
Megan's Island
Night Cry
The Other Side of Dark
The Sandman's Eyes

## *SCHOOL LIBRARY JOURNAL* BEST BOOKS FOR CHILDREN

After the Rain
All About Sam
Angel's Mother's Wedding
The Blossoms and the Green Phantom
The Bone Wars
Born into Light
Borrowed Children
The Boy Who Reversed Himself
Building Blocks
The Burning Questions of Bingo Brown
Class Clown
Come a Stranger
Come Sing, Jimmy Jo
Cracker Jackson
Deep Wizardry
Dogsong
The Duplicate
Edith Herself
Fallen Angels
A Fine White Dust
The Goats
Good-bye and Keep Cold

A Good Courage
The Hero and the Crown
I'll Meet You at the Cucumbers
In Summer Light
Interstellar Pig
In the Year of the Boar and Jackie Robinson
Invincible Summer
The Kid in the Red Jacket
A Kindness
Legend Days
M. E. and Morton
Midnight Hour Encores
The Moonlight Man
More Stories Julian Tells
The Moves Make the Man
On My Honor
Permanent Connections
Princess Ashley
Probably Still Nick Swansen
Quentin Corn
Ramona Forever
Rear-View Mirrors
Remembering the Good Times
The Return
Return to Bitter Creek
A Rumour of Otters
Sarah, Plain and Tall
Sex Education
Sirens and Spies
So Far from the Bamboo Grove
Sons From Afar
Stay Away from Simon!
Tancy
The 25¢ Miracle
The Village by the Sea
The Whipping Boy
Wolf of the Shadow
The Year Without Michael

## WESTERN WRITERS OF AMERICA SPUR AWARD

Prairie Songs
Trapped in the Slickrock Canyon

## GEORGE G. STONE CENTER FOR CHILDREN'S BOOK RECOGNITION OF MERIT AWARD

Fran Ellen's House
Stone Fox

## WESTERN HERITAGE AWARD

Prairie Songs
Stay Put, Robbie McAmis

# INDEX

Names and titles in ALL CAPITAL LETTERS refer to the actual entries of the dictionary, and page numbers in *italics* refer to the location of the actual entries in the dictionary.

163; gentle, unsensational, 26; hyperbole, 274; ironic, 75, 80, 169; mild, 46; point of view, 70; relief, 208, 209, 239; situation, 14, 26, 274; situation and outlook, 114; situation, hyperbole, 38; taking statements literally, 11; various kinds, 66, 70, 224; wordplay, one-liners, quips, 266
humorous novels
—boy and girl: 223–25, 265–66
—boys: 10–11, 37–38, 45–46, 126–27, 155–56, 160–61, 225–26, 273–75
—family: 14–15, 25–26
—girls: 7–8, 24–25, 69–70, 113–14, 145–46, 204–5, 261–62
—pig: 201–2
*The Hunger*, 245
Hunter family, 11, 53, 166, 168
Hunter, Miz, 48, 57
hunters: arrive during nuclear cold storm, 278; Eskimo, 60; father and daughter, 27; Indian girl, 139; pioneer boy, 241; steal plane, 278; wolves drive away, 278
HURMENCE, BELINDA, *105*, 249
HURWITZ, JOHANNA (FRANK), 45, *106*
husbands: abandons doctor wife, 239; abusive, 11, 53, 166; beats up alleged harasser of wife, 207; cleared of charge of theft, 150; fondling other woman, 227; hen-pecked, 258; indulgent, 10, 249; kind, gentle, loving, 211; murdered, 143, 150; of cook-housekeeper, 165; old man fears wife, 94; political prisoner, health failing, 150; run-away, 90; stern, 8, 195; uncouth, treacherous, 244; wimpish, 36
huts: mud, in kraal, 226; rude, for ex-slaves, 181; sod, disliked, 195; Virginia mountains, 44. *See also* homes; houses; mansions
hybrids, space people and earth people produce, 30
hymns, "I come to the garden alone . . . ," 66
hypnosis: of abused child by amateur psychiatrist, 146; of boy suspected of murder, 220
hypochondriacs, father, 96
hypocrisy, of whites: as seen by Indians, 139; as seen by South African blacks, 270

*I Am the Cheese*, 52
Ian Jackson, 111
"I come to the garden alone . . . ," hymn, 66
idealists, political, 78, 104
identification: by lisp, 253; driver in accident by picture, 4; of body, not son's, 282
identity: cards, forged, 21; clone assumes, 62–63; mistaken, 13, 166, 260, 265; revealed, handyman is rebel leader, 108
idioms, fun poked at, 202
*If I Asked You, Would You Stay?*, 37

*If You Were an Ant*, 34
*Iliad*, 57
Illinois: Chicago, 44, 130, 155; Pineville, 123; Starved Rock State Park, 178
illiterates, black ex-slaves, 181
*I'LL MEET YOU AT THE CUCUMBERS*, *107–8*, 160
illnesses: agoraphobia, 189; arthritis, 169, 177, 211; asbestosis, 6; blamed on black Ethiopian Jews, 208; boy falls ill and can't feed cat, 177; brain tumor, 192; cancer, 6, 93, 115; caused by guilt, 254; cholera, suspected, 241; cold, 87, 105; comas, 85–86, 153, 179, 254; considered punishment for sin, 36, 91; consumption, 240; depression, 203; dog's, burst heart, 243; Down's syndrome, 229; drug overdose, 164; emotionally disturbed, 57, 166, 195; epilepsy, 8, 65; fever, 257; flu, 31, 227; from drink and drugs, 110; heart attack, 5, 28, 97; heart palpitations, 96, 206; hemorrhaging after giving birth, 30; infected ear, 235; leukemia, 114, 212, 275; malnutrition, 194; measles, 263; mental, 129, 220, 226; mental and physical collapse, 242; mental breakdown claimed, 192; mononucleosis, 111; mysterious, 67; old age weakness, 273; operation, 32; over revelation of infidelity, 90; post-traumatic stress disorder, 57; seizures, 27; siblingitis, 205; smallpox, 139; spinal meningitis, 94; stroke, 82, 163, 168, 177, 186; tonsilitis, 46; tuberculosis, 8, 103, 226; typhoid fever, 228, 246; vomiting from overdrinking, 3. *See also* accidents; injuries; invalids; wounds
illusions, stage, 78
illustrators: Allen, Thomas B., 162; Apple, Margot, 14; Barrett, Jennifer, 198; Carrick, Donald, 239; deGroat, Diane, 10; Egielski, Richard, 11; Ginsburg, Max, 82; Hamanaka, Sheila, 45; Hays, Michael, 88; Himler, Ronald, 65; Johnson, Pamela, 201; Pate, Rodney, 155; Rogers, Jacqueline, 25; San Souci, Daniel, 255; Sewall, Marcia, 242; Shaw, Charles, 240; Simont, Marc, 113; Sis, Peter, 273; Stock, Catherine, 126; Strugnell, Ann, 160; Tiegreen, Alan, 204; Wooding, Sharon, 107; Zudeck, Darryl S., 195
Illyria, 108
*Illyriad*: information in epic proved true, 109; 12th century epic, 108
*THE ILLYRIAN ADVENTURE*, 9, *108–9*
IMELDA, 69, *109*, 179
imitations, girl of slow brother's behavior, 153
Imjon River, 102
immigrants: black to Missouri from Tennessee,

puppets, business making, 266
puppies: in garbage dumpster, 26; named
   Buddy, 245
Purple Hearts, 5
pursuits: junior high boy by outlandish girl,
   117; of mute girl by girl playing
   psychiatrist, 146
Purvis family, 144, 168, 173, 245
pushers, drugs, 271
pushes, of man down cliff, 256
pygmies: ancient relics of, 253; Pacific Island,
   234
pyromania, girl's, 144

Q: nickname for pig, 201; purple, inside red
   heart, 202
Q-T ranch, 126
quarrels: family, 49, 263; sweethearts', 99; to
   protect girlfriend, 232; with girlfriend, 3
quarries, body found in, 110
quarters, given to street musician, 275
quartets, string, 69
Queen Augusta of Westmark, 20, 79, 138,
   156, 252, 272
*Queen of Hearts*, 230
queens: abdicates to supporter and pretender,
   21; deposed, Westmark, 138; flees from
   throne, 21; urchin, 20
Queen's Gambit, 124
Quentin Corn, 13, 67, 166, 167, 201
*QUENTIN CORN*, 201–202, 242
questions: about love, 169; burning, boy's, 38;
   tactless, 281
quests: for brother, 151; for freedom from
   religious persecution, 208; for mermaid, 12;
   for pirate treasure, 12; to find father, 142; to
   find mother, 272; ultimate, to find lost
   necklace, 265. *See also* journeys; searches;
   trips; voyages
quick sand, 256
Quigley, Farmer, 201
quills, porcupine, 98
quilt pattern, choosing, symbol of readiness
   for marriage, 257
quilts, family peace offering, 211
Quimby family, 204
Quinn family, 43, 51, 94, 120, 230
quotations: about facts and fiction being true,
   152; from Wordsworth, 79; mysterious, 69;
   "of the week," boy makes, 115

rabbits: baby, pet, 161; care of, 91; groom-to-
   be dresses as for shower, 14; hunted, 241;
   pet, named Ophelia, 36, 217; pet, warned
   against, 217
Rabble Starkey, 203
*RABBLE STARKEY*, 145, *203–204*
races: bug, 154; dogsled, 242; foot, 30; to find
   doctor in Arctic, 60–61

Rachel Cooper, 6
Rachelle, 48–49
racial mix, studied, 114
racism. *See* prejudice
radio: husband works for, 227; on plane, 97
rafts, constructed, 98
RAGS O'LEARY, 14, *204*
raids: for horses, among Indians, 139; on
   marijuana growing farm, 189
railroads: employee blackballed, 166;
   magnates, 29; transcontinental, 140
Rainey, Ty, 36, 91, 193, 217
*Rain of Fire*, 20
rainstorms: intense, repeated, 278; on
   Memorial Day Parade, 14
Ralphie, sister's sweetheart, 26
rambunctiousness, interpreted to mean like a
   male sheep, 46
*Ramona and Her Father*, 47
*RAMONA FOREVER*, *204–205*, 47
Ramona Quimby, 204
*Ramona Quimby, Age 8*, 47
*Ramona the Pest*, 47
Ramoom, 34
ranchers: 28, 256. *See also* farmers
ranches: Missouri, 126; sheep, New Zealand,
   214. *See also* farms; sheep ranches
ranch hands: old Maori, 215; young, 215
ranch life, novels of: Missouri, 126–27; New
   Zealand, 214
Randy Broughton, 82, 185
Randy Hicks, 222
Randy the antiquarian shop owner, 133
*Ransom*, 62
ransom: cutthroats seek for prince, 274; sought
   to finance scientific project, 225
rapelling, from mesa top, 256
rapes: attempted, 63; attempted by white
   brother of black slave sister, 249; avoided
   by ruse, 139; prevented by strafing plane,
   235; threatened, 23; thwarted, 163;
   witnessed, 235
Rapidan River, 43
Rap Stevens, 29
raptor rehabilitation center, 71
raspberries, survival food, 97
rat catchers, 274
*Rated PG*, 277
Ratliff family, 173, 245
rats: attack cutthroats, 274
Rawlings family, 125
Ray Bannister, 23
RAYFORD, 180, *205*
Raymonda Smiths, 10, 49
Raymond Bond, 232
Raymond Szyznowski, 232, 239
reading: girl teaches pig, 201; learning to, 181;
   teaching cousin, 229; teaching of, 91, 218,

273; teaching self to, 162; whipping boy does, 274

reading aloud: Bible to long underwear, 12; father to daughter, 159; *Ivanhoe*, 93; Mother Goose to doll, 12; mother to daughters, 150; teacher in classroom, 7; to blind veterans, 5, 93; to toy animals, 12

realtors, mother, 110

*REAR-VIEW MIRRORS*, 76, *205–207*

rebellions: against king, 108; against principal's ban on T-shirts, 38; Illyrians, 108; in Damar, 101; in Westmark, 21; quelled, 272. *See also* revolts

rebels: against disorganized family, 66; blacks, South Africa, 270; disguised as gypsies, 108; in Westmark, 138; old, ailing, 21; threaten government of Austar IV, 99

Rebels, American Civil War, 43, 180

rebirths, with ability to see myriads of colors like dragons, 100

receivers, of stolen goods, 25

recipes: for best biscuits, 126; for ointment against dragon fire, 101

recitations, poem by Tennyson, 195

recluses: Mad Mary, 26; widow, 246. *See also* hermits

reconciliations: boys, 214; girl engineers, 104–5; grandmother and granddaughter, 257; of king and rebel leader, 109; prickly, 211

Reconstruction, 250

recording device, assumed to be cosmic power, 113

records: family, 143; of birth of slave girl, 249; of number of songs sung, 266; request to falsify school, 54

recruiters: American Revolution, 52; for black rights in South Africa, 122

rectors: daughter of, 67; small town, 201. *See also* ministers; preachers, priests

rectory, painting of, 201

red, car painted for wedding gift, 204

Red Cross camp, Sudan, 209

*Red Dragonfly on My Shoulder*, 42

red-haired persons: boy, crossing guard, 7; cutthroat, 274; explorer, 244; graduate student, 111; guardian, 166; Irish boy, 43; sister and brother, 154; woman, 252

Red Hawk, 244

red herrings, numerous, 180

red paint, all over, 14

Red Sox, Boston, 96

REEDER, CAROLYN, *207*, 228

reform schools: psychiatric, 219. *See also* prisons; schools, reform

refrigerator, grandfather buys, 194

refugee camps, 235

refugees: black Ethiopian Jews in Sudan, 11; Japanese in Korea, 134, 235, 283; Japanese,

World War II, 102; starving, in Sudanese Red Cross camp, 209; Vietnam, 251

refuges: barn, 65; boat in squall, 257; dilapidated tree house, 180; for girl on beach, 16; in dragon's body, 100

Reggie, 163

Reggie Taylor, 110

Regia, kingdom of, 21

regiments, black, in Civil War, 273

Regina Stone, 265

*A Regular Rolling Noah*, 147

Rehab Station, 265

rehabilitation, of raptors, 71

rehearsals: chamber group, 179, 194; refusal to attend, 50

rejections: girl by mother, 129; of Caribbean past, 125; of daughter, 16; of sweetheart, 38

relapses, from leukemia, 115

relationships: aunt-nephew, much improved, 267; bossy sister-slow brother, much improved, 162; boy-father, improved, 74–75; boy-grandfather, acknowledged, 186; boy-mother, joking, 124; boy-mother's lover, gradually improving, 277; boy-mother's lover, mutual distrust, 276; brother-sister, discovered, 186; daughter-father, filled with rage, 142; daughter-father, finally resolved, 205; family, tense, 281; father-daughter, competitive, 111; father-daughter, improved, 57; father-daughter, strained, 55; father-daughter, strained, reversed, 159; father-daughter, very close, 27, 232; father-son-grandson, 125; father-son, growing understanding, 36; father-son, improved, 37, 75, 131; father-son, remote, 56; girl-grandfather, changing, 6; girl-great-grandmother, close, 33; girl-mother, warm and appreciative, 72; girl-music teacher, very close, 67; girl-parents, improved, 103; husband-wife, on prairie, strained, 195; improved when sister comforts older brother, 7; interpersonal, explored, 38; mother-daughter, improved, 153; mother-daughter, strained, 5, 129; mother-grandmother, antagonistic, 211; mother-son, ruined, 91; musical brother-sister, close, 263; older sister-younger brother, close, 195; parent-child, conflict ridden, 190; samurai lord-boy, ambivalent, 8; sister-sister, improved, 73; slow brother-bossy sister, improved, 153; stepfather-daughter, loving, 15; unmarried but permanent, 41

relatives: barely known, 264, 267; foreign, bogus, 115

*The Relatives Came*, 216

release forms, forged, 32

religion, novels of, 75–76, 91–92, 208–9

religions: different ideas of, 214; fanatic, 91, 122; important in family, 177

## About the Authors

ALETHEA K. HELBIG is Professor of English Language and Literature at Eastern Michigan University. A former president of the Children's Literature Association, she has received the State of Michigan Award for Outstanding Teaching and Publication. She has published over one hundred articles in professional journals such as *Children's Literature* and *The Children's Literature Association Quarterly* and reference books such as *American Women Writers*, *Writers for Children*, and *Masterplots*.

AGNES REGAN PERKINS is Professor Emeritus of English Language and Literature at Eastern Michigan University. She has published numerous articles in journals and reference books, including *A Tolkien Compass*, *Unicorn*, *Children's Literature*, *The Children's Literature Association Quarterly*, *Writers for Children*, and *Masterplots*. She is co-compiler of the poetry anthologies *New Coasts and Strange Harbors* (with Helen Hill), *Straight on Till Morning*, and *Dusk to Dawn* (both with Hill and Alethea Helbig).

Everett